Currency Internationalization and Macro Financial Risk Control

International Monetary Institute

Currency Internationalization and Macro Financial Risk Control

palgrave
macmillan

Editor
International Monetary Institute
Renmin University of China
Beijing, China

ISBN 978-981-13-0697-6 ISBN 978-981-13-0698-3 (eBook)
https://doi.org/10.1007/978-981-13-0698-3

Library of Congress Control Number: 2018948149

Printed on acid-free paper

This Palgrave Macmillan imprint is published by the registered company Springer Nature Singapore Pte Ltd.
The registered company address is: 152 Beach Road, #21-01/04 Gateway East, Singapore 189721, Singapore

Preface

The year 2015 was an eventful year. After the Federal Reserve officially started the interest rate increase, the dollar index continued to rise, dollar assets were sought after by many, international capital flow experienced large-scale adjustment, and China faced an increasingly sharp pressure of capital outflow. Refugee crisis slowed down the economic recovery in Europe, the risk of "British Exit" further increased the uncertainty of its prospects, and the European Central Bank announced to implement the negative interest rate policy. Since the EU is China's largest trading partner, a substantial depreciation of the euro hit heavily the export trade of China. Such international circumstances worsened the Chinese economy which was itself in a difficult transformation. For one thing, issues including over-capacity, decline in private investment, and non-performing bank assets have become increasingly prominent. For another, the domestic financial market was in turmoil: the first half of the year witnessed the stock market disaster propelled by high leverage and private funding, ending up with an market value evaporation of over 20 trillion yuan; and the second half experienced a panic exchange rate overshoot in the foreign exchange market, and a cliff-like liquidity crunch of the offshore renminbi market. Domestic and international confidence in China's economic growth and financial stability has been shaken.

RMB internationalization still maintained a good momentum. By the end of 2015, the international use of RMB index marked by the RII reached 3.6, an increase of over ten times over the past five years. The ratio of RMB settlement in China's foreign trade was nearly 30%, and that in global trade was pushed up to 3.38%. RMB foreign direct investment reached 736.2 billion yuan, registering an increase of 294.53% from the previous year. Meanwhile, the share of RMB in international credit, international bonds, and bill business also increased rapidly, pushing the share of RMB in international financial transactions to 5.9%. The currency swap agreement signed by the People's Bank of China registered a balance of 3.31 trillion yuan.

On November 30, 2015, the International Monetary Fund (IMF) announced to include RMB into the SDR basket of currencies, which would enter into force on October 1, 2016, officially with the weight of RMB in the new currency basket reaching 10.92%. This is an important milestone in the integration of the Chinese economy into the global financial system, a win-win for both China and the rest of the world. Although renminbi was officially identified as a "freely usable currency", its "official status" may not necessarily lead to the "market position" as an international currency. Joining the basket does not mean that the RMB internationalization has achieved its goal, because the ultimate goal is to match the currency status with China's economic and trade status in the global stage. That is destined to be a long historical process. Whether the RMB could become one of the major international currencies depends on how much renminbi the international market will use and hold in the actual situation.

In general, the issuer of a major international currency should meet a number of conditions: integrated economic strength, trade status, currency stability, free movement of capital, and macro-management capacity. A review of the past few years show that the first few factors that support the internationalization of the RMB perform soundly in China, but macro-management may present a weakness in the long run. As macro-management capacity affects other factors such as currency stability and free flow of capital, China needs to pay special attention to this aspect through study and making improvement, so as to win the lasting confidence in the RMB from the international community.

RMB Internationalization Report, which is themed at Currency Internationalization and Macro Financial Risk Management, takes a deep look into macro-management issues and explores the macro-financial policy adjustment and the potential macrofinancial risks as the internationalization of RMB has entered a new stage. The report suggests that a macro-prudential policy framework should be built based on the national strategic perspective, which can effectively prevent the systemic financial crisis and provide a fundamental guarantee for the steady growth of the real economy and the ultimate realization of RMB internationalization.

The international financial classic theories hold that the monetary authorities of an open economy can only choose two out of the three macro-financial policy objectives, namely, the independence of monetary policy, the fixed exchange rate system, and the complete free flow of capital. The history of Germany and Japan shows that in the process of the climbing level of currency internationalization, the monetary authority must adjust policy objectives to major changes in cross-border capital flows and exchange rate regimes. Germany and Japan launched internationalization of their currencies from similar starting points, but the different decisions on policy adjustment have had profound but distinct impact on the domestic economy and finance, resulting in the opposite results of currency internationalization of the two countries.

At the initial stage of currency internationalization, Germany regarded exchange rate stabilization as its primary target. It even resorted to the measures including capital controls, the suspension of financial market development, and the use of foreign exchange reserves for market intervention. As a result, it created favorable external conditions for maintaining the advantages in trade, enhancing industrial production competitiveness, and consolidating the domestic development of the real economy, and provided a strong support for the long-term stability of the mark exchange rates. Japan was too radical because it over-estimated the ability of its real economy in coping with the impact of the appreciation of the exchange rate, thus failing to keep the yen exchange rates stable. Coupled with the mistakes made in internal macro-economic policies, Japan has fundamentally undermined its real economy, making the international level of yen temporarily rise before the sharp decline.

The level of RMB internationalization has improved steadily in recent years, and will embark on a new stage of development after joining the currency basket. This marks that China has entered a sensitive period of policy adjustments in the area of macro-management. The difference in the policy adjustment that Germany and Japan made and the distinct impact on the currency internationalization provide us with an important historical lesson. The experience of the two countries reminds us that China should not implement policy adjustment too speedily; rather, the exchange rates and capital account can be liberalized only after the real economy, financial market, and management departments are fully prepared.

Therefore, in the transition of the macro-financial policy mix from the "partial independence of monetary policy + managed floating exchange rate + limited liberalization of capital account" to "independent monetary policy + floating exchange rate + free flow of capital", China must manage the impact of the exchange rate fluctuations on the economic and financial operations, and adapt as soon as possible to the new interaction mechanism between cross-border capital flows and the domestic financial market, financial institutions as well as the real economy, with particular attention to preventing and managing systemic financial risks. Based on study on historical experiences, literature and theoretical research, empirical research, and policy research, especially on the above-mentioned key issues that have great impact on the process of RMB internationalization, this book argues that a macro-prudential policy framework should be put in place as the institutional guarantee, the exchange rate management should be the focus of macro-financial risk management, the capital flow management be the key entry point for macro-financial risk management, with the ultimate goal of preventing and resolving the devastating systemic financial crisis and realizing the internationalization of the RMB. Specifically, we have come to the following core conclusions and recommendations:

First, on the RMB exchange rate system and exchange rate management issues. The defining factors of renminbi exchange rates have clearly shifted as the long-term exchange rates are determined by the fundamentals and the short-term exchange rates are mainly affected by the cross-border capital flows and other countries' policy spillovers, but market arbitrage can lead to a return to long-term equilibrium. With the increasing flexibility of exchange rates, the volatility of it has a significantly greater effect on the stability of economic growth.

China should further promote the market-oriented reform of exchange rates, improve the RMB exchange rate system, and shift gradually from the managed floating to free floating. Exchange rate policy should attain its goals by means of from indirect intervention rather than direct intervention, management of market expectation should be strengthened, and long-term exchange rates should maintain basic stability at the equilibrium level. China needs to pay attention to the effect of policy spillovers, strengthen international policy communication and coordination, and pursue such exchange rate policy objectives as in line with the optimal monetary policy objectives.

Second, on the relationship between cross-border capital flows and the stability of domestic financial market, financial institutions and the real economy. Liberalization of capital account should be coordinated with the reform in the exchange rate system; follow the principle of taking gradual, controllable, coordinated steps; and adapt to the needs of China's economic and financial development and the changes in the international economic situation.

Study shows that since the exchange reform on August 11, 2015, the relationship between the capital market prices, the leverage rate, and the net inflow of cross-border capital has shifted from the previous one-way relation to a cyclical interaction, as the short-term capital flows are sufficient to affect the capital market prices and leverage levels. Asset prices have been more connected between domestic financial subsidiary markets and between financial markets at home and abroad, and financial risk has been more contagious, and the impact on cross-border capital flows has been more sensitive. China should not be aggressive into the capital account liberalization; rather, it should strengthen the overall capital flow monitoring.

Due to the capital account liberalization, Chinese-funded banks can access greater international development space, but they must withstand the dual challenges both domestically and internationally and confront more difficulties in balancing market expansion and risk control. Banks of systematic importance should seize this opportunity to expand cross-border operations while improving risk management mechanisms to avoid becoming an amplifier of external impact or a flashpoint for systemic risks.

Capital flows are having more complex and frequent impacts than ever before, exacerbating the volatility of the real economy. China needs to set the supply-side reform as the starting point, promote technological progress from both the internal and external, provide financial services to the real economy, and watch out for bubbles and virtualization, so as to solve the problems faced by the Chinese economy, such as inappropriate models, backward innovation capacity, wide but weak trade, and reduction in private investment, among other issues, and to reduce the risks of the real economy. RMB internationalization can positively interact with the supply-side reform through direct investment, technological progress, trade upgrades, and so on, and together the two can turn risks into opportunities and promote the restructuring, transformation, and upgrading of China's economy.

Third, on the macro-financial risk management in the process of RMB internationalization. Financial stability is the necessary prerequisite to realize the ultimate goal of the RMB internationalization. Therefore, the core task in macro-financial management of the monetary authorities is to build a more comprehensive, targeted macro-prudential policy framework.

Cross-border capital flows and other external shocks intertwine with and reinforce the risks in domestic financial market, institutions, and the real economy, spreading a single market or local risk into a chain of risks and a likely systemic risk. China needs to plan a systemic risk index which includes assessment and monitoring. A China-specific macro-prudential policy framework should be put in place so as to prevent and manage systemic risk from the institutional level.

In order to solve the problem caused by multi-pronged regulators, such as the overlapping of policies and regulated duties and powers and unified standards, China should draw from the international experience, set clear principles for the current financial regulation reform, and build a China-specific macro-prudential policy framework as an institutional guarantee for managing system risk. Specifically, it is necessary to add the element of "macro-prudential" in the existing financial regulatory framework, and to clarify the enforcers of the macro-prudential policy. In addition to maintaining monetary stability, the central bank should perform the function of securing financial stability and strengthening financial regulation. China should straighten out the relationship between monetary policy, macro-prudence, micro-prudence, and behavioral regulation from the perspective of functions and mechanisms, and enhance coordination between each other. It also needs to improve the availability and accuracy of financial data so as to provide comprehensive and timely information for monitoring, analyzing, and evaluating systemic risks. An effective crisis disposal mechanism should be put in place and financial consumers should be well protected.

The internationalization of RMB, as one of the important plans put forward by China in the twenty-first century as an emerging power, shoulders the dual historical mission of realizing the interests of China and reforming the international monetary system. Therefore, China must stand at the height of the national strategy to implement macro-financial risk management and improve the monetary authorities' macro-management capacity, with the ultimate goal of realizing internationalization of RMB.

International currency diversification is a dynamic process, the structure of which could be adjusted with the changes in international trade patterns and international financial market volatility. The more international economic and financial situation is complex and uncertain, the more China should stand firm, so as to calmly deal with policy adjustment and macro-financial risks and hold the bottom line of avoiding systemic financial crisis. The steady improvement China makes in the internationalization of the RMB is the best response to all the doubts and skepticism.

Beijing, China International Monetary Institute

Contents

List of Figures

List of Tables

CHAPTER 1

Internationalization Index of Renminbi

International Monetary Institute

In 2015, with global economic recovery tortuous and financial market dynamic, Chinese economy moved into a new normal. In spite of current domestic and international economic stress from an increasingly stronger dollar, renminbi (RMB) depreciation, and capital outflow, the internationalization of renminbi is still gaining momentum. Great achievements were made. Cross-border RMB policies under capital account were enforced, the first phase of Cross-border Interbank Payment System (CIPS) launched, and "the Belt and Road" initiative carried out. Especially in November RMB was approved to be included into the special drawing rights (SDR) basket, a milestone of the internationalization of RMB. In the past five years, due to the wider use of RMB in international trade, financial transaction, and international reserves, RMB's internationalization has been moving on smoothly, with international index of RMB (RII) growing by more than ten times.

International Monetary Institute (✉)
Renmin University of China, Beijing, China
e-mail: imi@ruc.edu.cn

International Monetary Institute (ed.), *Currency Internationalization and Macro Financial Risk Control*,
https://doi.org/10.1007/978-981-13-0698-3_1

1.1 Analysis on RII and Its Variation

1.1.1 Status Quo of RMB's Internationalization Index

In 2015, the growth of global economy remained sluggish, and the Fed's announcement of raising interest rate together with a stronger dollar disturbed the world financial market. At the same time, China's economic development has now entered a new normal, with tough tasks of sustaining economic growth and restructuring. After the "8.11" exchange rate reform, the stress of RMB depreciation increases and daily trading band widened, bringing negative impact on RMB internationalization. However, short-term fluctuation does not conceal its long-term prospect. RMB's internationalization went smoothly on the whole and made some breakthroughs. Cross-border RMB strategy was improved, the first phase of Cross-border Interbank Payments System launched, and "the Belt and Road" initiative carried out. Especially in November RMB was approved by the board of the International Monetary Fund (IMF) to be the fifth currency in the SDR basket after dollar, euro, yen, and GBP, opening a new chapter for the internationalization of RMB. In 2015, the use of RMB as international currency broadened in payment and settlement, financial transaction, and international reserves, driving the RII higher. As Fig. 1.1 shows, by the end of the third quarter of 2015, RII reached 3.87, a year-on-year growth of 83.9%; by the end of the fourth quarter it reached 3.60, a year-on-year growth of 42.9%. A minor setback of growth rate did not reverse the upward trend. In the past five years, RII grew by more than ten times.

In 2015, the RIIs in four quarters were 2.48, 2.76, 3.87, and 3.60, respectively. RMB's internationalization entered a stable yet expanding stage, which, along with the increasing stress in the second half year, resulted in a drop in RII growth, with average growth per quarter falling to 37.8% (as is shown in Fig. 1.2).

1.1.2 Major Impetuses for RMB's Internationalization

With global economic recovery tortuous and financial market dynamic, domestic economy is confronted with downward pressure. Faced with complicated and tough economic environment both at home and abroad, the growth rate of RII edged down, but remained promising on the whole. In 2015, the RII was driven to a higher level mainly by the following five factors:

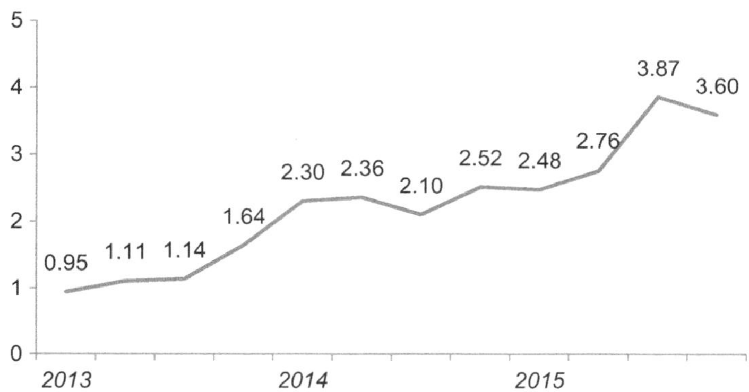

Fig. 1.1 The RII. Note: RII has been subject to the following adjustments. (1) Offshore market has developed rapidly, and the statistics system about renminbi assets improved. Our indicators of RMB international credit include not only the former statistics about the mainland and Hong Kong, but also statistics about Macau, Taiwan, Singapore, and London. (2) Chinese International Balance of Payments Statistics shifted to *BPM6* standard in 2015; as a result, the caliber about direct investment included in RII shifted from *BPM5* standard to *BPM6* standard. (3) RII is modified along with the statistical adjustment of the raw statistics

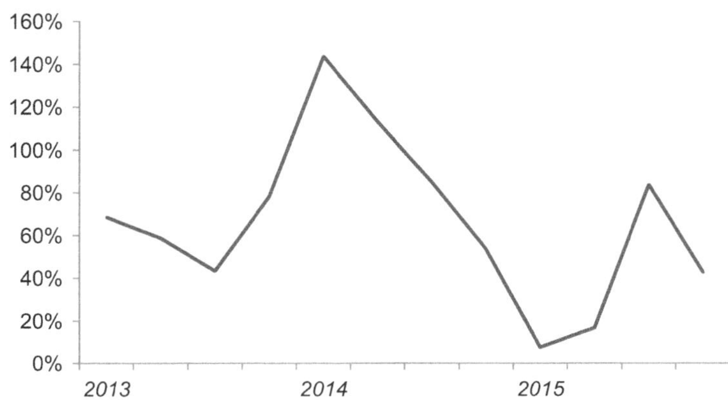

Fig. 1.2 RII quarter annual growth

Firstly, Chinese economy remained stable on the whole and financial reform was advanced smoothly. In 2015, although faced with downward pressure, China remained one of the most stable economies, which laid a solid development foundation for RMB's internationalization. As a flagship of emerging markets, China boasted a GDP growth rate of 6.9%, one of the fastest in the world; China reinforced structural reforms, kept its monetary policies robust, and its economic and financial system remained resilient against risks, all of which provided RMB's internationalization with sustaining momentum; the current account realized a surplus of $293.2 billion with a year-on-year growth rate of 33.5%, overseas direct investment (ODI) increased by 14.7% year-on-year, the international payments account stayed balanced basically, and cross-border capital outflow converged to the fundamentals. As for the financial reforms, China seized the opportunity to lift the ceiling of floating interest rate of commercial bank and rural cooperative financial institutions and canceled the interest rate control; improved the regime of central parity rate of RMB; increased the liberalization level of exchange rate; and narrowed the difference between central parity rate and market exchange rate and between onshore and offshore exchange rate. Meanwhile, the publishing of China Foreign Exchange Trade System (CFETS), the improvement of People's Bank of China (PBOC) exchange rate market management, and the maneuver against the short-selling of RMB abroad helped the market expectations to return to a rational level. By encouraging innovation and following successful patterns nationwide, the RMB convertibility under the capital account was advanced smoothly. The RMB's admission to the SDR basket represented the acknowledgment to China's monetary financial reform by the international community.

Secondly, the policies of RMB cross-border business under capital account improved. Although the volatility of financial market both at home and abroad was heightened and the stress of capital outflow increased, China still made outstanding progress on the policies of the RMB cross-border under capital account, which broadened the backflow channels of RMB, optimized the capital allocation, and supported the real economy. In 2015, China relaxed external debt regulations of enterprises and the two-way cross-border RMB cash pooling, which improved the independence and convenience of cross-border financing; China permitted foreign currency authorities, official reserve managers, global financial organizations, and sovereign wealth funds to enter China's interbank market and conduct foreign exchange business including spot, forward, swap and options transactions, which improved the representative of RMB exchange rate and enhanced the function of international reserve;

the trial of Qualified Domestic Investment Enterprise established in Qianhai Zone of Shenzhen, Shanghai-Hong Kong Stock Connect run smoothly, and the allocation of asset became more diversified. At the same time, China (Shanghai) free trade zone played a leading and exploratory role in capital account convertibility, inspired innovation in the trials, and applied successful patterns to the rest of the country, which accelerated the achievement of capital account convertibility.

Thirdly, infrastructure construction of RMB improved, and the relative supporting system started to be subject to the international standards. In 2015, China was integrated into the global financial system and management framework. Besides, the infrastructure and relative supporting system for finance improved, providing comprehensive hardware and software support for the use of RMB on an international scale. In October 2015, it was great progress for the modern RMB payment to launch the first phase of CIPS as the strategic financial infrastructure, offering clearing and settlement service on RMB business to the financial institutions both at home and abroad, which covered the major financial centers except the United States. Meanwhile, China got closer to the international standards in statistical management: it adopted the Special Data Dissemination Standards of the IMF, joined the CPIS of the IMF, the International Bank Statistics (IBS) of Bank for International Settlements, and the survey of composition of foreign exchange reserves; converted to The sixth edition of the Balance of Payments and International Investment Position Manual (*BPM6*); improved the statistical approach, the regime of declaration and examination; and enforced the standardization and publication. In addition, the index system on financial market became abundant: CFETS, BOC Credits Investing & Financing Environment Difference Index and the BOC RMB bond trading index, UBS international bank demand index, and DBS RMB diving index (DRIVE) were published, providing global investors with better reference of RMB investment and use.

Fourthly, with the development of "the Belt and Road", China-EU economic and financial cooperation was on the rise. From the beginning of "the Belt and Road", China signed agreements and MOUs with 31 countries and regions, many construction projects were implemented, and the deepening of the regional economic communication and the establishment of the Asian Infrastructure Investment Bank provided a foundation for the use of RMB along the "Belt and Road". In 2015, Sino-Australia FTA and Sino-Korea FTA were implemented. China signed international cooperation agreement on production capacity with more than ten countries, and signed currency swap deals with the currency authorities of Suriname,

Armenia, South Africa, Chile, and Tajikistan separately. The domestic free trade area and financial experimental zone were constructed at high speed, which helped to further consolidate the RMB function of payment, settlement, investment, and financing. In addition, on the 40th anniversary of establishment of diplomatic ties between China and EU, their financial cooperation continued its positive momentum: European Union became the largest trade partner, the most important source of imported technology, and a great investment cooperation partner for China; the business cooperation scale between China and EU in 2015 reached $169.2 billion; the top leaders of both sides made frequent visits to each other, which helped to enhance the dialogues on economy and finance, supported the development of offshore RMB market, and deepened the cooperation on market access, cross-border securities regulation, investment platform, and supporting facilities. At the same time, RMB opened the gate of Sino-Central and Eastern European Countries (CEEC) cooperation: the fourth China-CEEC Leaders Meeting was held in November; the participants advocated the establishment of 16+1 Financial Company, discussed the possibility of building up the China-CEEC cooperation fund, and agreed to support the setup of RMB clearing regime, offering good external environment for the CEEC offshore RMB market.

Fifthly, under the circumstances of the fluctuating financial market and a stronger dollar, the use of RMB in denominating commodities became more frequent. With the international oil price low and petrodollar tightened, the level of RMB use in Middle East increased. In 2015, RMB clearing center in Qatar was set up, and MOU was signed between China and UAE, making RMB the common currency used in the payment from UAE and Qatar to Chinese Mainland and Hong Kong, with proportions of 74% and 60%, respectively, an annual growth rate of 52% and 247%. Serbia started its RMB projects. The Russian acceptance of RMB constantly improved, making RMB its third popular currency after USD and euro, and the Moscow bourse launched ruble-denominated RMB futures trading. London Metal Exchange accepted RMB as a pledge currency. China (Shanghai) free trade area started cross-border RMB spot commodity transaction in July. The use of RMB in commodity denomination was enhanced.

1.1.3 Major Challenges for RMB's Internationalization

In 2015, the growth of RII slowed down. Offshore RMB deposits and issuance of RMB-denominated financial products were lackluster. In the short term, RMB's internationalization was facing some stress coming from the following three aspects:

Firstly, the temporary depreciation of RMB had negative effects on the confidence of RMB holders and users. With the United States tightening its monetary policies and the implementation of "8.11" exchange rate reform, RMB was confronted with temporary depreciation pressure instead of the former trend of unilateral appreciation, and the exchange rate against the dollar fell by 4.5% through the year. The outflow of capital and the shorting on RMB abroad increased the exchange rate fluctuation, bringing the shocks to RMB's internationalization and capital account opening. Chinese citizens adjusted their assets and liabilities arrangements, and repaid the debt ahead of schedule, while non-residents cut their holdings of domestic RMB assets. Both offshore RMB deposits and the issuance of RMB bonds shrunk. In 2015, offshore RMB deposits in Hong Kong fell to 851.11 billion yuan, with a drop of 15.2% year-on-year; the issuance of dim sum bonds in Hong Kong fell to 126.51 billion yuan, with a drop of 42.8% year-on-year. The severe fluctuation of exchange rate brought negative impacts on RMB's function in payment, settlement, investment, and financing. The negative interest rate spread between abroad and the domestic market restrained the use of RMB. Foreign exchange rate market, financial products system, the market participants' awareness of risk management, and the ability and policy portfolio of monetary authority financial management still needed to be improved.

Secondly, the downward risk of China's economy increased and the China bears were growing louder. In 2015, China's structural reform advanced zigzag through hardship, the pressure of cutting overcapacity, reducing inventory, and de-leveraging accumulated, and the downward risk of economy emerged, resulting in the GDP growth rate falling to 6.9%, with a 0.4% drop year-on-year, which was the lowest in recent 25 years. The Chinese economy was at a crucial stage of transition from old to new growth drivers: the release of financial risk speeded up; the issues of non-performing loans in traditional banks, domestic debt problem, Internet finance, stock market turbulence, and the outflow of capital broke out intensively; trade and investment became sluggish. Aging population, severe fluctuation of the return on investment of finance assets, structural conflictions of supply and demand, and slowing growth rate of total factor productivity had a negative effect on the economic vitality and RMB's internationalization. Meanwhile, the international situation was more complicated and tougher, the clash and conflicts increased, and China bears became louder. And some controversies blamed other countries' economic turbulence and currency wars on

China, and even exaggerated Chinese exchange and debt problems, to mislead market expectation and flow of capital, and to reduce the attractiveness of RMB.

Thirdly, the USD was becoming stronger, hindering RMB internationalization. The rebalance of international monetary system was a process of repetitive gaming, and the growth of one currency's status was often accompanied by the decline of another currency's status. Since the international financial crisis struck in 2008, a weaker USD provided a chance for RMB's internationalization. In 2015, with the Fed tightening its monetary policy and starting interest rate hike cycle, the USD was becoming stronger, which disturbed the international market and capital allocation on a global scale. From 2015, emerging market currencies entered the longest depreciation cycle ever since 1997. With the risk aversions of investors heightening, the net outflow of capital reached $735 billion. As a typical emerging market currency, RMB confronted even more complicated environment, making its holders less confident. The share of dollar rose significantly in payment, settlement, investment, financing, foreign exchange transaction, and international reserves, which posed a great challenge to RMB's internationalization.

Column 1.1 The Importance of the Reform of Central Parity System

On July 11, 2015, the PBOC announced the decision to improve quotation of the central parity of RMB against USD and finished the correction between the central parity and the market rate within the next three trading days. According to the new regulations, the market makers might quote to the China Foreign Exchange Trading Center before the opening of interbank FX market every day, referring to the closing rate of the previous day, the market demand and supply, and the changes of major international currencies exchange rates. Compared with the former quotation of the central parity, the new one emphasized the reference to the closing rate of the previous day and the market demand and supply, which was beneficial to correcting the divergence between the market rate and the central parity, the onshore and offshore rate, the exchange rate against the dollar and its effective exchange rate, making the quotation more transparent and market-oriented, as well as improving its function as a benchmark for the market.

Judging from the market response, the depreciation trend of RMB was confirmed after the one-time correction of the divergence, which strengthened people's expectation of depreciation, enabled the self-realization of the expectation. The stress of RMB depreciation increased, bringing a great shock to the global macro economy and capital flow. However, the depreciation of RMB this time was a correction of exchange rate to some extent as well as a necessary stage during the improvement of exchange rate regime. RMB would still be a strong currency in the long run, and there was no basis for persistent depreciation; RMB might meet depreciation pressure in the short term and experience temporary de-valuation. The new regime of quotation would fix some imbalance in the economy and finance, and might bring some fluctuation, which, however, were all under control. RMB exchange rate would become normal after brief friction.

The adjustment of quotation was of great significance for RMB's internationalization. The reform was a key step to realizing the market-based reform of RMB exchange and the PBOC gave up the normal currency intervention. On one hand, this regime helped the exchange rate to reflect the market supply and demand, eliminate the accumulated problems in the long-term development, correct the divergence between the market price and central parity, and improve the basic system construction of RMB internationalization. On the other hand, this adjustment helped to close the gap between the offshore and onshore exchange rate, reduce the mismatch of capital and prevent unusual arbitrage, and achieve the sound development of RMB offshore market. The offshore exchange rate converged to the onshore price, further helping to enhance its national pricing power, and to guarantee the national financial security. At the same time, RMB was at a critical period of SDR assessment review, and the improvement of exchange rate regime was an essential condition for it to be committed into the SDR basket. The reform made RMB more market-oriented and more consistent with the international practice, making it easier to gain the recognition of the market and build up the holders' confidence in RMB in the long run.

1.2 Structural Analysis of RMB Internationalization Index Changes

According to the computing methods of the RMB internationalization index, the variation of trade settlement, financial transactions, and foreign exchange reserve proportion all influence RII. At the original period of RMB's internationalization, the main influence came from trade settlement. With RMB's internationalization, RII started to be driven by both trade settlement and financial transaction. In 2015, RII rose sharply, though fluctuated in the meanwhile. Financial transaction became the most important factor to RII, and its contribution exceeded that of trade settlement. At the same time, the proportion of RMB as the foreign exchange reserve grew slower. In a comprehensive view, the international trade settlement and financial transaction were the two main drivers of the RII, while the acceptation of RMB as a reserve currency still needed to be promoted. There was still a long way to go for RMB to become an international reserve currency.

1.2.1 The Function of RMB International Trade Settlement Was Further Consolidated

RMB cross-border trade settlement was the launch pad and the cornerstone for RMB's internationalization. In 2015, the cross-border RMB receipt and payment scale expanded to 12.1 trillion, with a growth of 22% year-on-year, among which the actual receipt is 6.19 trillion while actual payment is 5.91 trillion. Under the impact of the exchange rate fluctuation and arbitrage reversal, the receipt-payment ratio reached 1:0.96, a sharp increase of receipt compared to the 1:1.4 of last year. RMB cross-border trade settlement in 2015 was 7.23 trillion yuan under current account, including goods trade settlement of 6.39 trillion and service settlement of 0.84 trillion, growing at 8.31% and 29.73% respectively. At the end of 2015, the proportion of RMB settlement in world trade rose to 3.38%, with a growth of 110.4% year-on-year and almost five times the figure at the end of 2010 (Fig. 1.3).

In conclusion, there were two main drivers in promoting the proportion of RMB settlement in international trade:

On one hand, Chinese international trade performed relatively well, regional trade cooperation accelerated, and FTA strategy was being put into practice. Because of the international trade demand slumping,

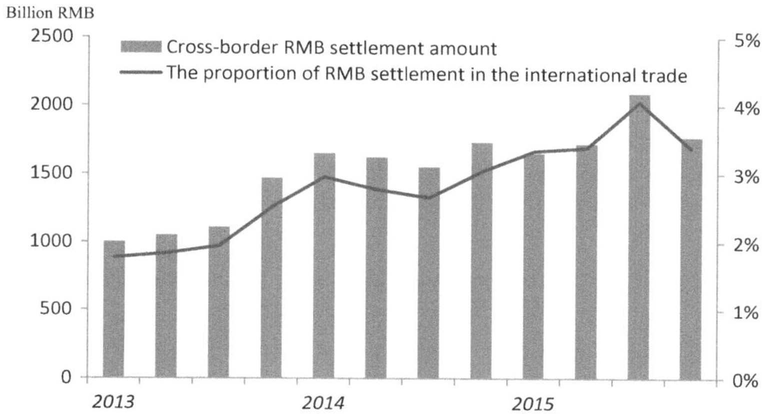

Fig. 1.3 Cross-border trades settled in RMB

primary commodity prices dropping, and other cumulated influence, the total value of foreign trade fell to \$3.9586 trillion in 2015, declining by 8% year-on-year, but the figure was still better than other major economies on the whole. Moreover, China's international market share increased and foreign trade quality improved as well. In recent years, China signed Free Trade Agreements (FTAs) with ASEAN, Singapore, Pakistan, New Zealand, Chile, Peru, Costa Rica, Iceland, and Switzerland, and Sino-Australian FTA Agreement and Sino-Korean FTA Agreement were also formally implemented on December 20, 2015. Until now, regional economic and trade cooperation has involved 22 economies across Asia, Latin America, Oceania, Europe, and other regions, creating good environment for China's trade scale expansion and trade restructuring. At the same time, China stepped forward to optimize the FTA overall arrangement and enhance the level of its development, put "the Belt and Road" strategy into practice, and strengthened the top-level design and regional economic cooperation, greatly promoting the acceptance of RMB in cross-border trade settlement.

On the other hand, RMB cross-border trade settlement and relevant service became increasingly more convenient and efficient. China (Shanghai) Free Trade Account System further reinforced the connection between FTA and offshore market, providing the domestic enterprises with better ways to enter overseas and facilitating trade settlement, cross-border investment, and financing for real economy. In October 2015, the first phase of CIPS was launched in Shanghai, which facilitated cross-border RMB business such as cross-border good and service settlement, direct investment, financing, and personal remittance. Besides, the enhancement of financial transaction also promoted the use of RMB in cross-border trade, helping to establish a positive cycle of trade, industry investment, and financial investment.

1.2.2 RMB's International Financial Transaction Function Has Been Greatly Enhanced

The international financial transaction function of RMB was greatly enhanced and its financial transaction scale continued expanding quickly in international credit, direct investment, and international bonds and notes. By the end of 2015, the comprehensive proportion of RMB-denominated international financial settlement was 5.9%, with a growth of 107.3%, and 50 times the figure at the end of 2010. In general, RMB direct investment became the most significant driver to the rise of the comprehensive index for RMB-denominated international financial settlement (Fig. 1.4).

1. RMB International Credit

In 2015, RMB international credit scale maintained stable. By the second quarter of 2015, the proportion of RMB international credit in global was 0.66%, five times more than that in 2010. Although the index was sluggish in the second half year, it still remained on a high level (Fig. 1.5).

There were two factors behind the fluctuation of international credit scale—one being the expansion of RMB stock in offshore markets and the other the scope of the trial for RMB cross-border credit. According to incomplete statistics, the scale of offshore RMB deposits in Hong Kong, Taiwan, Macau, Singapore, and Korea reached 1497.1 billion yuan by the end of 2015, among which the deposits in Hong Kong was 851.1 billion yuan, with a drop of 15.2% year-on-year, Taiwan 319.5 billion yuan with a growth of 5.7%, and Korea 4.68 billion yuan. And the RMB deposit in Macau by the end of November was 71 billion yuan, and Singapore by the end of September was 225 billion yuan. Influenced by the volatility of exchange rate and other factors, the scale of offshore RMB deposits shrunk a little, but the distribution range of overseas RMB broadened, and the

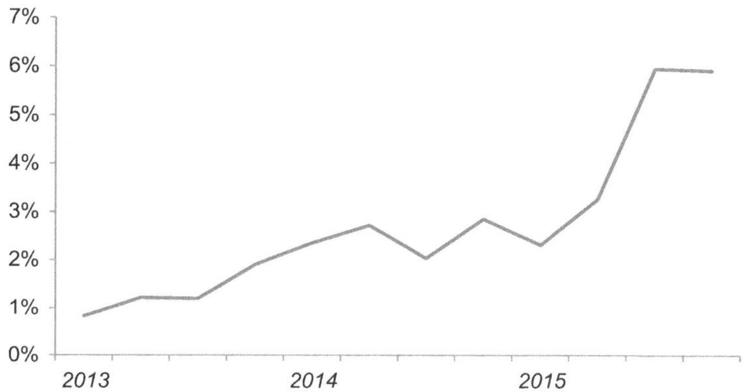

Fig. 1.4 Comprehensive index for RMB-denominated international financial settlement. Note: The comprehensive index for RMB-denominated international financial settlement consists of the proportion of RMB overseas credit in international credit, the proportion of RMB security in announced issuance of international bonds and notes, the proportion of RMB security in amounts outstanding international bonds and notes, and the proportion of RMB direct investment in international direct investment

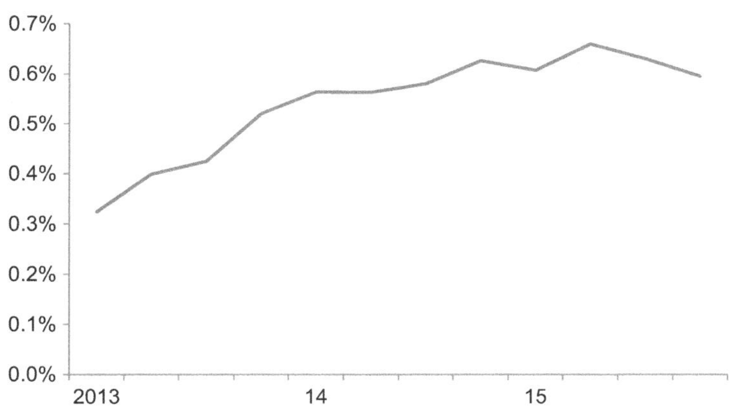

Fig. 1.5 RMB's proportion in international credit

products and market became diversified. In addition, the scope of the trial for RMB cross-border credit expanded: the trials of cross-border RMB debt in Hengqin Nansha free trade zone made the investment and financing between the mainland and the Hong Kong-Macau more convenient; the trials in Quanzhou financial reform experimental area and Xiamen developed the RMB debt business between the mainland and Taiwan, broadened the investment and backflow channels of RMB in Taiwan, and accelerated the development of RMB offshore market.

2. RMB Direct Investment

RMB direct investment can be divided into RMB foreign direct investment (FDI) and RMB ODI. With the development of "going out" of Chinese enterprises and international cooperation on production capacity, the scale of RMB direct investment kept expanding rapidly. RMB FDI in 2015 was 2.32 trillion yuan with a growth of 121.6%. At the end of 2015, the proportion of RMB direct investment in global FDI was 16.56% (Fig. 1.6).

Although the risk of economic downturn rose, Chinese GDP growth rate and return on assets still took the lead around the world, attracting even more foreign investment. Due to the relaxation of the FDI limitations,

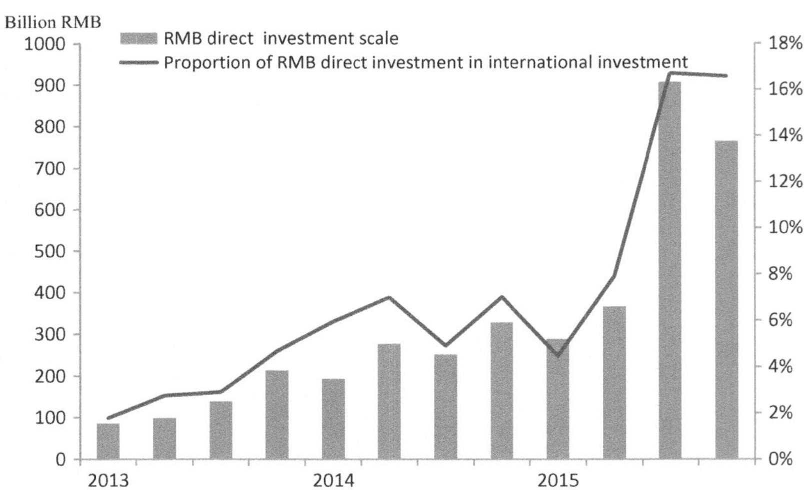

Fig. 1.6 Global RMB direct investment

the conversion from administrative approval system to registration system in the introduction of foreign capital, and the boost of the free trade strategy, the FDI increased by 6.4% in 2015, the actual use of direct foreign capital reached 126.2 billion yuan, among which the RMB FDI was 1587.1 billion yuan, with a growth rate of 84.1% and the total FDI of RMB from 2011 was 3275.8 billion yuan. In addition, the pace of ODI quickened: "the Belt and Road" enhanced the mutual investment and trade, facilitating the ODI. Meanwhile, the domestic economic transition accelerated the "going out" of China-funded enterprise, and Chinese enterprises' mergers and acquisitions overseas were on the rise due to the downturn of the international economy. According to preliminary statistics, there were 593 cases of overseas mergers and acquisitions across all industries in 2015, with transaction amount of $40.1 billion. The non-financial ODI of domestic investors reached $118.02 billion in 2015, with a growth rate of 14.7% year-on-year, and the total amount of RMB ODI from 2011 was 10638.3 billion yuan. The 13th Five-Year Plan emphasized the supporting for overseas investment; the "going out" of equipment, technology, standards, and services; the integration into the global industry chain, value chain, and logistics chain; and the aim of building up commodity production overseas and multinational enterprise. In the future, China will usher in a new era of overseas investment, which will provide lasting power for the RMB direct investment.

3. RMB International Bonds and Bills

The international bond market is an important component of international financial market, the proportion of which is one of the vital indicators of evaluating the degree of a country's currency used in international scope. In 2015, the balance of RMB international bonds and bills was $124.79 billion, rising by 30.8% year-on-year, meanwhile with its global percentage up to around 0.59% from 0.08% in the end of year 2010. Although the scale of using RMB in international bond market rapidly increased, it accounted for a relatively small portion in global market, which also limited RMB's influence worldwide (Fig. 1.7).

In 2015, the issuance scale of RMB international bonds and bills significantly surged owing to the following three main aspects:

Firstly, the spread variations between the domestic and foreign impelled market entities to choose autonomously and onshore, offshore RMB

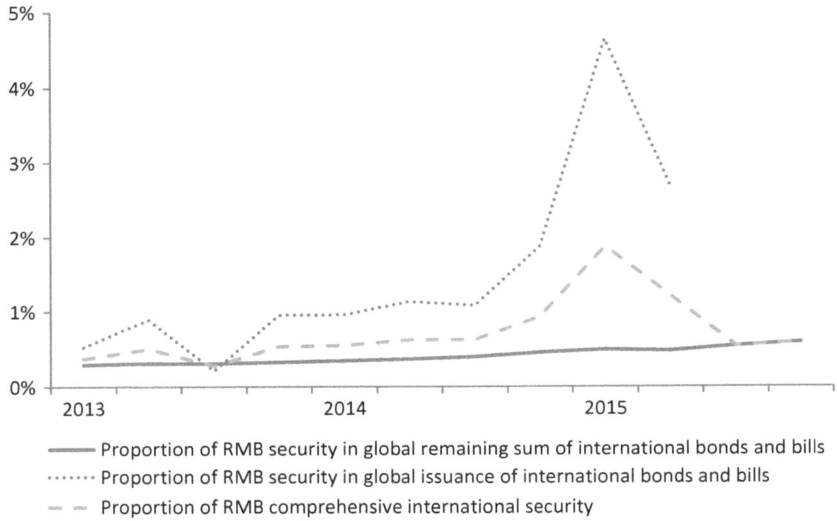

Fig. 1.7 The comprehensive index of RMB international bonds and notes

bonds market to develop complementarily. In early period, the level of domestic interest rate within China was generally higher than that of the overseas market; therefore, numerous institutions chose overseas financing to reduce the cost of capital, which significantly promoted the development of offshore RMB bonds market such as dim sum bonds; then, the PBOC cut the requirement reserve ratio and lowered key interest rates for several rounds; meanwhile the USD stepped into interest rate hike cycle, and as a result the domestic and overseas spread of interest rate continuously diminished and the yield of overseas RMB bond was even higher than that of domestic RMB bond. Furthermore, the Panda Bond circulation exploded with market chasing in frenzy. Overall, onshore and offshore RMB bond markets complemented each other and were subject to fluctuation, which had positive significance for developing real economy and strengthening RMB's functions of investment and financing. With the development of China's economy and the promotion of RMB's internationalization, the total issuance of RMB international bonds showed a rising tendency, which implied huge long-term growth potential.

Secondly, infrastructure of RMB bond and related indicators were gradually improved and perfected. The related infrastructure and indicators were increasingly completed as RMB international bonds market gradually was developed. In 2015, South Korea launched RMB bond real-time settlement system, and China Taiwan began to publish the yield curve of RMB Formosa bond and others, which had positive significance for constructing offshore RMB market in South Korea and Taiwan region. The establishment and launching of market indexes such as CIFED and RMB bond trading index by Bank of China (BOC), providing market entities with quantitative references for financing choices, effectively mirrored onshore and offshore RMB bond market yields spread and volatility.

Thirdly, restrictions on the issuance of RMB bonds were relaxed, and the market openness was further improved. In 2015, China further liberalized market access restrictions: in April, more than 30 overseas financial institutions including HSBC, Morgan Stanley, and BNP Paribas were permitted to enter the interbank market; by the end of 2015, there were 292 foreign institutions such as Central Bank sovereign wealth funds (SWF) participating in the interbank market; in June, the PBOC authorized offshore RMB clearing banks and some overseas banks to participate in bond repurchase transactions in interbank bond market, which narrowed the gap between RMB onshore and offshore markets to some extent, attracted foreign institutions to enter the domestic bond market, and expanded their bond investment and liquidity management needs as well. Furthermore, from another aspect, regulatory authority further loosened management policies: in September, the PBOC abolished quota approving mechanism for foreign debt issued by enterprises, and implemented registration system management, thereby realizing macro supervision on foreign debts' amount, and boosting the growth of RMB international bonds.

Column 1.2 CIPS Officially Launched: Cross-Border RMB Transactions More Secure and Convenient

On October 8, 2015, the first phase of CIPS, organized and developed by the PBOC, was officially launched, which was the milestone in China international payment system development, and laid a solid foundation for the internationalization of RMB. The first batch of directly participating institutions included 19 Chinese and foreign-funded banks within China, such as ICBC, ABC, BOC, CCB, and BOCOM; 179 overseas banks located abroad indirectly participated by synchronously running the system. On the first day online, 336 transactions with total value of 676 million yuan funds were accomplished through the system in only 45 minutes.

In recent years, the continuous development of China's international trade and capital account liberalization made capital flow more frequent. The RMB's international status improved significantly, and affected by a variety of factors, cross-border RMB payment and settlement demand gradually increased. The original Chinese modern payment system (CNAPS) for RMB cross-border and offshore clearing and settlement was problematic with low review efficiency, ununified standard, insufficient running time coverage, and low system security, and can hardly support the growth of cross-border RMB payment and settlement needs. Against this background, CIPS was invented upon the call of the time. The current CIPS (phase I) applied real-time lump-sum settlement mode and converged direct and indirect participants in a top-down pyramid management structure, providing customers and financial institutions with clearing and settlement services in cross-border goods and service trade, cross-border investment and financing, and cross-border personal remittance business. China International Payment Service (Shanghai) Co., Ltd. took responsibilities for the CIPS (phase I) system operation, participant services, and market development, with business hours in legal workday between 9:00 and 20:00. Direct participants could use their unique ID number to do their businesses with their account in the system; indirect participants could accomplish RMB cross-border businesses through multiple direct participants. The PBOC and the operating agencies were responsible for formulating relevant system regulations (The Cross-Border RMB Payment System Business Provisional Regulations, The Cross-Border RMB Payment System Participants Service Agreement, The Cross-Border RMB Payment System Operational Guidelines, The Cross-Border RMB Payment System Operating Rules, and The Cross-Border RMB Payment System Technical Specifications) to supervise and manage CIPS. According to the PBOC's blueprint, CIPS would launch phase II system in the future, employing a more liquidity-efficient mixed settlement and one-stop processing methods, to further improve business efficiency, and meanwhile to expand the direct and indirect participants scale to facilitate businesses.

As infrastructure of cross-border RMB payment, the direct significance of CIPS is to improve the existing RMB cross-border clearing and settlement patterns, expand service coverage through the pyramid structure of participants, improve Chinese processing standards, increase the conversion efficiency of the message, cover more of the world time zones, integrate resources, and improve efficiency. And on a deeper level, the establishment of CIPS dominated by the PBOC can effectively avoid the excessive dependence on the SWIFT system, improve the RMB cross-border settlement safety, ensure the financial security of China, and pave the way for the internationalization of the RMB.

1.2.3 Reinforcement of RMB's Foreign Exchange Reserve Function

As Chinese economy strengthened and international status improved, RMB became more popular as a reserve currency. In 2015, the PBOC initially signed currency swap agreements with monetary authorities of Suriname, Armenia, South Africa, Chile, and Tajikistan, and renewed currency swap agreements with central banks of Australia, Malaysia, Belarus, Ukraine, England, Turkey, and the United Arab Emirates. By the end of 2015, the PBOC already signed 3.31 trillion-yuan worth of currency swap agreements with monetary authorities of 33 countries and regions, which supplemented the existing monetary system defects, offered a buffer, and strengthened market confidence of RMB liquidity worldwide, especially in emerging economies. According to the IMF statistics, from 2010 to 2014, the foreign exchange reserves in RMB accounted for 1.1% of global foreign exchange reserves, meaning the status of RMB as reserve currency rapidly improved, in spite of a big lag compared with the 65.3% of USD. On November 30, 2015, the IMF Executive Board announced that China's currency would be accepted into the SDR currency basket, with RMB as the fifth currency after USD, euro, yen, and GBP. RMB accounted for 10.92% in the basket, third to the USD and the euro. RMB joining the SDR was a symbol of RMB being integrated into international currencies and being endorsed by the IMF on an international scale, which greatly boosted the confidence of the market and helped RMB to become one of the important choices of global central banks' foreign exchange reserve currency. RMB gained increasingly wider recognition from other countries. In November, British Columbia of Canada initially registered to issue panda bonds of 6 billion yuan in China's interbank bond market, which was the first issuance of panda bonds in China led by a foreign government; in December, South Korean government was granted the qualification to issue 3 billion yuan of panda bonds; Russia and some other countries and regions declared that they would consider to recognize RMB as a reserve currency.

1.3 Comparison of the Internationalization Indexes of Major Currencies

Diversification of international currency is a dynamic development process. Changes in both international trade patterns and the international financial markets will lead to corresponding adjustments in international monetary structure, which is presented as some currencies gaining popularity in the globe, while some others losing it. In order to objectively evaluate the gap in the level of internationalization between the RMB and major currencies, this report has also compiled internationalization indexes for USD, EUR, JPY, and GBP (Table 1.1). The US economy maintained a strong recovery momentum and the Fed started to raise interest rate. A strong dollar drove the internationalization index of USD up to 54.97 from 54.17 in 2014. The USD's international currency status rose again. A modest recovery appeared in the Eurozone; however, each member country's economic performance was uneven. Dragged down by the severe challenges from Greece's problems, refugee crisis, the euro continued to depreciate, hitting international confidence in the euro. Hence the internationalization index of euro continued slipping to 23.71, and would be stuck in a rut for a while. Global economic stress and inadequate demand resulted in slight weakness of Japanese economy, but the characteristic of yen as a safe-haven currency was strengthened. Thus the internationalization index was held at

Table 1.1 Internationalization indexes of the world's major currencies

	2014Q1	*2014Q2*	*2014Q3*	*2014Q4*	*2015Q1*	*2015Q2*	*2015Q3*	*2015Q4*
USD	53.58	53.47	54.78	54.17	55.66	55.91	54.56	54.97
EUR	26.57	25.00	24.30	24.69	24.09	22.39	24.68	23.71
JPY	4.44	4.40	4.11	4.33	4.12	4.08	4.10	4.29
GBP	5.58	4.56	4.54	4.25	4.79	4.74	4.83	4.53
Total	90.17	87.44	87.74	87.44	88.66	87.12	88.17	87.49

a stable level of 4.29. The UK economy performed better than expected, and trade and investment relatively increased rapidly. However, with the UK's EU referendum approaching, British political and economic situation became more uncertain. Meanwhile the GBP exchange rate continued to decline, and GBP internationalization index dropped from the beginning of 4.79 to 4.53 this year (Fig. 1.8).

1.3.1 Analysis of the Variation of Dollar's International Index

In 2015, US economy experienced a moderate expansion with GDP growth rate of 2.4%. The job market continued to recover, unemployment rate fell from 5.7% early in the year to 5%, a record low in the past 7.5 years, and the prospect of inflation rate was also comparatively optimistic. On December 16, 2015, the Federal Reserve raised its benchmark interest rate by 0.25%, officially launching the process of raising interest rates, and exiting from quantitative easing (QE) monetary policy. The America-dominated Trans Pacific Partnership eventually reached an agreement in October 2015, and it involved 12 countries: the United States, Japan, Australia, and so on, which represented more than 40% of the world's GDP, and provided great confidence for American trade and the subsequent economic growth. However, the US economy outlook was not always good. Manufacturing

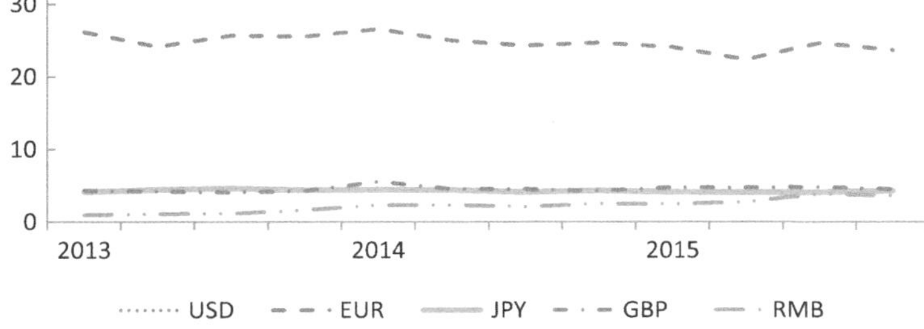

Fig. 1.8 The internationalization indexes' changing trend of the world's major currencies

activity index fell to 48 in December, and this weakness brought risks to economic recovery; the Fed's raising interest rates and a stronger dollar exacerbated the global economic and financial volatility, as well as created "spill-back effects", weighing down American economy.

With the support of the US economic recovery, in 2015 the global market continued to digest the impact of expectation of the rising dollar rate, which led to a substantially strong dollar. USD index once rose from 90.3 at the beginning of the year to 100.47. Global funds accelerated flowing back to the US market, which made USD as the world's best performing currency. In the second quarter of 2015, the balance of USD–denominated international bonds and notes accounted for as high as 43.73% in the whole world, and the share of global official foreign exchange reserves of USD also rose sharply to 63.38%. In 2015, USD international index was 54.97, an increase of 1.47% year-on-year, rising by 6.68% compared with 51.53 in the year 2010. The dollar's role as a leading international currency was further consolidated.

Column 1.3 USD Interest Rate Hike Stirred the Global Capital Markets

Since the Fed proposed to exit from QE in 2013, the expectation of rising dollar interest rate was increasingly stronger, especially after October 30, 2014 when the US Federal Reserve announced its exit from QE and constantly implied to raise interest rates to stimulate the international capital inflow to the United States and enhance the vitality of the US market investment and attractiveness. In 2015, with the recovery of the US economy and the expectation of dollar interest rates rising, the dollar index surged and hit the highest point in the past 12 years of 100.412 on December 2, 2015. All parties gave a high degree of concern about the Fed's monetary policy, and different opinions about the tendency of dollar interest rates resulted in a large range of market volatility. Global commodity markets and financial markets fluctuated. Commodity prices, stock markets of major countries, and the international currency exchange rates suffered different degrees of shock.

Finally, the Federal Reserve announced to raise the federal funds rate by 0.25% on December 16, 2015, and declared the low interest rates would remain for long. In the future the Fed would adjust the process of interest rate hike according to future economic data performance. It was the first time in nearly ten years to raise the federal benchmark interest rate, terminating the situation where official interest rate wandered around zero for 84 months. After the announcement, the dollar index rose to 99.2898 in short term. Although the global financial market had long expected this event and braced itself for the interest rate rises, and the stock market, bond, and foreign exchange markets of the main developed countries were without drastic fluctuations, emerging markets reflected intensively: Argentine Peso plummeted by 30%; the Russian ruble, the Brazilian real, and South African rand declined to different extents; even the RMB exchange rate also depreciated for ten consecutive days.

In the short term, a stronger dollar would attract back overseas capital that out-flowed due to QE, exerted pressure on the global monetary policy, and imposed a negative effect on the world's major economies through three channels: capital flow, exchange rate, and trade. First, economies with their currencies pegged to the dollar would adjust interest rate automatically, such as Hong Kong. Second, the economies affected by the fall in commodity prices, such as Argentina, Brazil, Russia, and South Africa, as well as economies suffering from high debt rate and international trade deficit, such as some of the southern European countries, had to raise interest rates, depreciate their currencies, impose capital controls, or take other measures to deal with the situation, which suppressed real economies' confidence and vitality. Finally, some developed economies such as the EU and Japan were still in economic downturn and their monetary easing space would be restricted. Easing policies would likely make more capital flow to the United States for relatively higher returns, thus weakening the effect of easing policies.

The impact of the dollar rate rising would gradually fade out. In a long-term view, if the US economy further recovered in the process of raising interest rates, it would produce positive effect through the trade to economic situation of major US trading partners including China, European Union, Japan, South Korea, Mexico, and ASEAN countries; support commodity prices; and further boost the economy of Russia, South America, Middle East, Africa, and other regions. If the US economy was impeded by raising interest rates, the process of interest rate rising would slow down and even reverse.

1.3.2 Analysis on the Variation of Euro's International Index

In 2015, European economies showed signs of recovery, inflation bounced back, and the GDP growth rate in the euro area for the year was 1.6%. However, the foundation of the Eurozone economic recovery was relatively fragile, the statuses of the member countries were uneven, and there were still many uncertainties, especially the distress of refugee crisis which troubled the European economy and society. A flood of refugees into Europe not only increased financial burden on the government, but also brought hidden dangers to the security situation and social order in Europe, which weakened the basis for the Eurozone economic recovery. The European Central Bank continued to implement a QE monetary policy, which led to the euro continual depreciation. Recently, the risk of Brexit rose. Once Britain exits from the EU, it will fuel the already-severe economic and political problems of EU. The scenario, which would further dim euro and the Eurozone, made investors hesitative and undermined EU's momentum of recovery.

Suffering from the impact of fragile economic recovery and continued QE monetary policy in Europe, euro took a nosedive to a record low since the outbreak of financial crisis, which triggered large-scale evacuation of international capital. In the traditional euro-dominated international bond markets, euro international bonds and notes balance proportion fell to 38.48% in the fourth quarter of 2015, dropping by 7.21% year-on-year. The proportion of euro in official foreign exchange reserves dropped to 19.91% over the same period; euro's proportion in cross-border trade slowly declined. In the fourth quarter of 2015, the euro internationalization index fell to 23.71, decreasing by 14.44% compared with 27.71 at the end of 2010. The euro's international status was seriously frustrated.

Column 1.4 The Influence of European Refugee Crisis on European Economic Recovery

In recent years, the situation of West Asia and North Africa were in shocks, and continued to deteriorate; the religious factions and tribal internal conflicts continued to ferment; the extremist terrorist organizations took the opportunity to make a profit in troubled situation, and made terrorist incidents frequently. People became homeless and large scale of refugee flows emerged. Due to proximity and the open-door immigration policy of Europe, increasing numbers of refugees flowed from the Mediterranean and land into Europe. According to the latest UNHCR data, as of December 29, 2015, the number of refugees flowing into Europe through Mediterranean and land exceeded 100 million, far more than the 21.9 million in 2014, posing a more serious problem. Millions of refugees flooded to the fragile borderline of European countries. Some countries were unable to effectively control the border. In addition, tensions in West Asia and North Africa region could not be abated shortly. The number of refugees in Europe would further increase; the EU expected that, by the end of 2016, the influx of refugees in Europe would exceed 3 million. Refugee crisis brought many uncertainties to the economy in Europe, and the economic and social development in Europe faced greater challenges.

On the one hand, the Europe recovery was still weak, and the refugee crisis would undoubtedly bring enormous economic pressure. Influx of refugees would increase the financial burden on European countries, and create negative impact on public finances of European countries. The EU planned to spend 9.2 billion euro to deal with the refugee crisis within two years, but the large expenditure still could not crack the refugee problem. According to agency estimates, refugees cost German government around 21 billion euro, equivalent to nearly 0.7% of German GDP. Greek refugee cost might reach 40 billion euro, equivalent to 2% of its GDP. Meanwhile, the refugee crisis would further exacerbate social insecurity in Europe, thereby affecting the investment environment. This was obviously not good news as EU was in urgent need of outside investment to revitalize the regional economy. Also, new refugees might occupy the already-stretched jobs, worsen the problem of unemployment, and encroach upon the public welfare of local people. Rapid population growth accompanied by economic weakness is very dangerous. Continuous European refugee crisis would not only hinder the Eurozone economic recovery to a certain extent, but also bring challenges for regional security situation and social stability. This caused panic among investors, impacted the international economic and trade exchanges in Europe, increased downward pressure on the euro, and also weakened the international position of euro. If handled improperly, it might intensify the contradiction between EU members, and even cause some divisions.

On the other hand, the positive effect of the refugee flow into the European economy cannot be ignored. Research shows that since government expenditure on refugee matters could stimulate domestic demand, the inflow of refugees boost economic development slightly in EU countries; the GDP of 2017 was expected to increase by 0.1%. Austria (+0.5%), Sweden (+0.4%), and Germany (+0.3%) that received more refugees would benefit more. Meanwhile, local residents and refugees worked in different fields of employment, and therefore refugee inflows would not produce greater competition and conflicts. A recent study of the IMF showed that refugee crisis had limited impacts on the development of the European economy, the job market, and the national financial market. Impact of refugee inflow on long-term economic development of Europe depends on how quickly the refugee integrates into the labor market. Therefore, countries should take a series of measures to help refugees to be integrated into the European society, including providing the subsidies of wage costs, temporary reduction in minimum wage, reducing the burden of self-employed refugees, relaxing migration restrictions, and providing supports of housing and education.

1.3.3 Analysis of the Variation of Yen's International Index

Due to the impact of the decline of external demand caused by weak consumption, global economic slowdown, and other factors, Japan's economic recovery was weak in 2015, with growth in fits and starts. Benefiting from the growth of capital expenditures and residential investment caused by corporate income rises, the actual GDP growth rate in the first quarter reached 1%, showing a modest recovery. But due to the unexpected decline in capital expenditures, the actual GDP of the second quarter decreased by 0.3% quarter-on-quarter, hindering the recovery. In the third quarter, the actual GDP growth was 0.3% quarter-on-quarter, and the escalating capital expenditure was the main reason. In the fourth quarter, Japan's GDP was dragged down by weak demand by 0.4% quarter-on-quarter. Japan's unemployment rate in 2015 fluctuated around 3.3% and maintained at a low level. The employment figure was sound. Owing to import decrease caused by lower oil prices and export increase caused by depreciation of the yen, Japan's trade deficit shrank dramatically, plummeting from 12.78 trillion yen in 2014 to 2.83 trillion yen in 2015, and the international balance of payments improved. However, the trade deficit was not reversed for five years, and the dim prospects for exports also fueled controversy about whether Japan's foreign trade could continue to improve or not.

In 2015, Bank of Japan maintained easing monetary policies, and nominal yields were anchored while Japan inflation expectations increased, which compressed real rate of return of yen. But the JPY gradually highlighted its features as a safe-haven currency and performed well overall in the fierce fluctuation of the exchange market. In the fourth quarter of 2015, the balance of international bonds and notes in the yen accounted for 1.91%, decreasing by 4.02% year-on-year; compared with the same period, the share of official foreign exchange reserves in the yen rose slightly, accounting for 4.08%. The yen's internationalization index was 4.29, declining slightly year-on-year.

1.3.4 Analysis of the Variation of Pound's International Index

In 2015, Britain's economic growth decelerated, with GDP growth of 2.2%, receding to the lowest level of economic growth in nearly three years. The unemployment rate continued to decline. At the end of the fourth quarter, the unemployment rate fell to 5.1%, but the salary growth and unemployment compensation application rate were lower than expected; average inflation rate was 0 in 2015, and the United Kingdom accordingly decided to terminate the position of rising interest rates. Britain's trade deficit for the year hit a six-year peak, reaching 125.028 billion pounds, which had a negative impact on macroeconomic growth. Britain's economic slowdown, Brexit expectation, postponed interest rises, and other factors aggravated the bearish sentiment in the market and the investors' anxiety, impacting capital flow. GBP thus took a nosedive. However, Britain had a relatively good performance among major developed economies, and was better than expected. In the fourth quarter of 2015, GBP-denominated international bonds and notes balance accounted for 9.55% in the international market, an increase of 3.02% year-on-year. In the fourth quarter of 2015, the GBP internationalization index was 4.53, climbing up by 6.59% year-on-year, and the international status of the GBP was enhanced.

CHAPTER 2

Status Quo of Renminbi Internationalization

International Monetary Institute

In 2015, RMB's internationalization speeded up its process. During the past years, the amount of RMB used as a settlement currency for trades increased significantly on a larger scale, and the offshore market was booming. Meanwhile, international financial cooperation was deepening, and the RMB exchange rate regime reform was promoted steadily. Under the new normal of economy, structural adjustment and institutional reform were pushed forward in an orderly manner, and market-oriented reform of capital pricing further cleared institutional obstacles for RMB's internationalization. On November 30, 2015, the IMF announced that the RMB would be included in the SDR, which started a new journey of RMB's internationalization.

2.1 RMB Cross-Border Trade Settlement

1. RMB was used on a larger scale with the proportion of RMB settlement fluctuating.

International Monetary Institute (✉)
Renmin University of China, Beijing, China
e-mail: imi@ruc.edu.cn

International Monetary Institute (ed.), *Currency Internationalization and Macro Financial Risk Control*,
https://doi.org/10.1007/978-981-13-0698-3_2

In 2015, the scale of cross-border trade settlement by RMB expanded steadily. The annual cross-border trade settlement in RMB reached 7.23 trillion yuan, increasing by 680 billion yuan and 10.38% compared with the figure in 2014. The proportion of cross-border trade settlement in RMB in total international trade was 29.36%, increasing by 4.6% compared with the last year.

Influenced by the weak recovery of the global economy and downward pressure, China's import and export exhibited for the first time a double down situation since 2009. Although the external environment was grim, the scale of RMB as a settlement currency still maintained a growth momentum on the whole in 2015, with characteristics of significant slower growth rate and fluctuating proportion in settlement through the year. Cross-border trade settlement in RMB grew from 3.04% in the fourth quarter of 2014 to 3.38% in the fourth quarter of 2015, with a slower growth rate of 11.18%.

Since the dollar came into a strong period, RMB continued to depreciate. Especially after the reform of the RMB exchange rate regime, a substantial decline of the RMB trade settlement scale occurred in the third quarter, the proportion of which declined by 10%. With the expansion of international trade scale in the fourth quarter, the RMB exchange rate tended to be stable, and the proportion of RMB settlement rebounded to September level. In the third quarter, the share of RMB settlement in global trade reached 4.06%, a record high (Fig. 2.1).

2. RMB was mainly used in goods settlement, with RMB used in service settlement edging up.

In the cross-border RMB settlement structure, goods trade dominated. In 2015, cross-border goods trade settled in RMB reached 6.39 trillion yuan, accounting for 88.34% of cross-border RMB trade settlement. RMB settlement in service trade and other items under current account reached 843.2 billion yuan, accounting for 11.66% of cross-border RMB trade settlement. RMB settlement in service trade was in a slow yet steady growth, and in the fourth quarter increased considerably. In the environment of global economic downturn, in October and November 2015 international trade volume fell significantly, resulting in a corresponding decrease in the scale of cross-border trade settlement. With cross-border goods trade sliding far faster than service trade, the RMB settlement of service trade slightly increased in terms of proportion. In December, cross-border trade both in goods and services rebounded (Figs. 2.2 and 2.3).

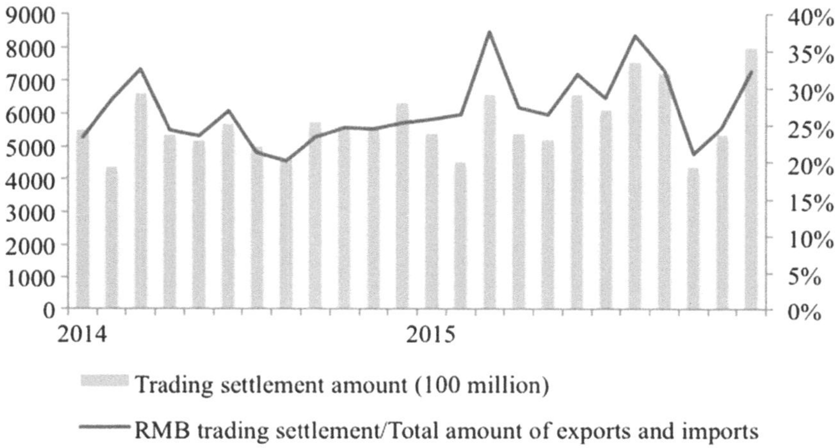

Fig. 2.1 Scale of RMB cross-border trade settlement. (Source: People's Bank of China; the Ministry of Commerce)

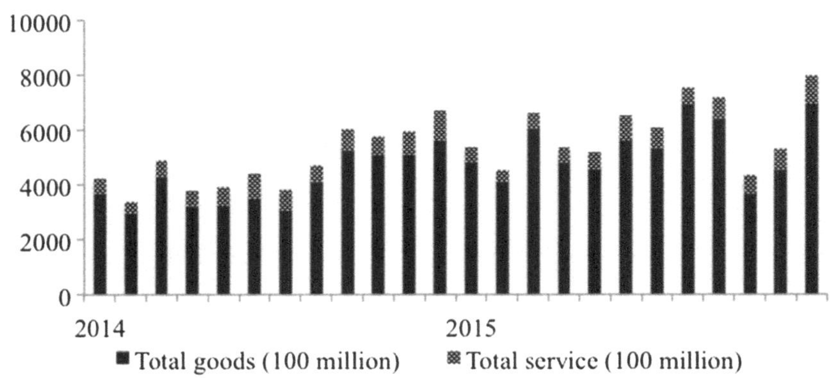

Fig. 2.2 Settlement volumes of goods and service trades in RMB. (Sources: The People's Bank of China; the Ministry of Commerce)

3. RMB payment exceeded RMB receipt for the first time, and RMB settlement in export rapidly increased.

By the end of 2015, the actual receipt in cross-border trade RMB settlement was 6.19 trillion yuan, representing an increase of 3.46 trillion yuan compared with 2014, an increase of 126.74%; actual payment was

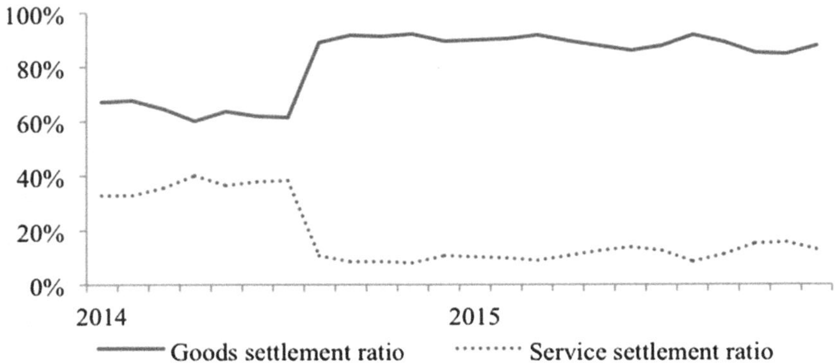

Fig. 2.3 Settlement ratios of goods and service trades in RMB. (Sources: The People's Bank of China; the Ministry of Commerce)

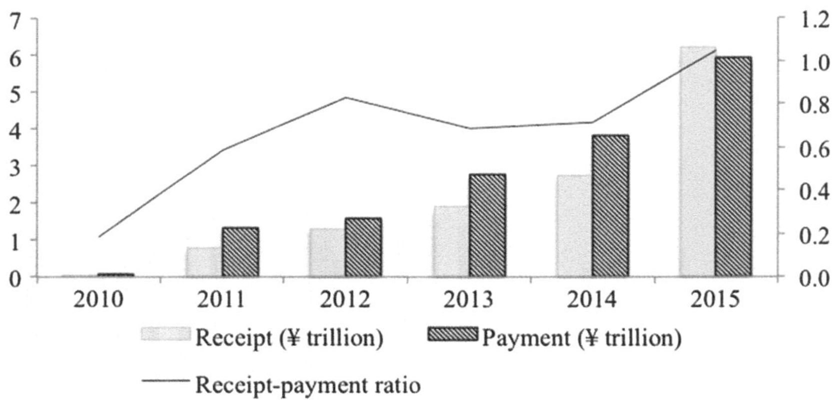

Fig. 2.4 Receipt-payment ratio of RMB settlement in cross-border trade. (Sources: The People's Bank of China)

5.91 trillion yuan, representing an increase of 2.09 trillion yuan in 2014, an increase of 54.71%. The receipt-payment ratio decreased significantly from 1.4 in 2014 to 0.96, which meant that cross-border RMB actual receipt was less than actual payment appeared for the first time since the internationalization of RMB, reflecting foreign enterprises' confidence in Chinese economy and a long-term stable RMB. The internationalization of RMB further deepened (Fig. 2.4).

Column 2.1 "The Belt and Road Initiative" Countries Are More Willing to Use RMB

Trade facilitation is one of the main objectives of "the Belt and Road Initiative". In 2015, with the deepening of cooperation willingness and continuous progress of pragmatic cooperation between China and neighboring countries, the Belt and Road neighboring countries increased the scale of trade with China.

According to the Ministry of Commerce statistics, in 2015 China and the Belt and Road neighboring countries' bilateral trade amounted to $995.5 billion, accounting for 25.1% of China's total international trade in the same period; and countries that were highly dependent on trading with China included Mongolia, Laos, Republic of Yemen, and so on. Meanwhile, in order to promote the growth of trade, in 2015 Chinese enterprises put a total of $14.82 billion of direct investment to the 49 Belt and Road–related countries, with a year-on-year growth of 18.2%, and the investment mainly flowed to Singapore, Kazakhstan, and Laos.

With expanding trade scale between the Belt and Road countries and China, the former showed stronger willingness to use RMB as a settlement currency. According to a 2015 survey by BOC on whether enterprises of the Belt and Road countries would like to use RMB, 73% of corporate respondents believed that the RMB would become an important international currency, in contrast with 64% in 2014. Forty-four percent of enterprises believed that the international status of the RMB would be closer to the USD and the euro, 11% higher compared with 2014. Seventy-two percent of respondents expressed their willingness to use RMB to settle trades with China.

China is the largest trading partner of most countries along the Belt and Road, for which better economic cooperation in trade, investment, and other aspects with China could bring capital, technology, comparative trade benefits, and higher revenue. If the enterprises used more RMB rather than a third-party settlement currency in trades with China, price stability would help them to expand their exports to China. Using RMB could also avoid exchange rate risk that third-party currency may bring. Therefore, more overseas enterprises tended to use RMB.

2.2 RMB Financial Transactions

2.2.1 RMB Direct Investment

1. RMB overseas direct investment

In 2015, China's overseas investment and RMB foreign investment increased significantly. According to the Ministry of Commerce statistics, in 2015 Chinese domestic investors put direct investment to 6532 foreign enterprises in 155 countries or areas, and the cumulative non-financial direct investment was 735.08 billion yuan (USD 118.02 billion), increasing by 16.3% compared with 2014, among which the amount of ODI in RMB was 736.2 billion yuan, a year-on-year increase of 549.6 billion yuan and 294.53% compared with 2014.

Chinese economy was undergoing industrial restructuring and the supply-side reforms, which needed rational allocation of domestic and external resources, and better capacity cooperation with other countries. In 2015 mergers and acquisitions (M&A) activities and overseas investment were active, and overseas RMB direct investment scale registered a record high. As is shown in Fig. 2.5, in 2015 the scale and proportion of RMB-denominated ODI exhibited an inverted V-shape: from January to August, the scale of RMB ODI climbed up slowly; from August to

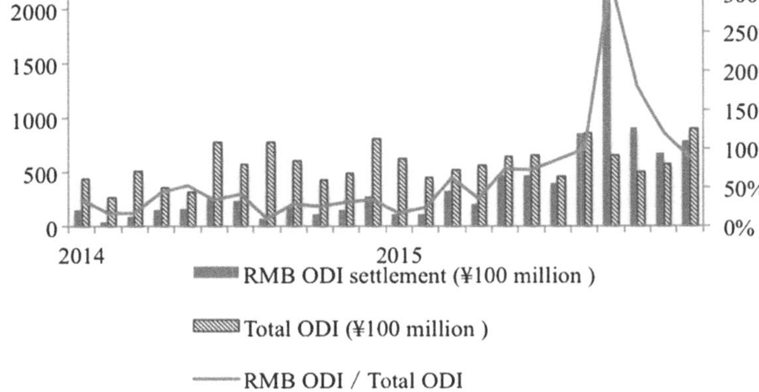

Fig. 2.5 RMB ODI's ratio in the total Chinese ODI. (Source: People's Bank of China; the Ministry of Commerce)

September, influenced by the impact of the RMB exchange rate regime reform, RMB depreciation accelerated, and many enterprises accelerated global asset allocation to reduce the exchange rate risk of holding RMB, which led to a sudden rise of RMB ODI from 85.1 billion to 207.8 billion yuan, reaching a peak since the start of the RMB internationalization. The proportion of RMB ODI accordingly increased rapidly. After September, the expectation of de-valuation of the RMB was weakened, and RMB ODI also gradually declined. Coupled with China's recovering overseas investment, the reduction of the proportion of RMB settlement slowed down.

2. RMB Foreign Direct Investment

In 2015, the actual use of FDI reached \$126.25 billion, an increase of \$6.692 billion and 5.6% over the previous year. The offshore direct investments were mainly from Hong Kong, Taiwan, Singapore, Japan, and other countries or regions, engaging in the manufacturing, real estate, financial services, and wholesale and retail trade. With the continuous improvement and expansion of the offshore RMB market, RMB FDI increased significantly in 2015 with an amount of 1.5871 trillion yuan, a year-on-year increase of 725.1 billion yuan and 84.12% (Fig. 2.6). Affected by the RMB exchange rate regime reform in August, foreign investors used a large amount of RMB in direct investment to avoid exchange rate risks, so in September RMB FDI peaked.

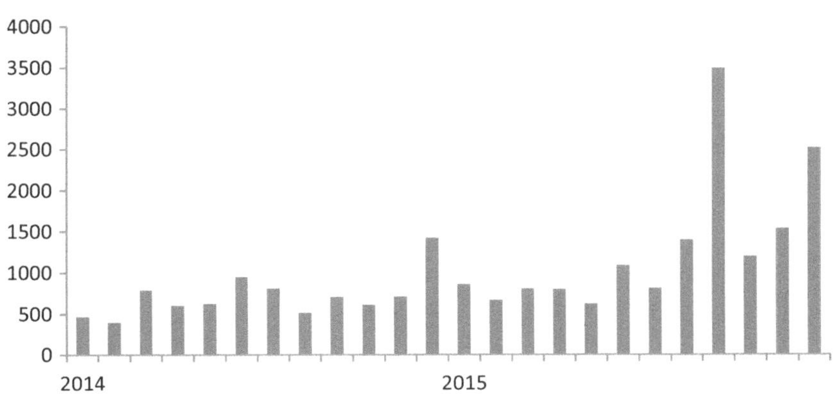

Fig. 2.6 FDI RMB settlement (¥100 million). (Source: People's Bank of China, the Ministry of Commerce)

Column 2.2 International Capacity Cooperation Promotes the Rapid Growth of China's Overseas Direct Investment

In economic globalization and an increasingly competitive international market, many developing countries along the Belt and Road had an urgent demand for growth. But limited by their poor infrastructure and technical conditions, they could not reach their goal. In March 2015, the Chinese government issued "Vision and Action to Promote the Silk Road Economic Belt and the 21st Century Maritime Silk Road", putting forward an idea to strengthen all-round cooperation interoperability with neighboring countries; in May of the same year, the Chinese government put forward "Guiding Opinions on Promoting the International Equipment Manufacturing Capacity and Cooperation", which raised the international cooperation capacity to a national strategic level.

The Chinese government strengthened pragmatic cooperation with the national governments along the Belt and Road, established capacity cooperation fund, and jointly developed a capacity cooperation plan with Brazil, Peru, and other ten more countries. There is no doubt that countries along the Belt and Road are the focus area of China's international capacity cooperation at this stage. According to the Ministry of Commerce statistics, in 2015 China's non-financial ODI amounted to $118.02 billion, an increase of 14.7% compared to the same period last year. International capacity cooperation has made a great leap forward. Chinese enterprises allocated direct investment to 49 countries along the Belt and Road including Singapore, Kazakhstan, Laos, Indonesia, Russia, and Thailand, with a total amount of $14.82 billion and an year-on-year growth of 18.2%; and China signed 3987 new outsourcing project contracts with 60 countries along the Belt and Road, with a total contract amount of $92.64 billion, which accounted for 44.1% of China's new contract amount of outsourced contracted projects, with an year-on-year growth of 7.4%; operating income reached $69.26 billion, which accounted for 45% of the total and achieved an increase of 7.6% compared to the same period last year.

Carrying out international capacity cooperation based on comparative advantages and local market demand can bring mutual benefits and collaborative development, which contributes to the national development of technology and improves business environment in those cooperation countries to achieve faster growth.

2.2.2 RMB Securities Investment

1. International bonds and notes market

With the internationalization of the RMB and the liberalization of the capital market, the panda debt market ushered in the first wave of issuance since the market was established ten years ago. In 2015, six domestic and foreign institutions issued panda bonds with a total amount of 15.5 billion yuan in interbank bond market, a record high.

In September 2015, the Chinese government issued "Notice on the Promotion of Foreign Corporate Debt Issuance Registration System for Management Reform", which relaxed the regulations on enterprises' issuing overseas bonds, canceled the amount approval of issuing foreign debts, and carried out the registration system management. And the document encouraged enterprises to finance in overseas market with lower interest rates, allowed capital to be freely used at home and abroad, and supported restructuring and upgrading in key areas and industries. External debt management system reform was conducive to enhancing the offshore bond issuance and to improving the convertibility under capital account.

In 2015, the amount of international RMB bonds and notes increased steadily. By the end of 2015, the value of RMB international bonds and notes was $ 124.792 billion, a year-on-year increase of $ 29.409 billion and 30.8%. The proportion of RMB rose to 0.59% in outstanding international bonds and notes (Fig. 2.7). International bonds are the most impor-

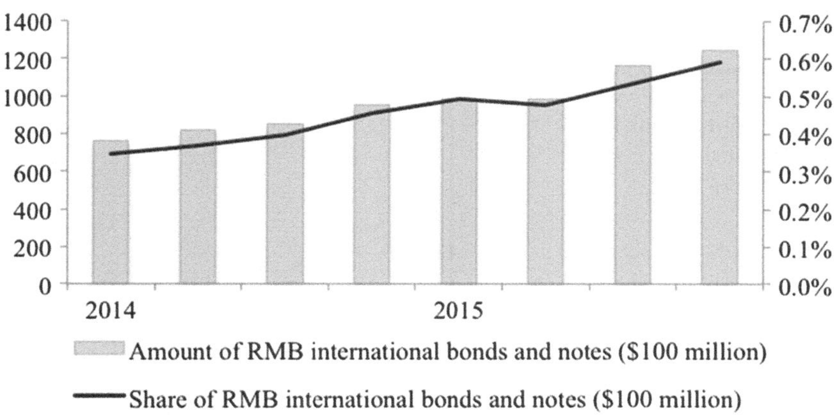

Fig. 2.7 Amount and proportion of RMB international bonds and notes. (Source: Bank for International Settlements)

tant part of the international capital markets, so the steady growth of RMB international bonds and notes meant that the RMB was gradually accepted in financial transactions.

RMB's internationalization achieved a remarkable success since its start in 2009. But in the financial market it was still faced with strong hindrance caused by network effect. There was still a large gap between RMB and mainstream currencies. By the end of 2015, in outstanding global international bonds and notes, dollar accounted for 43.73%, the euro 38.48%, the pound 9.55%, and the yen 1.91% (Fig. 2.8). RMB's internationalization still has a long way to go, and needs to be continuously expanded and improved.

Offshore market is the main place for RMB international bond issuance. In 2015 many global financial centers carried out offshore RMB business, resulting in the rapid expansion of offshore RMB deposits and creating good conditions for the issuance of RMB international bonds. Apart from Hong Kong, in Singapore, London, Taiwan, Seoul, Frankfurt, Luxembourg, and other places, RMB offshore market participants and products became more diversified, and the size of the market was significantly expanded. Of course, Hong Kong was still the largest offshore RMB market. In 2015, the stock of RMB bonds in Hong Kong rose to 397.116 billion yuan from 386.087 billion yuan by the end of 2014, an increase of 2.85%. Among RMB bonds, the most obvious change was in outstanding RMB financial bond, which rose to 120.324 billion yuan in 2015 from 111.227 billion yuan in 2014, and its market share increased by 5 percentage points (Table 2.1).

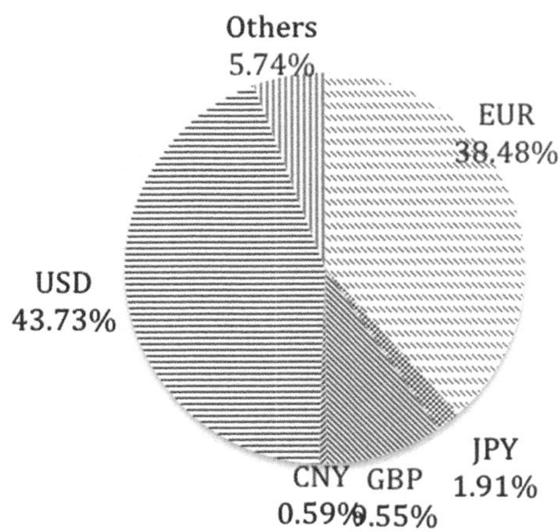

Fig. 2.8 Currency structure of the stock of international bonds and notes by the end of 2015. (Source: Bank for International Settlements)

Table 2.1 Amount and structure of RMB bonds in Hong Kong in 2015

Categories	*Outstanding amount (100 million RMB)*	*Share (%)*	*Number of bonds*	*Share (%)*
Corporate bonds	1761.22	44.35	154.0000	43.87
Government bonds	934.00	23.52	37.0000	10.54
Financial bonds	1203.24	30.30	152.0000	43.30
Convertible bonds	72.70	1.83	8.0000	2.28
Total	3971.16	100.00	351.0000	100.00

Source: Wind database

Dim sum bond issued by local investors in Europe accounted for 47% of the total amount of the bond, and investors from the United States, China, and other regions accounted for 14%, 5%, and 34% respectively. Outside the Asian market, Luxemburg became the first major offshore center of the dim sum bonds. In 2015, 31 offerings of dim sum bond were made with a total value of 11 billion yuan. The number of bonds issuance rose by 34.78% compared to 2014.

2. Stock market

China's financial structure was suited to the economic restructuring; the financing mode gradually changed from indirect financing to direct financing, and capital market's financing function was enhanced. By the end of 2015, the total value of the stock market (A-, B-share) totaled 53.1 trillion yuan, a year-on-year increase of 15.9 trillion yuan and 42.61%. By the end of 2015, the market value of Chinese stock market was 41.8 trillion yuan, a year-on-year increase of 10.2 trillion yuan and 32.41%. The sharp rise in the overall level of the stock price made trades more active, and the volume set a record high. In 2015, Shanghai and Shenzhen markets accumulated turnover of 255.1 trillion yuan, a year-on-year increase of 180.7 trillion yuan and 242.85%. Average daily turnover was 1.045303 trillion yuan, a year-on-year increase of 741.665 billion yuan and 244.26% (Fig. 2.9).

In 2015, China's stock market exhibited irrational volatility. The high gearing and securities margin trading enlarged the leverage, and the optimism in the market propelled the boom in the stock market. On June 12, 2015, the Shanghai Composite Index reached an annual record high of 5178.19. After the China Securities Regulatory Commission (CSRC) forbade OTC gearing and regulated the margin trading activities, the stock

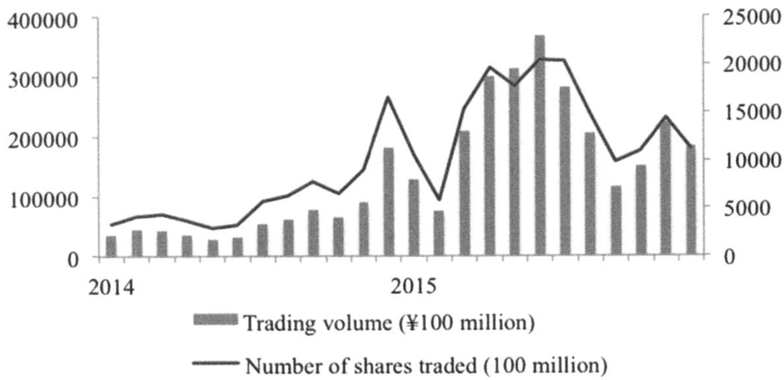

Fig. 2.9 Chinese stock market transactions. (Source: China Securities Regulatory Commission)

Table 2.2 Chinese stock market financing volume

Year	*IPO amount*			*Refinancing amount*					
	A-share (¥100 million)	*B-share ($100 million)*	*H-share ($100 million)*	*A-share (¥100 million)*				*B-share ($100 million)*	*H-share ($100 million)*
				Public offering	*Private placement*	*Rights offering*	*Warrants exercised*		
2013	0	0	113.17	80.42	2246.59	475.75	0	0	59.51
2014	668.89	0	128.72	18.26	4031.3	137.98	0	0	212.90
2015	1766.91	0	236.19	0	6709.48	42.33	0	0	227.12

Source: China Securities Regulatory Commission

market plummeted. The Shanghai Composite Index reached the lowest point of the year of 2850.71 on August 26, 2015. In just two months the index dropped by 44.9%, and the turnover volume dropped.

In 2015, a total of 224 companies were newly listed, among which 90 were listed on the Shanghai Stock Exchange main board, 45 were listed on the Shenzhen SME board, and 86 were listed on GEM. Newly listed companies financed 176.691 billion yuan through the stock market. The amount of private placement of listed companies also increased significantly compared with 2014. The annual issuance amounted to 670.948 billion yuan, with an increase of 66.43% (Table 2.2). Capital market's financing function strengthened.

On November 18, 2015, China Europe International Exchange co-funded by the Shanghai Stock Exchange, the Deutsche Börse group, and China Financial Futures Exchange with proportions of 40%, 40%, and 20%, respectively, was established in Frankfurt, in which RMB financial products were traded. Products included RMB-denominated and China's A-share index-based exchange-traded fund (ETF) products, as well as RMB financial bonds issued by Bank of China. Twelve Chinese market-related ETF previously listed on the Deutsche Börse and more than 180 RMB bonds were transferred to the China Europe International Exchange trading platform.

Column 2.3 International Strategy and Overseas Business Development of Bank of Communications

1. International strategy of Bank of Communications

Bank of Communications was founded in 1908, and it was one of the first domestic commercial banks to explore the international market. As early as it was established, Bank of communications went global. Saigon representative office and Hong Kong branch were set up in 1909; Singapore and Yangon branch were established in 1910; management office of Japan was established in 1918; Liangshan Communications office and the Philippines branch were set up in 1939; Calcutta branch was established in 1941. All overseas branches enjoyed a good reputation in the host countries.

In 2009, after restructuring and IPO, Bank of Communications established the "walking an international and integrated path, and building the first-class public bank group featuring wealth management" development strategy (referred to as the "two paths and one bank" strategy). It constantly improved the overseas business management system; continued to enhance the capacity of cross-border financial services; created a global financial services platform, cross-border wealth management platform as well as a clearing, settlement, and financing center; promoted steady and rapid international development; connected domestic and foreign markets; won competitive advantage of cross-border RMB business; and built an overseas network of "exploring the global market with Asia and Pacific region being the main market, and Europe and America being two wings" to achieve sound development.

By the end of 2015, Bank of Communications set up 15 offshore banking institutions in Hong Kong, New York, Tokyo, Singapore, Seoul, Frankfurt, Macau, Ho Chi Minh City, London, Sydney, San Francisco, Taipei, Toronto, Brisbane, and Luxembourg, including 14 branches and one representative office. The bank's overseas business outlets were up to 56 (excluding representative offices). In May 2015, the bank and the BBM Bank of Brazil signed a BBM bank equity transfer agreement, which became the first time for the bank to set up an overseas institution through M&A. The bank extended its business network to Asia, North America, Europe, Oceania, and Latin America. At present, the bank is promoting institution building in Hong Kong, Europe, North America, and other places, and strengthening planning studies in Africa, the Middle East, Eastern Europe, and other countries along the Belt and Road. The international layout of "One Body, Two Wings in Global Market" is being completed.

2. Overseas business development of Bank of Communications
   (a) Following the Belt and Road strategy. Bank of Communications conducted overseas institutions layout closely around the Belt and Road strategy. Based on its own advantages, the bank identified target customers and projects, and gave full play to the corresponding product system and service ability; the bank prioritized risk management, by not only investigating risks for the project alone, but also analyzing risks according to the location of the project and putting forward comprehensive and reliable safety measures. The bank served various financial needs of the Belt and Road strategy under the premises of safety.
   (b) Adhering to the "following customer" strategy. The bank adhered to the principle that equal attention should be paid to both Chinese "going out" corporate clients and foreign corporate clients, both large corporate customers and SME customers, both grassroots customer and high-end customers. The bank took opportunities to serve "going global Chinese enterprises", "foreign enterprises in China, and local enterprises". The bank combined global customer expansion strategy with overseas local customer maintenance. It selected an appropriate entry point to expand the domestic market

and increased the share of local business in total asset; it strengthened the cooperation with overseas banks. Around the Belt and Road strategy, the bank strengthened the cooperation with the CDB, China Exim Bank, CITIC, and other policy-oriented financial institutions and explored opportunities for cooperation with BRICS banks.

(c) Using the overall group synergies by connecting domestic and international markets. Bank of Communications adhered to "one Bank, one customer" philosophy. With domestic and overseas institutions sharing network resource, client resource, channel resource, and brand resource, the bank could use the synergy to provide comprehensive and integrated service for clients both in domestic, foreign currencies, and in onshore and offshore markets.

(d) Fully using the advantage of the opportunity brought by RMB internationalization. In the field of cross-border trade, Bank of Communications used both domestic and overseas markets, providing client-oriented comprehensive service programs around the whole transaction chain, and expanding cross-border RMB funds services; in cross-border investment and financing, the bank seized the opportunity of RMB capital business, pushing the use of RMB in project financing, and supporting enterprises to carry out cross-border RMB loan business at home and abroad based on regional finance innovation policy; in financial markets, the bank accelerated research and development to promote currency swaps, interest rate swaps, and other offshore market derivatives, to promote the development of the RMB "panda bonds" business, and to promote the development of RMB bond trading in the secondary market.

Promoting international development with "two paths and one bank" strategy is a major strategic decision of Bank of Communications. The bank will continue to combine the internal and external situation with overseas business practice, and adhere to the principle of combining efficiency with scale, common services with differentiated services, comprehensive linkage with localization of business, and business development with risk control, to promote the further implementation of the international strategy.

3. Derivative Market

By the fourth quarter of 2015, the value of outstanding global OTC interest rate derivative market was $3.84 trillion, where the dollar, euro, Japanese yen, and British pound accounted for 36.19%, 30.69%, 10.05%, and 9.93% respectively. Compared with the same period last year, the balance and market share of the dollar and the yen increased significantly; meanwhile the euro dropped. The market share of pound-denominated derivatives registered the fastest growth, but their outstanding value declined (Fig. 2.10).

Since China's derivative market lagged behind and had a relatively small scale, there was still a big gap between China and developed countries and RMB derivatives were listed under "derivatives of other currencies" by BIS.

As is shown in Fig. 2.3, compared with 2014, one of the trends of the global OTC interest rate derivative market in 2015 was that the outstanding balance and the market value of other currencies' interest rate derivatives on the global OTC market both increased, the proportions of which went up from 8.47% to 10.25% and from 5.06% to 6.63% respectively. This showed that in addition to the main international reserve currency, other currency hedging tools were used more widely (Table 2.3).

In 2015, the liberalization of RMB interest rate was basically completed; the regime of the RMB exchange rate was more market-oriented,

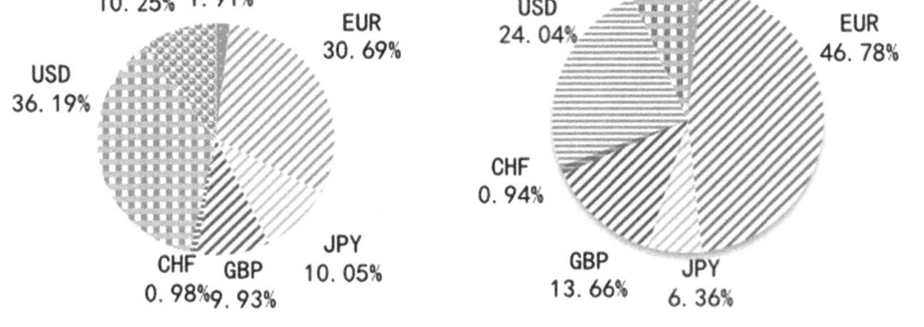

Fig. 2.10 The currency structure of interest rate derivatives on the global OTC market in 2015. (Source: Bank for International Settlements)

Table 2.3 Currency structure on the global OTC interest rate derivatives market

Currency	*Outstanding balance proportion of global OTC interest rate derivatives market*		*Market value proportion of global OTC interest rate derivatives market*	
	2014Q4 (%)	*2015Q4 (%)*	*2014Q4 (%)*	*2015Q4 (%)*
Canadian dollar	2.00	1.91	1.05	1.60
Euro	33.09	30.69	52.44	46.78
Yen	9.13	10.05	5.11	6.36
Pound	11.28	9.93	11.71	13.66
Swiss France	0.94	0.98	0.82	0.94
USD	34.14	36.19	23.07	24.04
Others	8.47	10.25	5.06	6.63

Source: Bank for International Settlements

and the volatility of RMB exchange rate and interest rate increased obviously. In order to meet the urgent needs of the market to avoid the exchange rate risk, the offshore RMB market derivative innovation continued to emerge. For example, on March 17, 2015, the Moscow Stock Exchange launched CNY/RUB futures trading. On July 20, the Taiwan Futures Exchange listed two RMB exchange rate futures, including the "USD-denominated RMB futures contract with small value" with a contract size of $20,000 and the USD-denominated RMB futures contract with a contract size of $100,000. Currently, there are two kinds of RMB derivatives traded in Hong Kong: USD-denominated RMB futures and the China 120 index futures. In 2015, 262,433 contracts of USD-denominated RMB futures were traded, a year-on-year increase of 67,384 and 34.55%; 27,427 contracts of China 120 index futures were traded, and the turnover per quarter showed a decreasing trend (Table 2.4).

In 2015, the money market continuously saw a vigorous activity in RMB interest rate swap, with increasing trading enthusiasm. The total transaction of interest rate swap reached 8.22 trillion yuan, a year-on-year increase of 4.18 billion yuan and of 104% (Table 2.5).

In 2015, the transaction of CSI 300 stock index futures increased significantly, reaching a total of 439.67 trillion yuan, a year-on-year increase of 276.54 trillion yuan and 170%. The turnover of CSI stock index futures and the fluctuation of CSI 300 index were synchronized, which indicated that the CSI 300 stock index futures played an active role in hedging. Treasury bonds were the main investments of overseas institutional

Table 2.4 USD-denominated RMB futures and China 120 index futures transactions summarized (unit: contract)

	2014				2015			
	Q1	*Q2*	*Q3*	*Q4*	*Q1*	*Q2*	*Q3*	*Q4*
USD against RMB futures	75,498	33,359	42,843	53,349	58,303	34,390	86,580	83,160
China 120 index futures	9824	8678	10,935	10,756	14,375	9403	3363	286

Source: Hong Kong stock exchange

Table 2.5 Interest rate swap transactions on interbank market (unit: 100 million yuan)

	2014				2015			
	Q1	*Q2*	*Q3*	*Q4*	*Q1*	*Q2*	*Q3*	*Q4*
Interest rate swap	8044.5	8908.53	9577.68	13786.59	16597.79	19319.37	22519.47	23721.98

Source: China Foreign Exchange Trading Center

Table 2.6 Stock index futures and treasury bond futures transactions (unit: 100 million yuan)

	2014				2015			
	Q1	*Q2*	*Q3*	*Q4*	*Q1*	*Q2*	*Q3*	*Q4*
CSI 300 stock index futures	272,821	275,356	348,607	734,601	882,766	1,546,583	977,621	989,717
Treasury bond futures	1083.95	1078.99	1322.63	5299.58	6778.97	7167.55	4334.30	25314.17

Source: China Financial Futures Exchange

investors. After the completion of the interest rate liberalization, treasury futures that could hedge interest rate risk became popular in the market. In 2015, treasury bond futures trading totaled 4.36 trillion yuan, with an increase of 396% over the previous year (Table 2.6).

4. Non-resident investors invested in RMB financial assets

With the liberalization of Chinese financial market, non-resident investors' enthusiasm increased, and they gradually expanded the scale of investment in stock and bond market. There were three channels for investors to invest in RMB stocks: qualified foreign institutional investors (QFII), RMB qualified foreign institutional investors (RQFII), and Shanghai-Hong Kong Stock Connect Program. The previous two approaches apply to institutional investors, and individual investors can invest in stocks through the third channel.

In 2015, QFII and RQFII increased fast. QFII increased to 295, an increase of 20 and 7.27% over the previous year. RQFII increased to 186, an increase of 68 and 57.63% over the previous year.

Up until the end of 2015, China's interbank bond market permitted the following institutions: 40 QFII, 131 RQFII, 84 foreign banks, and 16 foreign insurers. In 2015, 177,625 transactions were made by overseas institutions in interbank bond market, with a total value of 15, 931.655 billion yuan (Fig. 2.11).

Affected by the huge shock in stock market and the RMB de-valuation expectation in 2015, the scale of non-resident investment in Chinese stocks dropped, and the scale of resident investment in overseas market skyrocketed. According to the data from HKEx, the turnover of SH Equities was 62.527 billion yuan in December 2015, a year-on-year

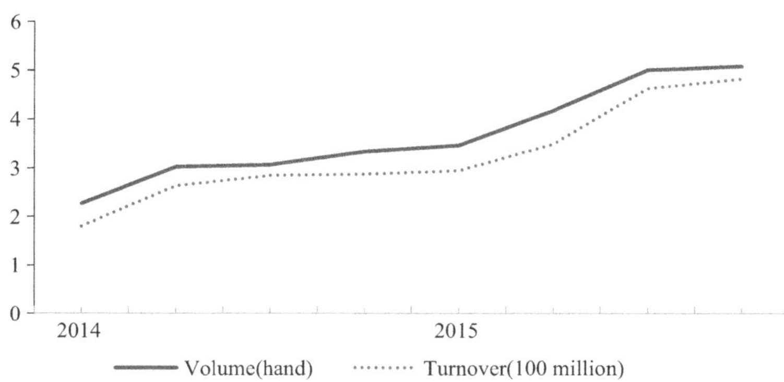

Fig. 2.11 Transactions by overseas institutions in interbank bond market. (Source: China Foreign Exchange Trade Center)

decrease of 46%; the turnover of HK Equities was 45.235 billion Hong Kong dollar in December 2015, a year-on-year increase of 145%.

Overall, RMB financial assets are increasingly internationally attractive. The amount of domestic RMB financial assets held by foreign institutions and individuals was basically stable. In the first half of 2015, domestic stocks, bonds, and loans held by overseas investors increased due to the boom of Chinese stock market. But the stocks and deposits decreased because of the failure of stock market and the depreciation of RMB exchange rate in the second half year (Table 2.7).

2.2.3 RMB Overseas Credit Market

Up until the end of 2015, the balance of RMB overseas loans of domestic financial institutions reached 315.347 billion yuan, increasing by 58.49% over 2014. The new loans reached 13.974 billion yuan, increasing by 2.784 billion over compared with 2014. The ratio of RMB overseas loans to total loans borrowed by the financial institutions was 0.34%, an obvious rise over 2014. This was due to the decrease of RMB overseas interest rate and the de-valuation expectation of RMB. To lower the financing cost, enterprises needed more RMB overseas loans, and this trend became particularly evident after the exchange rate reform in August, which increased the scale of RMB overseas loans largely, as well as their ratio to total loans (Fig. 2.12).

RMB overseas loans include overseas loans of domestic financial institutions, as well as the RMB loans issued by overseas financial institutions to domestic companies. The overseas RMB interest rate was lower, so domestic institutions were willing to use overseas RMB loans. In 2013, the People's Bank of China (PBOC) approved this practice in Shanghai FTZ, Shengzhen Qianhai zone, and Kunshan pilot area, and this practice expanded to more areas in 2014, including Tianjin, Guangxi, and Yunnan. Some enterprises had access to southeastern Asia and other RMB offshore market to get overseas RMB loans. In 2015, the PBOC approved this practice in Guangdong Nansha and Hengqin FTZ, meaning enterprises in these areas could borrow RMB from banks in Hong Kong and Macao. The funds should be used within these areas or abroad to support local production, operation, project construction, and overseas project construction of local enterprises. Besides, the funds should be used in areas consistent with the national macro-policy and industrial orientation. These policies and strategies in liberalizing credit market were also the reasons for the large increase in the balance of RMB overseas loans in 2015.

Table 2.7 RMB financial assets held by foreign institutions and individuals (unit: 100 million yuan)

	2014Q1	*2014Q2*	*2014Q3*	*2014Q4*	*2015Q1*	*2015Q2*	*2015Q3*	*2015Q4*
Stock	9790.76	10,426.99	13,332.98	15,313.38	20,121.46	24,325.43	16,782.28	16,513.76
Bond	14,003.20	16,295.90	17,979.59	19,600.92	21,345.98	22,478.36	23,402.83	22,718.63
Loan	21,299.51	24,945.63	26,129.73	24,900.87	26,174.44	26,899.73	28,661.28	26,942.65
Deposit	55,576.06	60,215.43	65,126.38	70,538.32	63,386.11	63,844.34	54,574.54	46,635.06

Note: The balance of stock market value was adjusted according to the balance of stock value held by non-resident investors through the Shanghai-Hong Kong Stock Connect Program

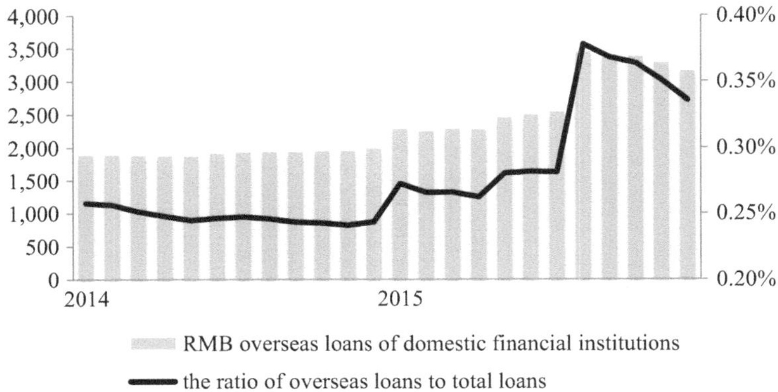

Fig. 2.12 RMB overseas loans and the ratio of domestic financial institutions. (Source: The People's Bank of China)

2.2.4 RMB in Foreign Exchange Market

The PBOC reformed the regime of RMB exchange rate in 2015. Since August 11, 2015, the price provided by market makers to the China Foreign Exchange Trading Center before the daily opening of interbank foreign exchange market referred mainly to the last closing exchange rate in interbank foreign exchange market, and adjusted the bidding rate slightly according to the changes in exchange rates of major international currencies as well as the supply and demand of foreign exchange on the last day. Basically, the goal of liberalization reforms came true. Due to the fluctuations of exchange rate and the influence of Fed rate hike expectations, market expectations of RMB exchange rate became divided, which resulted in different trading volume of RMB against different currencies in foreign exchange market in 2015. In 2015, the spot transaction of RMB foreign exchange reached USD 4.86 trillion, with an increase of 18.23% year-on-year (Table 2.8).

Derivatives became increasingly important in exchange rate risk management. Swap is the major product in the RMB foreign exchange derivatives market, and its trading currency is mainly USD. The transaction of RMB foreign exchange swaps accumulated to USD 8.34 trillion, with an increase of 86.8% over 2014. The RMB foreign exchange forward accumulated to USD 37.199 billion, decreasing by 29.6% year-on-year.

Table 2.8 RMB against other currencies transaction in interbank FX spot market (unit: billion yuan)

currency	*USD*	*Euro*	*Japanese yen*	*Hong Kong dollar*	*British pound*	*Australian dollar*	*New Zealand dollar*	*Singapore dollar*	*Canadian dollar*	*Ringgit*	*Ruble*	*Swiss franc*
Volume	46,131	678	537	278.97	1245	160	27	605	20	2	35	23
% year-on-year	19	33	−27	−15	−44	−34	−39	345	818	23	−11	−44

Source: Wind

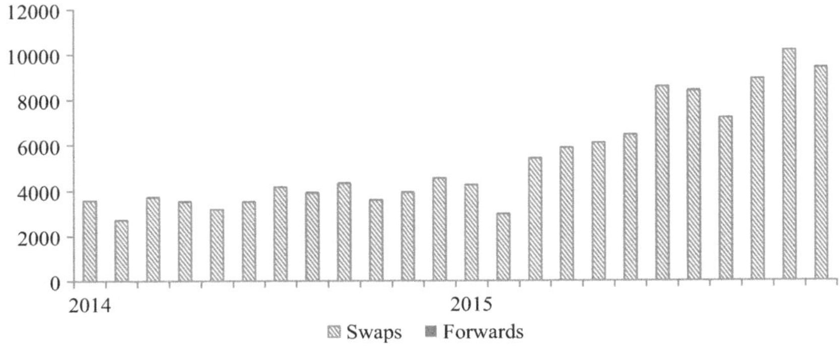

Fig. 2.13 2014–2015 derivative market of RMB foreign exchange. (Source: China Foreign Exchange Trade Center)

In 2015, the turnover of foreign currency swaps for RMB reached USD 191.518 billion, increasing by 16.24% year-on-year. The biggest share went to swaps of USD for euros, whose trading volume reached USD 84.141 billion, accounting for 43.93% in the market (Fig. 2.13).

On September 30, 2015, the PBOC announced that overseas central bank (monetary authorities) and other official reserve management agencies, international financial institutions, and sovereign wealth funds were allowed to trade in the China interbank foreign exchange market in obedience with laws and regulations. Besides, varieties of foreign exchange trading were also permitted, including spot trading, forward trading, swaps, and options. This was an important step toward full convertibility of RMB under capital account and RMB internationalization, and enabled foreign central banks to hold RMB assets as official reserves. The participation of important international financial institutions, including central banks, in China interbank foreign exchange markets greatly increased the turnover of RMB onshore market and improved the significance of RMB exchange rate in the interbank market.

2.3 RMB in Global Foreign Reserves

2.3.1 Enhancing Monetary and Financial Cooperation Between Central Banks

By the end of 2015, the PBOC signed the currency swap agreements with monetary authorities from 33 countries and regions, with a balance of

RMB 3.31 trillion yuan. It was the second time that the PBOC signed the agreement with Belarus, United Arab Emirates, Turkey, Australia, Ukraine, and the United Kingdom, and the third time with Malaysia. Compared with 2014, there were five more countries and regions, including Suriname, Armenia, South Africa, Chile, and Tajikistan. These agreements, aiming to maintain regional financial stability and promote bilateral trade and investment, were different from what were signed among developed economies to deal with crisis.

In addition to currency swap agreements signed by central banks, RMB settlement banks also guaranteed RMB liquidity on the market. In 2015, the PBOC authorized the establishment of RMB settlement banks in Kuala Lumpur, Bangkok, Sydney, Qatar, Chile, and South Africa, to facilitate and support the local use of RMB. On November 30, 2015, financial and business leaders in the United States announced the setting up of the RMB trading and clearing work group to explore the establishment of the RMB trading and clearing mechanisms in the United States, which aimed to facilitate US institutions to use and accept RMB payment, reduce transaction costs, and improve efficiency (Fig. 2.14).

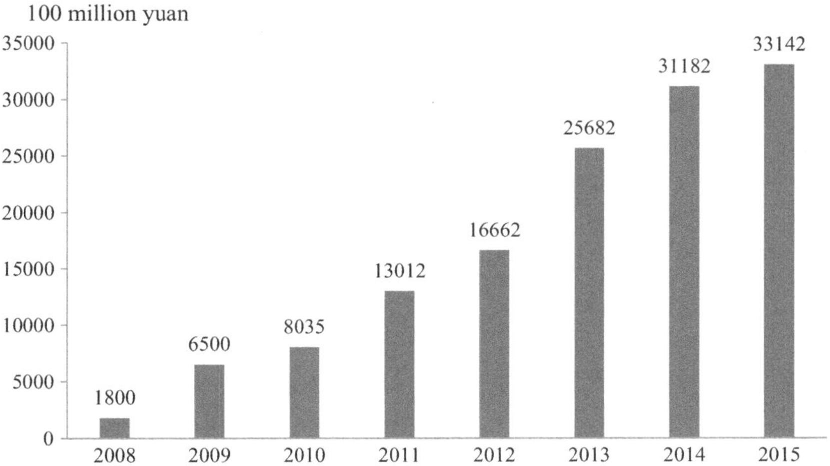

Fig. 2.14 Amount of currency swap between the PBOC and other monetary authorities. (Source: The People's Bank of China)

2.3.2 *Diversification of International Reserve Currencies*

The IMF categorized official reserves into "Allocated Reserves" and "Unallocated Reserves". Any currency accounting for more than 1% in the official reserves fell into the category of "Allocated Reserves". By the end of 2015, "Allocated Reserves" were $6.81 trillion, accounting for 62.3% in the global official reserves. In addition, "Unallocated Reserves" were $4.11 trillion, accounting for 37.7%, decreasing by approximately 10% over 2014.

Among the "Allocated Reserves", USD reserve was $4.36 trillion, accounting for 64.06%; euro was $1.35 trillion, accounting for 19.91%; British pound was $0.33 trillion, accounting for 4.88%; Japanese yen was $0.28 trillion, accounting for 4.08%; Swiss franc was $21.034 billion, accounting for 0.31%; Canadian dollar was $0.13 trillion, accounting for 1.88%; Australian dollar was $0.13 trillion accounting for 1.90%. Compared with 2014, percentage of USD and British pound reserves increased by more than 1%; while the percentage of euros decreased by more than 2.3%, and other currencies remained stable (Table 2.9).

Table 2.9 Percentages of currencies in global foreign exchange reserves (%)

	2014				*2015*			
	Q1	*Q2*	*Q3*	*Q4*	*Q1*	*Q2*	*Q3*	*Q4*
Global reserves	100	100	100	100	100	100	100	100
Allocated reserves	52.69	52.65	52.56	52.45	53.02	58.14	58.96	62.30
USD	60.8	60.73	62.37	62.88	64.17	63.77	63.98	64.06
Euro	24.33	24.09	22.6	22.21	20.8	20.5	20.34	19.91
Japanese yen	3.93	4.03	3.96	3.96	4.2	3.81	3.77	4.08
British pound	3.86	3.88	3.85	3.8	3.91	4.69	4.72	4.88
Swiss franc	0.26	0.27	0.27	0.28	0.29	0.3	0.28	0.31
Canadian dollar	1.87	1.99	1.93	1.91	1.84	1.92	1.89	1.88
Australian dollar	1.89	1.92	1.88	1.81	1.73	1.9	1.89	1.90
Other currencies	3.05	3.1	3.14	3.14	3.07	3.11	3.19	2.99
Unallocated reserves	47.31	47.35	47.44	47.55	46.98	41.86	41.04	37.70

Source: IMF COFER Database, International Financial Statistics released by IMF

Notes:

(1) Data of allocated reserves come from IMF COFER database: proportion of each currency is the ratio of the amount of reserves denominated by this currency to the amount of total allocated reserves, a way of calculation consistent with the IMF

(2) The amount of unallocated reserves is equal to the difference between total global reserves and allocated reserves

On November 30, 2015, IMF Executive Board decided to absorb RMB into the SDRs, which enlarged the SDR basket to USD, euro, RMB, Japanese yen, and British pound. RMB accounts for 10.92% in the SDRs, and USD, euro, Japanese yen, and British pound account for 41.73%, 30.93%, 8.33%, and 8.09% respectively. The new SDRs will come into use on October 1, 2016. The acceptance of RMB into SDRs could help to enhance the significance and attractiveness of SDRs and perfect the existing international monetary system.

RMB entered the official reserves in dozens of countries. On June 24, 2015, the Mongolian government issued offshore RMB bonds for the first time, with the amount of 1 billion yuan, with maturity of three years. The bonds were issued at par value with the coupon rate and yield both at 7.50%. On November 27, Chinese Interbank Market Dealers Association accepted the registration request by British Columbia, Canada, to issue RMB bond (6 billion yuan) in Chinese interbank bond market. On December 15, the Korean government issued three-year 3 billion yuan of RMB bonds in Chinese interbank bond market with the bid rate at 3.00%. This was the first foreign sovereign state issuing "panda bonds" in China. Foreign governments absorbed RMB into foreign currency reserves by issuing RMB-denominated bonds, which indicated that the function of RMB as a reserve currency was getting stronger.

Column 2.4 RMB Assets Became More Internationally Attractive

With the development of RMB's internationalization, RMB capital account was gradually liberalized and the RMB became stable against a basket of currencies, which attracted more global financial institutions and investors, making RMB assets more internationally attractive.

Firstly, the convertibility under capital account continued to increase. Administrative approval of foreign exchange management under the direct investment was nearly canceled. Except from few projects involving individuals and hot money, 85% items under capital account became convertible. Overseas funds could be used for stock trading through QFII, RQFII, and Shanghai-Hong Kong Stock Connect. International financial institutions, including foreign central bank, were permitted to participate in the Chinese interbank bond market, and the scale of RMB stocks and bonds held by non-residents increased greatly.

Secondly, RMB entering the SDR basket showed that RMB became an official reserve currency, which helped to improve the international confidence on RMB and increase the competitiveness of RMB in the international monetary system. There were more RMB offshore products and more participants, and the demand for RMB assets of financial institutions, enterprises, and individuals increased.

Thirdly, the capital market was liberalized. The common policy of the Chinese capital market liberalization was to attract foreign long-term funding to invest in A-shares, optimize the investors' structure, and promote a stable capital market development. On June 9, 2015, MSCI published the results of "the Global Market Classification Review" in Geneva, and claimed that China A-shares were to be absorbed in the Global Benchmark Index. In the semi-year report issued on November 12, 2015, MSCI absorbed 14 Chinese Concept Stocks into its China Index and Emerging Market Index for the first time. China A-shares' acceptance into an internationally renowned index enlarged the international impact of Chinese capital market, and encouraged foreign long-term institutions to invest in A-share market.

2.4 RMB Exchange Rate and the Opening of China Capital Account

2.4.1 Improvement of RMB Exchange Rate Regime

China managed to improve the RMB exchange rate regime since 2005. Guided by the market, China increased the flexibility of the RMB exchange rate. On August 11, 2015, the PBOC reformed the regime of RMB exchange rate again. Market makers could provide the central parity rate to the China Foreign Exchange Trading Center before the daily opening of interbank foreign exchange market. The price should base on the last closing exchange rate on interbank foreign exchange market, the changes in exchange rates of major international currencies as well as the supply and demand of foreign exchange overall. This regime made the central parity rate between RMB and USD a market-based benchmark. Afterward, the Chinese government seldom intervened into the foreign exchange market directly and let market decide the RMB exchange rate. Because of the changes in the pricing mechanism, the reference currency for exchange rate targets changed from the previous single USD to a basket of currencies. The criteria for selecting currency basket were currencies of main countries and regions that accounted for a large proportion in China's foreign trade, foreign debt, FDI, and other economic activities. Market participants needed time to adapt to these changes, which resulted in the RMB exchange rate fluctuations in the second half of 2015 and great externality.

To support the liberalization of the RMB exchange rate, Chinese government took measures to improve the development of the foreign exchange market, such as enriching foreign exchange products, liberalizing foreign exchange market, extending the foreign exchange trading time, and introducing qualified foreign market players to promote and form a mechanism where onshore and offshore RMB exchange rate were interconnected. According to the development of the foreign exchange market and the overall financial environment, two-way floating elasticity of the RMB exchange rate should be enhanced and the RMB exchange rate should be maintained at a reasonable and balanced level.

The reform on the exchange rate regime in August 2015 helped the market exchange rate expand its influence and improved the current managed floating exchange rate regime which was based on the market supply and demand with reference to a basket of currencies.

2.4.2 RMB Exchange Rate Level

1. The central parity rate of RMB

By the end of 2015, the number of currencies traded with RMB directly in the domestic foreign exchange market increased from 11 in 2014 to 12, namely, the USD, HK dollar, Japanese yen, euro, British pound, Ringgit, ruble, Australian dollar, Canadian dollar, New Zealand dollar, Singapore dollar, and Swiss franc.

Since the reform of RMB exchange rate regime in July 2005, RMB exchange rate against USD maintained an appreciation trend. Because of the improvement of US economy as well as the Fed rate hike in 2015, global capital flowed back to the United States and the RMB started to depreciate against USD. Before the reform of RMB exchange rate regime in August, the central parity rate of RMB against USD fluctuated between 6.1 and 6.2. After the PBOC announced to change the quotation method of central parity rate on August 11, the central parity rate of RMB against USD rushed to 6.4085, with a narrower appreciation margin but a more significant fluctuation. The closing exchange rate was 6.4936 on December 31 and RMB against USD depreciated 5.77% over 2014 (6.119). Since the Hong Kong dollar against the USD exchange rate was subject a linked exchange rate system, the trend of RMB against Hong Kong dollar was basically similar with RMB against USD. The exchange rate mainly stayed at the ceiling of the boundary, and the central parity rate of RMB against Hong Kong dollar depreciated by 5.84% in the year.

The exchange rates of RMB appreciated dramatically against ruble, Ringgit, Canadian dollar, New Zealand dollar, and Australian dollar. By the end of December, 2015, the central parity rates of RMB against ruble, ringgit, Canadian dollar, New Zealand dollar, and Australian dollar were 11.31, 0.66051, 4.6814, 4.4426, and 4.7276 respectively, and the appreciation rates were 24.92%, 16.42%, 12.69%, 8.12%, and 6.13%, respectively, year-on-year.

By the end of 2015, the central parity rates of RMB against euro, 100 Japanese yen, Singapore dollar, and British pound were 7.0952, 5.3875, 4.5875, and 9.6159 respectively. Compared with that in 2014, the rates against Euro and Singapore dollar appreciated by 5.08% and 1.14% respectively; on the contrary, the rates against Japanese yen and British pound depreciated by 4.65% and 0.75% respectively. These four exchange rates fluctuated more dramatically during 2015, which meant a larger spread between the highest and lowest prices. The annual fluctuation range, the annual spread between the highest and lowest exchange rate divided by the exchange rate of the last year, of the exchange rates against euro, British pound, Japanese yen, and Singapore dollar were 12.26%, 11.12%, 9.41%, and 4.72% respectively.

On November 10, 2015, RMB could be used to trade directly with Swiss franc. During the period, the central parity rate of RMB against Swiss franc went through few fluctuations. By the end of 2015, RMB appreciated slightly by 0.92%, against Swiss franc (Fig. 2.15).

2. Nominal effective exchange rate and real effective exchange rate

According to the data from BIS, by the end of 2015, nominal effective exchange rate of RMB was 125.9, up by 3.66% over the same period of the

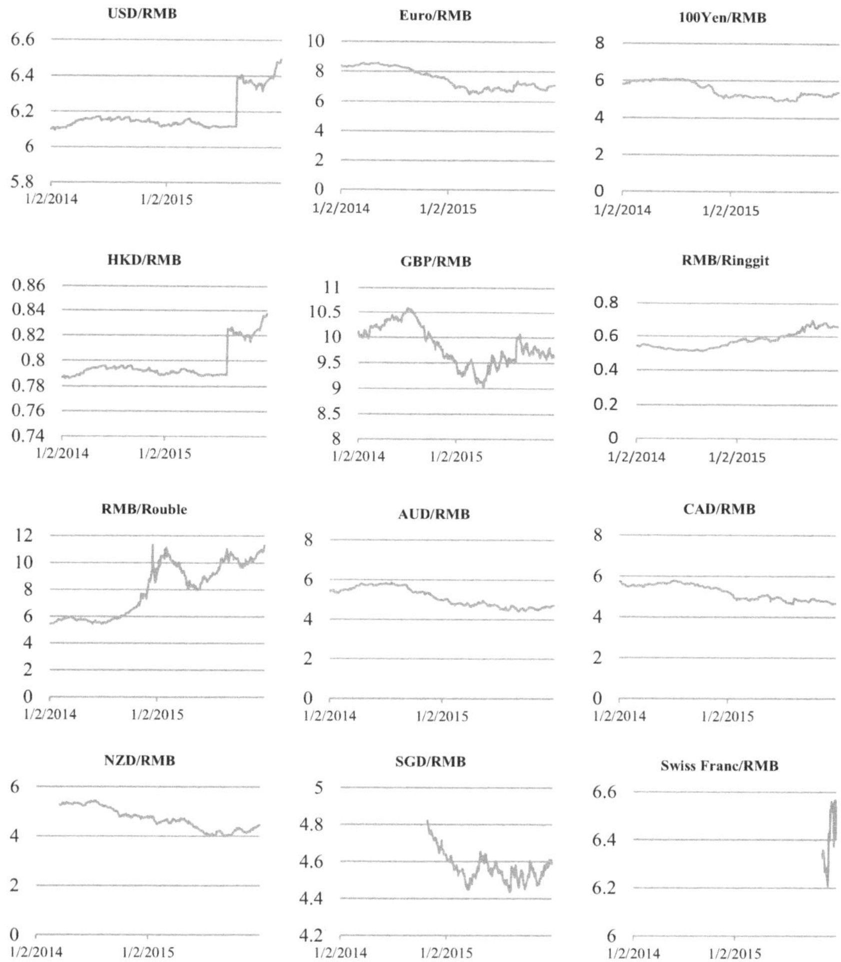

Fig. 2.15 The monthly central parity rates of RMB against 12 foreign currencies during 2014–2015. (Source: State Administration of Foreign Exchange)

last year; adjusted for the effects of inflation, real effective exchange rate stood at 130.11, up by 3.93% over the same period of the last year. This fact indicated that RMB was still strong compared with a basket of trade-weighted currencies of Chinese major trading partners. Starting from July

2005 when the exchange rate regime reform began, nominal and real effective exchange rates rose by 43.14% and 53.34% respectively (Fig. 2.16).

By the end of 2015, the nominal effective exchange rates of Japanese yen, euro, British pound, and USD were 78.52, 96.4, 114.75, and 120.1 respectively. Japanese yen, British pound, and USD appreciated dramatically and remained strong, rising by 5.17%, 5.31%, and 10.82%, respectively, compared with 2014. In contrast, euro was weak, with the nominal rate dropping by 4.42% (Fig. 2.17).

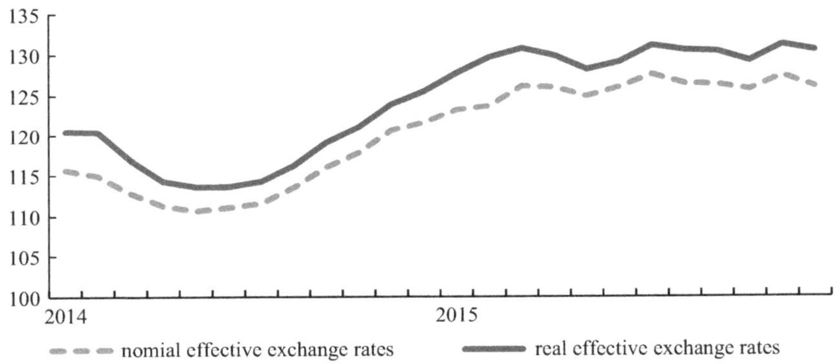

Fig. 2.16 RMB effective exchange rates movements. (Source: Bank of International Settlements)

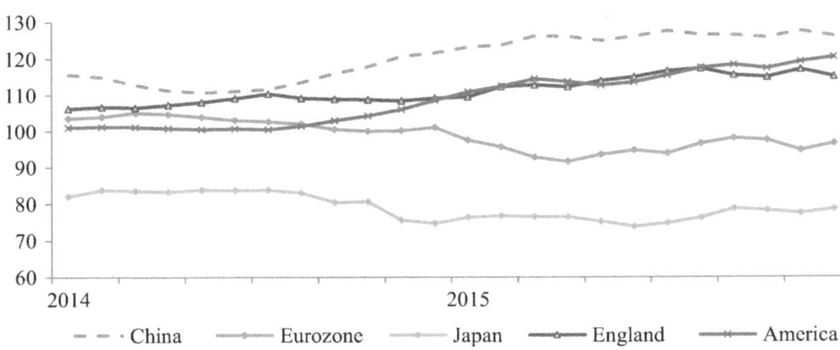

Fig. 2.17 Nominal effective exchange rate movements of five major economies. (Source: Bank of International Settlements)

3. Offshore Chinese RMB (CNH)

In 2015, offshore exchange rate of RMB against USD took a fall before climbing up: the exchange rate fluctuated between 6.6123 and at 6.0150 with a fluctuation range of 9.93%. By the end of December, 2014, the exchange rate was 6.5687, down by 5.42% compared with 6.2128 in late 2014.

Onshore and offshore markets' being separate caused CNY and CNH experiencing different fluctuations and there was a price difference between the two. The price difference fluctuated with changes in supply and demand and interest rates. On September 7, 2015, CNY was 1130 BP lower than CNH; on September 29, 2015, CNY was 116 BP higher than CNH. The price difference peaked at 1296 BP. Overall, the price difference between CNY and CNH went through an inverted "V" shape throughout 2015. Moreover, CNY was lower than CNH most of the time, which indicated that RMB depreciated greater than CNH.

With the substantial completion of RMB interest rate liberalization, the change in price difference between CNY and CNH had a great impact capital flows. On the one hand, the narrowed interest margin dampened motives for cross-border RMB arbitrage. On the other hand, under the condition of RMB's temporary depreciation against dollar, the widened exchange rate difference exerted a stronger influence on RMB cross-border flow (Fig. 2.18).

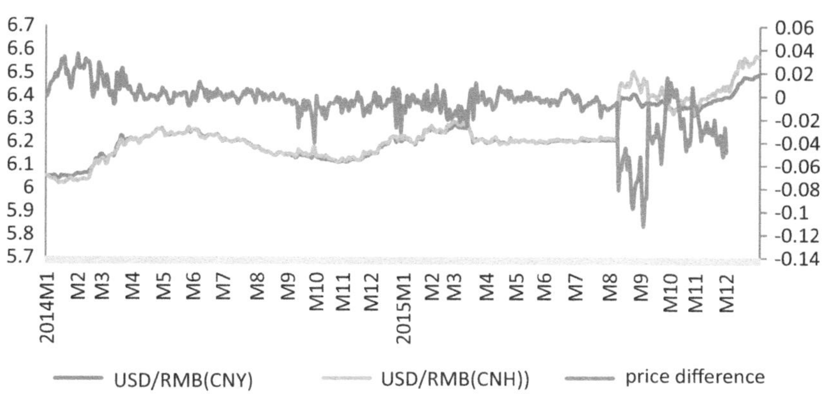

Fig. 2.18 Exchange rate and price difference of onshore and offshore RMB. (Source: Wind)

4. RMB NDF

In countries with foreign exchange control where currencies cannot be freely converted, non-delivery forward (NDF) was created in the 1990s to avert risks that come with foreign exchange fluctuations, and it was used in emerging markets like China, Vietnam, India, and the Philippines.

Singapore and HK are the two most important NDF markets in Asia. The market reflects international expectations of RMB exchange rate changes. Main participants of the market are large banks and investment institutions from Europe and America, and their clients are mainly multinationals with a lot of RMB revenue and HK-headquartered mainland enterprises.

NDFs of different maturities rose continuously in 2015 as in 2014, but they fluctuated in a wider range. Specifically speaking, NDF exchange rate rose sporadically in the first quarter and fell sporadically in the second quarter. In the third quarter, it was stable at first. After the RMB rate formation mechanism reform, NDF exchange rate rose rapidly. In the fourth quarter, NDF experienced small adjustments and exchange rate continued to rise.

In the end of December 2015, closing rates of RMB NDF of one-month, three-month, six-month, and one-year maturities were 6.5600, 6.630, 6.705, and 6.79, respectively, depreciating against the USD by 6.26%, 6.42%, 6.63%, and 6.44% respectively. This meant the depreciation expectation of RMB NDF was still higher than that of onshore and offshore markets.

In summary, influenced by a strong dollar and the RMB rate regime reform, expectations of RMB one-way appreciation were averted, and various influencing factors were reflected in the market. Two-way fluctuations of RMB exchange rate against other major currencies appeared, with a larger range and better elasticity. The difference between onshore exchange rate and offshore exchange rate gradually returned to a normal scope, and the effective exchange rate of RMB appreciated a little, and the stability of RMB did not change (Fig. 2.19).

2.4.3 The Measurement of Chinese Capital Account Openness

Epstein and Schor (1992) first put forward the use of Annual Report on Exchange Arrangements and Exchange Restrictions (AREAER) to

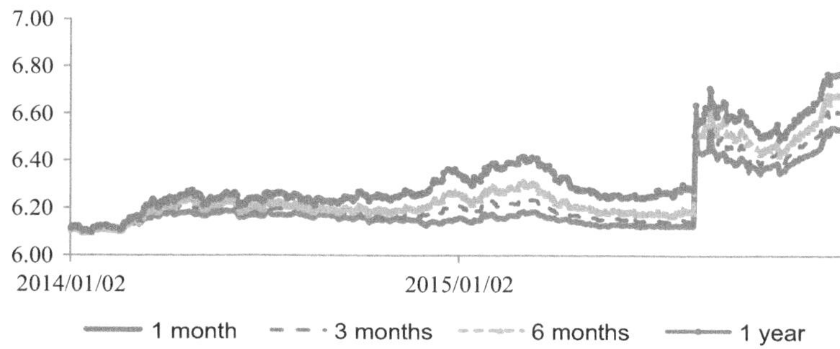

Fig. 2.19 Daily closing prices of RMB NDF in the 2014–2015 period. (Source: Wind)

Column 2.5 CFETS RMB Exchange Rate Index Published
On February 11, 2015, China Foreign Exchange Trade Center released CFETS RMB exchange rate index, which was significant for transforming society's way of observing RMB exchange rate. According to the calculation method, CFETS RMB exchange rate referred to CFETS currency basket, specifically including the foreign exchanges listed in China Foreign Exchange Trade Center (in which dollar's weight is 26.40%, euro 21.39%, Yen 14.68%, HKD 6.55%, GBP 3.86%, AUD 6.27%, NZD 0.65%, SGD 3.82%, CHF 1.51%, CAD 2.53%, MYR 4.67%, RUB 4.36%, THB 3.33%). The weights of sample currencies were designated by trade-weighted method, which considered intermediary trade factors. Sample currency pricing referred to the central parity rate of the RMB and the reference transaction price. Index base period was December 31, 2014, with a base of 100 points.

For a long time, the market perspective on the RMB exchange rate was primarily focused on bilateral exchange rate of RMB against the USD. As exchange rate fluctuations were to adjust trades and investments between multiple trading partners, only observing the bilateral exchange rate of RMB against the USD did not fully reflect the international parity of trade. RMB exchange rate should refer not only to dollar, but also to a basket of currencies. As a weighted average exchange rate, exchange rate index is mainly used to comprehensively calculate the changes of one currency against the weighted average exchange rates of a basket of currencies, and it can reflect the changes in the value of a country's currency. In comparison, reference to a basket of currencies can better reflect a country's comprehensive competitiveness of goods and services, and exchange rate can better play a role in regulating the import and export, balance of payments, and international investment. The release of CFETS RMB exchange rate index provided a quantitative indicator for the market, changing the perspective on RMB exchange rate and reflecting changing market conditions comprehensively and accurately.

Judging by the international experience, some exchange rate indexes are issued by the monetary authorities, such as the Fed, ECB, and Bank of England; some are issued by intermediary agencies, such as the dollar index published by Intercontinental Exchange (ICE), an important reference index for international markets. The release of the RMB exchange rate index by China Foreign Exchange Trade Center is consistent with international practices.

Since 2015, the overall trend of CFETS RMB exchange rate index was relatively stable, and on December 31 the rate was 100.94, appreciating by 0.94% compared with the rate at the end of 2014. This suggested that although the RMB depreciated against the USD since 2015. From a more comprehensive perspective, RMB still slightly appreciated against a basket of currencies. Among major international currencies, RMB was still a strong currency.

In order to facilitate observing of changes in the effective exchange rate of RMB from different angles, the China Foreign Exchange Trading Center also listed RMB exchange rate indexes based on BIS and SDR currency basket. At the end of December, compared with the end of 2014, the two indexes respectively appreciated by 1.71% and depreciated by 1.16%.

The fact that China Foreign Exchange Trade Center regularly published CFETS RMB exchange rate index helped to change the practice of mainly focusing on the bilateral exchange rate of RMB against the USD, and helped the market to refer to the effective exchange rate calculated based on a basket of currencies. This would contribute to keeping the RMB exchange rate stable at a reasonable and balanced level.

measure the degree of capital regulation. Cottarelli and Giannini (1997) quantified the information of AREAER capital regulation into binary variables,[1] working out the capital account openness by arithmetic methods. Because of its imprecision, the credibility of the conclusion has been questioned a lot. This report employs the current mainstream capital openness measuring approach, namely, the Qinn method,[2] to measure the openness of nominal capital account in China.

According to the description of *Annual Report on Exchange Arrangements and Exchange Restrictions 2015* on China's capital account regulation in 2014, following the trend in 2013, there were three inconvertible items under capital account in 2014, mainly centering on non-residents investing in domestic money market, collective investment securities, and the sales and issuance of derivatives. Some convertible items were bond market trading, stock market trading, real estate trading, individual capital trading, and so on. China's capital openness in 2015 was 0.6302 using the calculation of fourth gear constraint approach, considering subtle changes, and comprehensively quantifying the description in *Annual Report on Exchange Arrangements and Exchange Restrictions 2015* (Table 2.10).

2.4.4 *Items Under Capital Account Whose Degree of Openness Changed*

Compared with 2013, seven items were further liberalized, including "Restrictions on securities trading in capital market", "Restrictions on

[1] 0/1 virtual variables: 0 for regulated items under capital account; 1 for unregulated ones.

[2] Calculation formula:

$$\text{open} = \sum_{i}^{n} p(i) / n$$

"open" stands for the degree of capital account openness, within a range from 0 to 1. Smaller value means larger regulation. "n" stands for the total amount of capital trading items considered in measuring capital account openness. In this report n means the 40 capital trading sub-items under 11 major capital items. "p(i)" means the openness of the "i"th sub-item. Values of sub-items are assigned with the Qinn method. "p(i) = 1" means no regulations over the discussed item, in terms of either real trading under capital account or exchange trading; "p(i) = 1/3" means some regulations for the majority of trading parties or items under capital account; "p(i) = 2/3" means few regulations over the discussed item with regulations only imposed on few trading parties and items under capital account; "p(i) = 0" means strict control. The trading is forbidden, either de jure or de facto; in addition, in AREAER a few items are labeled "regulated" without further details, a case 1/2 applies.

Table 2.10 Current situation of China's capital regulation in 2014 defined by IMF

Capital trading items	*2014*
1. Regulation on securities trading in capital market	
A. Trading of stocks or other securities related to stock holding	
(1) Non-resident purchase in China	QFII's investment on domestic A-shares must be in line with the following requirements: (1) the ownership of foreign individual investors in a listed company through QFII cannot exceed 10% of the company share, and A-shares held by all foreign investors in a listed company cannot exceed 30% of its total; (2) the total investment limit of QFII is USD 150 billion; (3) the main lock-in period of pension fund, insurance fund, and mutual fund issued though QFII is three months B-share, denominated in USD or HKD and listed on stock exchanges, can be bought by foreign investors RQFII can invest in domestic security market using RMB raised overseas From November 17, 2014, Hong Kong investors can invest in Shanghai security market when meeting the requirements of certain provisions and quotas
(2) Non-resident sales and issuance in China***	Non-residents can sell A-share and B-share; but they cannot issue A-share or B-share
(3) Resident purchase overseas**	Insurance company can participate in overseas investment activities with investment size not surpassing 15% of its total assets in the last quarter. All types of foreign investments are included, such as stocks, bonds, and funds Company can invest in overseas and domestic stocks and stock funds with investments size not surpassing 30% (previously 20%) of its total assets in the last quarter Qualified domestic institutional investors (QDII), including banks, fund management companies, securities companies, and insurance companies, can purchase foreign stocks and other investment products within their approved foreign exchange quotas From November 17, 2014, Chinese domestic investors can invest in Hong Kong security market if they met the requirements of certain provisions and quotas

(*continued*)

Table 2.10 (continued)

Capital trading items	*2014*
(4) Resident sales and issuance overseas***	To issue or sell foreign shares, domestic residents and companies should be approved by CSRC and also register in State Administration of Foreign Exchange (SAFE)
B. Bonds and other debt securities	
(5) Non-resident purchase in China**	QFII and RQFII can invest in financial instruments denominated by RMB: (1) stocks, bonds, and warrants traded or transferred by exchanges; (2) fixed-income products traded in interbank bond market; (3) security investment funds; (4) stock index futures; (5) other financial instruments allowed by CSRC All investments above are subject to requirements of quotas and locked periods
(6) Non-resident sales and issuance in China**	Approved by the Ministry of Finance, the PBOC, and the National Development and Reform Commission (NDRC), international development institutions can issue bonds denominated by RMB. Foreign-funded companies in China can also issue bonds
(7) Resident purchase overseas**	QDII, including banks, fund management companies, securities companies, and insurance companies, can purchase foreign bonds within their foreign exchange quotas and regulations Since February 19, 2014, the book value of a single investment of fixed-income assets or equity assets cannot be over 5% of the total assets of the insurance company at the end of last quarter From November 1, 2014, investments overseas in RMB by RMB Qualified Domestic Institutional Investors (RQDII) are not limited by quota
(8) Resident sales and issuance overseas***	The application of foreign currency bonds issued overseas with maturities over one year must be registered at NDRC The application for issuing RMB bonds overseas with maturity over one year must be approved by the PBOC
2. Regulation on money market instruments	
(9) Non-resident purchase in China***	QFII can purchase money market funds within the shortest lock-in period. QFII cannot directly participate in the trade of interbank foreign exchange market. Lock-in period refers to the deadline of investor's remittance for investment From May 28, 2015, overseas RMB settlement bank and non-residents participating bank who acquired quotas can conduct repurchase agreement in interbank bonds market

(*continued*)

Table 2.10 (continued)

Capital trading items	*2014*
(10) Non-resident sales and issuance in China*	Non-residents cannot sell or issue money market instruments
(11) Resident purchase overseas***	QDII can purchase money market instruments within the limitation of respective foreign exchange quotas and regulations. The investment on bonds of unsecured enterprises and securities investment funds at home and abroad cannot exceed 50% and 15%, respectively, of the total assets of the insurance company at the end of last quarter
(12) Resident sales and issuance overseas***	Approved by SAFE, residents can issue overseas money market instruments, such as bonds and commercial papers with maturity of less than a year
3. Regulation on collective investment securities	
(13) Non-resident purchase in China***	QFII and RQFII can invest domestic closed-end and open-ended fund
(14) Non-resident purchase in China**	From July 1, 2015, public funds in Hong Kong can be sold in approved regions
(15) Resident purchase overseas***	Subject to respective foreign exchange quotas and regulation, QDII can buy overseas collective investment securities. Unsecured corporate bonds and security investment funds within and without China shall not exceed 50% and 15% of the total assets of the insurance company at the end of last quarter
(16) Resident sales and issuance overseas***	From July 1, 2015, public funds in Hong Kong can be sold in approved regions
4. Regulation on derivatives and other instruments	
(17) Non-resident purchase in China***	If the trade is to maintain asset value, QFII can invest domestic stock index futures, subject to specific regulations and size requirements

(*continued*)

Table 2.10 (continued)

Capital trading items	*2014*
(18) Non-resident sales and issuance in China*	Forbidden
(19) Resident purchase overseas**	Institutions regulated by China Banking Regulatory Commission can buy and sell derivatives approved by the Commission to: (1) hedge the inherent risks in balance sheets. (2) make profits. (3) provide customers (including institutions) with derivative trading services For the sake of customer interests, commercial banks shall not invest in commodity derivatives by financing in overseas market QDII can purchase foreign derivatives within their foreign exchange quotas With the approval of State-owned Assets Supervision and Administration Commission (SASAC), the state-owned enterprises can operate offshore derivative businesses
(20) Resident sales and issuance overseas**	Subject to rules and laws on overseas purchase of derivatives
5. Regulation on commercial credit	
(21) Provided to non-residents by residents	
(22) Provided to residents by non-residents	
6. Regulation on financial credits	
(23) Provided to non-residents by residents***	Certain regulation allows domestic affiliated businesses of multinational corporations to directly issue loans to overseas affiliated businesses or through domestic banks From November 1, 2014, multinational corporation groups can transfer and allocate profit and loss among domestic and overseas non-financial members

(*continued*)

Table 2.10 (continued)

Capital trading items	*2014*
(24) Provided to residents by non-residents**	Residents and enterprises borrowing long-term foreign debts (more than one year) should be approved by NDRC Institutions and Chinese joint stock companies which are allowed to borrow foreign debts can borrow short-term foreign debts (no more than one year) within the quotas set by SAFE. All foreign debts shall be registered at SAFE In 2014, the total quota approved by SAFE was USD 37.3 billion. There is no need to further examine or approve details. All foreign debts shall be registered at SAFE From November 1, 2014, multinational corporation groups can transfer and allocate profit and loss among domestic and overseas non-financial members
7. Regulation on guarantee, warranty, and provisional financing facilities	
(25) Provided to non-residents by residents***	From May 12, 2014, SAFE approval was canceled when residents provided assurance to non-residents PBOC approval was canceled when non-financial residents provided RMB assurance to overseas non-residents
(26) Provided to residents by non-residents***	From May 12, 2014, SAFE approval was canceled when non-residents provided assurance to residents Foreign non-financial institutions can use the fund in RMB settlement account as collateral for financing in China
8. Regulation on FDI	
(27) FDI***	From November 27, approval of FDI by residents and enterprises was canceled except in cases of investment to sensitive countries, regions, and industries There are no foreign exchange restrictions on FDI by domestic enterprises. They are allowed to purchase foreign currency for FDI, but the capital outflow should be registered at the managing bank
(28) Inward direct investment**	Four classifications of IDI: (1) favorable, (2) permissible, (3) restricted, (4) prohibited Non-residents can invest in and establish businesses in China if they act in accordance with the laws and regulations on foreign investment and are approved by the Ministry of Finance or local commercial departments

(*continued*)

Table 2.10 (continued)

Capital trading items	*2014*
9. (29) **Regulation on liquidation of FDI*****	A-share stocks of listed companies shall not be transferred within three years Liquidation during the operating period shall be examined and approved by the original authorities or be subject to judicial opinions
10. Regulation on real estate transactions	
(30) Overseas purchase by residents***	Domestic institutions' buying overseas real estate is regarded as ODI. An insurer's investment in foreign real estate shall not exceed 15% of the company's total assets From February 19, 2014, the book value of overseas and domestic real estate investment shall not exceed 30% of the insurer's total assets. Total book value does not include real estate bought with self-owned fund for the insurers themselves. The differences of the real estates' book values shall not exceed 50% of the insurer's total net assets
(31) Domestic purchase by non-residents***	Foreign residents shall follow the principle of actual needs for their own use when buying commercial properties. To pay the seller, they can exchange foreign currencies to RMB at designated foreign exchange banks
(32) Domestic sales by non-residents***	After registering at SAFE, non-residents can remit proceeds from selling properties through certain banks. The foreign exchange approval procedures have been canceled
11. Regulation on personal capital flows	
Loan	
(33) Provided to non-residents by residents***	Without specific authorization, residents shall not issue loans to non-residents
(34) Provided to residents by non-residents***	Without specific authorization, non-residents shall not issue loans to residents
Gifts, donation, bequeath and heritage	

(*continued*)

Table 2.10 (continued)

Capital trading items	*2014*
(35) Provided to non-residents by residents***	Residents with effective proof of identification can buy foreign exchanges (no more than USD 50,000 a year) at banks to aid or help overseas direct relatives. For larger amount, individuals shall show the banks effective proof of their identification and the information of their direct relatives which has been approved by relating departments or notary authorities
(36) Provided to residents by non-residents***	With effective proof of identification, individuals can collect their income (no more than USD 50,000) from endowment funds, bequeath, and inheritance at banks. For larger amount, proof of identification, relevant documents, and payment vouchers are required
(37) Debt settlement of foreign immigrants within China	n.a.
Asset transfers	
(38) Outbound transfers by immigrants***	Retirement funds and old-age funds can be remitted to other countries. Before natural persons move abroad or to Hong Kong and Macao and get permanent citizenship, their legitimate assets in Chinese mainland can be liquidated through exchange purchase and remittance
(39) Inbound transfers by immigrants	No governing laws at present
(40) Transfers of lottery income	No governing laws at present
Openness level of capital	0.6502

Source: Annual Report on Exchange Arrangements and Exchange Restrictions 2015, IMF

Note: *denotes forbidden, **denotes more restrictions, ***denotes less restrictions collective investment securities", "Restrictions on financial credits", "Restrictions on guarantees, pledge and standby financing facility", "Restrictions on direct investment", and "Restriction on real property trading". More specifically, ten sub-items of all the 40 on the capital accounts saw obvious changes, meaning China's capital accounts were further liberalized.

Take "Restrictions on security trading in capital market" as example.

Under "stock trading or convertible securities", the first sub-item "non-resident purchase in China" told that the total investment quotas of RQFIIs rose to 970 billion RMB in June 2015, from 770 billion RMB in 2014. Following QFII, RQFII was gradually expanded.

Regarding the third sub-item under of the "trading of stocks or other convertible securities", namely, "Resident purchase overseas", "Comprehensive investment in stocks and stock funds overseas should not exceed 30% of the total asset of the company" was changed to "The restrictions and quotas of RMB overseas investment by QDII have been canceled".

Since the *Annual Report on Exchange Arrangements and Exchange Restrictions 2015* published by the IMF depicts the capital restrictions in 2014, there is a one-year lag. As a result, compared to the current value in 2014, the estimated degree of capital account in the report is relatively conservative. On February 18, 2014, the first rule of "FTA 30 Financial Regulations" released by the PBOC was implemented, and cross-border RMB payment through payment institutions in China (Shanghai) FTA was started; on February 21, 2014, a meeting was held to promote cross-border RMB payment in payment institutions in China (Shanghai) FTA; on March 16, 2014, foreign non-financial enterprises issued RMB bonds for the first time; on April 10, 2014, the CSRC issued a public notice to set forth the principles and the system of the Shanghai-Hong Kong Stock Connect program; on November 17, 2014, Shanghai and Hong Kong stock market were connected with each other. These facts indicate that China's capital account was further deregulated with larger efforts, and the PBOC and other relevant agencies made large adjustments to the description of the capital account liberalization. Larger changes in capital account openness are to be expected in 2015 (Chart 2.1).

Chart 2.1 Changes of capital accounts control in 2014 compared with 2013

Capital account	*2013*	*Changes in 2014*
1. Restrictions on securities trade in capital market	Returns in foreign currencies from overseas companies controlled by Chinese shareholders shall remit their profit back to China within two years	The words in left chart disappeared
A. Trading of stocks or convertible securities		
(1) Non-resident purchase in China	(1) In listed companies, the ownership held by foreign individual investors through QFII should not exceed 10% of the company's shares. Accumulated shares held by foreign investors shall not exceed 30% of a listed company. (2) The total investment quotas of QFII were $150 billion By the end of 2013, 251 institutions were approved, with total investment of $49.701 billion	Hong Kong investors can invest in Shanghai Security market By the end of May 2015, there were 271 QDIIs approved, with total investment of $77.474 billion By the end of June 2015, total investment quotas of RQFII were 970 billion RMB, exceeding the amount at the end of 2014, which was 770 billion RMB
(2) Non-resident sales or issuance in China		Unchanged
(3) Resident purchase overseas	Comprehensive investment in stocks and stock funds overseas should not exceed 30% of the total asset of the company. The book value of the single investment in fixed-income assets or stock assets should not exceed 5% of the total assets of the last quarter of the insurance company	The restrictions and quotas of investing overseas in RMB by QDII have been canceled Chinese domestic investors can invest in Hong Kong security market
(4) Resident sales or issuance overseas		Unchanged

(*continued*)

Chart 2.1 (continued)

Capital account	*2013*	*Changes in 2014*
B. Securities and debt securities		
(5) Non-resident purchase in China	In 2013, RQFII-investable security markets started in Taiwan from June 21st, in the UK from October 15th, and in Singapore from October 22nd	In 2015, RQFII-investable security markets started in Australia, Canada, Chile, France, Germany, Hong Kong, Hungary, Luxemburg, Qatar, Korea, and Sweden
(6) Non-resident sales or issuance in China		Unchanged
(7) Resident purchase overseas	From February 19, 2014, the book value of the single investment in fixed-income assets or stock assets should not exceed 5% of the total assets of the last quarter of the insurance company	From November 1, 2014, the quotas of investing overseas in RMB by RQDII were canceled
(8) Resident sales or issuance overseas		Unchanged
2. Restrictions on monetary market		
(9) Non-resident purchase in China		Unchanged
(10) Non-resident sales or issuance in China		Unchanged
(11) Resident purchase overseas		Unchanged
(12) Resident sales or issuance overseas		Unchanged
3. Restrictions on group investment securities		
(13) Non-resident purchase in China		Unchanged

(*continued*)

Chart 2.1 (continued)

Capital account	*2013*	*Changes in 2014*
(14) Non-resident sales or issuance in China		From July 1, 2015, public funds in Hong Kong could be sold in approved areas in mainland
(15) Resident purchase overseas		Unchanged
(16) Resident sales or issuance overseas		From July 1, 2015, public funds in Hong Kong could be sold in approved areas in mainland
4. Restrictions on derivative instruments and other instruments		
(17) Non-resident purchase in China		Unchanged
(18) Non-resident sales or issuance in China		Unchanged
(19) Resident purchase overseas		Unchanged
(20) Resident sales or issuance overseas		Unchanged
5. Restrictions on commercial credits		
(21) Resident provides to non-resident		Unchanged
(22) Non-resident provides to resident		Unchanged
6. Restrictions on financial credits		
(23) Provided to non-residents by residents	Certain regulation allowed domestic affiliated businesses of multinational corporations to directly loan to overseas affiliated businesses through domestic banks	From November 1, 2014, multinational corporation groups can transfer and allocate profit and loss among domestic and overseas non-financial members

(*continued*)

Chart 2.1 (continued)

Capital account	*2013*	*Changes in 2014*
(24) Provided to residents by non-residents	In 2013, the short-term external debts approved by the SASAC reached $37.3 billion. Specific details were no longer subject to review or approval. All external debts must be registered at the SASAC	From November 1, 2014, multinational corporation groups can transfer and allocate profit and loss among domestic and overseas non-financial members
7. Restrictions on guarantees, pledge, and standby financing facility		
(25) Provided by residents to non-residents	Domestic banks providing external financial guarantees shall be approved by SAFE, and individual transaction is not subject to approval; domestic banks can provide external non-financial guarantees without approval. Domestic banks providing foreign guarantees shall be registered at SAFE. Within the limits of the SAFE, non-bank financial institutions and enterprises can provide external financial and non-financial guarantees	From May 12, 2014, there is no need to be approved by SAFE when residents provide assurance to non-residents
(26) Provided by non-residents to residents	Borrowing from domestic financial institutions, foreign enterprises approved by Ministry of Commerce according to foreign investment law (including but not limited to foreign-owned enterprises, joint ventures, Sino-foreign cooperative enterprises, etc.) can accept guarantees from foreign institutions. Chinese enterprises in some pilot areas that issue loans to domestic financial institutions may accept guarantee from foreign institutions within the limitations of SAFE	From May 12, 2014, SAFE approval was no longer required when residents provide assurance to non-residents

(*continued*)

Chart 2.1 (continued)

Capital account	*2013*	*Changes in 2014*
8. Restrictions on direct investment		
(27) Foreign Direct Investment (FDI)	FDI program: (1) favorable, (2) permissible, (3) prohibited. The foreign capital source of FDI should be registered and outward remittances of the FDI capital are not subject to approval but should be registered	Except investment to sensitive countries, regions, and industries, FDI by residents and enterprises is no longer subject to approval, but should be registered. The basic material for remittance of investment profits less than \$50,000 no longer need to be checked, and to remit the excess part, enterprises only need to provide resolutions of the board and proof of tax payment The settlement process of RMB FDI is simplified, and only needs to be examined by the managing bank
(28) Internal direct investment		Unchanged
9. (29) **Restriction on the liquidation of direct investment**		Unchanged
10. Restriction on real property trade		
(30) Resident purchase overseas	The book value of property investment at home and abroad should not exceed 20% of the total assets of the insurance company	From February 19, 2014, the book value of property investment at home and abroad should not exceed 30% of the total assets of the insurance company. The total book value does not include the capitals used by the insurance company itself and its book value gap should not exceed 50% of its net assets

(*continued*)

Chart 2.1 (continued)

Capital account	*2013*	*Changes in 2014*
(31) Non-resident purchase in China		Unchanged
(32) Non-resident selling in China		Unchanged
11. Restriction on individual capital mobility		
Loans		
(33) Provided by residents to non-residents		Unchanged
(34) Provided by non-residents to residents		Unchanged
Gifts, donations, bequests and heritages		
(35) Provided by residents to non-residents		Unchanged
(36) Provided by non-residents to residents		Unchanged
(37) Debt settlement of foreign immigrants in China	–	–
Capital transfer		
(38) From immigrants to overseas		Unchanged
(39) From immigrants to China		Unchanged
(40) Lottery and gamble income transfer		Unchanged

Source: Annual Report on Exchange Arrangements and Exchange Restrictions 2014, Annual Report on Exchange Arrangements and Exchange Restrictions 2015, IMF

CHAPTER 3

Event of the Year: The RMB's Inclusion into the SDR Basket

International Monetary Institute

On November 30, 2015, the IMF Executive Board completed its regular five-year review of the basket of SDR currencies. A key focus of the 2015 review was whether the RMB met the existing criteria to be included in the basket. The Board decided that the RMB met all existing criteria, recognized it as a freely usable currency, and included it in the SDR basket as a fifth currency, along with the USD, the euro, the Japanese yen, and the Great Britain pound. The new SDR basket would take effect on October 1, 2016, to provide sufficient lead time for the IMF, its members, and other SDR users to adjust to the changes.

3.1 A Win-Win Result for China and the World

3.1.1 SDR Becomes More Representative and Attractive

The SDR, regarded as a super-sovereign currency created by the IMF, is a potential claim on the freely usable currencies of IMF members. It acts as a reserve asset and unit of account. SDR was created in 1969 to supplement

International Monetary Institute (✉)
Renmin University of China, Beijing, China
e-mail: imi@ruc.edu.cn

International Monetary Institute (ed.), *Currency Internationalization and Macro Financial Risk Control*,
https://doi.org/10.1007/978-981-13-0698-3_3

a shortfall under the Bretton Woods system of preferred foreign reserve assets, namely, gold and the USD. After the system collapsed, the SDR was officially defined as a supplementary reserve asset and the unit of account of the IMF and other international organizations.

The SDR was created as result of the reform of the international monetary system. In the 1960s, under the par value system, the international monetary system faced three threats to its normal operation: first, the shortage of international liquidity supply became more evident; second, against the severe balance of payments disequilibrium, especially the continuous trade deficit of the United States, aggregate demand management policies were ineffective; third, the use of the USD as a global reserve currency faced the Triffin Dilemma where the dollar reserves of other central banks exceeded the value of the US gold reserve. The confidence in the USD faltered. If banks and enterprises in other countries were not willing to increase their dollar holdings, international liquidity squeeze and global economic crises would follow. To ensure future economic growth and the stability of the international monetary system, it was necessary to undertake in-depth and systematic reforms. Against this backdrop, the IMF adopted the suggestions of the Group of Ten (G10) and created the SDR, a super-sovereign currency.

Upon its creation, the SDR was entrusted with special historical responsibilities. The short-term goal was to supplement foreign reserves and relieve the tensions caused by the Triffin Dilemma. The United States may then adjust the par value of the dollar and rectify its balance of payments disequilibrium. The institutional arrangements and basic operations of the par value system could thus be sustained. The long-term goal was to ensure at the same time both the international liquidity and confidence in foreign reserves when official dollar reserves around the world exceeded the US gold reserve by multiple times. As a result, the SDR served as an alternative to the USD and the international community was in charge of international liquidity and foreign reserves. In this way, the supply of international liquidity could be kept at an appropriate level, with no surplus or shortage, to satisfy the needs of international trade and capital flow. The introduction of the SDR was, in essence, intended to establish a mechanism for issuing global reserve currencies, so that the supply of international liquidity would be no longer dependent upon the current account deficit of one or several countries. The confidence in global reserves could thus be boosted and the governance of the international monetary system could become more representative.

However, regarded at best a unit of account among IMF members, the SDR did not replace gold as a measure of value. Neither did the SDR become a major reserve asset of central banks. After four rounds of allocation, SDR accounted for only about 2% in global reserve assets. SDR had extremely limited functions and influence. The reasons are as follows: first, monetary authorities of major industrial countries refused to hand over the control over global reserves to the IMF and make the IMF a "super-sovereign central bank". Second, after the Bretton Woods system collapsed, the dollar was no longer pegged to gold and the Triffin Dilemma ceased to exist. The USD was provided globally as the credit currency of a sovereign nation, and liquidity deficit disappeared naturally. The original international monetary reform was thus upset and the effort to partially replace the USD with the SDR failed. Third, the international monetary system gradually entered an era of floating exchange rates and diversified reserve currencies. The euro emerged as a counter-balance to the USD, showing to some extent that the SDR was not the only choice to regulate and manage international liquidity. Fourth, against financial and economic globalization, financial liberalization and innovation gave a strong boost to the international financial market. Speculations became increasingly harmful and international financial crises erupted frequently. The IMF thus focused mainly on the management of financial crises and paid less attention to providing global liquidity, adjusting balance of payments, and managing global reserves.

The 2008 financial crisis gave rise to people's concern about the sustainability of the current international monetary system. People observed that the United States was still providing global liquidity by maintaining trade deficits, roughly the same scenario as half a century ago. For the United States, the volume of its real economy accounted for one-fifth of the world's total and its trade volume slipped to one-tenth of the world's total. However, the USD was unapologetically a super-currency as it accounted for about two-third of all countries' official reserve assets. As the USD was no longer pegged to gold, global excess liquidity became more evident. The USD's status as a supreme currency was based on US trade deficit, which would only lead to real problems like excessive domestic liquidity, bubbles in dollar assets, the escalation of domestic crises of sub-prime mortgages into global crises, and the spillover impact of the US monetary policies on the global economy. Developing countries were extremely concerned about the current international monetary system. These countries saw their economic volume and foreign trade grow dramatically but were, due to severe currency mismatches, often attacked by speculative capitals. International financial crises frequently erupted. To fend off crises, these countries accumulated more foreign reserves and thus fell into the dollar trap, having to pay for other countries' financial crises. Therefore, the international monetary system was again at a critical juncture for reform. But this time, the appeal came from developing countries rather than from the G10.

The SDR is closely related to the international monetary system as its valuation is based on a basket of major international currencies. The adjustment of the SDR basket itself reflects the direction of international monetary reform. The development of RMB internationalization is the best demonstration of the ongoing changes in the international monetary system. Therefore, including the RMB into the SDR basket would both make the SDR more representative and attractive and enhance the IMF's credibility. To be specific, (1) China is the largest developing country. After the inclusion of the RMB, the SDR basket would have currencies of both developed and developing countries, making it more diversified, balanced, and more representative of major international currencies. (2) China and the United States are each other's largest trade partners. Their unequal currency positions are the main reason for the long-term disequilibrium of balance of payments. The inclusion of the RMB represented that the internationalization of RMB gained the IMF's recognition. As the RMB became more widely used, the excessive reliance on the United States for international liquidity supply and the risk of the dollar trap faced by countries with trade surpluses can both be mitigated. (3) The issuing countries of the four currencies in the current SDR basket adopt a freely floating exchange rate regime, while China, the issuing country of the RMB, adopts a managed floating system. This difference could help offset the value changes of major currencies, mitigate SDR fluctuations, and enhance its stability and attractiveness. The SDR could thus better perform its role as a measure of value and become widely used, and its position in the management of international reserves could be further enhanced.

The inclusion of the RMB may be a starting point to a checked competition among diversified international currencies. Developing countries could have the opportunity to choose safer international currencies and avoid the risks of relying excessively on the USD. In terms of the international monetary system, this competition is in line with the adjustment of international economic and trade and conducive to changing the deadlock of either imbalance of the global economy or balance of terror in global finance. The competition could effectively relieve the pressure of systematic global financial crises and contribute to the SDR's mission of reforming the international monetary system.

3.1.2 *The RMB's Inclusion Is Monumental in RMB Internationalization*

Since 2009 when cross-border RMB business were first undertaken, RMB internationalization has gone through nine years. In this short period, the international use of the RMB expanded substantially. By 2015, the RMB has become a major international currency as the second largest currency for trade financing, fifth largest currency for international payment, sixth largest currency for forex transactions, and sixth largest currency for international interbank lending. Against this background, the inclusion of the RMB was only natural and rational. It was also monumental. Christine Lagarde, IMF's Managing Director, pointed out: "The Executive Board's decision to include the RMB in the SDR basket is an important milestone in the integration of the Chinese economy into the global financial system. It also marks the recognition of the progress that the Chinese authorities have made in the past years in reforming China's monetary and financial systems. The continuation and deepening of these efforts will bring about a more robust international monetary and financial system, which in turn will support the growth and stability of China and the global economy."

1. The IMF officially recognized RMB as a freely usable currency

According to the IMF's Articles of Agreement, the Executive Board reviews the composition of the SDR basket every five years. The reviews cover key elements of the SDR methods of valuation and are intended to ensure that the SDR basket reflects the relative importance of major currencies in the world's trading and financial systems. These elements include the criteria and indicators used in selecting SDR basket currencies, the number of currencies in the basket, and the methodology for determining currency weights. The financial instruments comprising the SDR interest rate basket are also generally covered.

The Board at the 2015 SDR Review reconfirmed the existing two substantive criteria (exports and freely usable) while expanding the size of the basket from four to five currencies. The export criterion, which acts as a "gateway", aims to ensure that basket currencies are issued by five members or monetary unions with the largest product and service export value over a five-year period. This criterion has been in place since the 1970s. The criterion for currencies in the SDR basket to be freely usable was incorporated in 2000 to formally reflect the importance of financial transactions.

A "freely usable" currency is defined in the IMF's Articles of Agreement as a member's currency that the IMF determines is, in fact, widely used to make payments for international transactions, and is widely traded in the principal exchange markets. The concept of a freely usable currency is different from a currency that is either freely floating or fully convertible.[1] The concept of a "freely usable currency" seeks to ensure that a member can use the currency received from the IMF either directly or indirectly (by exchanging it into another currency without disadvantage) to meet balance of payments financing needs.

The inclusion of the RMB went through two procedures: first, the assessment and recommendation of the staff; second, the policy judgment of the Executive Board.

The IMF staff recommended to the Board the inclusion of the RMB into the SDR basket of currencies for reasons in the following areas: first, international use and trade. Since the last SDR review in 2010, the use of the Chinese renminbi (RMB) in international payments has risen substantially. RMB activities in foreign exchange markets covering two of the three major trading time zones have increased significantly and can accommodate the transaction scales involved in IMF operations. This provided, in the judgment of staff, a basis for the RMB to be considered "widely used" to make payments for international transactions and "widely traded" in the principal exchange markets. Second, operational considerations. While operational issues are not formal requirements for the inclusion, the staff assess that the IMF, its members, and other SDR users are now able to conduct operations in RMB without substantial impediments, and this can ensure smooth IMF-related operations. China's authorities made great efforts in this term, principally their decision to grant full access for

[1] A currency can be widely used and widely traded even if it is subject to some capital account restrictions (in the past, currencies such as the pound sterling, and Japanese yen were determined freely usable when some capital account restrictions were in place). On the other hand, a currency that is fully convertible may not necessarily be widely used and widely traded.

official reserve managers and their agents to the onshore fixed income and foreign exchange markets. The Ministry of Finance started to issue three-month treasury bills on a weekly basis to improve the return rate curve and the CFETS announced exchange rates five times a day and identified the reference rate for SDR. The authorities have also fully liberalized domestic interest rates, taken steps toward a more market-determined exchange rate, and implemented a new cross-border interbank payment system. Third, complementary steps to enhance data disclosure. While data disclosure is not a formal criterion for a currency's inclusion in the SDR basket, issuers of these currencies generally meet high transparency standards. Now China has joined the Special Data Dissemination Standards in its data disclosure.

The IMF's Executive Board decides whether the RMB should be included in the SDR basket. Since there are no pre-set thresholds or benchmarks, the decision ultimately required a subjective judgment by the Executive Board based on the "freely usable currency" concept and quantitative indicators under the IMF's Articles of Agreement. The report prepared by the staff provided a rigorous technical assessment with a clear recommendation in order to inform Executive Directors. The Board endorsed staff's analysis and recommendation and made the final decision.

As the Executive Board's decision was made pursuant to statutory procedures and criteria, the judgment that the RMB is freely usable is clear-cut and cannot be compromised. The decision can be regarded as the IMF's official endorsement for the RMB to be widely used in the international market and international payment. Previously, businesses, institutions, and even monetary authorities were not confident in RMB assets due to opaque information disclosure. The inclusion of the RMB in the SDR basket could eliminate such doubts and hesitations. RMB could thus better play its role as a medium of financial transactions and a reserve asset.

2. RMB internationalization would face new challenges and opportunities after the inclusion.

The inclusion of the RMB in the SDR basket represents IMF's official recognition of the RMB as an international reserve currency; it is also a key symbol of RMB being a major international currency. But the inclusion's influence is far more than just symbolic. According to the IMF, the RMB's inclusion would boost the ever-increasing use of the RMB in international transactions and payments.

The RMB's weight in the new SDR basket, 10.92%, took effect on October 1, 2016, which offers a reference to various actors in the international financial market in their asset allocation and leaves sufficient lead time for necessary preparation and adjustment. As the IMF collects and discloses information on RMB reserves, more official institutions of IMF members will hold RMB assets. The RMB can make new breakthroughs in serving as an international currency in terms of trade settlement, financial transactions, and official reserves, and RMB internationalization can gain further momentum. Official and non-official players will gradually increase their holdings of RMB assets, which is undoubtedly good news to RMB offshore markets around the globe. There will be more RMB-denominated financial assets and the RMB will take up a larger proportion in international financial transactions. RMB usage and RMB-denominated transactions will expand and witness in-depth development. With the RMB's inclusion, the RMB can gain its due position in the international monetary system in line with China's economic strength. China can thus effectively avoid the dollar trap, safeguard the economic gains made by its people, and ensure economic and financial security of the nation.

China's entry into the WTO in 2002 was considered a milestone because ever since then, China's integration into the world economy has substantially accelerated. The entry laid a solid foundation for China to become the largest trading nation of the world. The RMB's inclusion in the SDR basket was also a milestone because it was a harbinger that China's integration in the international trade and economic system would also accelerate. At the current stage, the functions and use of the SDR are limited. Even so, the inclusion of the RMB, the currency of a developing country, is still unprecedented and inspiring. We believe that as RMB internationalization continues to progress and the use of the SDR is expanded in a planned and phased manner,[2] the reform of the international monetary system will be promoted.

The RMB's inclusion is an affirmation of the progress made in China's economic development and reform and opening up, especially the primary progress of RMB internationalization. The inclusion also shows the international community's high expectations on China to play a more important

[2] Zhou Xiaochuan, Governor of PBOC, pointed out at the High-level Seminar on the International Financial Architecture in March 2016 that China would release foreign exchange reserve data denominated in the SDR in addition to the USD and would also explore issuing SDR-denominated bonds in the domestic market.

role in the world economy and finance. However, as a developing country, China still lags behind in terms of the width and depth of its financial market. After the RMB's inclusion, the cooperation and interaction between China and the international monetary and financial system will widen and deepen. As a result, China will face new challenges in terms of domestic institutional arrangements, policy decisions, the operation of the whole financial system including financial markets and institutions, and the development of the real economy. If China can successfully tackle these challenges and perform its obligations as the issuing country of an international currency, it can broaden the prospect of RMB internationalization. Therefore, the top priority after the RMB's inclusion should be identifying future challenges and making early and effective preparations.

First, the ever closer interaction between China and the international monetary and financial systems would definitely result in changes of cross-border capital flow and draw closer attention of the global market to the RMB exchange rate. In this term, the RMB exchange rate volatility and the PBOC's exchange rate management are the most challenging issues. As the RMB is taking up more of the functions of an international currency, the RMB exchange rate will not only influence the economic and financial activities in the domestic market but also have a spillover effect on the exchange rate of neighboring countries' currencies, regional trade, and investment and even the international financial market.

As the exchange rate reform progresses, the formation mechanism of the RMB exchange rate is constantly improving. On one hand, the formation mechanism becomes evidently more market-oriented. As a result, the RMB exchange rate becomes more flexible and can swing in both directions. On the other hand, from December 2015, the CFETS began to release a new RMB index regularly. The index represents a weighted exchange rate based on a basket of currencies. Compared with the traditional practice of observing the RMB's exchange rate against the USD, the index can better reflect the external value of a currency based on the overall competitiveness of the goods and services of the issuing country. The extent and direction of the RMB index fluctuations may not be in line with those of the RMB exchange rate against the USD. Over-emphasis on the RMB/USD rate may risk exaggerating the fluctuations of RMB exchange rate or even misjudging the trend of the RMB exchange rate.

In terms of the exchange rate regime, China's proper choice now is still the managed floating regime. Currently, China's capital account is not fully liberalized, and certain restrictions still exist. Meanwhile, the PBOC's monetary policy is not fully independent from the influence of policies adopted by central banks of other countries. Under these circumstances, choosing a regime between fixed and freely floating systems makes perfect sense. The key is how to manage the exchange rate to realize exchange rate objectives in line with the optimal monetary policy. More importantly, the PBOC should be able to guide market expectations and give full play to the market mechanism. In this way, the PBOC can realize the objectives of exchange rate adjustment without undue interference. In the future, when RMB internationalization reaches a certain level, restrictions on capital flow will be further relaxed and the PBOC will pursue more independent monetary policies. In this case, the exchange rate regime will become fully floating. The PBOC will then be pursuing exchange rate objectives through the indirect influence of monetary and fiscal policies.

Second, during globalization and financial liberalization, the financial markets of emerging economies are vulnerable against external shocks and susceptive to financial crises. When crises happen, the domestic financial system will be disrupted, economic growth may come to a halt, and long-term social and economic disturbances may follow. China's financial market is as vulnerable and susceptible to crises as that in any other emerging economy. As the financial reform continues to deepen, China's financial market is open to more foreign investors. The co-movement among sub-markets and domestic and international markets becomes more evident; so does the transmission of financial risks. All these pose another severe challenge to the ultimate completion of RMB internationalization.

Cross-border capital flows, especially short-term ones, evidently influence the price of RMB-denominated underlying assets and the transmission of financial risks. Therefore, capital account liberalization must be undertaken in a gradual, stable, and orderly manner and in coordination with the reform of China's domestic financial system. The pressing priority is to explore effective tools to manage short-term cross-border capital flows. Meanwhile, China should establish at the earliest juncture a comprehensive supervision system, prioritize financial legislation, and innovate in risk management technologies. It should also pay close attention to the co-movement and contagion among financial markets so as to avoid the accumulation of financial risks and the eruption of systemic crises.

Third, the prudent operation of systemically important banks is key to the security of China's financial system and a key variable in RMB internationalization. As RMB plays a more important role in the international market, these large banks will definitely go global and enjoy a huge space for international development. As the banks serve more clients and offer more products, they will expand the scale and income sources of their overseas business. However, these banks will also face more complex market environment and supervision. The amount and structure of the banks' risk exposure will also change substantially. It should also be noted that despite external risks when going global, at the current stage, these systemically important banks face more risks in their domestic business. Therefore, when going global, these banks face challenges from both the domestic and the foreign markets. As China further integrates into the international monetary and financial system, it must pay special attention to the risk control mechanism of systemically important banks and make efforts to prevent individual incidents from becoming systemic financial crises or disasters to the real economy.

Fourth, the stable and sound development of the real economy is key to realizing RMB internationalization. At the current stage, China's economy faces multiple challenges. The supply-side reform will inject new vitality to the sustainable development of China's real economy if it can transform the growth model, break the bottlenecks in social and economic development, and boost industrial upgrading and technological innovation. Only then will the confidence of the global market in RMB internationalization be established and enhanced. In short, without the support of a strong real economy, RMB internationalization will only face a dim prospect. Therefore, uncertainties in the real economy constitute a major challenge to the ultimate realization of RMB internationalization. It is worth noting that China's domestic reform is deepening when it becomes more open to the outside market. Therefore, as China integrates more into the international economic and financial system, China needs to both fend off external risks on one hand and develop the domestic market on the other, so as to build the capacity to tackle all kinds of shocks. In deepening the supply-side reform, China also needs to notice the fact that problems in the real economy often show themselves in financial risks. If not addressed in time, these risks may transfer, transmit, or even lead to systemic financial crises.

Systemic financial crises are extremely damaging. In addition to hurting the economy and people's lives, these crises may well disrupt the strategy of RMB internationalization. In China, systemic risks have temporarily risen several times but have not led to crises. Recently, systemic risks emerge from the co-movement of several markets rather than any individual market. China needs to pay great attention to this trend and take effective measures to monitor and assess systemic risks. In preventing and tackling systemic risks, China needs to catch up with the global trend of macro-prudential regulation. In financial regulation, China should add a long-awaited macro-dimension, and adopt both macro- and micro-prudential regulation to form synergy, so as to fend off systemic risks, prevent their transmission, and secure financial stability. By establishing a policy framework of macro-prudential regulation in line with China's conditions, China can tackle systemic risks, hold the bottom line that no systemic financial crisis should happen, and create favorable conditions for RMB internationalization and other major national strategies.

3.2 The RMB's Inclusion Does Not Mean China's Capital Account Is Fully Liberalized

3.2.1 We Need to Clarify the Relationship Between RMB Internationalization and Capital Account Liberalization

Concerning the relationship between RMB internationalization and capital account liberalization, we need to clarify the two popular, but not necessarily correct, opinions. One is that capital account liberalization is the prerequisite for RMB internationalization; as the RMB is not yet fully convertible, it is not universally accepted or used in international trade and settlement; RMB internationalization under capital account restrictions is doomed. This opinion was popular when China first put forward its strategy of RMB internationalization, and was representative of the opposition to RMB internationalization and its rationality and legitimacy. As RMB internationalization made rapid progress, this opinion vanished.

Another opinion was popular when the IMF considered whether to include RMB into the SDR basket. Some people believed that capital account liberalization was key to meeting the criterion of a freely usable currency. They thus held a negative prospect for the RMB's inclusion. When the RMB's inclusion did happen, these people changed their minds and held that the RMB's inclusion was a harbinger that China would fully liberalize its capital account very shortly. Currently, many institutions and individuals from both home and abroad still hold this opinion.

Past international practices indicate that capital account liberalization is not a sufficient condition for the internationalization of a currency; it is not even a necessary condition at the early stage of internationalization. In the 1990s, many emerging economies opened their capital accounts, but rarely were their currencies recognized and used widely around the world. The idea that capital account liberalization is the prerequisite of a currency's internationalization has been proven wrong: the RMB is included in the SDR basket as a fifth currency, but China's capital account has yet to be fully liberalized. Meanwhile, the IMF has clarified that a freely usable currency is not necessarily linked with the opening of the capital account or full convertibility. Therefore, there is not sufficient evidence to support the prediction that after the RMB's inclusion, China will fully liberalize its capital account.

Instead of regarding capital account liberalization as the prerequisite of a currency's internationalization, we may reason as follows: a currency becoming a hard currency in the international market pushes forward its internationalization and all this in turn requires further capital account liberalization.[3] Currently, the booming RMB offshore markets not only meet businesses' demand for RMB settlement under capital account restrictions and increase liquidity supply, but also provide financial services like investment, financing, and hedging through diversified markets and product innovation to satisfy non-residents' need to preserve and increase the value of their RMB-denominated assets and enhance attractiveness of and confidence in the RMB. On offshore markets, the RMB is convertible to some extent and using the RMB is very convenient. As a result, RMB internationalization quickly gained momentum. RMB offshore markets now serve as a transit arrangement before capital account liberalization. These markets provide favorable conditions for us to push forward the capital account reform based on domestic and foreign economic conditions and in a timely and prudent manner.

Therefore, at the early stage of RMB internationalization, it is not necessary for China to fully liberalize its capital account only to meet the needs of RMB internationalization. If we were to generally analyze the reason and timing of capital account liberalization, we should consider both the advantages of the liberalization and the fact that financial crises frequently happen after emerging economies liberalize their capital accounts. Arteta et al. (2011) and Gu and Huang (2011) hold that under incomplete financial regulation, premature liberalization of the capital account would substantially increase the risk of financial crises. Ma Yong and Chen Yulu (2010)

[3] Lu Lei, 2014. Monetary Theory and Optimal Policy Based on Micro-Level Analysis, China Finance (22).

discover through empirical studies that although over the longer term, financial crises are not triggered by capital account liberalization, radical liberalization does greatly increase their incidence. These analyses also offer another perspective in proving that capital account reform should not and need not be influenced by RMB internationalization.

3.2.2 Both De Jure and De Facto Liberalization Should Be Concerned

People do not have a clear-cut perception of capital account liberalization. For instance, some believe that liberalization is zero regulation; that developed countries are more liberalized in this regard than developing ones; that liberalization is a state rather than a process; or that liberalization is irreversible. In fact, none of these ideas are right.

Capital account liberalization is a dynamic process. In practice, no country has completely removed capital control, including those who claim to have fully liberalized their capital accounts. There are two dimensions to assess a country's capital account liberalization: the de facto dimension (based on promulgated laws and regulations) and the de facto dimension (based on facts).

The AREAER of the IMF is the major measuring method under the de facto dimension. Chart 3.1 shows the 2015 assessment of the 11 items in the capital account of G20 countries using a binary variable. According to the assessment, India imposed restrictions on each of the items. China, Argentina, and South Africa imposed restrictions on all but one items. Japan, Italy, and Canada were the most liberalized, imposing restrictions on only two items. People always thought that the United States was the most liberalized, but most surprisingly, the United States imposed restrictions on seven items. So did Germany and Brazil.

The measuring method using a binary variable is not that precise. The mainstream measuring method of de jure liberalization is the four-variable model. According to the RMB Internationalization Report, in 2014, China's de jure capital account liberalization degree reached 0.6502, a substantial progress compared to 0.5045 in 2010.

Kraay (1998) proposed to use the balance of payments information to establish the indicators of capital account liberalization. Capital account liberalization is assessed based on the proportion of capital inflow and outflow under the items of FDI, securities investment, and other investments in a nation's GDP. Based on this proportion, Chart 3.2 shows the

Chart 3.1 AREAER binary variable assessment of the capital account of G20 countries (2015)

	11 items under the capital account										
Country	*Capital market*	*Monetary market*	*Collective investment*	*Derivatives*	*Commercial credit*	*Financial credit*	*Warranty and guarantee*	*Direct investment*	*Liquidation*	*Immovables*	*Personal trading*
Indonesia	•	•	•	•	•	•	•	•	•	•	
China	•	•	•	•		•	•	•	•	•	•
India	•	•	•	•	•	•	•	•	•	•	•
Argentina	•	•	•	•		•	•	•		•	•
Mexico	•	•	•	•		•	•	•		•	•
Australia	•		•		•			•		•	•
Russia	•	•	•					•			
Saudi Arabia	•	•	•	•	•	•	•	•		•	•
South Africa	•	•	•	•	•	•	•	•		•	
South Korea	•			•				•			
Germany	•	•	•	•		•		•		•	
The US	•	•	•	•			•	•		•	
Brazil	•	•	•	•		•		•		•	
Japan	•							•			
France	•	•	•					•			
Italy			•					•			
Canada	•							•			
Britain	•	•	•					•		•	
Turkey	•	•	•	•	•	•		•		•	

Source: 2015 AREAER, IMF
Note: • for restrictions imposed

Chart 3.2 De facto capital account liberalization in some G20 countries

	Australia	*Brazil*	*Canada*	*China*	*EU*	*France*	*Germany*	*India*	*Japan*	*South Korea*	*Russia*	*South Africa*	*Britain*	*USA*
1985	0.000	0.054	0.056	0.040	0.000	0.046	0.083	0.014	0.000	0.050		0.031	0.253	0.036
1990	0.076	0.019	0.073	0.016	0.000	0.184	0.096	0.021	0.000	0.044	0.000	0.025	0.304	0.044
1995	0.118	0.048	0.085	0.061	0.000	0.074	0.110	0.018	0.000	0.107	0.026	0.068	0.315	0.104
1996	0.114	0.050	0.132	0.055	0.000	0.108	0.118	0.054	0.093	0.122	0.097	0.074	0.538	0.122
1997	0.100	0.045	0.144	0.114	0.000	0.180	0.211	0.046	0.137	0.073	0.126	0.171	0.592	0.142
1998	0.093	0.094	0.173	0.095	0.000	0.181	0.309	0.038	0.124	0.072	0.111	0.156	0.322	0.092
1999	0.144	0.096	0.129	0.078	0.152	0.386	0.359	0.023	0.231	0.074	0.126	0.201	0.460	0.135
2000	0.136	0.083	0.225	0.101	0.227	0.369	0.410	0.036	0.089	0.063	0.152	0.061	0.998	0.161
2001	0.153	0.066	0.173	0.078	0.174	0.347	0.292	0.022	0.114	0.097	0.030	0.191	0.610	0.110
2002	0.194	0.077	0.120	0.053	0.113	0.234	0.222	0.028	0.091	0.040	0.046	0.047	0.289	0.104
2003	0.244	0.058	0.093	0.065	0.128	0.323	0.195	0.031	0.142	0.079	0.149	0.056	0.599	0.111
2004	0.267	0.061	0.112	0.070	0.149	0.419	0.200	0.036	0.139	0.089	0.144	0.056	0.890	0.217
2005	0.283	0.038	0.130	0.115	0.236	0.594	0.320	0.047	0.231	0.084	0.166	0.091	1.139	0.142
2006	0.347	0.082	0.203	0.139	0.285	0.551	0.341	0.075	0.181	0.134	0.170	0.168	0.867	0.249
2007	0.293	0.115	0.257	0.126	0.298	0.531	0.461	0.104	0.252	0.180	0.256	0.115	1.302	0.259
2008	0.194	0.055	0.149	0.082	0.083	0.240	0.145	0.084	0.235	0.309	0.262	0.142	1.163	0.155
2009	0.403	0.079	0.153	0.057	0.184	0.358	0.173	0.056	0.246	0.263	0.128	0.100	0.790	0.139
2010	0.281	0.122	0.150	0.107	0.099	0.266	0.287	0.083	0.275	0.184	0.099	0.072	0.487	0.157
2011	0.245	0.093	0.149	0.097	0.102	0.299	0.152	0.065	0.239	0.159	0.153	0.238	0.223	0.100
2012	0.201	0.069	0.165	0.074	0.112	0.197	0.218	0.079	0.194	0.155	0.139	0.222	0.304	0.149
2013	0.217	0.081	0.117	0.083	0.134	0.324	0.237	0.067	0.253	0.142	0.159	0.187	0.296	0.128
2014	0.210	0.123	0.158	0.080	0.098	0.203	0.125	0.071	0.308	0.145	0.112	0.217	0.187	0.113

Source: IMF

assessment results of de facto capital account liberalization in some G20 countries. It is not difficult to find that capital account liberalization is a dynamic process. The de facto liberalization of any nation changes constantly and in both directions. Generally speaking, developed countries are more liberalized than developing countries. But the de facto liberalization degrees vary among developed countries. For certain countries, they are not as liberalized as people expect.

Figure 3.1 shows the trend of China's de facto capital account liberalization. Since the reform and opening up, China's cross-border capital flow has maintained a steady and rising trend. But during global financial disturbances, the capital flow witnessed sharp declines. The proportion of overall capital flow in GDP rose as the restrictions on international capital flow were loosened, and the proportion dropped (or overall capital flow decreased substantially) as the restrictions were intensified. This further demonstrates that China is very flexible in coping with the shocks from international financial capital.

It is worth noting that since 2010, China's capital account liberalization has continued to rise in the de jure dimension; but in the de facto dimension, it rose after falling. This shows that even for the same economy, the

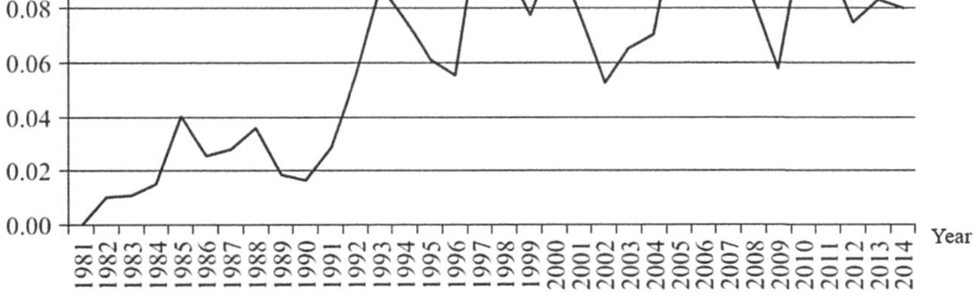

Fig. 3.1 The trend of China's de facto capital account liberalization. (Source: IMF)

de jure and de facto dimensions of capital account liberalization may change not in lockstep, or even in opposite directions sometimes.

This reminds us that China's reform should neither focus only on the de jure dimension nor rush to a complete removal of all restrictions. First, China should notice IMF's change of mind concerning capital flow management. Capital control was not considered a policy option but is now considered an important part of the policy toolkit managing capital flow. Under specific circumstances, capital control could be deemed appropriate. IMF advised countries to establish three lines of defense in managing their capital flow, namely, adjustment of macro-economic policies, macro-prudential management, and temporary capital control. Therefore, we should not hold prejudice against capital control. Capital control covers at least three aspects: control to fight against money laundering, terrorism financing, tax havens, and national security threats; control to various degrees due to macro-prudential considerations; temporary control in the case of large-scale hot money flows and severe balance of payments disequilibrium. Second, we need to draw upon developed countries' experience in managing capital flow and foreign investment. We should especially learn from the countries whose capital account liberalization degree is high in the de jure dimension but low in the de facto dimension, so as to address the problem that China's capital account liberalization, for a long time, remains low in the de jure dimension but high in the de facto dimension. Before supportive measures for capital account reform are fully in place, we should not liberalize China's capital account prematurely.

Column 3.1 The Current US System of Foreign Investment Management

The United States liberalized its capital account in as early as 1969. The United States has always been open to foreign investment and offered it national treatment. Meanwhile, specific systems as follows exist to manage capital flow:

1. The national security and investment review

The Foreign Investment and National Security Act of 2007 amended Section 721 of the Defense Production Act of 1950 (*Code of Laws of the United States*). Since then, the Committee on Foreign

Investments in the United States (CFIUS) has been responsible for reviewing foreign investment. The CFIUS specifically supervises and assesses foreign investment and undertake investigations based on the investment's impact on the national security of the US. It may recommend that the president make the final decision and block a foreign acquisition.

Criteria for the CFIUS review cover the supply of goods and services important to the US economy, key resources and technologies, critical infrastructure, and so on. The CFIUS includes representatives from multiple departments and agencies including the Council of Economic Advisers and the National Economic Council. How to interpret national economic security and whether to expand relevant reviews are at the discretion of the CFIUS.

2. Supervision on the security industry

In terms of securities supervision, the United States regulates securities issuance pursuant to the Securities Act of 1933 and securities exchange pursuant to the Securities Act of 1934. Public offerings should be registered; the issuers need to submit registration forms and applications to the SEC. After the SEC's approval, they can proceed with their offerings. Foreign investors just need to fill in different forms and meet different requirements of information disclosure. For private offerings, there are fewer restrictions. Foreign and domestic issuers basically go through the same procedure. Under the registration system, the SEC undertakes strict and rigorous reviews of registration materials, and those who fail to meet the SEC's requirements cannot register their offerings, so the registration may take a long time.

3. Restrictions on the banking industry

In October 1978, the United States adopted the International Banking Act (IBA), its first federal law concerning foreign banks, which marked that the US banking regulation system initially took shape. The Foreign Bank Supervision Enhancement Act of 1991 established the principles of national treatment and reciprocity, amended the IBA of 1978, and set up a unified standard for foreign banks to enter the United States and expand their business. The 1991 Act enhanced the federal supervision on foreign banks and imposed strict restrictions on their business scope.

General requirements are the same for foreign and domestic investment banks. Special requirements are in the aspects of market access and business operation. Under the IBA, the Office of the Comptroller of the Currency is authorized to raise different capital requirements for foreign banks of different countries and regions. If foreign banks apply to establish branches or offices at the federal level, they have to put a certain amount of capital in cash or qualified securities in designated banks. There are certain restrictions on foreign banks' fund use. According to the US law, foreign banks are not allowed to use business operation as an excuse to involve in politics or to provide politics-related (e.g., elections) loans and investments. These banks are also not allowed to acquire or purchase the stocks of non-bank US companies.

4. A negative list system based on Model BIT

Model BIT (Bilateral Investment Treaty) is the blueprint for US outward investment. The United States signs all its BITs and FTAs based on this model and extends national treatment to the pre-entry stage using a negative list. However, to ensure some leeway, Article 14 of Model BIT provides non-conforming measures concerning national treatment, most-favored-nation treatment, performance requirements, senior management, and boards of directors. These measures are incorporated in the annex as a negative list. In the United States, a negative list usually includes three attachments: the list of the first, second, and third categories of excluded sectors. In the second category, only specific sectors and relevant legal bases are specified with the wording like "reserving the right to adopt or maintain any measures". Therefore, the non-conforming measures of a signatory country can be expanded to the largest extent. In the third category, non-conforming measures for financial services are singled out, covering issues like the ownership of financial institutions, the limits of business, and policy treatment. In this list, two types of non-conforming measures exist based on whether they are binding or not.

First, a negative list mainly covers sectors concerning the national and economic security. The restrictions can be divided into six categories: first, on the use of land and other natural resources; second, on energy; third, on maritime and air transportation; fourth, on broadcast and communication; fifth, on finance, insurance and real estate; sixth, on the ownership level in all sectors. The restrictions show the basic intention and purpose of the US investment protection. The first five categories are closely linked to national security while the sixth offers space for the US government to adopt supportive policies in favor of domestic industries and businesses. Meanwhile, the negative list of the United States does not cover any manufacturing industries. In this model, exceptions are also made for foreign investors' national treatment in terms of clauses concerning major security issues, financial services, and tax.

Second, a negative list emphasizes restrictions on the financial sector. As the financial services of the United States are highly competitive in the international market, in recent years, the United States has singled out the financial services as a third attachment of the BITs and FTAs that it has signed, so as to pursue a high level of financial liberalization. The emphasis on financial services in the negative list can be seen in the following aspects: first, financial services cover the most non-conforming measures and are singled out as an independent attachment; second, non-conforming measures related to financial services cover issues like the ownership of financial institutions, limits on business, and transactions and policy treatment.

3.3 The RMB's Inclusion Does Not Equal the Realization of RMB Internationalization

The ultimate goal of RMB internationalization is for the RMB to become a major international currency and to a gain a status that matches China's economic and trade strength. But under the current international monetary landscape, RMB internationalization will be a long and difficult journey.

The RMB's inclusion shows the IMF's recognition of the RMB as a freely usable currency. This means that the RMB is officially recognized as an international reserve asset. But whether the RMB can become a major international currency still depends on the actual use and holdings of RMB in the international market. The yen's experience after its inclusion shows that the official recognition as an international currency may not necessarily lead to market strength. Therefore, it is necessary to explore the yen internationalization and draw upon lessons and experience. We need to be objective in evaluating the RMB's current functions as an international currency and put forward valuable policy advice for the next stage of RMB internationalization.

3.3.1 Why the Yen Waned After Its Inclusion in the SDR Basket

As the Bretton Woods system and the fixed exchange rate system collapsed, in 1974, the SDR began to derive its value from a basket of currencies. The original basket included 16 currencies, the issuing countries of which respectively accounted for more than 1% of global export. At this stage, the Japanese yen first entered the SDR framework.[4] A basket of 16 currencies would definitely make it difficult to calculate the value of the SDR, making the development and promotion of the SDR more difficult. In 1981, the IMF decided to limit the basket to five currencies of major developed countries, namely, the USD, the British pound, the French franc, the Deutsche mark, and the Japanese yen. It also decided to review the weights of basket currencies every five years. These decisions marked that the Japanese yen became a true international reserve currency.

Table 3.1 shows that after its official inclusion into the SDR basket in 1981, the Japanese yen maintained ten years of rapid growth as an international reserve currency. The yen's internationalization peaked in the late 1990s and then started to wane. In the latest review of SDR basket currencies, the yen's weight further dropped to a historic low of 8.09%, a decrease of 55.1% compared to its peak weight of 18%.

[4]The 16 currencies in the 1974 basket include the USD, the Deutsche mark, the Japanese yen, the French franc, the British pound, the Dutch guilder, the Canadian dollar, the Belgian franc, the Swiss franc, the Australian dollar, the Danish krone, the Spanish peseta, the Norwegian krone, the Austrian shilling, and the South African rand. In 1978, the IMF adjusted the SDR basket and replaced the Danish krone and South African rand with Iranian riyal and Saudi Arabian riyal.

Table 3.1 The weight of the Japanese yen in the SDR basket (%)

	USD	*EUR*	*FRF*	*DEM*	*GBP*	*JPY*	*CHN*
1981–1985	42	–	13	19	13	3.3.1.1. 13	–
1986–1990	42	–	12	19	12	3.3.1.2. 15	–
1991–1995	40	–	11	21	11	3.3.1.3. 17	–
1996–2000	39	–	11	21	11	3.3.1.4. 18	–
2001–2005	45	29	–	–	11	3.3.1.5. 15	–
2006–2010	44	34	–	–	11	3.3.1.6. 11	–
2011–2015	41.9	37.4	–	–	11.3	3.3.1.7. 9.4	–
2016–2020	41.73	30.93	–	–	8.33	3.3.1.8. 8.09	10.92

Source: IMF

The track record of the Japanese yen in global asset allocation (Appendix 1) fully demonstrates how yen internationalization waxed and waned. Japan has long been the second largest economy and the third largest trading country. However, yen internationalization rapidly waned after a peak in the 1990s. Today, no one still recalls the past honor of the yen. This is because that the Japanese government was short-sighted and took a wrong method in yen internationalization.

1. Explanations at the policy level

In the 1980s, most of Japan's financial management institutions were established before the Second World War. These institutions were better at politics, management, and coordinating special interest groups, but they faced excessive constraints when tackling economic issues, and were highly inefficient. For the yen internationalization, the Japanese government recognized its importance and urgency too late. The Japanese government failed to make full use of the most precious five years after the yen's inclusion. From 1980 to 1985, the government was excessively conservative on the financial market liberalization and yen internationalization. It was until after 1985 that a large number of supportive policies were adopted. But at this juncture, Japan's economy started to show problems. Yen internationalization finally failed due to domestic recessions.

In the bond market, Japan's government bonds are less liquid than American and German ones. By the end of 1998, Japan's bond market volume reached 423 trillion yen, 280 trillion yen of which was government bonds, only second to the volume of the US government bonds. But

Chart 3.3 shows that the non-resident holdings of Japan's government bonds accounted for only 10%, lower than the level in other G10 countries. In the United States, the figure was as high as 37.5%. This indicates that though Japan's bonds witnessed a high growth in volume, they lacked liquidity in the international market. The situation was also harmful to the yen as a medium of transactions.

Another reason for the insufficient government bond liquidity was that a withholding tax was imposed on the interest income of non-residents (Murase 2000). Non-residents could invest in Japan's government bonds through three channels: 63% through the transfer settlement system, 36% through the registration system, and 1% through holdings of qualified securities. The withholding tax could be spared if non-residents chose the transfer settlement system, but not if non-residents chose the registration system. This differentiated treatment was a major hindrance toward the integration of Japan's bond market. It was not until the end of 1999 that the Japanese government removed the withholding tax.

Another factor restricting the liquidity of Japan's bond market is that the government's public sector held too many bonds, and often held them

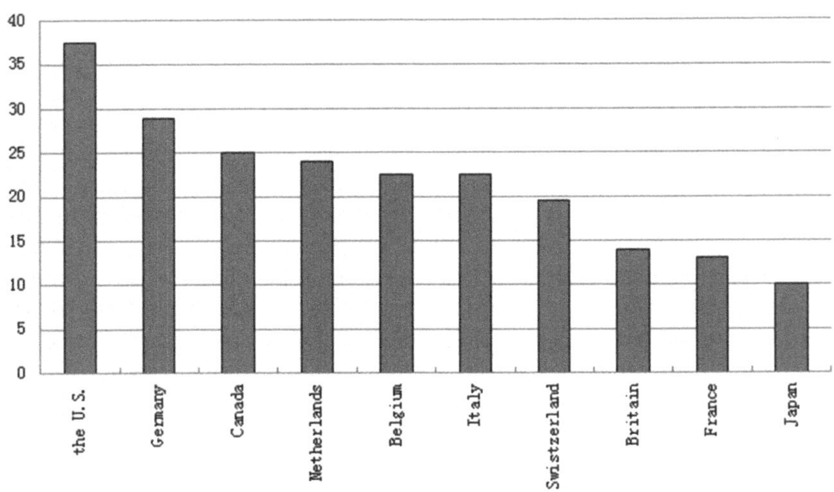

Chart 3.3 The 1997 non-resident holdings of government bonds in G10 (10%). (Source: Bank of Japan, Murase, Tetsuji (2000) "The Internationalization of the Yen: Essential Issues Overlook", Pacific Economic Papers, No. 307)

to maturity. This went against the development of the market price formation mechanism in the secondary market, and many non-resident investors began to lose confidence in Japanese government bond in the late 1990s. An attempt to boost non-residents' interest in domestic bonds—the abolishment of the withholding tax by the Japanese government in 1999—ended in vain. As depicted in the following table, by the end of 1997, public sectors held nearly 50% of the government bonds, 36% held by the Japanese government, and 11% held by the BOJ. But at the same time, this proportion in the United States and Germany was much lower, especially Germany, the government of which only held 3% and Deutsche Bundesbank held no government bonds. The majority of government bonds were purchased by financial institutions which had a high participation in the market. The US government held 25% of government bonds, the majority of which, however, were non-tradable ones issued by social welfare trusts, exerting no impact on the demand and supply in the market (Table 3.2).

Besides, the Japanese government failed to provide a "continuous settlement system" for bond investors. The transactions of bonds issued by the US government can be completed and settled in the next workday; but in Japan, settlement is only allowed six times per month, which undoubtedly increased the transaction risks for investors (Garber 1996[5]).

2. Explanation from the theoretical perspective

Since its inclusion into the basket of SDR currencies, the Japanese yen developed slowly as an international settlement currency and a transaction medium, but its value maintenance function developed rapidly. The lack of

Table 3.2 Government bonds holding structure (%)

	Government	*Central bank*	*Financial institutions*	*Non-resident*	*other*
Japan	36.0	11.0	26.0	10.0	17.0
USA	25.0	8.0	11.0	37.5	18.5
Germany	3.0	0.0	53.5	29.0	14.5

Data sources: Ministry of Finance of Japan, Murase (2000)

[5] Garber, Peter M., The Use of Yen as a Reserve Currency [J]. Monetary and Economic Studies, 1996 December: 1–21.

liquidity renders yen-denominated financial assets a stronger performance in the long-term capital market than in the short-term currency market. This imbalance in the yen's three international functions contributed to the failure of the yen's internationalization. The decade from 1970 to 1980 saw a rapid increase of the yen's share in the settlement of Japan's export from 0% to 40%. However, no breakthrough was achieved since 1980, no matter how hard Japan promoted the settlement function of the yen after it was included into the basket of SDR currencies. The proportion even dipped to 35% in 2004. The causes behind such lagged development of the yen's settlement function were analyzed profoundly by Kawai (1996),[6] Frankel and Wei (1994),[7] Taguchi (1994),[8] Fukada and Ji (1994),[9] Sato (1999),[10] the Ministry of Finance (1999),[11] Takatoshi (2010), and others. They concluded that six restricted factors played a part (see Table 3.3).

Table 3.3 Major factors restricting the development of the yen's international settlement function

Factor 1	The existence of inertia of USD
Factor 2	No market for direct trade between Yen and South Asian currencies
Factor 3	Relatively small financial market in Japan
Factor 4	South Asian countries reserve USD as anchor currency
Factor 5	Japan's high trade dependence on the United States (See Chart 3.4)
Factor 6	Many Japanese general trading companies have huge foreign currency loan

[6] Kawai, M., The Japanese Yen as an International Currency: Performance and Prospects [J]. Organization, Performance and Equity Research Monographs in Japan – US Business & Economics, 1996 (1): 305–355.

[7] Frankel, Jeffrey. A. and Wei, Shang-Jin, Yen Bloc or Dollar Bloc? Exchange Rate Policies of the East Asian Economies, in Takatoshi Ito and Anne O. Kruger, eds. Macroeconomic Linkage: Savings, Exchange Rates, and Capital Flows, Chicago: University of Chicago Press, 1994: 295–329.

[8] Taguchi, H., On the Internationalization of the Japanese Yen, in Takatoshi Ito and Anne O. Kruger, eds. Macroeconomic Linkage: Savings, Exchange Rates, and Capital Flows, Chicago: University of Chicago Press, 1994: 335–355.

[9] Fukuda, S. and Cong, J., On the Choice of Invoice Currency by Japanese Exporter: The PTM Approach [J]. Journal of the Japanese and International Economies, 1994 (8): 511–529.

[10] Sato, K., The International Use of the Japanese Yen: the Case of Japan's Trade With East Asia [J]. The World Economy, 1999, 22 (4): 547–584.

[11] Ministry of Finance, Council on Foreign Exchange and Other Transactions, Internationalization of the Yen for the 21st Century—Japan's Response to Changes in Global Economic and Financial Environments, 1999.

As is shown in Chart 3.4, Japan's trade dependence on the United States was much greater than that of other developed capitalist countries, especially the dependence on export which stayed at a level of around

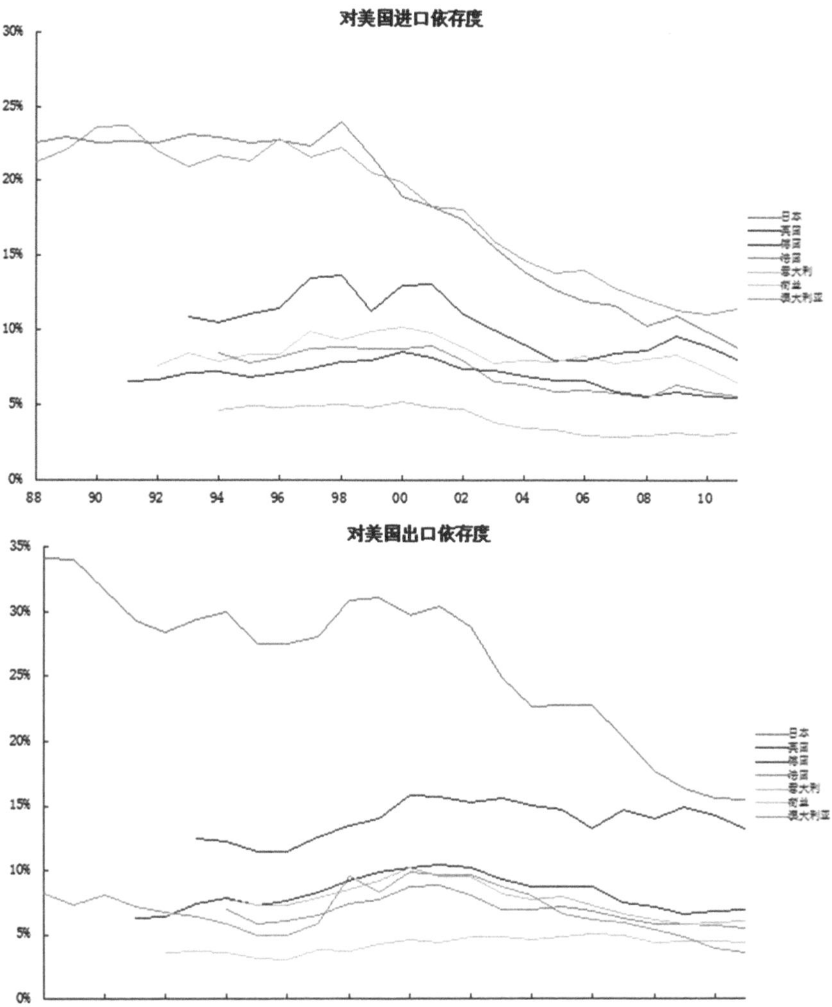

Chart 3.4 Dependence on the trade with the United States. (Data source: Calculation based on statistics of UN Comtrade)

30% in the two decades before 2000. In contrast, Germany kept a rather low reliance on import and export, creating a benign external environment for the rapid rise of DEM after its inclusion into the basket. Japan's excessively high dependence on the United States hampered, to a large extent, the internationalization of the yen. Fukuda and Cong (1994) analyzed with the general equilibrium model the yen's function as an international transaction medium and concluded that whether a company desired to adopt the yen as its settlement currency was decided by the shape of the profit function. When the profit function took the shape of a concave function, the high relevance between the exchange rate and the export price settled in the domestic currency was too high, leading to highly fluctuation risks, and enterprises tended to adopt the importing country's currency in settlement; in contrast, when the profit function took the shape of a convex function, enterprises were more willing to settle accounts in domestic currency. But for different regions, differences in the market demand curves would cause changes in export enterprises' profit curves. Fukuda and Cong (1994) further studied some of Japan's export industries, such as television, video recorders, and automobiles, which shared one feature in common: when Japan exported to the United States, the dominant clearing currency was the USD; but when Japan exported to the South Asian countries, the yen was used for settlement. The profit function of the corresponding firms in these two markets also changed. These enterprises saw a concave profit function when exporting to the United States and a convex function when exporting to the Southeast Asian market. This conclusion by Fukuda and Cong (1994) was further confirmed by the findings of Sato's (1999) research on Japanese semiconductor component export industry. According to Sato, the increasing share of Japan's export of integrated circuit components was a significant contributor to the decline in the settlement ratio of the yen.

It is safe to infer from the partial equilibrium model and the general equilibrium model that the major factors affecting the choice of the corporate settlement currency include exchange rate fluctuations, the degree of differences in export products, the market size, the size of the national economy, and money supply stability. Oi et al. (2003) found that the Japanese money supply in the 1990s was relatively stable compared with other countries, but the use of the Japanese yen was still limited and did not rise significantly. Therefore, the indicator of money supply does not apply in the analysis of the share of the yen in settlement.[12] Although the models and data prove that the size of the country is an important factor, Japan is an exception. Japan was the world's second largest economy in the 1970s, but in its domestic trade settlement the proportion of the yen was relatively low. Therefore, the following analysis focuses more on exchange rate volatility and product differentiation.

1. Exchange rate fluctuations and the choice of settlement currency strategy

In choosing the settlement currency, a firm will compare the fluctuation degree of the exchange rate between the domestic currency and the importing country's currency with that between importing country's currency and a third country's currency. If the latter is less than the former, the firm will adopt the third country's currency for valuation and settlement. As can be seen from Table 3.4, the yen and the Italian lira had the

Table 3.4 Exchange rate fluctuations and the choice of the settlement currency in export trade

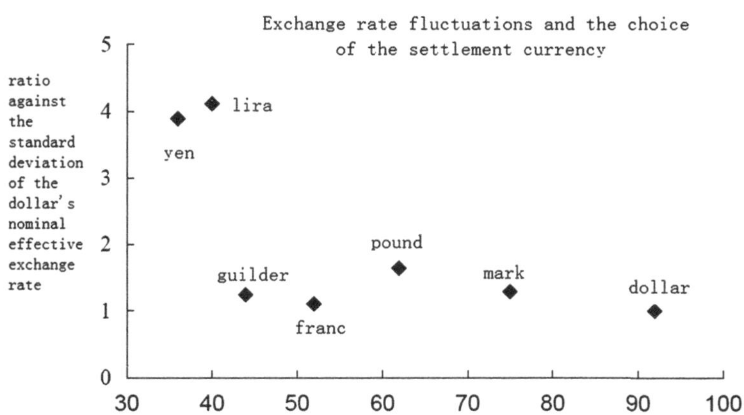

Data source: Bekx (1998), CEIC database
Note: The computation interval for standard deviation of nominal effective exchange rate is from January 1991 to December 1995

[12] Oi, Hiroyuki, Otani, Akira and Toyoichiro Shirota. The Choice of Invoice Currency in International Trade: Implications for the Internationalization of the Yen [J]. Monetary and Economic Studies, 2003 (October): 27–64.

largest fluctuation degree compared to the USD, so in the two countries the proportion of local currency in cross-border trade settlement is relatively low, while the proportion of dollar in settlement is higher. Among several major international currencies, the Deutsche mark had the lowest fluctuation degree relative to the USD. Therefore, we can infer from Table 3.4 that the stable value of the Deutsche mark laid a solid foundation for its rapid rise in the 1980s and 1990s.

2. Product differentiation and the choice of the settlement currency strategy

Product differentiation is a key concern in new open economy macroeconomics, and many studies explain the failure of the yen's internationalization from the perspective of product differentiation, such as Hamada and Horiuchi (1987),[13] Tavlas and Ozeki (1992), Iwami and Sato (1996),[14] Hooper et al. (1998),[15] Hummels (1999),[16] Oi et al. (2003), Bacchetta and Wincoop (2002),[17]and Fukuda and Ono (2006).[18] Hamada and Horiuchi (1987) analyzed a 1984 survey of major Japanese importers and exporters, and concluded that one of the main reasons why firms did not want to use the yen for settlement was the excessive pressure from international markets. Japan's products were generally more homogeneous than their international counterparts. Hooper et al. (1998) found that Japan's export price elasticity was higher than that of other major industrial countries, which means that Japan's product differentiation was too low. Empirical evidence also shows that Japan's product substitution elasticity was the highest in these countries. Iwami and Sato (1996) found that Japanese exporters were over-reliant on the US market, and they had

[13] Hamada, K. and A. Horiuchi, "The Political Economy of the Financial Market", In Kozo Yamamura and Yasukichi Yasuba, (ed.), The Political Economy of Japan, The Domestic Transformation: Stanford University Press, Vol. 1, 1987.

[14] Iwami, T. and Sato, K., The internationalization of the yen: with an emphasis on East Asia [J]. International Journal of Social Economics, 1996 (23): 192–208.

[15] Hooper, P., Johnson, K. and Marquez, J., Trade Elasticities for G-7 Countries [R]. International Finance Discussion Papers, No. 609, 1998.

[16] Hummels, D., Toward a Geography of Trade Costs, mimeo, University of Chicago, 1999.

[17] Bacchetta, Philippe and Van Wincoop, Eric, 2002, "A Theory of Currency Denomination of International Trade", ECB Working Paper, No. 177.

[18] Fukuda, S., Ono, M. On the Determinants of Exporters' Currency Pricing: History vs. Expectations [R]. NBER Working Paper, No. 12432, August, 2006.

to settle in the USD to ensure export growth. Oi et al. (2003) found that the proportion of products with a high degree of differentiation, such as automobiles, which were settled in the yen, was significantly higher than Japan's average in cross-border trade settlement. In Japan's export to the United States in 1998 only less than 20% was yen-denominated export, but the share of yen-denominated export to Southeast Asian countries was relatively high, exceeding 50%. Oi et al. (2003) studied the product categories of Japanese exports to Southeast Asian countries, and found that products which had dominant market shares, such as food, general machinery, transportation equipment, and precision instruments (see Table 3.5), were more likely to be settled in the yen.

Although Japan's yen-dominated export had a low share in Japan's export to developed countries like the United States, in the export to South Asian countries, its proportion in industries with high product differentiation is dominantly high. Figure 3.2 shows a clear negative correlation between export price elasticity and the share of the yen in the export trade settlement. For larger industries with relatively high export price elasticity, such as chemical products, metals, and minerals, the proportion of settlement in the yen is comparatively low. For industries with relatively low export price elasticity, such as automobiles and precision instruments, the proportion of settlement in the yen is higher than that in other industries, even as high as 80% in the automobile industry.

Table 3.5 The proportion of Japanese export to Southeast Asian countries denominated in local currencies (%)

	1993	*1994*	*1995*	*1996*	*1997*
All products	52.0	47.2	44.1	45.5	48.4
Food	52.5	63.8	67.7	65.8	59.2
Textile	29.5	26.3	28.4	31.0	28.2
Chemical products	23.6	19.2	20.7	22.0	29.8
Non-metallic mineral products	37.6	28.9	24.9	34.8	53.1
Metals and minerals	20.1	17.9	17.5	21.5	23.2
General machinery	69.0	66.8	59.9	59.7	59.7
Electronic machinery	41.8	37.0	39.7	37.9	42.7
Transportation equipment	78.4	71.5	58.5	72.3	81.3
Precise instruments	79.0	71.6	59.3	49.5	61.5
Other	34.1	32.8	32.6	37.2	40.3

Data source: World Bank

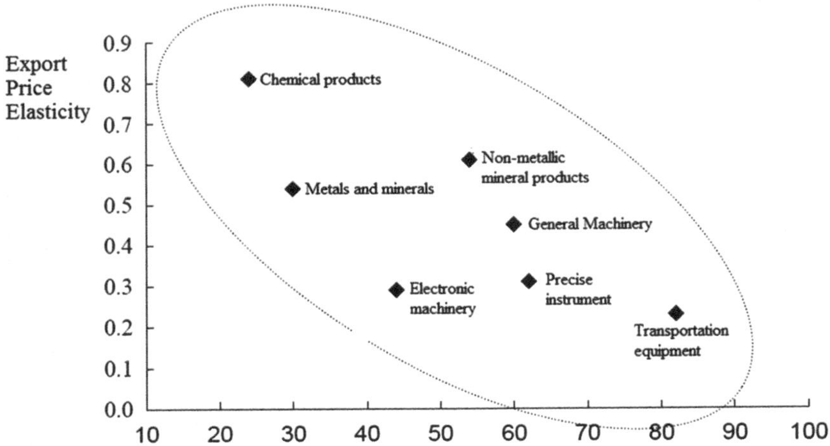

Fig. 3.2 Export price elasticity and the selection of settlement currency in export trade. (Data source: Bekx (1998), Oi et al. (2003), CEIC database)

3. Explanation from the perspective of the international monetary competition game

After the JPY joined the SDR as one of the major competitors for the status of an international reserve currency, the United States regarded the containment of the internationalization of yen as an important defense practice in the internationalization of the USD.

After becoming the world's second largest economy, Japan gradually began to possess a strong financial strength, which can be seen from the following aspects: (1) Japan became the world's largest creditor country, with overseas assets amounting to USD 2035.2 billion; (2) The competitiveness of Japanese multinationals in the global business system rose dramatically. More than 120 Japanese companies were among the "Fortune 500", and the top 30 enterprises in Asia were almost all Japanese companies; (3) Japan's financial institutions ranked top among industries globally. In the late 1980s, the world's top ten commercial banks were all Japanese banks. In 1990, the Bank of Japan accounted for 13% of all US bank assets (loans). The Bank of Japan accounted for a quarter of all loans in California. (4) The rapid rise of Japanese investment banks meant active competition against their American counterparts in traditional underwriting, M&A, trading business, and other areas. (5) The crazy rise of Japan's real estate industry and stock market resulted in unprecedented phenomenon: the total market value of Tokyo's real estate even exceeded that of the whole United States. (6) With huge capital export (loans, aid, foreign investment, etc.), Japan began to seek its say in political, economic, financial, and monetary areas internationally.

These changes were enough to draw the attention of the United States. The US containment strategy against the yen was immediately implemented with quick results. By taking advantage of its financial and monetary instruments, the United States orchestrated Japan's dazzling bubble economy. The burst of asset bubbles rendered Japanese banks and companies in heavy debts. The Japanese economy was completely overwhelmed by bad debts and many Japanese banks and businesses were forced to shrink or even go bankrupt. Then, the BIS, led by the United States, adopted the Capital Accord to raise banks' capital adequacy ratio which caused almost all Japanese banks to fail to meet international regulatory standards and to return home. In January 1990, the Japanese stock market crashed. In 1994, 70% of the market value vaporized. The real estate market plunged into a long-term decline for 14 consecutive years. From 1990 to date, Japan's recession has lasted for more than 20 years, a record in human history. Japanese banks gradually faded out in the international arena. The Japanese yen accounted for less than 3% of world's reserve currency.

The US containment strategy undoubtedly played a key role in the yen's "short-lived" participation in international currency competition. The United States checked the yen's international development by specific means as follows: (1) Suppressing the Japanese economy by taking advantage of Japan's high degree of dependence on the US economy. The United States used trade disputes as an excuse and threatened Japan with trade sanctions, and maintained the high pressure of "Japan bashing". (2) Preventing the yen with all means and at any time from becoming an international currency or a dominant regional currency. The United States has never allowed Japan to dominate international financial institutions. During the Asian financial crisis in 1997, Japan proposed to establish the "Asian Monetary Fund" to be led by Japan to deal with the Asian financial crisis, and the United States opposed. The United States insisted that all international debt be handled by the IMF. (3) The US financial institutions used financial instruments to short Japanese capital market. An important cause behind the collapse of the Japanese stock market in 1990 was the "Nikkei Index Put Options" invented by Goldman Sachs. The US companies first bought large amounts of put warrants and then pressed the stock market to make huge profits. (4) The US financial institutions actively did long the yen and boosted the expectation on its appreciation. As a result, on one hand, the policies of Japanese banks were influenced and constrained by international hot money; on the other hand, the Japanese central bank accumulated a large amount of foreign exchange reserves, forming large quantity of funds outstanding of foreign exchange and resulting in liquidity overflow in Japan—a liquidity trap hard to get over in the long run.

3.3.2 *A Comparison Between the Levels of Internationalization of the RMB and the JPY*

1. The function as an international currency in the period of inclusion into the basket.

(1) The comparison of the functions in trade settlement

First of all, we conduct an investigation into the domestic currency settlement of the two countries at the time. When the yen was included into the SDR in 1980, the JPY settlement accounted for only 15% of Japan's total trade. However, the RMB settlement accounted for nearly 30% of China's total trade in 2015 (see Fig. 3.3). The amount of RMB

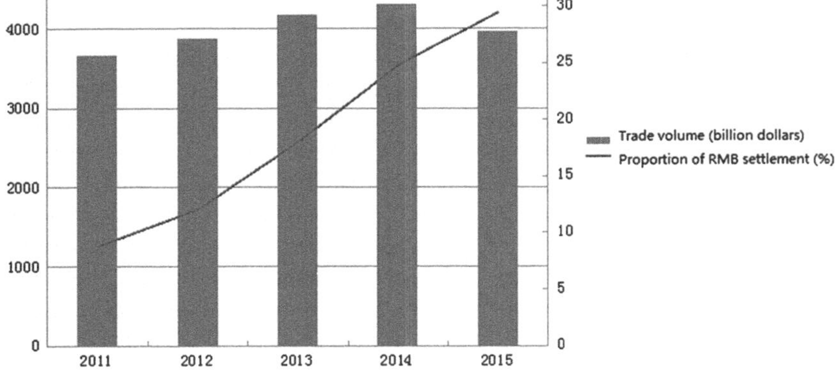

Fig. 3.3 The proportion of RMB settlement in total trade. (Data source: People's Bank of China, the Ministry of Commerce)

settlement reached 7.23 trillion yuan, up by 10.4% on a yearly basis. As can be seen from the data, the RMB's function in trade settlement was more powerful than the yen at its inclusion in SDR basket.

Second, we study the dependence of both countries' foreign trade on the United States and the level of product differentiation. As mentioned in previous analysis, the lag in the development of the JPY's settlement function was largely relevant to Japan's over-reliance on the US economy and its low differentiation of domestic products.

China's import dependence on the United States is relatively low, but its export dependence on the United States surpassed that of Japan from 2008, now standing at 17% (see Fig. 3.4). Though it is still far behind Japan's export dependence on the United States in the 1980s (close to 35%), the United States is China's largest export trade partner, which means that China's dependence on the United States has exceeded that of other countries. This shows that China is facing the same problems that Japan once went through. Too much dependence on the US market may restrict the development of RMB's functions in trade settlement to some extent.

Table 3.6 shows the dependence of ASEAN countries on the major imported products from China and Japan. It is not difficult to find that the ASEAN countries' dependence on imported products from China, such as footwear, miscellaneous products, textile products, stones, fur products, wood products, and mechanical products, exceeds 20%. The market share seems considerable, but all of them except mechanical products are low-tech and can easily be substituted. The ASEAN countries mainly import from Japan base metals, vehicles, precision instruments,

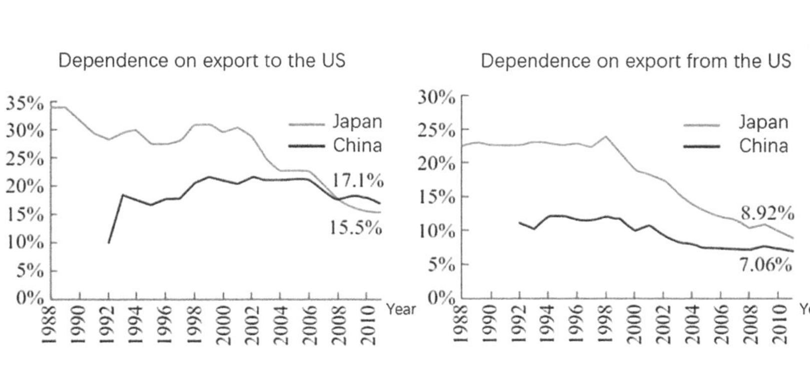

Fig. 3.4 Comparison of China's and Japan's dependence on trade with the United States. (Data source: Calculation according to statistics on UN Comtrade)

Table 3.6 Dependence of ASEAN countries on major products imported from China and Japan (2011)

	China		*Japan*	
No.	*HS category*[a]	*Dependence %*[b]	*HS category*	*Dependence %*[c]
1	Footwear, hats, umbrella	52.28(1.01)	Base metal and its products	22.80(15.63)
2	Miscellaneous articles	40.63(10.10)	Vehicles, aircraft, ships	21.28(6.75)
3	Textile raw materials and textile products	31.73(4.86)	Special goods and unclassified commodities	19.41(4.65)
4	Backward stone, gypsum, cement	27.70(17.37)	Optical, photographic, and precision instruments	18.81(11.05)
5	Raw hides, leathers, and their products	25.67(1.88)	Stones, gypsum, and cement	17.37(27.70)
6	Wood and wood products	21.49(1.63)	Plastics and its products	16.12(10.08)
7	Machinery, mechanic equipment, electrical equipment	20.09(14.81)	Machinery, mechanic equipment, electrical equipment	14.81(20.09)
8	Base metal and its products	15.63(22.80)	Natural or cultured pearls, precious stones	12.37(2.26)
9	Products of the chemical industry and related industries	13.28(9.81)	Art works, collectibles, and antiquities	10.51(6.96)
10	Plant products	12.51(0.44)	Miscellaneous articles	10.10(40.63)

Data source: Based on statistics on UN Comtrade

Note:

[a]Means the classification of international trade products in accordance with the Customs Co-operation Council HS2000 Code

[b]Stands for dependence on such products imported from Japan

[c]Stands for dependence on such products imported from China

mechanical products, gypsum and glass products, and rubber products, which are high-tech and have a high degree of product differentiation.

It is noteworthy that in Japan's trade with Asian countries in 2008, the proportion of settlement by the JPY was close to 50%. However, the proportion of settlement of trade by the RMB between China and Asian countries in 2012 was about 24%, which was relatively low compared with the level of domestic currency settlement of major international currency issuers.

At present, the most important factor restricting the development of RMB's international settlement function is China's low degree of product differentiation. This will lead to large export price elasticity that reduces the bargaining power of enterprises. However, if we look in the long run and along with the implementation of "One Belt and One Road" initiative, there is much room for growth of RMB's trade settlement functions.

(2) The comparison of functions of financial transaction and reserve

China's bond market in 2014 issued a total of 11 trillion yuan worth of bonds, an annual increase of 22.3%. According to the BIS, as of the end of 2014, RMB-denominated international bond had a balance of 535.118 billion yuan, accounting for 0.45% of the world's total. The balance of RMB bonds issued by overseas institutions in the offshore market was 530.48 billion yuan, and the balance of panda bonds issued in China was 4.63 billion yuan. Statistics show that RMB bonds still have a very limited influence in asset allocation in the global financial market.

In contrast, the yen's performance in the international bond market is clearly more prominent. Before its inclusion into the SDR basket, the JPY's share in the international bond market reached 4.8%; this share grew to 9.1% in 1985. From this perspective, the RMB is weaker than the yen in its development in the international bond market at the time of inclusion into the SDR basket. Whether the share of transactions conducted in RMB in the international financial market can be increased steadily will be key to determining the RMB internationalization process in the future.

By the end of 2015, the PBOC had signed bilateral currency swap agreements with central banks or monetary authorities of 34 countries and regions, with a total size of about 3.255 trillion yuan. The substantive role of the bilateral currency swap agreements had been significantly enhanced. In 2014, foreign central banks or monetary authorities initiated RMB currency swap transactions with a total volume of 1.1 trillion yuan, and used a total amount of RMB of 38 billion yuan. By the end of 2014, overseas central banks or monetary authorities initiated RMB swap transactions with a total volume of about 2.3 trillion yuan and used a total amount of RMB 80.7 billion yuan; the PBOC initiated RMB swap transactions equivalent to RMB 4.1 billion yuan and used the currencies of counterparts equaling RMB 1.58 billion yuan.[19] If the bilateral currency swap

[19] PBOC, Report on RMB Internationalization 2015, 2015.

agreements are regarded as the foreign exchange reserves of other countries, the amount of the RMB as foreign exchange reserves, by the end of 2015 and if converted into USD, was USD 522.71 billion.[20] According to IMF statistics, the total global foreign exchange reserves in the third quarter of 2015 added up to USD 11,203.357 billion. Then, it can be roughly estimated that the amount of RMB as foreign exchange reserves accounted for about 4.67% of global foreign exchange reserves in 2015.

Upon its inclusion into SDR basket, the JPY accounted for 4.2% of global foreign exchange reserves. This proportion has fallen to 3.78% now. It can be deemed that the RMB and the JPY had similar functions as foreign exchange currencies at the initial stage of inclusion into the SDR basket. Generally speaking, an international currency's financial transaction function and reserve function are highly relevant. Therefore, as its influence in the international financial market gradually increases, the RMB will see its share rise correspondingly in official foreign exchange reserves globally.

2. Influence on the exchange rate of major ASEAN countries

China and Japan are geographically adjacent, and the areas covered by their outbound economic, trade, and financial activities overlap. The international currency competition between the RMB and the yen is also reflected in the competition for the position of the regional core currency.

We selected four major Southeast Asian countries, namely, Singapore, Thailand, the Philippines, and Indonesia, as our research subjects. We construct a decision model for the exchange rate formation mechanism and estimate the weight of the impact of each regional core currency on the intrinsic value of the target currency exchange rate, and judge the status of the regional core currency on this basis.

We use the decision model for intrinsic exchange rate formation mechanism developed by Frankel and Wei (2007, 2008),[21] Frankel (2009),[22]

[20] The RMB/USD exchange rate adopted here is from the 2015 Statistical Data of the PBOC.

[21] Frankel, Jeffrey A., and Shang J. Wei. 2007. "Assessing China's Exchange Rate Regime" *NBER Working Paper*, No. 13100. Frankel, Jeffrey A., and Shang J. Wei. 2008. "Estimation of de Facto Exchange Rate Regimes: Synthesis of the Technique for Inferring Flexibility and Basket Weights" *NBER Working Paper*, No. 14016.

[22] Frankel, Jeffrey A. 2009. "New Estimation of China's Exchange Rate Regime" *NBER Working Paper*, No. 14700.

Ma and McCauley (2010),[23] and Fang et al. (2012).[24] We set the SDR as the base currency and assume that the core currencies that affect the intrinsic value of the four currencies are the USD, the Deutsche mark (euro after 1999), the Great Britain pound, the JPY, and the RMB. The specific model is as follows:

$$\Delta \log TC_{i,t} = c_i + \alpha_i \Delta \log SDR_t + \sum_{j=1}^{5} \beta_{j,i} \left[\Delta \log X_{j,i,t} \right] + u_{i,t} \tag{3.1}$$

TC_i represents the target currency i, and c_i is a constant which represents the intersect term in the equation of target currency i, and $X_{j,\,i,\,t}$ represents the No. j currency of the major currency portfolio which decides the intrinsic value of exchange rate of target currency i. $\beta_{j,\,i}$ represents the weight of corresponding currency j in deciding the intrinsic value of target currency i. In addition, the paper assumes that $\alpha_i = 1 - \beta_{1,\,i} - \beta_{2,\,i} - \beta_{3,\,i} - \beta_{4,\,i} - \beta_{5,\,i}$, and the Eq. (3.1) can be further converted into $\Delta \log TC_{i,t} - \Delta \log SDR_t = c + \sum_{j=1}^{5} \beta_{j,i} \left[\Delta \log X_{j,i,t} - \Delta \log SDR_t \right] + u_{i,t}$:

$$\Delta \log \left(\frac{TC_i}{SDR} \right)_{t,n} = c_{i,n} + \sum_{j=1}^{5} \beta_{j,i,n} \Delta \log \left(\frac{X_{j,i}}{SDR} \right)_{t,n} + u_{i,t,n} \tag{3.2}$$

It is assumed that X_j represents the USD, the euro, the GBP, the JPY, and the RMB respectively. We use the logarithmic difference in the exchange rates of the target currency between term t and t-1 as the explanatory variable in the model for the purpose of eliminating the possible non-stationarity in the time series data of the target currency exchange rate. The inherent decision mechanism of exchange rate has a time-varying characteristic. To reflect this characteristic, Frankel and Wei (2007) divide the whole sample into N sub-samples of equal time duration of four years each and then carry out the regression of model (3.2) respectively, and obtain estimated values corresponding to N different time periods. To

[23] Ma, G., and Robert N. McCauley. 2010. "The Evolving Renminbi Regime and Implications for Asian Currency Stability" *BIS Working Paper*, No. 321.

[24] Fang, Y., Shi C. Huang, and L. Niu. 2012. "De Facto Currency Baskets of China and East Asian Economies: The Rising Weights" *BOFIT Discussion Paper*, No. 2/2012.

reflect more accurately and systematically the time-varying structure in weight coefficients, we use in our model computation the time period of one year as a sub-sample to obtain the weighing factors of major currency in the currency portfolio in its influence on the intrinsic value of target currency i by taking advantage of the daily data of the exchange rate of each currency. In model (3.2), Δ is the difference operator. $(TC_i/SDR)_{t,n}$ represents the exchange rate of the target currency i to SDR on the tth day of the nth year. The corresponding $\beta_{j,i,n}$ represents the weighing factors of currency No. j that influence the intrinsic value of the exchange rate of target currency i in the nth year.

We selected the daily data of exchange rate of target currency to SDR during the period from January 1, 1982, to December 31, 2012. Since we will establish models for the daily data of each year separately, we can get the weight changes of the 31-year core currency portfolios through the model computation. All exchange rate data is from the Bloomberg database. The results of model estimation are as follows:

As can be seen from Table 3.7, Southeast Asia was a real dollar area when the yen was included into the SDR basket. The dollar was the only core currency in the region. The weight of the USD against the value of the Singapore dollar and the Thai baht was consistently high, especially that against the Thai baht, which had an average weighting of over 85%. The excessive reliance on the dollar of ASEAN countries constrained the regional development of the yen during that period. Before the Asian financial crisis broke out in 1997, the yen had the highest weighting of 8.3% in the core currency portfolio that determined the intrinsic value of the Singapore dollar exchange rate. According to the definition by Cao Tong and Zhao Ran (2014) of "core currency in the multi-core currency area", the yen at that time could only be defined as "core currency in the multi-core currency area", the yen can only be called a "regional low-level core currency". After the crisis, Asian countries universally realized that they must get rid of the excessive reliance on the dollar in order to effectively avoid the spread of systemic financial risks. Many countries began to expect and call for intra-regional currency cooperation. Many Southeast Asian currencies including Thai baht began to change from the fixed exchange rate regime pegged to the USD into a managed floating exchange rate regime. Therefore, at least in Southeast Asia in recent years, RMB internationalization received less pressure from the dollar than yen internationalization in the 1980s.

Table 3.7 The weight of core currencies determining the intrinsic value of target currency exchange rates (100%)

	1982	*1985*	*1988*	*1989*	*1992*	*1993*	*1994*	*1995*	*1996*	*2006*	*2007*	*2008*	*2009*	*2010*	*2011*	*2012*
Singapore dollars																
USD	87.2	89.6	91.3	98.7	91.7	51.6	61.2	33.4	70.3	44.9	34.4	40.9	53.1	48.5	26.8	30.8
RMB	–	3.0	–	–	–	–	–	–	–	**16.8**	**31.2**	**19.1**	**28.9**	**25.2**	**44.6**	**34.9**
JPY	**5.6**	**7.4**	–	–	**6.1**	**4.5**	**10.3**	**7.8**	**8.3**	25.1	–	–	–	–	5.8	5.0
R^2	44.0	35.0	78.0	76.0	72.3	62.4	77.5	73.0	66.6	68.3	52.1	55.8	74.8	59.8	67.7	56.3
Thailand Baht																
USD	99.5	81.3	–	98.1	93.2	84.6	82.7	82.2	81.5	50.7	85.6	70.3	67.7	73.6	55.5	39.1
RMB	0.06	2.3	–	–	–	–	–	–	–	**10.4**	–	**14.9**	**8.1**	**14.8**	**21.3**	**23.4**
JPY	**0.26**	**3.7**	**4.2**	–	**4.7**	–	–	–	**3.3**	18.8	–	–	–	4.9	3.5	4.2
R^2	99.6	20.0	89.0	88.0	83.4	72.4	88.6	72.5	88.8	25.7	13.8	41.1	71.5	62.4	51.3	42.5
Philippine Peso																
USD	N/A	N/A	N/A	N/A	–	–	62.7	99.2	98.5	35.6	−0.8	60.1	57.8	48.8	49.3	29.3
RMB	N/A	N/A	N/A	N/A	–	–	–	–	–	62.6	67.3	19.1	33.7	42.6	28.8	44.5
JPY	N/A	N/A	N/A	N/A	–	–	–	–	–	–	6.9	–	–	–	–	–
R^2	N/A	N/A	N/A	N/A	9.7	10.2	21.9	68.9	95.0	43.9	22.4	31.1	46.0	41.1	37.4	28.9
Indonesia Rupiah																
USD	N/A	N/A	N/A	N/A	96.6	98.8	–	90.8	98.1	–	–	56.5	49.8	59.4	52.9	77.3
RMB	N/A	N/A	N/A	N/A	–	–	–	–	–	–	**64.4**	**24.0**	**43.5**	**36.1**	**30.0**	**31.7**
JPY	N/A	N/A	N/A	N/A	–	–	–	–	–	–	6.2	2.9	–	–	–	–
R^2	N/A	N/A	N/A	N/A	94.6	90.2	82.9	88.9	70.0	30.1	21.2	16.4	17.4	55.0	27.5	21.9

Note: "N/A" represents incomplete data of the year and failure to collect statistics and conduct verification. "–" represents insignificant statistics regarding the value of weight estimation of the year. All the values in the table are significantly above 10%

During the period from the outbreak of the Asian financial crisis to 2006, the core leading currencies of the Southeast Asian region changed from the USD to a portfolio of the USD, the RMB and the yen. But after 2006, due to Japan's continuous economic downturn and the strong promotion of RMB internationalization, the core currency structure determined by Southeast Asian currency exchange rates changed again—the weight of the RMB rose quickly and the RMB began to gradually replace the yen as a leading core currency in ASEAN region, next only to the USD.

Singapore is an important international financial center in Southeast Asia. In 2012, the weight of the USD in core currency portfolio that determined the value of the Singapore dollar exchange rates dropped to 30.8%, while the weight of the RMB increased to 34.9%, making the RMB a "moderate core currency" that determined Singapore currency exchange rate.

The United States has a very far-reaching economic and cultural impact on the Philippines. Before 1997, the intrinsic value of the Philippine peso was almost entirely determined by the dollar. After 1997, the intrinsic value of the peso gradually decoupled from the dollar. In 2012, the dollar's weight dropped to 29.3%. With increasingly close economic and financial cooperation between China and the Philippines, the impact of the RMB on the value of the peso gradually increased with the weight of the RMB in 2012 reaching 44.5%, much higher than that of the dollar, making the RMB a "moderate core currency" that determined the value of the Philippine peso. At the same time, the Philippine peso became the currency most affected by the RMB among ASEAN countries.

In addition, the above empirical analysis has also led to an important conclusion: the impact on the intrinsic value of the exchange rates of Southeast Asian currencies exerted by RMB was significantly higher than that by the JPY at the initial stage of its inclusion into the SDR. In 1982, the weight of the yen in determining the intrinsic value of Singapore dollar's exchange rate accounted for only 5.6% and could only be called a low-level core currency. In 2012, the average weight of the RMB in determining the intrinsic value of the core currency portfolio of major currencies in Southeast Asia reached 34%, making the RMB a moderate core currency in the region.

Judging from the RMB's objective market performance, the influence of the RMB in Southeast Asia has far exceeded that of the yen, no matter whether some countries subjectively recognize the international status of RMB or not. The RMB has become Southeast Asia's core currency, next only to the USD.

It can be deemed that the RMB now has more favorable political and geographical conditions than the yen in the 1980s. As long as no significant adverse events occur after the RMB's inclusion into the basket, RMB internationalization can avoid the recurrence of the mistakes of the yen, and achieve steady progress toward the pre-set goals.

3.3.3 Problems to Solve at the Next Stage

1. Improving the degree of differentiation of export products and consolidating the RMB's trade settlement function

In international trade, the more competitive products are, the higher the degree of export product differentiation is, and the stronger the bargaining power enterprises will possess. Germany's exported products rapidly improved their international competitiveness, and the product differentiation degree also increased, which directly boosted the Deutsche mark to quickly become the main international pricing and settlement currency. Until now, Germany's exports are still highly competitive and maintain a high level of product differentiation, which ensures German export enterprises strong bargaining power and currency options in the international trade market. After comparing that with Japan's, Fukuda and Ono (2006) proposed that the decline of the international competitiveness of Japan's exports directly led to the retrogress of yen internationalization.[25]

Although China is already the largest commodity trading country, its irrational trade structure, the lack of competitive advantages, and the excessive reliance on the US market will restrict further development of RMB internationalization. Economic growth model featuring over-reliance on export is not sustainable. Neither could an economy with over-reliance on external demand maintain its economic and currency stability. China should learn from the experience of the yen, give full play to the role of trade in economic growth, but at the same time, it should proactively promote economic restructuring to strengthen its economy both internally and externally. Only in this way could a sound economic growth become the fundamental guarantee of RMB internationalization.

[25] Fukuda, S. and M., Ono, On the Determinants of Exporters' Currency Pricing: History vs. Expectations, NBER Working Paper, No. 12432, August, 2006.

2. Expanding the depth and breadth of the RMB international bond market

The international bond market is one of the most important international financial markets and an indispensable part of the international financial system. In recent years, the category structure and currency structure of the international bond market have undergone significant changes, and the size of European bonds is far greater than that of foreign bonds.

In 2012, the Eurozone accounted for 40% and 55% in the international bond market and the international monetary market, respectively, while the corresponding figures of the United States were only 26% and 7%. Eurozone countries issued mainly the European euro-denominated bonds in the international bond market, which largely contributed to the euro's international development. Zhao Ran and Wu Cong (2016)[26] proved that the only significant factor affecting the international pricing function of the JPY was the development of the international bond market in Japan. An increase of 1% in Japan's international bond market would lead to an increase of the international pricing function of the JPY by 0.99%. The expansion of the banks' overseas currency business did not significantly affect the internationalization of the yen, which was mainly due to the many restrictions set by the Japanese government for the Tokyo financial market.[27]

With the decline of its economic strength, Japan has been losing its ability to finance in the international financial market. The rapid shrinking of JPY debt held by European countries was the major reason for the sharp retrogress of JPY internalization. According to the experience of the JPY, although the JPY bond size was only second to the of USD, the fact that nearly half of the bonds were held by government and public sectors greatly influenced the formation of market pricing mechanism for JPY bonds on the secondary market, which increased the risks of investors and impacted the development of the JPY international bonds market.

[26] R. Zhao and C. Wu, The Role of Sub-financial Markets in the Development of the International Valuation Function of a Currency, Journal of Central University of Finance and Economics, 2016 (1): 50–60.

[27] The restriction on banks' domestic currency business development overseas is a major factor hindering the yen's internationalization.

In order to promote more effectively the internationalization of the RMB, China should increase the depth and breadth of the RMB offshore market; in particular, it should loosen the restrictions on the non-residents' issuance of RMB-denominated bonds in Europe, including expanding issuing institutions, easing issuance conditions, loosening quantitative restrictions, and expanding the scope of host banks.

3. Building a channel for RMB international circulation

The history of international currencies shows that the internationalization of major currencies cannot be possible without the development of the offshore market. According to the statistics of the BIS, in 2010, 80% of the foreign exchange transactions of the USD and the euro occurred in offshore markets, while that proportion of the JPY reached 72% in offshore markets outside Japan. In the internationalization of major international currencies, the role of offshore financial markets should not be overlooked. It can even be said that if there were no offshore financial markets, the internationalization of the dollar would not have reached the present level and the JPY would not have had the rapid development in the 1980s.

A general view of the offshore markets of the euro and the USD tells us that the biggest characteristic of these markets is that they can achieve self-circulation of monetary funds and have adequate investment instruments and channels to meet market liquidity requirements. Judging by this standard, the RMB offshore market in Hong Kong is far from complete. Although investors can invest in RMB in HK, with limited investment channels, the channels for international circulation have not been fully established. However, a complete "international circulation" channel is the pre-condition for the RMB to become an international currency in its real sense.

The construction of the "international circulation" mechanism requires coordination between offshore and onshore markets and some special policy arrangements. From the perspective of the offshore market, China should develop international capital markets for the RMB with Hong Kong as the center, so as to establish an RMB overseas circulation mechanism under capital accounts. China needs to issue RMB-denominated stocks and bonds on the Hong Kong Stock Exchange. At present, the issuance of RMB bonds faces no institutional and technical barriers, and this fact lays the foundation for the issuance of RMB-denominated stocks.

With the rapid development of cross-border settlement under trade accounts and the continuous improvement of the RMB remittance system for individual accounts, the problem of RMB liquidity shortage in Hong Kong market will be alleviated. In terms of institutional arrangements, the RQDII business can be considered as a priority, and consideration should also be given to allowing domestic securities and funds to directly participate in the close-end trading of RMB products on the Hong Kong Stock Exchange, thereby facilitating the construction of the RMB capital market in Hong Kong.

From a broader perspective, China shall spare no efforts to build a Greater China currency area and make the peripheral presence of the RMB as a strategic choice for this development stage. The Greater China currency area shall mainly include Mainland China, Taiwan, Hong Kong, and Macao. The signing of the ECFA agreement between Mainland China and Taiwan marked the beginning of a new stage in cross-strait economic and trade exchanges. The appropriate institutional arrangements for the RMB and the New Taiwan dollar will be another core task for the Greater China currency area besides the Hong Kong dollar dual-link exchange rate system. At present, the New Taiwan dollar and the USD have realized free floating. As long as the exchange rate between the RMB and the USD remains relatively stable, the free convertibility between the New Taiwan dollar and the RMB will not increase the exchange rate risk for participants in economic and trade activities. China's economic strength and foreign exchange reserves can guarantee the free convertibility between the New Taiwan dollar and the RMB.

From the policy perspective, China should first encourage local governments, businesses, and enterprises to issue bonds in Hong Kong and allow the financed RMB to return to the Mainland China. Second, China should promote FDI in RMB, and ask the foreign shareholders of foreign-invested enterprises to settle cross-border direct investment in RMB. Third, China should promote the development of cross-border lending business between Mainland China and Hong Kong banks. With Hong Kong's rising stock of RMB and the relatively low interest rate of the RMB, China should try to develop pilot projects under controllable risks to attract large amount of low-cost funds from HK back to Mainland China. Fourth, China should allow qualified institutions to raise RMB funds in Hong Kong to carry out domestic securities investment services (i.e., a small "QFII") to raise funds.

The arrangement of the RMB return mechanism provides many new historical opportunities for Hong Kong and Shanghai. The two areas can cooperate and complement the strength of each other according to their own advantages and needs, so as to jointly promote the internationalization of the RMB. The new pattern of onshore and offshore markets shall include the establishment of an offshore RMB market in Hong Kong and the establishment of an RMB market for non-residents in Shanghai FTA.

While developing the international financial markets for RMB, Shanghai and Hong Kong shall actively carry out cooperation at a deeper level, and coordinate especially in the arrangements for RMB return mechanism, according to which Hong Kong arranges for the return of the RMB and Shanghai promotes the outflow of the RMB and decides the destination of returned RMB, thus forming a virtuous circle mechanism. Onshore RMB market shall take the Shanghai Stock Exchange as the center to promote the construction of an RMB-denominated international market. China can also attract and propel excellent financial institutions and enterprises in the ASEAN region to issue RMB-denominated shares and bonds on the Shanghai Stock Exchange. Consideration can also be given to the setup of a joint listing mechanism with regional stock exchanges such as those in Hong Kong, Singapore, and Tokyo, so as to greatly reduce the pressure of qualification examination on listed companies.

Establishing an RMB outflow mechanism under the capital account through the development of the above-mentioned two mechanisms can ensure overseas RMB capital supply. At the same time, it can keep the balance in capital transactions within the controllable sphere of the USD foreign exchange reserves while controlling the process of IPO approvals.

CHAPTER 4

Macro-Financial Risks of RMB Internationalization

International Monetary Institute

As the internationalization of RMB enters a new era, the participation of China's economy and financial market in the global market has deepened, which poses even higher requirements for macro-financial management of China's monetary authority. As RMB's share in international trade, international financial trade, and foreign country's forex reserves increased from zero to a high level, the cross-border capital flow of China starts to show brand-new features. Therefore, the monetary authority must reconsider the choice of macro-financial targets and at the same time pay attention to how cross-border capital flow and policy adjustment trigger domestic financial risks, so as to prevent and solve destructive and systemic financial crises. Classical theories of the open economy tell us that with the internationalization of a currency, the issuing country will have to make a new choice between three macro-financial policies. As has been evidenced by Germany's and Japan's policy experience, improper policy choice will worsen domestic financial risks through a complicated trigger mechanism of cross-border capital flow; so apparently mistakes in macro-financial management will only divert currency internationalization to a path toward failure.

International Monetary Institute (✉)
Renmin University of China, Beijing, China
e-mail: imi@ruc.edu.cn

International Monetary Institute (ed.), *Currency Internationalization and Macro Financial Risk Control*,
https://doi.org/10.1007/978-981-13-0698-3_4

The internationalization of the RMB is a grand target, and China will have to walk a tough way to realize it. To facilitate RMB internationalization in a new era, it is urgent for China to readjust its macro-financial policies in a prudent manner, identify and monitor macro-financial risks in the course of internationalization, and construct an effective policy framework to address systemic financial risks. This chapter first analyzes the macro-financial policy adjustment and its influence on currency internationalization of Germany and Japan based on classical theories and historical experiences and conclude some practicable experiences and lessons; the chapter then discusses macro-financial risks that RMB internationalization must face, which is RMB exchange rate fluctuations and management at present and higher systemic risks caused by cross-border capital flow in the future; at last, the chapter concludes that the authority should conduct macro-financial risk management from the perspective of national strategy to realize the target of RMB internationalization.

4.1 Macro-Financial Policy Choices of International Currency Issuing Countries

Currency authorities of open economies are always faced with the problem of choosing macro-financial policy targets. They make choices between monetary policy independence, forex rate stability, and free capital flow based on their realities. In so doing they create different portfolios of policies and make adjustment upon requirements. With the internationalization of a currency, the issuing country will inevitably face changes of cross-border capital flow, forcing it to choose new policy targets and adjust the policy portfolios. On the theoretical level, there is of course more than one way to adjust the policy portfolios. But according to historical experience, policy adjustment paths chosen by Germany and Japan exerted different influences on their domestic economy and financial performance. And the two countries opened an apparent gap in their currency internationalization afterward.

4.1.1 Classical Theories and Policy Choice Strategies of the Open Economy

Back in the 1960s, Robert Mundell found that cross-border capital flow had significant influences on the choice of forex regime and currency policy independence. He pointed out when capital was kept from moving across borders, monetary authorities could always keep the independence of currency policies and solve economic problems under both a fixed exchange rate regime and a floating exchange rate regime; however, when capital was free to flow across borders, monetary policies were only effective and independent under a floating exchange rate regime and were totally ineffective in macro-control under a fixed exchange rate regime. This is the famous "Impossible Trinity" of Mundell widely known in the international financial arena: one can only simultaneously achieve two of the following three targets: completely free flow of capital, independent monetary policies, and a fixed exchange rate regime.

Mundell thought it was viable to achieve the three targets simultaneously, which, however, required limitless forex reserves. This is impossible in reality. The forex reserves of one country, however large, are not remotely comparable to tremendous international speculative capital. Once self-fulfilled expectation takes shape in the market, currency depreciation will gain great momentum that cannot be reversed by any amount of forex reserves. Therefore, in the case of completely free capital flow and monetary policy independence, the fixed exchange rate regime will eventually collapse.

The core of Mundell's "Impossible Trinity" is that in the case of completely free flow capital, one country's interest rate must be equivalent to the international interest rate to ensure a stable forex rate. We can analyze this topic from the perspective of uncovered interest parity (UIP):

$$R - R^{*} = \frac{S_{+1}^{e} - S}{S}. \tag{4.1}$$

The S in the equation, which stands for the exchange rate, is subject to direct quotation; the R stands for the interest rate of the concerned country; the R* stands for the interest rates of another country. UIP tells us only when two countries' interest rates equal the expected forex rate variation will market arbitrage stop. Otherwise, the possibility of arbitrage will remain.

If a country adopts a fixed forex rate regime and allows full convertibility under the capital account, the profit-pursuing nature of capital will cause capital inflow or outflow when R does not equal R*. When R is larger than R*, the spread will provide arbitrage opportunities in the market and attract a large amount of foreign capital. Under normal circumstances, a large amount of capital inflow will impose appreciation pressure on the domestic currency. However, under the fixed forex rate regime, to ensure forex rate stability, the central bank will have to intervene in the forex market by buying in forex and selling out domestic currency. Through money multiplier effect, the increase in monetary base will increase the liquidity in the whole monetary market and impose downward pressure on the domestic interest rate. In such cases, the central bank has in fact lost the independence of monetary policies.

Several decades later, Paul Krugman expanded Mundell's "Impossible Trinity" theory. He posed the "Trilemma" theory based on the forming mechanism of the 1997 Asian financial crisis and concluded the internal relationship between the three macro-financial policies in open economies. Chart 4.1 depicts the views of Krugman, in which the gray area represents the "Trilemma": among the three points—"free capital flow, monetary policy independence, and fixed forex rate"—only two are possible.

According to the "Trilemma" theory, there are three viable policy portfolios for open economies' monetary authorities:

Portfolio I: Deregulating capital accounts, allowing free capital flow, and keeping forex rate stable, but abandoning the independence of the monetary policy independence. As we can see in the UIP analysis, under a fixed exchange rate regime, the free flow of capital will force the central bank to intervene in the forex market and eventually influence money supply and market interest rates, which brings domestic market interest rates close to external interest rates and deprive the domestic currency policy of its independence. For example, Hong Kong, a small economy, allows free capital inflow and outflow and chooses a fixed forex rate instead of independent monetary policy. It has strict currency board arrangement, fixing the HKD-USD exchange rate at 7.8:1.

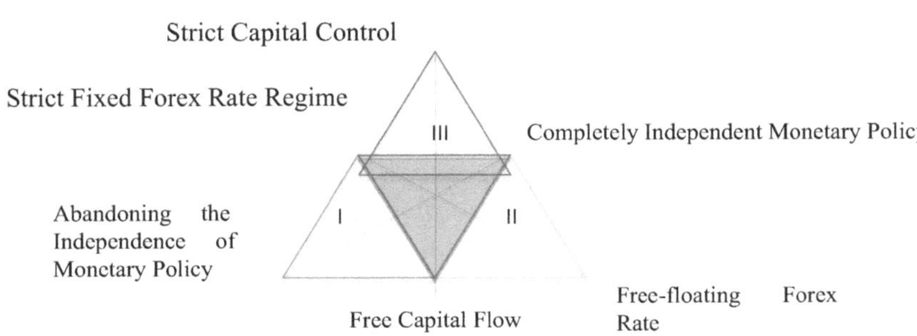

Chart 4.1 "Trilemma" triangle

Meanwhile, the currency policy of Hong Kong must keep pace with that of the Fed and is not able to determine market interest rates independently.

Portfolio II: Deregulating capital accounts, allowing free capital flow, and keeping the independence of the monetary policy, but giving up the fixed exchange rate regime and allowing the exchange rate to fluctuate. When capital flows in and out freely, changes in interest rates will inevitably cause major capital flow. The pressure of capital flow on the exchange rate can be lessened though the self-adjustment of the exchange rate and will not influence the size of the domestic monetary base, thereby not influencing the overall market currency stock and keeping the monetary policy independent. Advanced economies prefer such a policy portfolio, including the United States. It is one of the countries with the most liberalized capital accounts in the world. At the same time, the USD's position as the most important international currency requires the Fed to keep the independence of monetary policy and allow dollar's exchange rate to fluctuate.

Portfolio III: Keeping the independence of monetary policy, but not allowing free capital flow and imposing strict capital control. As has been pointed out in this chapter, Mundell's "Impossible Trinity" is based on liberalized capital accounts. Krugman enriched that theory by discussing policy choices under capital control: that is, capital control allows one country to independently determine its interest rates and keep the exchange rate stable; it artificially erases all economic factors causing exchange rate and interest rate fluctuations by sacrificing the liquidity of capital. At the beginning of the reform and opening up, China achieved the stability of the exchange rate and the independence of the monetary policy through strict capital control. This policy provided important institutional guarantee for long-term and fast growth and created precious space for stable development. It also resisted the impact of external financial market on China.

However, as China's economy continues to open up and the RMB is internationalized, its economy and financial market become increasingly interwoven with the global market. Under such circumstances, monetary authorities are obligated to readjust China's macro-financial policy portfolio in a prudent manner. As the second largest economy in the world, China cannot completely give up its independence of monetary policies, which excludes portfolio I from possible choices. So can China adopt portfolio

II? How can it achieve this policy portfolio? How to choose the right time to adjust policies and how to manage macro-financial risks in policy adjustments? Although international financial classical theories do not offer answers to those questions, Germany and Japan, who were faced with similar questions in currency internationalization, offer us a different policy experience which is of great preferential value for China.

4.1.2 Historical Experiences of Germany and Japan and Their Lessons

After the Second World War, Germany and Japan were faced with similar domestic conditions. Both countries were built on debris. Their economies and financial markets rose in an almost simultaneous way. However, different macro-financial policy choices made during opening up led their currency internationalization to completely different destinations. Take their currencies' shares in global official forex reserves for example: the share of the Deutsche mark rose steadily from less than 2% in 1973 to 13% before the birth of the euro, while the share of the Japanese yen rocketed from 0.5% in the early 1970s to 8.5% in 1991, and then started to plummet and fell to 4.8% at the end of 2015.

1. Germany's Experience

From the 1950s to the 1990s, as the German economy continued to open up, the country adjusted its policy portfolio on several occasions. We can divide its policy choices during the period into the following three stages based on the above-mentioned policy portfolios deduced from the "Trilemma".

Stage I (1950s–1960s): Germany chose portfolio I and deregulated the capital account, first allowing capital inflow and then capital outflow. Its capital account developed from a completely closed one to a basically liberalized one. During this period, the German economy grew fast and its manufacturing industry also recovered from post-war depression. Meanwhile, a large amount of capital started to flow into Europe from America, leading to the double surpluses on Germany's current account and capital account and imposing big pressure on the mark's exchange rate stability and domestic inflation. As the first step to release the pressure, Germany first loosened the control on capital outflow. In 1952, it removed the restriction on ODI of domestic individuals; in 1956 it allowed domestic individuals to buy foreign securities; in 1957 the country declared to achieve full convertibility under the capital account. By then, individuals no longer needed the authority's approval to invest overseas. Then Germany started to loosen the control on capital inflows. In July 1958, Germany started to allow foreign entity investment. We can see that in this stage the country basically liberalized its capital account. However, as the fixed exchange rate regime prevailed under the Bretton Woods system, as its capital account was liberalized, Germany gradually lost the independence of its monetary policy. Because once the interest rate of the domestic market rose above that of the external market, a large amount of foreign capital would flow in and threaten the stability of the mark's exchange rate. So Germany's monetary policies would have to keep pace with the issuing countries of central currencies.

Stage II (1960s–1970s): Germany restarted capital control, using portfolio III to ensure the independence of monetary policies and repeatedly adjusting management on short-term capital flows to transit to portfolio II. As has been evidenced by a large number of historical records, in less than six months from the end of 1968 to the beginning of 1969, global forex market became incredibly fervent about the mark, and Germany once had to temporarily shut down its forex exchange market.[1] The "sudden rise" of the Deutsche mark seemed hard to be explained by traditional economic theories but had a real background of the radically changing international economic and financial situation. From the end of the 1960s, we saw three USD crises, which undermined the USD's reputation and status as the central currency and international settlement currency in the Bretton Woods system. The international financial market urgently needed a new support, which brought the mark to the fore.

However, between the end of the 1960s and the beginning of the 1970s, under portfolio I, Germany's policy rate was highly synchronized with that of the United States (see Chart 4.2) and Germany totally lost the independence of its monetary policy. This brought great pressure onto Germany's central bank. Therefore, from the end of the 1960s, the Deutsche Bundesbank started to review its macro-financial policy choices. It planned to take three steps to ensure the independence of its currency policy: step one, giving up portfolio I, restarting capital control, and adopting portfolio

[1] Gray, W. Glenn, Number One in Europe: The Startling Emergence of the Deutsche Mark, 1968–1969, *Central European History*, Vol. 39, No. 1, 2006, pp. 56–78.

III to stabilize the domestic financial market; step two, allowing the mark's forex rate to float freely and adjusting policies toward portfolio II; step three, re-liberalizing the capital account and completely achieving portfolio II.

Specific measures included: in December 1968, Germany reinstalled control on the capital account to limit capital inflows and required German commercial banks to set a "special deposit reserve ratio" of 100% for new foreign liabilities; in September 1969, Germany decided to stop intervening in the market to maintain the official fixed exchange rate of 4:1 (the mark to the dollar); in October, the Bundesbank re-evaluated the mark-to-dollar exchange rate and the official rate was adjusted to 3.66:1, and the mark thus appreciated by 9.3%. After the re-evaluation, it rescinded the above-mentioned "special deposit reserve ratio" requirement.

It is noteworthy that after Germany canceled the fixed exchange rate, it did not transfer to portfolio II in a single step. It did not want the mark's value to skyrocket immediately and impact German economic competitiveness. Therefore, after the 1970s, the German government's management of the capital account went through a process of "control–deregulation–reinstalling control–removing control". Especially, the government imposed special reserve ratio requirements and cash deposit requirements on short-term speculative capital inflows to intensify control. For example: in April 1970, the government required German banks to set a special reserve ratio of 30% for new foreign liabilities; in May 1971, it forbade banks to pay interest for non-resident deposits and forbade non-resident investors to buy German current market products; in March 1972, it raised the special reserve ratio to 40%; in June it required non-resident investors to apply for approval before buying German fixed-income securities; in July 1972, it raised the cash deposit requirement and the reserve ratio to 50% and in June 1973, it raised the levels again. In addition to the above-mentioned measures, when indirect capital control was ineffective, Germany took even stricter direct capital control measures. For example, in February 1973, in addition to fixed-income securities, the government required non-resident investors to apply for approval to buy any credit instruments, including stocks, mutual funds, and loans (over 50,000 marks).

Stage III (1980s–): Completely achieving portfolio II and liberalizing the capital account. In the 1970s, the European Community established the "European Monetary System", which no doubt made the Deutsche mark a central currency of the system. By then the mark had already become a de facto international mainstream currency. Besides, after a decade of adjustment, the mark's exchange rate successfully transferred from a fixed interest rate regime to a floating interest rate regime. German financial institutions and enterprises were becoming increasingly internationalized and their resilience against international financial market impact was significantly improved.

Against such background, from 1981, Germany started to gradually rescind capital control. It first removed the control on capital inflows and canceled the restrictions on non-resident entities to invest in domestic securities. In 1984, the government allowed two-way capital flow, ending the on-and-off capital control adjustment and completely liberalizing capital account, which also meant Germany transferred from portfolio III to portfolio II in macro-financial policy choices. Most importantly, German monetary policy obtained independence. In the case of domestic inflation, it could adjust monetary policies without external interventions.

We can say that the mark achieved internationalization before completely liberalizing the capital account. Germany was stubborn in the pursuit for exchange rates and monetary policy stability, to achieve which the government could sacrifice a large amount of forex reserves and tolerate slow financial market growth. Compared to other western countries, up until the 1990s, Germany remained in the developing stage in terms of modern financial instrument application. Its financial market scale was not only far smaller than that of America and Britain, but also smaller than that of continental countries like France. But stable economic and financial growth won a golden stage for Germany to improve its core industrial competitiveness and prepared Germany to address financial market fluctuations after the internationalization of the mark by providing adequate techniques and policy tools. As a result, Germany's financial market became a late bloomer and Frankfurt became one of the most important global financial centers.

2. Japan's Experience

In comparison with Germany, Japan's macro-financial policy choice in the course of currency internationalization seemed more radical. It chose portfolio II since the 1960s, allowed JPY's exchange rate to float freely, and gradually liberalized the capital account. As Japan was not well prepared to address the impact of international capital, the yen's internationalization was only transient. Japan experienced three stages to achieve portfolio II.

Stage I (1960s–1970s): Allowing the exchange rate to float freely, liberalizing direct investment, and loosening control on security investment. In 1964, Japan liberalized the current account and signed the *Agreement on Recurrent Non-Trade Liberalization* and *Agreement on the Liberalization of Capital Flow*. Japan also revised the *Law of Foreign Capital* within the same year and allowed FDI, which meant Japan started the course toward full convertibility under the capital account. Within less than ten years from 1967 to 1976, the Japanese government adopted five policies to gradually cancel the industrial restrictions on FDI. By 1973, 96% of the industries in Japan were opened up. In 1971, the Bretton Woods system collapsed, and the international monetary system entered the "Jamaica Era". In 1972, Japan declared to rescind the fixed exchange rate between the JPY and the USD and adopted the floating exchange rate regime. It set a floating range of 2.5%, but with the large scale of international capital flow, Japanese government did not succeed in stabilizing JPY's exchange rate and its currency went into a lane of fast appreciation. In May of the same year, Japan canceled the forex concentration system, allowing residents and non-residents to hold foreign deposits. To address the decline of the current account surplus, the Japanese government again loosened the restriction on capital inflows, removed the restriction on non-residents to buy domestic securities, lowered the reserve requirement for non-residents' yen deposits, and opened the bond repurchase market to foreign institutional investors. Judging from Chart 4.2, during this period the degree to which Japanese monetary policy was intervened by the Fed was notably lower than that of the German policy. Japan had more independence in monetary policies. However, as yen's exchange rate appreciated sharply, Japan's current account difference became more fluctuated, which to some extent undermined Japan's real economy.

Stage II (the 1980s): Promoting financial liberalization and basically achieving convertibility under the capital account. In December, 1980, Japan adopted a new forex law named *Management Law on Forex and Foreign Trade*, changing the "overall prohibition with exceptions" to the "overall permission with exceptions". It provided that individuals could freely trade forex assets in government-approved commercial banks and security companies. The law also removed the cap on the number of foreign governments' JPY accounts, totally liberalized citizens' forex deposit, and allowed non-residents to invest in domestic securities. By then, Japan put an end to the 40-year-long isolation of the capital market, investment in both domestic and foreign securities were allowed, and foreign capital was allowed to enter Japan's capital market and security industry. During that stage, the opening up policy for capital accounts extended from direct investment to security investment and other investments, basically achieving convertibility

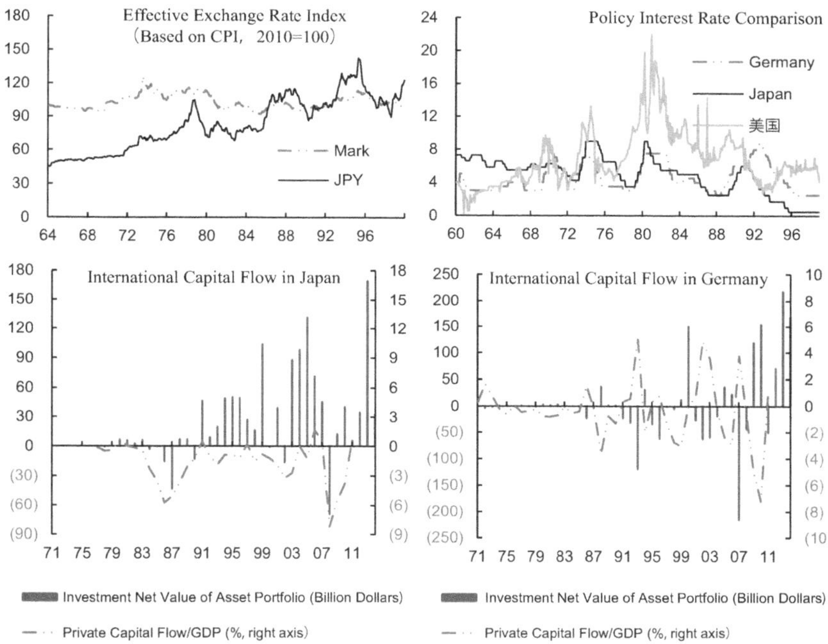

Chart 4.2 Currency internationalization and changes in economic indicators: the experience of Germany and Japan. (Data source: CEIC)

under the capital account. After the signing of the Plaza Accord in 1985, the JPY appreciated exponentially against the USD, which dragged back Japan's domestic industries and forced the government to take expansionary monetary policies in the late 1980s. This foreshadowed the burst of economic bubbles in the 1990s. As has been proved by history, Japan eventually fell into the liquidity trap and its real economy was shattered.

Stage III (the 1990s): Achieving full convertibility under the capital account. In the 1990s, Japan went through the "Lost Decade". Its manufacturing industry plummeted and JPY's share in the international market fell after peaking in the early 1990s. The international status of the yen fell far behind the Deutsche mark. After falling into the "liquidity trap", the Japanese government started the "Financial Big Bang" by intensifying the liberalization of the capital account and seeking new economic growth engines through introducing foreign capital. In May 1997, Japan passed a new forex law, changing the pre-approval and pre-reporting mechanism in capital trade to the ex post facto reporting system, rescinding prevailing laws on the forex bank system and exchange brokers, removing restrictions on forex forward exposure, and allowing e-cash payment. The implementation of the new forex law marked that Japan had canceled major measures in forex control and capital control put in place after the Second World War and achieved full convertibility under the capital account. But the "Financial Big Bang" did not attract a large amount of foreign capital as expected and Japan's economic problems remained unsolved. The long-term sluggish economy and excessively fluctuating exchange rate soon made JPY not so attractive among non-resident investors and as a result, the yen's international status inevitably fell.

We can see from the above analysis of Germany's and Japan's experience that both countries stood at similar start points in currency internationalization but ended differently. Although Germany started to liberalize its capital account in the 1960s, it was prudential in opening up and adjustment. It continuously improved its core competitiveness in industrial production and took dynamic adjustments in choosing macro-financial policy portfolios for the purpose of stabilizing the macro-economy and the forex rate, which eventually secured an important position for the mark and Germany in international financial market. In comparison, Japan was too radical. It liberalized its capital account in the 1960s, overvalued its real economy's resilience against the yen's appreciation, and failed to stabilize yen's exchange rate. As a result, its real economy was undermined. Although Japan started to stimulate its national economy through easy monetary policies and financial market opening up in the 1980s, the depression of the real economy became still inevitable. This not only made the yen's internationalization impossible, but also slowed down Japan's financial market development.

4.2 RMB Internationalization Is Faced with Macro-Financial Risks

Japan and Germany both paid high attention to the independence of monetary policies in its currency internationalization, because only when central banks can remain strong monetary policy independence can the financial market keep national economy growing steadily in opening up and control domestic inflation and unemployment. The monetary policy is an important measure to regulate the national economy, as well as a prerequisite to achieve national monetary policy targets. As an issuing country of an international currency, it is important for China to keep the independence of monetary policies. Currencies issued by a country without independent monetary policies can surely not win the recognition and trust of the international financial market and the currency's credibility would be undermined.

As major international currency issuers, Germany and Japan both adopted portfolio II. A more important lesson from their experience is their different policy adjustment paths and how their currency internationalization was influenced as a result. Their experience tells us that we cannot rush in policy adjustment. The forex rate and the capital account can be liberalized only after the national economy, the financial market, and regulatory institutions are prepared to address international capital impacts.

In recent years, the RMB has become more internationalized and will enter a new stage after the entrance into the SDR currency basket. We can learn from open economy classical theories and international experiences that China's macro-financial policy has undergone a sensitive period of policy adjustment. During the transition from portfolio III to portfolio II, China should identify and measure possible macro-financial risks, laying solid foundations for effective management of macro-financial risks and providing evidence for choosing the right timing and intensiveness of policy adjustment.

4.2.1 Current Policies Are Concentrated on Forex Fluctuations and Exchange Rate Management

In terms of policy adjustment, China is faced with the same problems as Germany and Japan in history. When a country's currency is being internationalized, the most immediate challenge is exchange rate fluctuations. For a trade power, increasingly fluctuating exchange rates bring uncertainty in foreign trade, increase transaction risks and costs, and probably break the existing trade balance, impacting the domestic market. For a developing country like China, the RMB exchange rate is definitely going to encounter more severe challenges: both long-term unilateral appreciation and short-term intensive depreciation can impose great pressure on the domestic macro-economy and the financial market. As exchange rate fluctuations are inevitable, how monetary authority manages the exchange rate becomes a key issue in currency internationalization.

In early stages of currency internationalization, unilateral appreciation always brings pressure. Before 2015, the RMB appreciated unilaterally against the USD for many years, a situation similar to Japan's experience.

During long-term currency appreciation, export in both countries suffered different impacts and year-to-year growth of export both decelerated on a monthly basis (see Chart 4.3). Unilateral appreciation will also squeeze the trade market, not only lowering national enterprises' international competitiveness, but also stimulating large amounts of capital to the forex market through the current account for arbitrage, forcing the central bank to increase money supply even with domestic over-production. Enterprises will be greatly discouraged from production and innovation, the real economy will be less active, and the country will be dragged into an abyss like Japan in extreme cases.

Maybe because Germany foresaw such dangers, it made different policy choices facing appreciation pressure: from the end of the 1960s, for a very long time, Germany stubbornly kept the mark's exchange rate stable. When internationalization started, the German monetary authority became nearly paranoid in maintaining the exchange rate stable, to achieve which the authority even restarted capital control, slowed down financial market growth, and used forex reserves to intervene the market. Exchange stability during that period created sound external conditions for Germany

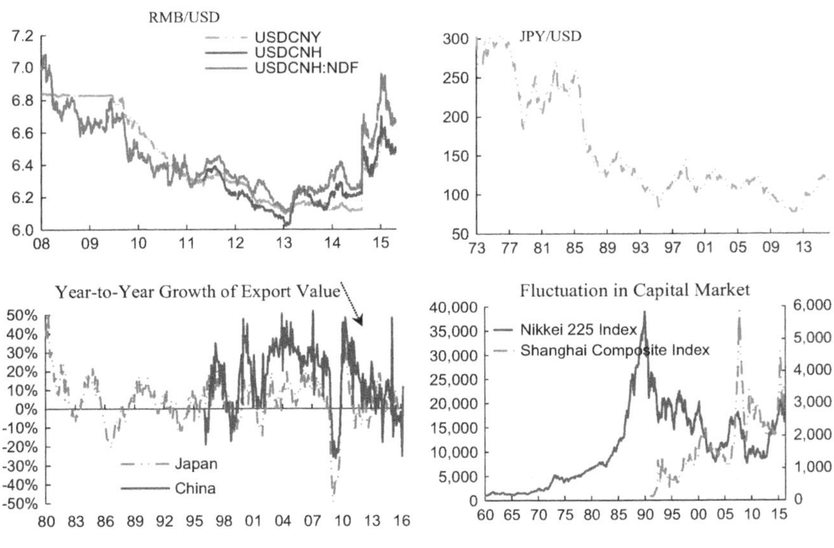

Chart 4.3 Unilateral appreciation's impact on economy: Japan and China. (Source: CEIC)

to keep trade advantages, improve industrial competitiveness, and consolidate national real economic growth. From a long-term perspective, the increase in industrial competitiveness and national real economy in turn provided a strong support for the stability of the mark's exchange rate. Germany kept a long-term surplus in international payment and occupied the dominating place in the global industrial chain. Its competitive export enterprises ensured the mark's share in international settlement so that after Germany liberalized the exchange rate it could keep stable demand for the mark in the international market. From 1980 to 1996, mark-denominated products in German export accounted for 82.3%, and in the same period, yen-denominated products accounted for only 29.4% in Japan's export. We can see from this fact that exchange rate stability is crucial for the real economy in the early stage of currency internationalization. From a long-term perspective, one currency's international status ultimately depends on the country's ability to create real wealth.

Continuous depreciation will also undermine the national economy. Especially for emerging markets, prolonged currency depreciation will lead to a sudden stop of international capital. Once depreciation expectation takes shape, the expectation will fulfill itself and profit-seeking short-term capital will flee in panic, which further accelerates currency depreciation. In such cases, on one hand, liquidity decrease in the domestic capital market will be a disaster for the security market; on the other hand, forex-denominated liability of domestic enterprises will skyrocket, forcing financially healthy companies to liquidate their assets in low prices. Great losses of enterprises will further undermine the growth of the national capital market, imposing a great threat to national economic security.

Since 2015, both domestic and foreign markets started to expect RMB to depreciate. After the "811" forex reform, RMB depreciated even faster and the impact from foreign markets on the RMB exchange rate grew. On January 1, 2016, RMB's NDF exchange rate on offshore market fell to 6.955, a record low since 2008 and the backwardation rate was as high as 6.49%. Although depreciation pressure on RMB lessened afterward, pessimistic sentiment and short sellers were still dominating the market. In effect, this pressure represented a test on the macro-financial management ability of the domestic monetary authority. If the authority could not properly address the fluctuating exchange rate and let monetary crisis burst out, RMB internationalization would inevitably become a short-lived flower just like that of the JPY.

On this issue, China should learn from Germany and prioritize exchange rate stability at the early stage of currency internationalization. Besides reinstalling capital control to stabilize exchange rate, Germany also used large amounts of forex reserves as the stabilization fund to stabilize the mark's supply in the market and the mark's exchange rate. So, China's current policy should center on how to further improve its managed floating exchange rate regime and make some space and time for the transformation and development of its real economy. Especially, China should make relentless efforts in communicating with the market and carry out effective exchange rate management by guiding market expectations. In addition, to facilitate exchange rate management, China should also consider adjusting measures in capital account management, especially in terms of short-term cross-border capital flow.

4.2.2 Cross-Border Capital Flow and Systemic Risks Are Major Threats in the Future

As has been evidenced by classical theories and international practices, when a country's currency becomes one of the international currencies, the monetary authority can only take portfolio II as its financial policy choices. This also applies to China. However, when domestic financial market is yet to be mature, the financial regulatory system is to be improved and measures to offset cross-border capital flow are limited and ineffective, an indiscreet liberalization of the capital account and the RMB exchange rate is most likely to cause systemic financial crises, harm the real economy and financial growth, and interrupt RMB internationalization. Therefore, when the emphasis shifts from portfolio III to portfolio II, China needs to simultaneously shift its emphasis of macro-financial risk management from preventing severe exchange rate fluctuation to preventing systemic crises caused by cross-border capital flow. In fact, as China's economy and finance are integrated into the global market, impacts of cross-border capital flow become frequent and the potential harm becomes bigger. So China needs to take full advantage of the time window brought by the partially liberalized capital account and RMB exchange rates to comprehensively study how cross-border capital flow influences domestic systemic financial risks and what counter-measures to take, improve monetary authority and regulatory institutions' ability to manage macro-financial risks, and pave the way for RMB internationalization in the future.

For China, the impact of cross-border capital is a real problem. America is the largest economy in the world as well as a trade partner of China. The USD currently dominates the international monetary system and America's monetary policy will inevitably have spillover effects on other countries. After the sub-prime crisis in 2008, after eight years of economic restructuring, America slashed financial leverage, increased residential deposits, rejuvenated the manufacturing industry, and improved export competitiveness and employment. Now America has basically passed the recovery period. The Fed declares to gradually exit QE, meaning the interest rate of the USD enters a rising cycle. Periodical changes in American monetary policies will inevitably enhance the appreciation expectation of the USD and cause a large amount of capital to flee to America. This poses pressure on many countries including China and increases the following risks: capital flees, decreasing capital formation, and disadvantages for industrial transformation and upgrade. Besides, the interest rate increase of the USD leads to international liquidity squeeze, which makes it harder for the EU to solve the immigration and refugee problem and makes financially vulnerable emerging countries like Brazil and Russia more prone to financial crisis. As half of the trade volume and the majority of FDI are associated with emerging economies, once financial crises break out there, international financial fluctuations are likely to impact China's national economy through a contagion mechanism. The impact increases the risk of unbalanced international payment and triggers domestic self-fulfilled financial crises.

China's integration into economic globalization creates conditions for optimized allocation of financial resources. When major economies like America, EU, and Japan are carrying out QEs and international financing cost is extremely low, gradually and prudentially liberalizing the capital account will make it easier for us to obtain cheap funds from the international market. On one hand, this relieves the problem of financing difficulty and high financing cost for Chinese companies and creates a sound financial environment for mass entrepreneurship and innovation. On the other hand, it enables China's outbound investment to give full play to its leading role and leverage effect, effectively channel international capital into the construction of "Belt and Road Initiative" and accelerate capacity transfer and industrial upgrade.

However, historical records tell us almost all the developing countries encountered monetary and financial crises shortly after liberalizing the capital account. China is also faced with three risks: first, according to the "Trilemma" principle, once RMB achieves full convertibility (which means to cancel the control on capital account), it will be necessary for China, the world's second largest economy, monetary policy independence of which is indispensable for macro-economic management, to adopt a floating exchange rate regime in the future. Exchange rate fluctuations are likely to lead to international trade fluctuations and bring unemployment and inflation pressure to the real economy; second, possible speculative capital flow or hot money impact may cause fluctuations in capital and asset prices, make financial system more vulnerable, increase liquidity crisis, and blow the asset bubbles through the interaction and transmission mechanism between the forex market, the monetary market, the capital market, and the derivative market; third, capital account liberalization and RMB internationalization promote each other, which expands the RMB offshore market. As the offshore market and the onshore market are different in terms of market players and operation mechanisms, exchange rate difference must exist in the two markets. This difference will inevitably lead to random flow in foreign and domestic RMB asset pools, and major fluctuations in RMB exchange rates make it more difficult for the central bank to manage the exchange rate and cause excessive consumption of China's forex reserves. This difference will also lead to major fluctuations in domestic money supply in the case of comprehensive intervention and undermine Chinese government's macroeconomic management ability.

Sustained short-term capital outflow is a financial risk that should be highly emphasized in both the short term and the long term in China's opening up process. Currently, a major reason for short-term capital flees is the reversal of RMB appreciation expectations. So stabilizing expectations helps to stabilize capital flow. However, with China's financial market being liberalized, Chinese citizens and enterprises are strongly motivated to invest in global assets due to worries about Chinese economic systemic risks. The scale of capital flee caused by this reason should not be underestimated. So besides liberalizing the capital account in a prudential, manageable, and gradual manner, the monetary authority should make efforts in monitoring and managing systemic financial risks and provide effective policy tools to prevent and address systemic financial risks.

China should also pay great attention to the risks of RMB cross-border arbitrage. First, international trade companies are indulged in manipulating capital. This will not only lead to exaggerated increases in trade figures and encourage hot money to transfer from forex reserves to offshore RMB inflow, but also make it difficult for the country to manage liquidity.

Second, the fast inflow and outflow of RMB cross-border arbitrage capital exert an impact on China's national economy. Large-scale cross-border arbitrage further exacerbates the fluctuation of China's cross-border capital flow. Especially, large amounts of arbitrage capital flow severely influence China's international payment balance and bring major impacts upon its national economic growth. Third, RMB cross-border arbitrage is associated with solvency risks. RMB cross-border arbitrage is not an isolated phenomenon and it is achieved through products associated with cross-border trade RMB settlement like forward Letter of Credit, overseas refinancing, agreement payment, deposit received, and payment deferred. But such transactions are temporarily not managed as foreign debts. Bad financial health and broken asset chains will lead to solvency risks.

4.3 Macro-Financial Risk Management from the Perspective of National Strategies

Diversification of international currencies is a dynamic process. Changes in the international trade landscape and the international financial market will lead to corresponding adjustment in international currency pattern. In this process, for the monetary authority of international currency issuing countries, the largest challenge is, without any doubt, how to carry out dynamic risk regulation and how to address the market fluctuations and influences on the national real economy. RMB has entered the SDR basket and become a de facto international currency, so how China formulates a macro-prudential management system to monitor and prevent systemic risks that may happen in different stages is of strategic significance for further opening its economy and promoting RMB internationalization.

4.3.1 Providing Fundamental Guarantees for the Ultimate Goal of RMB Internationalization

RMB internationalization shoulders double historical missions: realizing China's interest demands and reforming the international monetary system. It is one of the major plans of China, a newly emerging power in the twenty-first century. This strategy matches China's national interest and serves as an indispensable support for an emerging power; at the same time, it also matches the global interests, improves the current global economic order and the international currency system, and shows China's responsibility as an emerging power.

The RMB's growing into a major international currency and obtaining a status matching China's economic and trade position in the world helps the country move from the peripheral area to the center of global economic and financial equilibrium, escape from the "dollar trap," and guard its economic interests and people. This also helps China to offset the negative spillover effect of American monetary policies, enhance its resilience against external impact, and improve its soft international competitiveness.

Ever since the financial crisis in 2008, the call for international monetary system reform has grown louder. The core of the reform is to shake off the excessive dependence on the USD and give more say to developing countries in international currency governance. China, the largest developing country, should shoulder due responsibility in reforming the international currency system. The Chinese government welcomes wide use of the RMB in the international market and the RMB's inclusion into the SDR currency basket, and shows China's will and responsibility as a big country to provide public goods for the world. The rise of the RMB reshapes the international currency competition into a multiple-player arena, providing developing countries with opportunities to choose safer international reserve currencies and shake off the harms of over-dependence on the USD.

From the perspective of the general picture of the international currency system, the international currency arena with multiple competitors promotes the adjustment of international economy and trade and helps to break the stalemate of global economic imbalance and global financial terror balance. This situation is also a constraint mechanism where "the good money drives out the bad money", adding stabilizing factors to the international currency system and relieving the pressure of systemic global financial crises.

Generally speaking, currency internationalization should be based on the following conditions: comprehensive economic power, trade status, free capital flow, currency value stability, and macro-management ability. Based on the facts in the past few years, the first four factors supporting RMB internationalization had good performance, but the monetary authority's macro-management ability is yet to be enhanced. Especially, in terms of how to coordinate and manage capital flow and macro-financial risks with a more liberalized capital account, the authority probably needs systemic theoretical guidance and necessary practical experience. In the long run, macro-management may become the weakness dragging down

RMB internationalization. As macro-management ability also influences other factors like free capital flow and currency value stability, China needs to intensify its efforts in building this ability to win the international community's long-lasting trust on the RMB.

RMB internationalization needs healthy and stable macro-economic environment and a mature financial system. The stability and development of the financial market not only helps the real economy by allocating resources and sharing risks, but also acts as the best self-protection in the course of opening economy, and helps China to offset the large-scale impact brought by international capital. In the process of deepening financial development and internationalizing the RMB, macro-liquidity plays an increasingly influential role. Although present liquidity management tools help to stabilize prices and the operation of single micro-institutions, they are useless in the face of the accelerator effect of macro-liquidity pro-cyclicality and its impact on the entire economy. The capital market fluctuations in 2015 showed that China's regulatory institutions are not fully prepared to address severe fluctuations of the financial market and their management efficiency and modes are yet to be upgraded. If China cannot draw lessons timely and improve the methods and efficiency of its macro-financial risk management, then its backward risk management will be the largest hindrance in RMB internationalization.

According to the calculation of the BOC, when the RMB is included into the SDR basket, the adjustment of official asset allocation of other countries will lead to an increase in RMB demand of over 600 billion yuan. This will largely promote RMB internationalization and expand the use of the RMB in commodity denomination, financial transactions, asset allocation, and official reserves. Such multi-channel and multi-dimensional increases in RMB external demand will, in the case of a liberalized capital account, inevitably influence the supply–demand relationship in the domestic RMB market and may cause liquidity crises. The expansion in the demand and use of the RMB in the world enables Chinese enterprises and financial institutions to use more RMB in international trade, and their pricing ability and liability-asset structure will see big changes and their currency mismatch will decrease. But their source of liability and use of assets will be more internationalized and interest rate risks and national risks will grow. After the RMB is included into the SDR basket, the evaluation and interest rate pricing of the SDR pose new demands for RMB's market exchange rates and interest rates on the money market, which requires China to make quicker steps to liberalize the RMB exchange rate regime and the short-term market benchmark interest rate regime and solve other fundamental financial market problems. This no doubt poses new challenges for the macro-financial management ability of the central bank and increases the uncertainty of monetary policy efficiency and financial operation.

Strengthening macro-financial risk management and improving the monetary authority's macro-management ability are key to the success of the RMB internationalization strategy. To ensure successful RMB internationalization, China must improve its macro-financial risk management on the national strategic level.

4.3.2 *Taking the Construction of a Macro-Prudential Policy Framework as the Core in Financial Risk Management*

Classical international financial theories and the history of Germany and Japan show that with the internationalization of the RMB, the monetary authority must face the daunting challenge of adjusting macro-financial policies and the associated macro-financial risks. That is to say, in the transformation from portfolio III to portfolio II, China needs to address the impact of fluctuating exchange rates on the domestic economic and financial operation. China should also quickly adapt itself to the brand-new mechanism of how cross-border capital flow influences its domestic financial market, financial institutions, and the real economy. China should especially prevent and manage systemic financial risks.

Financial stability is the prerequisite for the ultimate goal of RMB internationalization. Therefore, to construct a more comprehensive and more targeted macro-prudential policy framework is the core mission of the currency authority in enhancing macro-financial management. On one hand, China should coordinate exchange rate policies with monetary policies and fiscal policies and unify policy targets like price stability, exchange rate stability, and stable macro-economic growth into the framework of financial stability. On the other, China should continuously improve micro-prudential regulatory policies, stress the risk management and control of financial institutions, and enhance the protection for financial consumers. China should also explore macro-prudential regulatory policies, pay attention to the sound operation of the financial system, enhance the harmonious development of finance and the real economy, and take the prevention of systemic financial risks as a major support for achieving financial stability.

1. Taking exchange rate management as a major leverage to manage macro-financial risks

As China's economy and financial market are further liberalized, the exchange rate is now playing a more important role in adjusting international payment balance and guiding capital flow. But excessive exchange fluctuations will have a negative impact on the financial market and harm the stable and sound growth of the real economy. So China should take exchange rate management as a major support of macro-financial risk management.

Now China should further improve the exchange rate formation mechanism, respect the market's fundamental role in determining the exchange rate, and take full advantage of the managed floating exchange rate regime. China should use the exchange rate as a leverage to adjust the international balance of payment, optimize resource allocation in both domestic and international markets, achieve the policy target of international capacity cooperation, as well as prevent excessive fluctuations of the exchange rate and related damage to China's financial market and real economy.

When China's exchange rate becomes more flexible, the monetary authority should phase out direct intervention in the exchange rate and use more market-based measures and combined policies to achieve the exchange rate policy targets. China should increase the monetary authority's specialty and public trust in macro-management and establish a guiding mechanism for market expectations. China should especially combine monetary policies, fiscal policies with exchange rate policies and achieve exchange rate policy targets through indirect management from the interest rate to the tax rate and then to the exchange rate.

As RMB becomes more widely used in the international market, the macro-economic policies of China, the second largest economy in the world, may have some spillover effects. This requires the PBOC to give priority to the needs of the domestic market in making and implementing monetary policies and exchange rate policies, and consider the interest demands of major trade partner countries through proper communication and coordination mechanisms to reduce policy frictions and achieve cooperation and win-win results.

In the current international monetary system with "one big power and multiple competitors", China, like other emerging countries, will inevitable be influenced by the changes in the macro-economic policies of America. In 2008, after the financial crisis, America took rounds of QEs and increased the dollar's interest rate in recent years, which triggered a large-scale capital flow in the world and impacted the forex market, the financial market, and the real economy of emerging countries. Such changes even triggered financial crises in some countries. The policy changes also resulted in abnormal changes of short-term cross-border capital flow in China and even caused great price fluctuations in the domestic housing stock markets, which brought difficulties to the transformation of the real economy and piled great pressure on the stability of the RMB exchange rate. Therefore, RMB exchange rate managers should pay close attention to the spillover effects of American macro-policies, give full play to the active role of the China-America Strategic and Economic Dialogue Platform, enhance the communication with American government, establish a coordinating mechanism between USD and RMB exchange rates, and reduce the negative effects of excessive exchange rate fluctuations on both countries' economy and financial markets.

In recent years, negative interest rate policies taken by the ECB and the BOJ and the "Brexit" referendum have enlarged the exchange rate fluctuations in the global forex market and may trigger a new round of global financial crises. Therefore, RMB exchange rate managers should also call for currency policy coordination among issuing countries of SDR basket currencies, so as to prevent exchange rate wars between major currencies, consider each other's interests, and together shoulder the responsibility and obligations to maintain the stability of the international financial market.

2. Taking capital flow management as a key starting point in managing macro-financial risks.

Since the 1990s, international capital has flooded into emerging countries, which brought economic prosperity but stimulated the formation of asset bubbles and made their financial systems more vulnerable. However, when the flow was reversed, none of those countries could escape from great economic and financial fluctuations, and even suffered from systemic crises. As China was integrated into the international market, it should learn lessons from those crises and stay highly alert against international capital flow, especially short-term capital flow.

In the next stage, when China's macro-financial policy choice shifts to portfolio II, forex market and capital market will probably become the major targets for foreign speculative capital. Therefore, macro-financial risk managers should take capital flow management as a starting point, identify and monitor the chain reaction in the domestic financial market caused by cross-border capital flows, enhance macro-prudential financial regulation, and prevent systemic financial crisis.

The liberalization of the capital account may increase cross-border capital flow in terms of scale and frequency. It involves areas like the financial market, financial tools, financial institutions, and financial infrastructure. The connectivity between financial sub-markets has become stronger. Traditional micro-prudential regulatory policies and tools cannot adapt to such changes and they are useless in the face of the accelerator effect of macro-liquidity procyclicality. With the fast growth of China's financial system and the promotion of RMB internationalization strategy, macro-liquidity exerts an increasingly larger influence on economic and financial operation. Only by constructing a macro-prudential policy framework; introducing macro- and anti-cyclical adjustment tools to achieve macro-prudential financial regulation; managing the liquidity in the financial system in a dynamic, comprehensive, and differentiated manner; and preventing systemic risks can China achieve the ultimate goal of financial stability and create a sound financial environment for the healthy development of the real economy.

CHAPTER 5

RMB Exchange Rate: Regimes and Policy Issues

International Monetary Institute

5.1 Improving RMB Exchange Rate Regime

5.1.1 Progress in the Market-Oriented Reform of Exchange Rate

The PBOC announced a decision to implement a market-based determination mechanism of the official fixing rate of RMB against USD in order to enhance the marketing and standard value of RMB on August 11, 2015. In the following three days, the official fixing rate of RMB against USD fell 4%. The release of the de-value pressure stimulates panic. In the expectation of de-valuation, the exchange rate volatility has increased and gap between the onshore and offshore exchange rate has further widened. The central bank faces greater difficulty in exchange rate regulation.

On December 1, 2015, director of the IMF Christine Lagarde announced to officially include RMB yuan in the benchmark SDR currency basket. The weight of the RMB in the reserve currency basket is

International Monetary Institute (✉)
Renmin University of China, Beijing, China
e-mail: imi@ruc.edu.cn

International Monetary Institute (ed.), *Currency Internationalization and Macro Financial Risk Control*,
https://doi.org/10.1007/978-981-13-0698-3_5

10.9%, after the USD and euro as the third weighted currency. After the RMB inclusion in the SDR, the demand for the renminbi assets will witness a sharp increase and fluctuation of the exchange rate will get bigger and cross-border capital flow will get stronger. It is a new challenge for the central bank to improve its policy-making mechanism for better supervision and crisis prevention and better shoulder its responsibility to maintain flexibility and stability of international currencies.

On December 11, 2015, China Foreign Exchange Trade System officially released the CFETS RMB exchange rate index. The RMB exchange rate is thus getting more market-based with USD and euros for reference. The weighting of different currencies in the basket is 26.4% for the USD, 21.39% for the euro, and 14.68% for the Japanese yen. The RMB exchange rate gets pegged to a basket of currency, instead of just one single currency. It can take a more flexible reaction to the USD while keeping relatively stable toward other emerging countries. However, the financial market and the foreign trade enterprises will still focus on the RMB exchange rate against the USD. How to strengthen information flow in the market and guide the exchange rate expectation is an urgent issue to be solved by the central bank.

In the past year, China has been deepening the reform of exchange rate and has improved the floating exchange rate mechanism with better orientation on the market demand and supply and regulation referring to the basket of currencies. In general, the RMB exchange rate mechanism has demonstrated five characteristics as below:

Firstly, RMB exchange rate becomes more market-based. After the reform of official rate on August 11th, the market maker should report the middle rate before interbank exchange market opening based on the close price and take the supply, demand, and the change of main currencies into account. Compared with the previous official rate, the reform weakens the power of government in the determination of the central parity rate. It can fully reflect the market opinions on the RMB exchange rate.

Secondly, RMB exchange rate turns from being USD pegged to referring to a basket of currencies. The CFETS RMB exchange rate index weakens USD's impact on the exchange rate. Getting rid of dependency on one single currency, RMB exchange rate can be more flexible and independent. It can also reflect the flexibility of exchange over the USD, euro, and the currency of emerging countries at the same time. The exchange rate is more close to the balanced rate.

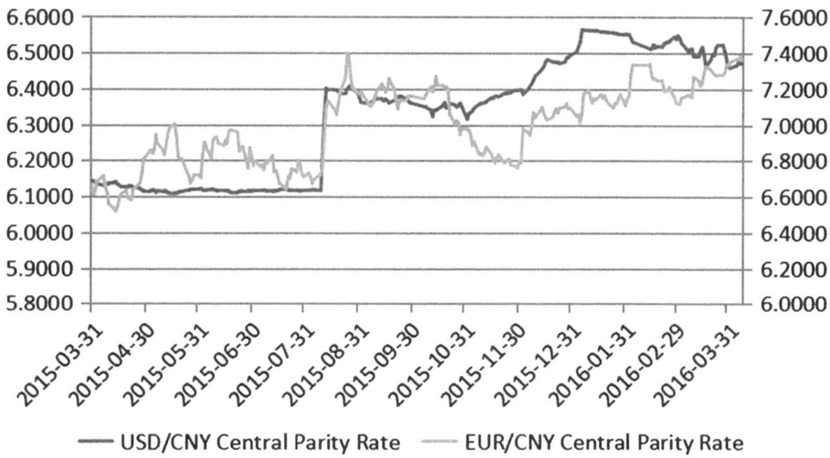

Graph 5.1 Trend of the exchange rate against USD and EUR

Thirdly, exchange rate becomes more volatile. According to Graph 5.1, renminbi exchange rate against the USD was almost between 6.11 and 6.14 before August 2015. But after the reform, the fluctuating range gets wider. The same relationship can be seen in the exchange rate against the euro in this period. However, compared to the USD/RMB central parity rate, euro/RMB rate fluctuates more sharply.

Fourthly, the relationship between exchange rate and the RMB assets strengthens. Before the reform, there is no significant impact on the stock and bond market. The trend of stock and bond market becomes more related to exchange rate after August 2015. Every de-valuation with RMB is associated with a plummet in the stock market (Graph 5.2).

Fifthly, the influence of exchange policy strengthens. In the currency background, the importance of currency policy spillover effects increases. The American Federal Reserve Committee's announcement to raise interest and the European's less-than-expected loose monetary policy both have great influence on the RMB exchange rate.

Faced with global economic downturn and major economies' different monetary policies, it is crucial to maintain the independence of monetary policy. China should continue this market-oriented exchange rate reform, gradually promote capital account liberalization, and explore appropriate exchange rate mechanisms to accelerate RMB internationalization.

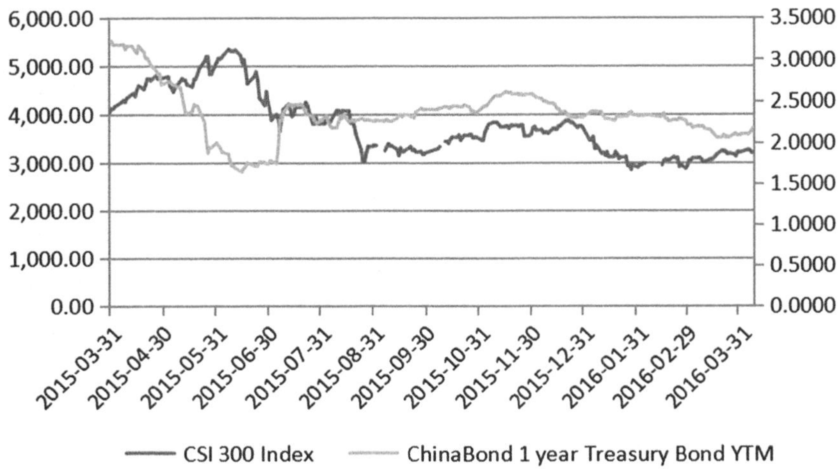

Graph 5.2 Trend of stock market and bond market

5.1.2 *Impacts Upon Exchange Rate Mechanism Under Currency Convertibility*

Currency full convertibility means that a country's currency can be converted to another currency at official or market exchange rate without limitation and control. First, local currency can be exchanged with any other currency, not just some specific ones. Second, such currency exchange is free from government control regardless of amount and purpose. Third, the rate of conversion is the official rate rather than the black market rate. As most countries' currency cannot reach the standard, we classify them into three categories: fully converted, partly converted, and unconverted. Judging from the content, currency convertibility can be classified into current account and capital account convertibility. Current account convertibility means that the currency can be fully converted in the trade associated with international goods and services export and import. Capital account convertibility refers to the currency exchange associated with the capital flow. The IMF put forward specific requirements for Member States that need free conversion under the current account. Most open economies have realized current account full convertibility so far. But as the capital account convertibility shows great differences. China accomplished current account convertibility in the 1990s, and the capital account convertibility is gradually being expanded.

With the development of exchange rate reform and capital account openness, RMB's convertibility gradually increases. At this time, how the exchange mechanism should be transformed to maintain balanced exchange rate with full convertibility is a heated question to be discussed. This book shows different characters of the exchange rate at different convertibility levels. The conclusion is that as the internationalization and macro financial risk contro convertibility level increases, the exchange rate mechanism will have a regime transformation. It is of great importance to analyze the turning point of the regime and examine the characteristics of different regimes. In this book, a threshold regression model is used to analyze how the exchange rate mechanism changes at different convertibility levels.

First of all, as the convertibility increases, determinants for short-term fluctuation change. When the currency convertibility is below a certain level, volatility of the exchange rate is mostly related to macro-economic factors such as economic growth rate, GDP per capita, and trade surplus. With increase of the currency convertibility, correlation of these factors decreases, and the deflation and interest difference factors become more important. It can be concluded that with opening of the capital account, exchange rates will not be closely related to macro-economic factors, but will greatly affect short-term capital arbitrage behaviors. Besides, when the currency is highly convertible, it is hard to use macro-economic factors to explain exchange rate changes. The exchange rate will be highly affected by market participants. Investors digging the arbitrage opportunities will push the exchange rate toward a balanced level.

In addition, the book discusses determinants of the real exchange rate. When a currency sees increased convertibility, will the determinant factors of the real exchange rate change? It is known that the most important explanatory variants for real exchange rate is the macro-economic background. Economic growth rate, economic volatility, and GDP per capita are highly correlated to the real exchange rate. The higher the convertibility level of the currency, the closer the relationship shows. It is because that the level of the real exchange rate is decided by a country's economy on the whole. Although the short-term capital flow may shock the real exchange rate and cause some variation, real exchange rate will return to the balanced level in the long run. And if the monetary department wants to intervene with real exchange rate, the influence must be short term. Besides, improvement of the real interest rate can also lead to an appreciation of the real exchange rate. It can be concluded that when the currency is convertible, high benefit, full investors' confidence, and so on as such can lead to the appreciation of the real exchange rate.

Last but not least, we discuss the explanatory factors of variation of exchange rate under different convertibility levels. According to the regression result, fluctuation of exchange is affected by different factors. And the impact of each factor is not that stable. Overall, the stability of macro-economy can decrease the fluctuation of exchange rate regardless of the convertibility level. But this stability effect is less significant when the currency is highly convertible. In the situation of low currency convertibility, easy monetary policy will strengthen the fluctuation of exchange rate. When the currency is convertible, the rise of real interest rate and capital inflows can decrease the fluctuation. It can be inferred that when convertibility level is low, the impact of capital flow is moderate. It is the reform of opening capital account that requires more supervision on the capital flow.

Our book uses threshold regression model to analyze the exchange rate mechanism. A regime change is discovered when the convertibility level improves. With the continuous exchange rate reform, RMB convertibility must pass the turning point in the future. Knowing the changes of exchange rate mechanism is highly important. There are some points worthy of attention in the following reform.

First, it is crucial to maintain stability of macro-economy to keep RMB exchange rate stable on a balanced level. With the development of currency convertibility, the real exchange rate is more closely related to the macro-economy. Stabilizing the economy level can also weaken exchange rate fluctuation. In the long run, developing economy and decreasing the shock of economy is the solid base of a stable exchange rate. Exchange rate mechanism is the policy base of economy and direct expression of economy. Therefore, China should pay attention to the fluctuation of exchange rate and continue to promote the reform while maintaining a stable exchange rate at the same time.

Second, the central bank should be more cautious with the exchange rate intervention. From the regression result, we can see that exchange rate can adjust toward the balance level gradually under influence of investors' arbitrage. Therefore, in the reform of capital account, the central bank should intervene less in the exchange market and allow the exchange rate to fluctuate freely in a certain range. These can help to discover the true price and release the power of market. The central bank can intervene in severe situations and make the intervention policies more powerful.

Third, pay more attention to the capital flow. With the development of currency convertibility, the amount of capital flow must increase. We have talked about this; the outflows of capital will strengthen exchange rate fluctuation. So the central bank should take actions to prevent the outflow capital from harming stability of the exchange rate. Measures to manage the capital flow include preventing the outflow and attracting the inflow. The government should supervise the capital flow closely and take suitable reactions.

5.1.3 Effects of Joining the SDR Basket

SDR is an international reserve asset and unit of account of the IMF created in 1969. Essentially, it is the potential claims right of all types of funds that the IMF allocated to the Member States. The Member States mainly convert SDR to the basket of currencies in two ways: (1) through voluntary exchange of membership, (2) the IMF selects a balance of payment–surplus membership state to exchange certain basket currency with a payment deficit state. Judging from effects, SDR is not a real estate reserve currency but a potential drawing right guaranteed by the IMF's basket currency. SDR is used to help members to balance their payment, prevent international liquidity shortage, and set up a system for risk sharing.

The renminbi became the fifth international payment currency, the second trade funding currency, the sixth international interbank loan currency, the seventh exchange trading currency, and the seventh exchange reserve currency by October 2015. Since then, RMB's international payment and reserve functions keep improving. The inclusion of RMB into SDR will strengthen the representativeness of basket currency and help improve the international trade and capital flow. From the point of RMB internationalization, joining the SDR will help improve the frequency of RMB use in international trade and financing activities. More importantly, the increased trading amount of RMB can improve convertibility of capital account and make a difference in the exchange rate mechanism.

In the case where currency convertibility significantly increases, the degree of increased capital inflows will reduce the level of exchange rate volatility, and increased capital outflows will cause instability of exchange rate movements. The interest spreads of RMB and USD get narrow as a result of the US economic recovery; the dollar interest rate increases expectation and causes easing of the domestic monetary. RMB's and USD's risk spreads continued to narrow; capital account deficit continued to emerge since the second quarter of 2014. The financial account deficit of former three-quarters of 2015 adds up to 121.9 billion yuan. When the macro-economic environment does not change significantly, the "current account surplus and capital account deficit will become the new normal of balance of payments." Reflecting on the RMB exchange rate is a substantial outflow of short-term capital leading to great de-valuation of RMB exchange rate against USD.

In order to avoid the potential risk caused by exchange rate fluctuation, it is of great importance to maintain healthy development of the macro-economy. According to the empirical result, when the currency is convertible, maintaining international payment surplus and appropriating capital return can neutralize the negative effects on exchange rate stability. Deepening trade integration will be a key factor in maintaining long-term stability of the RMB exchange rate after joining SDR. China's import and export growth rate has declined, because of the weak global economy and insufficient external demand. However, China's export growth rate performs better compared with other export-oriented countries such as Korea, India, Brazil, and Russia. China's international market share increased from 12.4% in 2014 to around 13% in 2015, maintaining the top one trading nation status. More importantly, the enhanced international payment and settlement functions after adding to SDR will contribute to the RMB internationalization strategy across borders. China can support the funding for one belt one road along. As the sponsor country of one belt one road, China can further enhance currency liquidity and facilitate international payment, leading to resource and trading flows over a higher level. In these cases, enhancing trade integration over relevant countries will effectively ease the level of volatility in exchange rates.

In terms of capital return, China needs an easy monetary policy to reduce financial cost and boost economic restructuring and development. Another significance of RMB joining SDR basket is the positive expectation of China's economy and stable exchange rate. GDP increase after the economic transformation will offset the exchange rate volatility caused by relative disadvantage of interest spread.

In the short run, RMB exchange rate is also affected by the separation of onshore and offshore renminbi market. Short-term volatility is expected to increase under the effect of the overshoot. The spread of capital return between onshore and offshore market shows a strict limitation on the capital flows. Since the beginning of 2015, onshore and offshore RMB exchange rates have maintained a slightly negative difference; and the spreads have become wider after exchange rate reform on August 11th. In the process of deepening market-oriented exchange rate, interexchange rate volatility increases. And in the period when capital account has not been opened, the presence of market overshoot expectation will strengthen the widening trend of offshore and onshore RMB exchange rate minus difference. Capital account convertibility can increase a degree after joining SDR, causing an increase in the capital flow. The volatility of offshore RMB will shock onshore and lead to de-valuation in the short run.

It can be seen that currency convertibility can significantly increase after joining SDR. Therefore, exchange rate mechanism will change and exchange rate can show more flexible characteristics. In the short run, RMB exchange rate will show great de-valuation effected by an appreciation of USD and easy monetary environment. The instability of exchange rate will further strengthen in the short run. But from the long-term view, short-term de-valuation and positive export will promote adjustment of exchange rate stability. And with the improvement of RMB expectation, RMB exchange rate will return to the balanced level in the long run.

5.1.4 Path and Risk of Exchange Rate Reform

This book presents that RMB exchange rate mechanism shows a significant difference at different currency convertibility levels. Therefore, reform of RMB exchange rate should be matched with gradual opening of the capital account. First of all, according to the IMF's Annual Report on Exchange Arrangements and Exchange Restrictions, the reform path of capital account will meet strict capital account limitation even in some developed countries like America, England, and Germany. When global economy becomes ever more closely related, the spillover effect of government policy strengthens. Only by maintaining the capital account restriction to a certain degree can the monetary policy's dependence and economic stability be guaranteed. Therefore, in the process of opening capital account, China should follow the principle of "gradual, controlled, and coordinated" development in managing the capital account based on the international situation. In the process of opening the capital account, maintaining prudential supervision and improving the central bank's financial market regulatory capacity can probably help control the crisis within a certain range. Meanwhile, the capital account liberalization should promote coordination with other Chinese economic system reforms, activating the financial markets, promoting Chinese enterprises to go abroad, while maintaining good external balance. Secondly, the reform of RMB exchange rate system should adhere to the market orientation, leaving the short-term exchange rate to fully reflect market supply and demand. When the fluctuation is too huge, the central bank should take an appropriate intervention to ensure macro-economic stability. It is important to strengthen the dependence of exchange rate and determine the exchange rate with reference to a basket of currency. Besides, China should allow the exchange rate to fluctuate within a certain range, strengthen the reform of China's financial market, and improve the enterprise's ability to avoid exchange rate in order to prevent financial system risk under fully floating exchange rate.

However, with deepening of the Chinese exchange rate reform and openness capital account, it is unavoidable to meet risks. China should have full knowledge of risk and take actions before the crisis to make sure reform promotes stability. Firstly, it should realize that exchange rate reform and open capital account will lead to huge exchange rate fluctuation for sure. According to the regression result in the previous section, short-term volatility is an inevitable process exacerbated by market participants' continuous push to the exchange rate toward balance. Therefore, the central bank should tolerate short-term volatility and take preventive actions when abnormal fluctuations emerge. What's more, judging from the exchange rate volatility after 811 reform, the volatility of RMB exchange rate is not that severe compared to other times. As for the huge currency reserve, the volatility of exchange rate is still within controlled range. Secondly, the capital flow will shock the domestic price determinant system. RMB exchange rate stands for the international price of the renminbi. Its volatility will certainly shock the price determinant of RMB assets. The expectation of RMB appreciation may cause a lot of capital inflows. To a certain extent, foreign capital can help improve the growth rate of the economy. But the capital flow into the stock and real estate market will promote the bubble and increase the systemic risk of China's economy. The central bank should supervise the capital flow and treat different types of capital inflows differently. Except that almost every devaluation of RMB is followed by a round of shock in the A-share market. The conductivity of RMB-denominated assets gradually strengthens. The central bank should set up a corresponding risk prevention system to avoid risks in the real estate, stock and bond market, the bank, trust, private financial community, and so on. Thirdly, the realization of expectation can lead to crises in the market-oriented exchange rate mechanism. It is inevitable to witness rounds of capital flow in the process of marketization. Since the prevailing speculation can cause deviations of the exchange rate in the short run, the central bank's attitude has a decisive role on the market expectation. And when the market expectation shows opposite severe deviation, the central bank should intervene strongly to avoid the second self-fulfilling currency crisis. Fourthly, the spillover effect can lead to huge volatility and low efficiency of central monetary policy. Experiences after "811 exchange reform" 2015 show that the Fed's monetary easing interest rates and the low expectation of euro area both caused fluctuations in the RMB exchange rate. Evidence proves that when the RMB exchange rate mechanism is more market-oriented, it will be easier to achieve a relatively balanced level with timely reaction to market information. On the other hand, it provides a stress test to the risk resistance of the central bank's regulation system, financial institutions, and relevant export enterprises. It is an urgent task for the central bank and relevant enterprises to learn to avoid loss and stabilize the market in front of different policy impacts of large economies (Graph 5.3).

5.2 Policy Goals for RMB Exchange Rate in the New Period

5.2.1 Exchange Rate Volatility and Its Impacts on Real Economy

1. Theoretical foundations for the relationship between exchange rate and the real economy

Based on the total demand theory, a country's GDP is equal to the level of consumption plus investment plus government spending and plus net foreign exports; that is, $Y = C + G + I + EM{-}IM$. The influence exchange rate fluctuation has on the real economy can be categorized into four aspects: consumption, investment, government expenditure, and net export. Since the government expenditure is independently determined by the government, it is assumed to have no effect on the exchange rate. In this part, we will analyze the relationship between

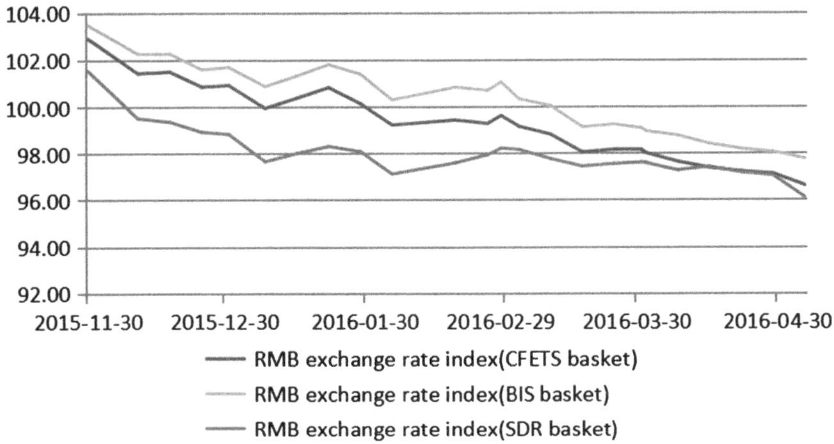

Graph 5.3 RMB exchange rate index

exchange rate fluctuation and real economy on a theoretic level, and then test the actual changes using an empirical model.

The effect of exchange rate changes on consumption is mainly reflected in the cost of production and the wealth effect. When a country's currency appreciates, the cost of domestic material remains unchanged while the price of imported material increases and cost reduces. The reduction of production causes a decline in goods' price. The purchasing power of consumers' currency increases, leading to a rise in consumption. And in terms of the wealth effect, since the appreciation of currency will lead to an increase in the relative wealth, it will lead to the increase in consumption expenditure. Therefore, an appreciation in exchange rate will stimulate consumption. From Graph 5.4, the effective exchange rate of RMB has a significant positive relation with consumption in China's society.

The effect of exchange rate changes on investment mainly lies on domestic loan, foreign capital, and fund through self-raising. If there is no limitation on capital flow, an appreciation of currency will lead to capital inflows, increase currency demand, and ease interest rate, all resulting in more domestic loans in the short term. And the appreciation of currency means relative high prices of domestic material, labor force, and assets. The increasing price will lead to a decline on investment return expectation, thus a reduction in foreign investment. The investment of

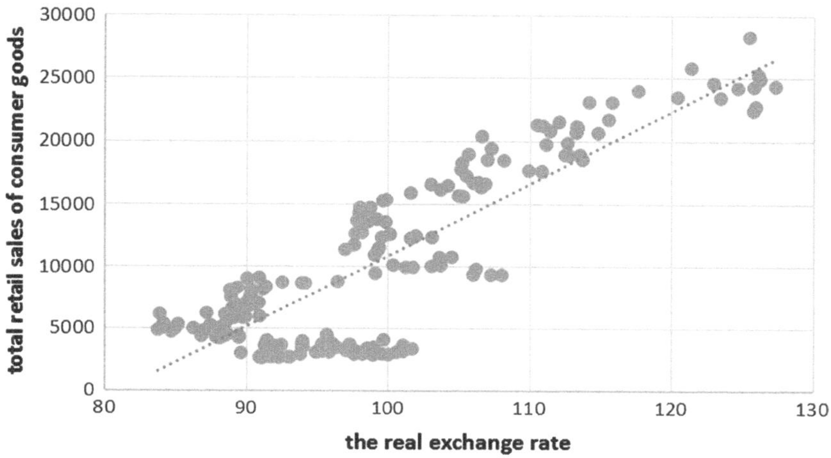

Graph 5.4 The effective exchange rate and total value of retail sales of social consumption goods

self-financed fund mainly depends on the interest rate. With the short-term capital inflows caused by domestic currency appreciation, a rise in monetary demand can boost a significant increase in self-financed funds. Apart from that, the effect of exchange rate change on investment is not simply reflected in the investment decision; the expectation volatility, capital flows, and the relationship between exchange rate and interest rate all have their impacts. Besides, the volatility of exchange rate has a negative effect on investment level. The instability of exchange rate means a currency hasn't reached a balanced level. Volatility of exchange market will relatively decrease the foreign investment level and the domestic investment may also flow away. From Graph 5.5, the effective exchange rate of RMB has been demonstrating a significant positive correlation with investment since 2000.

The effect of exchange rate volatility on net export is reflected on the relative price of domestic versus foreign goods. When a country's currency appreciates, the price of domestic goods would be relatively more expensive compared with the foreign counterparts, reducing competitiveness of domestic goods, causing less export and more import. On the other hand, when currency de-values, prices of domestic goods would be relatively lower than those of imported goods, leading to increasing export and

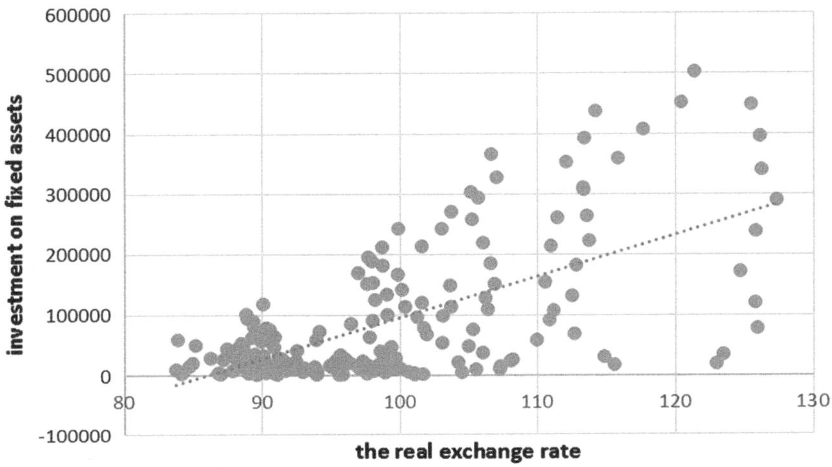

Graph 5.5 The real exchange rate and investment

decreasing import. Therefore, currency appreciation usually brings about reduction in net export while de-valuation causes growth. In more detailed analyses, we should consider how exchange rate changes impact prices of imported and exported goods. According to the Marshall-Lerner Condition, only when the export demand elasticity and the import demand elasticity equal one, controlling the exchange rate, by either raising or cutting its value, can help adjust the number in international trade and moderate the trade deficit.

Overall, regarding the influence exchange volatility has on real economy, there are usually several conclusions as follows. The most influential one is Balassa-Samuelson Hypothesis. It is pointed out that when a country's economy has maintained relatively rapid development for a certain long period of time, the productivity growth rate of its tradable departments would be higher than that of the non-tradable departments, causing frequent current account surplus and leaving pressure for the currency to appreciate. And then, in Mondale small open economy model, because of instability and fluctuation of monetary and exchange rate policy in small countries, a fixed exchange rate policy can moderate exchange rate volatility and help to boost development of trade, investment, and consumption, thus promoting economy on the whole.

2. The threshold regression of exchange rate and economy

Different currency convertibility decides different degree of impacts exchange rate appreciation has on economic growth. When the currency convertibility is relatively low, a 1% increase of the real exchange rate can cause 0.584% of economic growth. But when the currency 's convertibility increases, 1% increase in the real exchange rate can only lead to 0.18% growth in the economy. This means that the opening up of capital account may weaken the influence of exchange rate appreciation on economy growth. Although exchange rate appreciation can reduce net export, however with relatively low convertibility, capital flow would be limited under control. Confidence of the international community on a certain currency is mainly based upon its exchange rate; therefore, the de-valuation would batter international confidence and cause a sharp drop of consumption and investment. Appreciation of the actual exchange rate reflects growing confidence in the country's economy. So with currency convertibility, free flow of the capital gives way to greater volatility in the exchange rate. So the role of an increasing exchange rate may impact real economy through the chain of exchange rate, interest rate, investment, and consumption, instead of the assumption that investor confidence toward the economic development changes and economy responds with continuous action toward the actual exchange rate in the long run.

Different convertibility also leads to different impacts of exchange rate fluctuation upon economic growth. With tighter capital control and lower convertibility, a 1% growth in exchange rate volatility will reduce the real economy growth rate by 0.173%. When currency convertibility increases, the negative effect also grows. A 1% increase in volatility can reduce growth rate by 0.298%. It is because that when the currency is not fully convertible, a strict limitation lies on capital flows. The exchange rate market and the real economy are disconnected and the impact is controllable; the central bank can weaken the damage on the economy through monetary policies. But when the currency is fully convertible, the central bank can tolerate a higher degree of exchange rate volatility, thus more negative influence on the economy, and the central bank would find it harder to get control. When there is not strict control on capital account, the volatility of exchange rate can reflect the instability of currency price as well as the real economy. Foreign investors seeing the growing uncertainty of the economy will likely reduce their investment, thus less foreign capital inflow and more domestic capital outflow to avoid risks. This would harm the economy in the long run. It can be concluded that when the currency convertibility increases, it is more crucial to monitor the exchange rate volatility because of its more severe effects on the economy.

No matter the currency convertibility is high or low, appreciation of the actual exchange rate has no significant impacts upon real economy. This means high or low exchange rate has no say in fluctuation of the economy. Only a balanced exchange rate in line with the country's national conditions can bring lower volatility in the economy. Deviated from the level, be it appreciation or de-valuation does not matter. However, the fluctuating range of the exchange rate strongly affects volatility of the economy. When the currency convertibility is low, a 1% increase in exchange rate volatility leads to a 0.06% increase in economy growth rate volatility. And if the currency is convertible, the effect is stronger; a 1% increase in exchange rate volatility can increase the volatility of economy by 0.12%. Under strict capital account limitation and low currency convertibility, the fluctuation of the exchange rate has a delayed effect on the economy. Then the enterprises can adjust their investment and production decisions in a more timely manner. When the risk does spread to the real economy, its impact would be reduced because of all the measures taken ahead. But when the capital account opens up and when the currency is highly convertible, impacts of expectation effects and capital flow would quickly spread the risk to financial institutions and relevant enterprises, hence more direct and obvious impacts to the economy.

5.2.2 *Impacts of Exchange Rate Volatility Upon Cross-Border Capital Flow*

1. Theoretical foundation of the relationship between exchange rate change and capital flow

Cross-border capital flow refers to private or official capital flow between different countries for higher return, risk prevention, or international assistance. It is developed along with international trade and investment activities. Since the capital flow is closely related to capital investment return rate and the return is directly affected by the exchange rate changes, fluctuation of the exchange rate can impact cross-border capital flows.

Many scholars discuss the effect by quoting production cost effectiveness theory, capitalization rate theory, and relative wealth hypothesis. They think that in terms of capital flow, de-valuation of a country's currency can attract capital and increase investment. In terms of production cost, de-valuation of currency can decrease the production cost in that country, especially labor force cost. A relative low production cost can increase the country's competitiveness in international trade, thus increasing FDI. According to the capitalization theory, international capital will be directed toward countries with lower capital return. As Aliber pointed out in 1983, capital return is higher in countries with strong currency than those with weak currency. According to relative wealth theory, de-valuation of currency can boost additional return in assets transfer in international merger activities, thus increasing the FDI. But from return expectation theory, decision for foreign investment is determined by expectation of future return. The more robust the currency is, the higher expectation of the return foreigner investors will have, the more FDI inflows will follow.

As for those short-term capital flows pursuing return, they are mainly affected by the capital return rate after taxation. Capital flows from lower capital return country to higher ones to attain interest. De-valuation of a currency means same amount of foreign currency can change into more domestic currency. Expectation of return increases, causing more FDI. When the interest rate and expectation of currency stay constant, expectation of return increases may cause more FDI. But if the currency de-valuation causes the expectation of exchange rate to change, it will lead to capital outflow. Overall, the change of exchange rate will make a difference in both the long-term and short-term capital flows. It is negatively related to long-term capital while positively related to short-term capital.

However, because foreign investment is highly uncertain and risky, cross-border capital volatility is great and easy to shock a country's real economy. Most countries take measures to manage capital flows. Because of the limitations on capital flow, liquidity of capital flows can get blocked. The difference in capital return does not directly lead to capital flows. And the influence may be different in different countries, under different exchange rate mechanism and with different degrees of capital control. Capital flows are more sensitive to exchange rate in countries with less capital control.

The exchange rate mechanism has huge impacts upon capital flow. Generally speaking, with floating exchange rate, capital inflow will lead to currency appreciation and bigger deficit on current account, driving international account toward balance. With fixed exchange rate, the central bank will intervene to maintain the nominal exchange rate, which will definitely cause an increase on domestic asset price and the appreciation of the real exchange rate. The deficit of current account gets bigger and total demand further declines. A higher domestic price can also decrease total demand by real currency balance. It can be concluded that the balance of exchange rate market is usually attained at the sacrifice of balance in the domestic market. The exchange reserve is a tool to control exchange rate when capital can't flow freely. More foreign reserve means more room to adjust exchange rate. It is inevitable that capital inflow will cause pressure for currency appreciation unless there is a huge deficit in current account.

Different levels of control bring different impacts upon capital flow. For countries with tighter control, FDI may be limited by the designated quota. Even if there is a high return rate, there are many obstacles for cross-border capital flow. Therefore, capital flow is not very sensitive to exchange rate changes. For countries with an open capital account, the easy channel for capital flow also brings cross-border capital flow to greater impacts of exchange rate fluctuation.

2. The threshold regression of exchange rate impacts upon capital flow

When currency convertibility is at a certain low level, capital flow is controlled within certain ranges; the effect of exchange on capital flow isn't significant. Be it changes of the exchange rate growth rate or changes of its volatility, neither has a significant effect on FDI. However, FDI becomes more sensitive to exchange rate when the currency is convertible. With a 1% increase in real exchange rate growth rate, the FDI growth rate will decrease by 17%. And the exchange rate volatility has a stronger effect on capital flow. A 1% increase in the volatility will witness a 103% decline in net FDI, which almost means a full stoppage to capital inflows. According to the previous theory, exchange volatility increase can greatly add to risks of foreign investment. It has a detrimental impact on capital inflow. Based on the empirical result, the exchange fluctuation doesn't have a big impact upon cross-border capital flow when currency convertibility level is low. In this situation, foreign investors can't change their investment decisions and adjust the capital allocation with the change of exchange rate freely, because of the limitation of capital control. With the gradual opening up of capital account, change of the exchange rate becomes a major factor of FDI. Besides, we can also see that with the development of currency convertibility, capital flow is more sensitive to interest rate changes. As a major index for foreign capital investment return, interest rate has a significant effect on investment decisions. Higher interest can attract more capital inflow, while lower interest rate means more capital outflows. A 1% increase in interest rate can lead to a 0.25% increase of capital inflow. In addition, cross-border capital flow also becomes more sensitive to inflation and the growth rate of real economy.

Then, this book discusses the relation between short-term capital flow and the exchange rate change with the climbing of currency convertibility. The appreciation and volatility of exchange don't have a significant effect on the short-term capital flow regardless of the currency convertibility level. With low currency convertibility, the short-term capital flow is affected by real interest rate and deflation rate. It means short-term capital can be used in speculation and is more susceptible to expected return. Short-term capital flow is influenced by the expectation of risk and return, which promotes cross-border capital flow and drives exchange rate changes and fluctuation.

Special Column 5.1 RMB Exchange Rate and Capital Flow

Since reform and opening up, China has been accelerating its step outward and continues to attract foreign investment using different kinds of favorable policies measures. Capital inflow keeps increasing year by year and shows a prospective trend. Ever since the 1980s, the capital flow in China can be classified into three stages.

The first stage (1985–1992): China witnessed net capital inflow at a stable level. Starting from 1985, RMB exchange rate has been lowered for several times and caused continuous net capital inflow with growing volume. The amount of long-term capital inflow has maintained at around 10 billion and the capital net inflow generally keeps in surplus. The main reason is the rate of capital inflow keeps increasing; in particular overseas borrowing increases rapidly, to the extent that the annual amount of FDI always stands below that of borrowing. What's more, there are several occasions of deficit in current account during this period. But due to a huge capital inflow, deficit of the current account has been covered up for four years: 1985, 1986, 1988, and 1989. Deficit of short-term capital has been made up for and the international payment gets balanced. In this stage, attracting capital inflow emerges as a major measure to balance international payment.

The second stage (1993–1997): Capital inflow increases by big margins, multiplied by several times with tremendous changes taking place in financial projects and structure. During this period, capital inflow, current account, and international payment balance are of the same importance. First, the amount of total capital inflow grows by multiplied times. For instance, the amount of 1993 net capital inflow is 2.9 times that of 1991. And the 1994 net capital inflow is 130% more than 1993s. The amount of 1995 reaches USD 38.2 billion, more than 106% than that in 1994. Second, the amount of long-term capital inflow also grows rapidly. For example, long-term capital inflow of 1993 is nearly four times that of 1991 and is 1.8 times of 1992. Secondly, the growth rate and the volume of FDI far outshine those of external borrowing. It is the key point for the rapidly increasing capital inflow. Therefore, capital flow in this period is greatly different from that in the 1980s or the beginning of 1990s. Over the three years, capital account maintains a high level of capital inflow. The main reason is the excellent investment environment and great prospect for investment return after Premier Deng Xiaoping's speech during his inspection tour to south China.

The third stage (1998–now): After a downturn in 1998 affected by the Southeast Asian financial crisis, China's capital inflow increases again. Cross-border capital flows in this stage are more frequent, high level at a faster pace. Graph 5.7 shows the situations of China's financial account in 1998 Q1–2015 Q2. It can be seen that the amount of capital flow increases gradually from 1998 to 2004. Capital inflows and outflows are more stable; the financial account balance fluctuated through surplus and deficit. In 2004, China experienced an explosive growth of capital inflows and outflows, and capital inflows grew much faster than the outflow. The net inflow of capital of 2005 alone amounted to 159.4 billion yuan, compared with 2004s amount, 81.8 billion, nearly a double growth. After four-year rapid growth of capital flows and continuous increasing surplus of financial account, the 2008 global financial crisis caused a sharp decline in capital inflows and the financial account balance decreased. In the fourth quarter of 2008, net capital inflows added up to 131.2 billion, and then dropped sharply down to 16.973 billion in the second quarter of 2009, affected by the financial crisis. From 2008 to 2012, due to the impact of the international financial crisis, there were fewer capital inflows while the level of capital outflow diminished, and the capital account surplus decreased. In 2012, the level of capital inflows rebounded due to the debilitating impact of the financial crisis. The world's major economies are recovering from the crisis, and capital inflow and outflow channels are increasing; cross-border capital flows tend to be more active.

Graph 5.7 shows changes of the RMB real and nominal exchange rate during a same period. It can be seen directly that 2004 marks a key point for changes in capital flow. The RMB exchange rate is still pegged to USD in 2004, leading to a continuous decrease of the real exchange rate. But after 2005 exchange rate reform, the pressure of RMB appreciation gets released. We can see appreciation in both real and nominal exchange rate. And in the 2008 financial crisis, RMB real exchange rate has suffered a decline. As the crisis is over and economy starts its recovery, the real exchange rate grows even more. According to Graphs 5.6 and 5.7, the real exchange rate is more related to cross-border capital flows.

5.2.3 New Features of the RMB Exchange Rate Transmission Mechanism

Joining SDR has a symbolic significance to RMB internationalization. To a certain extent, it represents the endorsement of the IMF and other official agencies. It not only stands as a recognition of China's growing influence in the world economy, but also helps to enhance market confidence in the currency. SDR currencies are generally regarded as safe-haven currency. Obtaining this status will undoubtedly increase the use of RMB in public and private sectors across the world and increase the RMB proportion in international asset allocation. The inclusion of SDR will force RMB to take further exchange rate reform and open capital account. The convertibility of RMB will gradually increase, finally reaching the turning

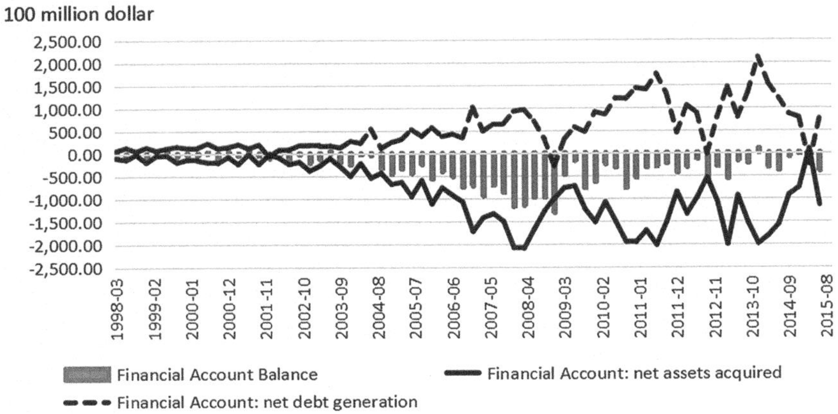

Graph 5.6 Capital flow in international balance account

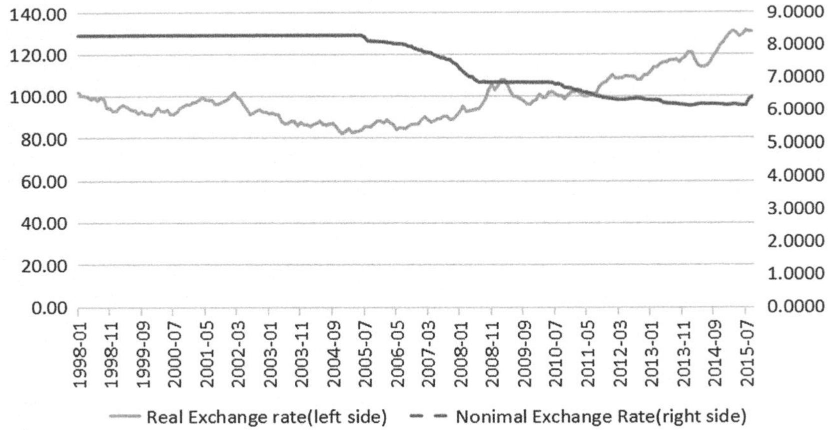

Graph 5.7 The real and nominal exchange rate

point and realizing the regime change. Thus, in the process of the gradual opening of the capital account and market-oriented exchange rate reform, China should pay attention to the transmission mechanism of the exchange rate and economy activity.

1. Growing sensitivity of real economy toward exchange rate changes and international environment

In the previous section, we mentioned that with the improvement of currency convertibility, real economy will be more vulnerable to changes in the RMB exchange rate. RMB appreciation will significantly improve the growth rate of China's economy, and decline in exchange rate fluctuation also accelerates economic growth rate and reduces macro-economic volatility. Inclusion of RMB in the SDR as an international reserve currency can enhance the prestige of RMB. The ratio of strong and stable RMB will create a favorable external environment to promote further development of the real economy. It is also conducive to the implementation of the RMB internationalization strategy and the goal of building an international financial center.

But every coin has two sides. We must realize that RMB's emergence as an international reserve currency also means more responsibilities. China should further open its capital account to meet the public demand in asset allocation. China should also consider the spillover effect of monetary policy, and build its image as a responsible big country. The reform and opening up policy has connected China more closely with the world. As China offers the world new risk-sharing approaches, it also increases its own risk-bearing abilities. China's real economy becomes more sensitive through a more market-oriented exchange rate transmission path.

Mussa (2000) believes that countries with weak macro-economic policies, inadequate capitalization, and fragile financial systems are likely to suffer from the impact of capital flows and may get thrusted into crises with direct accession into the international capital market. Many problems can be found in the central bank, financial agencies, and international trade enterprises. The central bank finds greater difficulty in supervision as it experiences the transitioning period of reform. It also runs into difficulty in learning from other countries' experiences as there are vagueness and discrepancy in policy. As for financial institutions, they are not as internationalized as their western counterparts. Against the complicated international environment, they show more vulnerability in their own system. Export-oriented enterprises have already grown used to stable exchange rate, hence only limited resistance against exchange rate fluctuation. Therefore, as China pushes forward exchange rate reform and capital account opening up, it must take it gradually with moderate control over risks. Throughout the process, the central bank, financial institutions, and relevant enterprises should all take an active attitude in learning, accumulate experiences, and fend off negative international impacts on themselves.

2. Improving role of the transmission mechanism of capital flow

With the gradual opening up of the capital account, convertibility of the RMB enhances, and capital flow will play a leading role in the equilibrium exchange rate. As capital flows are important market drivers to bring the RMB exchange rate to equilibrium in fluctuation, and major promoter of exchange rate fluctuations, policy regulators need to establish appropriate systems to enhance active roles of the capital flow and prevent impacts of negative effects.

As is mentioned in the previous section, capital outflows will increase China's exchange rate volatility and lead to macro-economic volatility. We must realize there are motives for capital outflow in China. First of all, decentralized and diversified investment can effectively share the risks. China has huge capital demands for global asset allocation. Although as an international reserve currency, the demand for RMB assets from international investors increased, the Chinese capital account controls prevented the realization of this demand to some extent. So overall, based on global asset allocation, China has pressure for capital outflow. Second, China is still lacking protection of private property, compared to other countries in the world. Without relevant legislation and management, just for protection of private property, capital would also flow out of China. Third, since 2005, due to the strong expectation of RMB appreciation and strict capital controls, a large number of foreign speculative capital has flown into China through false trade and long-term investments. The expectation of depreciation drives them out. From the historical view of capital flow, there is also pressure for capital outflow at the current stage. As such pressure for capital outflow accumulates, the central bank is urged to step up and safeguard stability and prevent sharp fluctuations of the RMB exchange rate in the short term so as to ensure relative safety of China's foreign exchange reserves. In the long run, China needs to adhere to reform and opening up to strengthen monitoring and supervision of capital flows.

In addition, regulation of capital flows doesn't only mean more attention to saving, but more importantly, China should seek more sources of earning, focusing on monitoring and supervision of capital inflows. Because financial innovations continue to emerge and some inevitably meet regulatory loopholes, capital may flow into China through a number of "legal" channels. Relevant regulatory agencies should stick to the principle of prudent supervision, centralized management of all capital flows, and special supervision on banking transactions, FDI and innovative financial instruments, as well as for large-volume capital flow and highly leveraged funds. In addition, Tobin tax can be imposed upon capital flow of the current account or that irrelevant to FDI. But Eichengreen et al. (1995) also pointed that Tobin tax has a limited effect on adding to the cost of capital flow. In the case of strong expectations, it can't stop capital flight. Then, financial innovations and offshore financial markets will also provide a means for tax avoidance. Therefore, China can consider other methods to increase the cost of capital flows, such as increasing time cost of capital flows—capital flows in and out of any country need to be frozen for two days by the PBOC—or increasing the system cost of capital flows. Only financial institutions (including central banks in the world and systemically important financial institutions) that meet certain credit standards can have large and frequent cross-border capital flow.

3. Higher connectivity between exchange and interest rates

Up to now, China's exchange rate and an interest rate linkage mechanism hasn't been put fully in place yet. Domestic and foreign capital markets are relatively segmented. Effects between changes in exchange rates and changes in interest rates are not significant. From the empirical analysis in the previous section, we can see that along with improvement of currency convertibility, we would witness more active cross-border capital flows, exchange rate, closer connectivity between interest rates and exchange rate as well as an enhanced connectivity mechanism.

The degree of openness of the capital is low; the correlation between the RMB exchange rate and interest rates is weak. The major reasons are the financial markets are not yet comprehensive; the "double rate" formation mechanisms are not yet fully market oriented; then, the capital account is not fully open; international capital flows face strict control; exchange rate lacks elasticity. All such institutional factors have limited the interest rate and exchange rate transmission in market economy. Adjustment of interest rate can't immediately reflect in the trend of exchange rate and neither can slight fluctuations in exchange rate show impacts on interest rate changes.

With the RMB joining the SDR basket, the process of interest rate marketization also needs to speed up. As exchange rate becomes more market oriented, so will the RMB interest rate. The correlation in between will also enhance. The central bank may eventually loosen its controls on interest and exchange rate, driving up both the degree of exchange rate fluctuations and interest rate sensitivity. In this case, interest rates and exchange rates affect each other through the market mechanism to balance domestic and foreign markets. Therefore, after RMB joining SDR, with a series of measures to promote capital account relaxation, market-oriented reforms for interest rates and exchange rate, connectivity in between will be strengthened, and the international environment will more directly affect the domestic market. Vice versa. As the central bank sets monetary policies, exchange rate, and interest rate policies, it should pay more attention to the linkage in between and make the policies mutually complementary to each other.

5.2.4 Rethinking Policy Goals for RMB Exchange Rate

With China's exchange rate reform and the gradual opening up of the capital account, RMB exchange rate would have significant impacts upon the macro-economy for a certain time in the future. Major impacts can be concluded as follows: firstly, increased volatility and de-valuation of RMB will bring pressure to the Chinese economic growth, adding the instability factors in macro-economic. Secondly, cross-border capital flows tend to be more active and short-term capital outflows will face persistent pressure. Thirdly, the impact of exchange rate volatility on RMB-denominated assets will strengthen. China should take measures to fend off systemic financial risks. Fourthly, the opening up of capital account will make economy exposed to the international shock.

Therefore, we hold the opinion that in the near future, especially as the exchange rate mechanism improves, the capital account opens up, and China's domestic economic reform steadily moves ahead, policies regarding the RMB exchange rate should focus on three goals. First, avoiding sharp fluctuations in the RMB exchange rate and ensure financial system stability. Stability of RMB exchange rate can create a good environment for economic development in a complex international environment. It will help prevent fluctuations in the value of RMB-denominated assets caused by huge exchange rate fluctuations. Second, stabilizing expectation of RMB exchange rate and improving government's credibility. The stability of RMB exchange rate expectation is a crucial foundation for stability of exchange rate and capital flow. The central bank should enhance its power of saying as well as its credibility, ensure its own capability to send positive signals, and stabilize the market to face major crises. Third, guiding the exchange rate to equilibrium and creating space for domestic economic reform and internationalization of the RMB. The central bank should actively explore the equilibrium exchange rate of RMB, while the stable external price system increases the intensity and effectiveness of policy tools and creates space for domestic economic reform and the implementation of the RMB internationalization strategy.

In order to realize the policy goal of RMB exchange rate, China should continue to develop the managed floating exchange rate regime based on market supply and demand with reference to a basket of currencies at first. This could be the anchor of the exchange rate. This anchor should be as transparent as possible to better manage the expectation of the exchange rate. And the stability of exchange rate could help to relax the short-term intervention and build a healthy and efficient market. Then, the central bank should lower the frequency of intervention but strengthen the intensity each time it does intervene. Frequent central bank intervention will hinder the market's self-formation and development and can't realize the effective price discovery function, which is not conducive to cultivating rational market players. However, the central bank should make strong intervention in face of speculative capital and international policy impacts. Intervention is needed to show confidence and avoid self-fulfilling currency crisis when the deviation is too large or fluctuations are too huge. Finally, the central bank ought to strengthen monitoring of capital flows and foreign exchange rate. Capital flow calls for special attention in the opening up of capital account and timely monitoring in the process can help with actions ahead of the actual crisis. It is crucial to take measures before the crisis to kill the danger in the bud. China's foreign exchange market size is still very limited compared to other mature foreign exchange markets. The central bank should strengthen its focus on the foreign exchange market to ensure healthy development under moderate pressure.

5.3 Strengthening Management of RMB Exchange Rate

5.3.1 *Choices Regarding Exchange Rate Systems*

According to the theory of impossible trinity, a country must sacrifice one of three targets: monetary policy independence, free capital flow, and exchange rate stability. In the beginning stage of China's economic development, domestic market-oriented reform is not comprehensive enough with heavy controls on capital flow. Selecting a managed floating exchange rate regime is helpful for maintaining internal and external stability of the RMB exchange rate. However, with RMB internationalization and capital account opening, demand for free flow of capital grows fast. Then, a country can choose either monetary policy independence or exchange rate stability. For a large economy like China, independence of monetary policy is crucial, since it is the major tool to regulate economic activities. Therefore, giving up the fixed exchange rate regime and gradually realizing currency convertibility becomes the only reasonable choice. And it is also conducive to achieving a more resilient and flexible exchange rate regime, which is a true reflection of the market price of the RMB, thus promoting the internationalization of the RMB. In addition, with growing financial liberalization, the spillover effects of major powers are more and more obvious. It is impossible to achieve independence of monetary policy without capital account controls. It can also be seen from the IMF's exchange rate regime where all the major countries maintain a certain degree of capital account control. Therefore, independent monetary policy, managed floating exchange rate regime, and limited capital account openness seem to be the best policy choice at this stage.

Judging from the three targets of impossible trinity, China must stick to the independence of monetary policy; therefore, a certain degree of capital control is needed. According to Tinbergen rule, certain capital account controls provide more management tools for the central bank, helpful for achieving multiple monetary policy objectives. Furthermore, Mundell-Fleming model also pointed that monetary policy will have a stronger effect under the floating exchange rate system. As a result, maintaining independence and effectiveness of monetary policy is just the choice to go for the central bank.

When China initiated the exchange rate reform in 2005, it decided upon managed floating exchange rate regime "based on market supply and demand, with reference to a basket of currencies". Managed floating exchange rate regime can fully reflect market supply and demand, and also make a strong intervention in extreme exchange rate fluctuations. It is the best choice of the RMB exchange rate regime currently. The central bank can set a range to allow the exchange rate to fluctuate. Allowing certain fluctuation of the exchange rate can help China accumulate experiences to fend off fluctuations, do pressure test in financial institutions, and promote deepening of China's financial market. Under the attack of speculative investment or crisis, the RMB foreign exchange market is vulnerable to devastating damages since it is still small in scale and immature in experience. Under such backdrop, the central bank is supposed to guide the expectation of the RMB and make strong interventions to stabilize the exchange rate in an appropriate time to prevent further spread of crisis and stabilize the exchange rate market.

China's exchange rate policy objectives must be coordinated with the objective of the government's work and monetary policy while the RMB exchange rate reform and capital account liberalization must be coordinated with the promotion of structural reform. According to the Mundell-Fleming model, effectiveness of fiscal policy and monetary policy is different under different circumstances of capital flow or different exchange rate regimes. Due to capital controls and fixed exchange rate regime in the past, fiscal policy has a stronger stimulating effect upon the economy. But with improvement of exchange rate reform and capital account liberation, the effectiveness of fiscal policy may gradually weaken while monetary policy becomes more effective. If the central bank still sticks to a proactive fiscal policy to boost the economy, it may impose pressure of depreciation in the foreign exchange market. In addition, China's current exchange rate is caught in a dilemma. On the one hand, RMB internationalization and the building of international financial hub need a stable exchange rate with prospective appreciation expectation. On the other, the downward pressure and the risk of debt and deflation call for RMB de-valuation so as to provide room for an easy policy. Therefore, reform of RMB exchange rate regime must be coordinated with domestic economic reform measures to improve resource allocation efficiency. Enhancing confidence in China's economy, maintaining the stable domestic macro-economic environment is the foundation for RMB exchange rate stability and appreciation in the long run.

With the gradual opening up of the capital account, capital flow becomes a more and more crucial element that can't be ignored. Among impacts of capital flow upon macro-economy, the most important is expectation and behavior of micro-entities. For them, the real interest rate determined by the deflation and nominal interest rate is crucial. But as the linkage mechanism between exchange rate and interest rate hasn't been put in place yet, risks are likely to be exposed in a complex environment. In mature economies, exchange rates are extremely sensitive to interest rates. The central bank can regulate the country's interest rates to indirectly impact on exchange rates through the market mechanism. Compared to direct intervention in the currency market, this measure cost less and does no harm to the central bank's credibility. Against current background, China needs to consider economic situations both at home and abroad, take the initiative for reform, steadily coordinate interest and exchange rate reform, liberate the capital account, and gradually make progress. In the meanwhile, it should pay attention to the construction and maintenance of government credibility, and improve the effectiveness of government guidance on exchange rate market through indirect involvement.

5.3.2 *Managing Exchange Rate Volatility*

With the gradual reform of exchange rate and opening up of capital account, volatility of exchange rate inevitably expands. Exchange rate reform is so complex that it may easily produce systemic risks. Therefore, with increasing currency convertibility, management of exchange rate fluctuations and maintenance of a robust exchange rate market is an important part of the central bank's policy goals. Specifically, China needs to enhance its managing capability from the following aspects.

1. Confirming the managed floating exchange rate system "based on market supply and demand with reference to a basket of currencies" to provide a clear "anchor" for the RMB exchange rate fluctuations. Major fluctuations of the exchange rate mainly come from inconstant market expectation against the actual level of balance. According to CFETS index, if we can specify the currency and its weight in the basket, we can to a certain extent stabilize market expectation.
2. The central bank should reduce the frequency of market intervention while enhancing the intensity of each to show its ability to maintain stability. In the gradual opening up of the capital account, it is inevitable that the exchange rate volatility will increase. With short-term, small-scale fluctuation of the exchange rate, the central bank should let the market decide, to fully reflect market demand and supply. Yet in times of crises, the central bank should take strong measures in intervention to demonstrate its confidence in maintaining the market stability.
3. Strengthening communication between the government, enterprises, and the market to clarify policy transmission and enhance

policy credibility. As the central bank maps its policies, it should initiate positive communication with the markets, financial institutions, and businesses so that the policies can better reflect the demands of the market players. In implementation of policies, the central bank should offer policy interpretation to help the market better understand the aims and expected utility. In this way, policies can better perform their roles and not cause fluctuations in the market because of public misunderstanding.

4. Developing the financial markets and improving resilience of the financial institutions and trade enterprises toward exchange rate risks. Organized training can make market players fully understand the RMB exchange rate fluctuations so that they can rationally use financial instruments to hedge and resolve exchange rate risks in daily operations. Stress tests on the financial markets can enhance their resilience against currency fluctuations and improve their operating stability.
5. Maintaining a prudent attitude toward capital account liberalization, and closely monitoring short-term capital flow. Capital account liberalization should follow the principle of being "progressive, controllable, and coordinated". China should not open it up once for all. Rather, it should implement full monitoring around the capital inflow and outflow and strengthen supervision of a large amount, highly leveraged, high-frequency trading. Local monitoring departments should collaborate with foreign counterparts to monitor capital flows together.
6. Speeding up the establishment of financial supervision system to improve the effectiveness of foreign exchange management and strengthening macro-prudential supervision and regulatory authorities' coordination to ensure that there is no risk of regulatory loopholes. China should constantly improve a systematic risk assessment system, build a sound exchange rate monitoring system, and monitor foreign exchange and capital flow. The systematic risk assessment system can help to assess stability of the financial system and issue early warnings to get China better prepared.

5.3.3 International Monetary Policy Coordination

With continuous deepening of economic globalization, the global economic landscape also witnesses great changes. Emerging economies began to play a more important role in international business. Especially after the

2008 international financial crisis, emerging markets have played a key role in boosting the global economy with stronger voice in the world market. The occurrence of the 2008 financial crisis made China aware of the strengthened ties between countries. No economy is a separate entity anymore. Each country's monetary policy will have an impact on that of another country, and the spillover effect of large countries' monetary policy is especially stronger. The spillover effect can spread to other economies through capital flow and now the spillover back from emerging economies to major economies also becomes more and more prominent.

Currently, the international environment is increasingly complex. The United States has entered the rate hike cycle by the end of 2015, while the euro area faces more downward pressure due to inflation and has taken more easy monetary policies. Japan has promoted negative interest rate policy to boost its economy. Monetary policies of major developed economies are quite diversified and inconsistent, lifting the market's preference for safe-haven assets and adding to the uncertainty and volatility of capital flow in terms of their direction and magnitude. The attitude of money worship of micro-entities becomes more prevalent and reduces the money multiplier, thus reducing the velocity of money derived. The whole globe fell into a deflationary environment. As for the emerging economies, the trend in different countries shows a great difference. Economic growth in India and Indonesia stably increases and excels in the emerging economy league. China's, Mexico's, and other countries' economic growth have declined in the complex global economic environment while Russia and Brazil were caught in a slump. Against the complicated international background, systemic risks of world economy increase. In this case, China should, through reform and opening up, improve its say in international negotiations and pay more attention to coordination in international policies and help create a favorable external environment for China's economic policy reforms.

1. Consolidating and enhancing international status of the RMB

RMB's inclusion in the SDR basket marks its official recognition of the world as an international currency. China is now the second largest economy after only the United States. It has maintained a high growth rate ever since reform and opening up and will maintain a medium high speed for a certain period of time in the future. This is a solid foundation for RMB internationalization. Stable domestic political environment, improving defense capabilities, and significantly enhancing comprehensive national strength all help to level up China's international status that gets China actively involved in international affairs on the world arena with a stronger voice. It will provide China with a greater stage in RMB internationalization in its negotiation with the IMF, World Bank, BIS, and so on. China should continue to implement the RMB exchange rate system reform and the gradual opening up of its capital account, comprehensively develop its offshore financial markets and international financial center to enhance the RMB international reputation, and promote the use of RMB in international trading, capital investment, and currency reserve. Only by enhancing the RMB international status of reputation and applying more flexible exchange rate regime can China effectively fend off the impacts of external shocks in the process of domestic economic development.

2. Expanding regional cooperation and currency in circulation

As Germany promotes internationalization for its currency mark, the country made good use of the currency cooperation mechanism in euro area, economic integration of the region, and central position of mark in euro area, and successfully solidified the position of mark in the international market. Different from the Japanese yen, the German monetary authorities chose to develop the non-dollar system, and reduced the blockade of the dollar to a certain extent. In its Belt and Road strategy, China cooperated with many countries in projects concerning infrastructure, energy, environmental protection, trade and investment, and so on, and used RMB as the currency for denomination and settlement, thus expanding the area of RMB circulation, increasing its usage offshore, and improving the currency mismatch. China should actively promote export of capital and other domestic capacity with an edge, so as to promote domestic industrial restructuring while promoting the development of surrounding areas and seeking the welfare of the regional economy at the same time. In the meanwhile, China should encourage issuing of RMB bonds and investment overseas in RMB to enrich RMB investment targets and promote currency swaps. However, we should note that Asia, unlike Europe, has big differences in cultures, economies, and levels of development with its boundary. Regional development still faces a lot of challenges. China should seek common ground for greater development as it promotes economic cooperation.

3. Actively responding to external shocks and avoiding "beggar thy neighbor" monetary policy through negotiations

With increasing complexity of the international environment, the United States and the euro zone's monetary policies will certainly have some impacts on the Chinese market. Faced with the spillover effect, China should actively construct a coordinated response mechanism to prevent their fatal impacts on its financial markets and macro-economy. Besides, China should actively issue policy advice and organize relevant training to enhance the market's capability of crisis-solving.

Those "Beggar thy neighbor" monetary policies, such as competitive de-valuation, have been proven to be harmful. It directly does harm to economic interests of neighboring countries. Although the country's economy will get better in the short term, it does not help improve its ultimate competitiveness and in the end, the country's economy will slide with trade and policy discrimination of surrounding countries. China as the world's second largest economy should assume more international responsibility and fulfill more obligations to avoid systemic impacts out of such policies upon its regional economy. China should step up coordination with its neighboring countries to further strengthen its saying in international negotiations, to avoid spillover effects of other currencies upon its own exchange rate market for systemic financial crises. At the same time, China should establish and improve its risk prevention mechanism, isolation mechanism, and, in particular, the crisis relief mechanism.

CHAPTER 6

The Price Linkage and Risk Conduction of RMB Underlying Asset

International Monetary Institute

China's market-oriented reform of interest rate was basically completed in 2015; by then the market-oriented reform of RMB had also made a breakthrough. More and more funds were allocated across markets under the command of market and price lever, and the price linkage and risk conduction mechanism began to form. So it is necessary to fully understand the development of finance under this new situation and accurately grasp the regularity and characteristics of cross-market financial risk conduction, so as to provide theoretical basis for strengthening the prudent macro-management and preventing systemic risk in the process of opening capital account.

6.1 Financial Market Risk and Its Infection Mechanism

6.1.1 *Changes of Financial Market Risk Factors*

Knight F., the founder of Chicago School, once put forward that the world is composed of three forms of things—certainty, risk, and uncertainty.

International Monetary Institute (✉)
Renmin University of China, Beijing, China
e-mail: imi@ruc.edu.cn

International Monetary Institute (ed.), *Currency Internationalization and Macro Financial Risk Control*,
https://doi.org/10.1007/978-981-13-0698-3_6

The certainty rules out the possibility for any events other than the specific results. Uncertainty means we cannot predict possible results for future or figure out their probability. While the risk means though unable to determine what exact would be the result, participants are able to get a fuzzy or accurate understanding of all possible results and their probability based on their experience or the objective laws. Specifically for the financial sector, risks can be divided into systemic risk and unsystematic risk according to the effect degree, or market risk, credit risk, liquidity risk, compliance risk, and so on according to the different causes.

Financial market risk refers to the probable future loss of assets caused by the financial market's price volatility. It is the main risk faced by various economic entities. Due to the unpredictable price fluctuation, the high debt ratio for financial institutions, and the wide use of derivatives, financial market risk has four typical characteristics of uncertainty, relativity, high leverage, and infectious. How to scientifically measure, resolve, and control financial market risk has been one of the major issues facing global enterprise, financial institutions, and governments.

Column 6.1 Evaluation and Management for Financial Market Risk

The general framework of financial market risk measurement can be divided into three levels: sensitivity analysis, value at risk (VaR), and pressure test. Sensitivity analysis is the basic module of the risk measurement. VaR provides a possible maximum loss for the portfolio combinations under a certain degree of confidence. Pressure test shows the effects of the risk factors under extreme situations. It's a rational supplement for the VaR measure.

1. Sensitivity analysis

The first step in risk measuring is to confirm the portfolio's sensitivity toward risk factors. Risk factors are market variables that can affect the value of securities or contracts, such as interest rates, exchange rates, stock index, and commodity prices. Taking bonds as an example, the adjustment duration is its sensitivity to interest rate. For stock, beta coefficient is its sensitivity to the stock index. For share option, delta is its sensitivity to underlying asset's price.

When using the sensitivity analysis method for risk management, we can make the value of the portfolio immune to all kinds of external sources of risks through immunization strategy. In this way, we will get rid of the dependence on risk factors, realizing zero exposure of single risk factor.

2. VaR

VaR is the mainstream measuring method for market risk. It can not only measure the portfolio's integrated risk, but also transform it into potential losses, that is, the biggest potential loss a certain financial instrument or portfolio can be faced within certain holding period and confidence degree. Differences of holding period and confidence level will cause the variation of VaR. The choice for confidence level reflects the risk aversion degree of the company and the cost they should pay when loss exceed the VaR value. For example, the Basel Agreement requires bank institutions to calculate VaR value of ten trading days under a confidence level of 99%. The logic is this they assume that it would take the managers ten days to find the problem and take remedial measures, while the confidence level of 99% can reflect the balance between the managers' desire to maintain a healthy financial system and the adverse effects for banks when venture capital is offset.

When solving the VaR value, we usually convert the asset's expected return into a combination of risk factors. Firstly, we should value the portfolio under current risk factors and simulate the probable changes for risk factors in the future. Then we simulate the portfolio's value and the distribution for its future earnings, based upon which the VaR value can be calculated. Methods for simulation mainly include historical simulation and Monte Carlo simulation. Historical simulation method directly estimates risk factors' future changes according to the historical data; the calculation is relatively simple. This method has been widely used by most institutional investors. While the Monte Carlo simulation uses statistical method to estimate the historical parameters for risk factors' movement. The calculation process is complex and difficult to conduct back-test, but its theoretical basis is better than historical simulation. Currently, more and more risk managers try to use this method to simulate the VaR value for risk monitoring.

3. Pressure test

Although VaR provides a more accurate method to measure the potential losses caused by different risks and their interaction, the occurrence of extreme events may bring a chain reaction far more than expected. This can lead to an outbreak of systemic risk causing bankruptcy for a large number of companies. So people use pressure test as a supplement to the VaR method under extreme conditions.

Pressure test is used to evaluate portfolio earnings or losses under extreme adverse market conditions which would almost never occur in normal situations. Compared to VaR, pressure test is less systematic and more informal. It has the advantage of fully considering the chain reaction between different markets and objectively analyzing a portfolio's expected earnings under extreme adverse market condition.

The causes of drastic financial market fluctuations tend to be various. First, the improvement of financial liberation and integration increases the freedom degree of market factors. The breakdown of Bretton Woods system, the canceling of many countries' interest rate control at the end of last century, and the two energy crises, for example, all reflected the increase of global market's volatility. Second, the rapid development of financial derivatives also widened the market volatility boundary. They not only created conditions for reasonable decomposition and shift of financial risks, but also increased the interaction among various market factors, making the volatility more uncertain.

Due to the smooth changes of the financial market before the 1970s, the main performance for financial risk was credit risk. However, since the 1970s, great changes have taken place in the international financial system. These changes, marked by the breakdown of Bretton Woods system, increased the volatility of the financial market. At the same time, the advancement of technology and economic globalization substantially increased the capital market's activity and accelerated the capital flow. This deepened the complexity and volatility of the financial market. The price entrainment among international financial markets made it possible for local fluctuations from different financial markets to quickly affect other markets. In addition, the competition between financial markets and the financial deregulation also increased the financial market risk.

Correctly understanding the determinants of financial risk can help us find the appropriate risk control indicators and strategies, so as to hold the bottom line of systemic risk and defend it.

Specially, financial market risk mainly refers to the possibility of future losses caused by the changes or fluctuations of asset's market price (including financial asset price and commodity price). According to different factors of market risk, it can be classified into interest rate risk, exchange rate risk, stock market risk, commodity price risk, and so on.

Since the 1970s, great changes have taken place in the international financial system. The influencing factors of market risk are shown as follows:

1. Since the breakdown of Bretton Woods system in 1973, the floating exchange rate regime has gradually become the choice of the world's major economies, leading to the exchange rate risk.
2. In 1979, the Federal Reserve changed the control target of monetary policy from interest rate to money supply. Western developed countries also gradually give up the interest rate control target during the next decade. These actions raised interest rate risk.
3. Two oil crises led to intensive fluctuations of oil prices and commodity prices, which had a great impact on national economy, causing the global commodity prices risk.

Since the 1990s, fundamental changes have taken place in the global financial market again. They mainly include the following several aspects:

1. The trend of economic globalization and financial integration promotes the globalization of enterprise market and resource allocation. Capital can flow worldwide in a swift and free method in large volumes, increasing the risk of market crisis transmission among different economies.
2. The fierce competition in the financial sector led to a wave of financial innovation. This resulted in government's deregulation of the financial sector, which in turn exacerbated market competition. In the backdrop of the technological revolution, this reflexivity amplifies the risk of the financial market.

Thus it can be seen that the influence factor of market risk plays different roles in different periods. With the changing of time, the key factor that influences the market risk is also in constant change.

6.1.2 *The Spreading of Financial Risks*

In the bid trend of globalization, material resources and financial resources are better matched internationally. However, closer economic links also bring higher risk for the outbreak of global financial crisis. When we go through the financial crisis taking place in recent years, it is obvious that the breadth and depth of financial crisis are increasing over time. The traditional theories can hardly explain how the risks are spreading across nations. Thus, more and more scholars begin to study this topic in the background of open economy. They focus on global transaction, the international capital flow, links between financial markets, and international economic co-operations. Their research covers how crisis in one country spreads to other countries, and what are the influences, in both quality and quantity, so as to better explain the inner mechanism of crisis spreading.

Academic search revealed that trade, finance, and expectation systems are the three conventional routes that pass risks.

Some foreign researchers have introduced one theory: if there is a financial crisis breaking out in one of the country's trade partners or competitors, the currency of this country will depreciate and the expectation of investors will consequently change. The economy thus becomes fragile and might lead to speculative attack and finally financial market crisis. What happened in Thailand in the Asian financial crisis in 1997 is an evidence of this theory.

Some researchers focus on the firm level. When regional financial crisis breaks out, the return of stock prices of firms who have foreign trade will deviate from other firms who don't trade with foreign entities. This will lead to an obvious difference between industries. The risk passes through firms in specific industries through competence of product, income, credit, and asset reorganization.

Meanwhile, the risk can be passed by the financial market. The turmoil in one country's financial system can also directly harm the stability of other countries' financial markets, especially may tighten the liquidity of the financial system, which will lead to the spreading of the crisis. The financial crisis will eventually hurt the real economy and aggravate the unbalance of asset and liability structure which will drain the liquidity of the financial market. And the financial intermediaries will have no choice but to decrease their lending causing short of funding in related countries.

What's more, it has been shown by research results that when a country has been influenced by financial crisis, there is always a deficit in capital account which, in fact, is capital flight. As the investors of risk-origin country have more information about the expectation of economy of their own country, they choose to withdraw from international financial market and the money inflow for other countries is suddenly cut off. A huge amount of capital withdrawal will cause turbulence of a country's financial market and lead to financial crisis.

Another way of passing risks is called expectation route. Sometimes, a country that doesn't have direct trading relation with the country in which a crisis happens may also be affected because of the changes in speculator's expectation.

Due to the existence of information cost and information asymmetry, the market tends to be similar, and investors often choose to follow the decisions of the others in the market. Even if the economic condition of one country differs greatly from that of another, foreign crisis can also lead to domestic crisis, which may affect their expectation to all markets, spreading the crisis.

6.1.3 Vulnerability and Susceptibility of China's Financial Market

Researchers usually study this topic from high inflation and deteriorated fiscal deficit. However, recently, these phenomena didn't show up in China; this method doesn't suit China. Considering the fact that the financial system in China developed from the traditional commercial bank system, residents have limited investment choices and deposit in banks takes the main part of their wealth. Against this background, it's easy to understand why commercial banks didn't attach much importance to the management of risks. Recent years have witnessed a great change in the environment of China's financial system: the rate of non-performing loan increases in large commercial banks owned by government; massive expansion of off-balance-sheet asset and interbank business; easier access to the banking industry; the interest rate liberalization; Internet finance begins to develop; shadow banking thrives. All of these changes contribute to the liquidity risk of commercial banks. Considering China's financial system is based on commercial banking system, the increase of liquidity risk is easy to cause vulnerability and susceptibility of the financial market.

First of all, the expansion of investment channels leads to a higher cost of liquidity. With the general adoption of the interest rate liberalization and the advance of Internet finance, financial products including stock, bonds, fund, and deviates are thriving. The supplement of investment channel attracts part of the money which used to be deposited in commercial banks. In the meanwhile, financial innovation, including co-operations between banks and trust, private lending, and other unconventional ways of finance, draws large amounts of money out of the banking system. This not only causes difficulty for banks to attract deposit but also for statistics gathering and risk management.

Secondly, the rising cost of capital pushed the preference of market risk to a higher level. Let's have a view of China's industry structure. Manufacturing industry still lacks sophisticated technique and adds little value to the products, thus their margin is narrow and they can't afford high cost for finance. Real estate industry has grown rapidly during the last decade thanks to speculating lands and the extremely high housing price in large cities. Their margin is high, they draw a large amount of money out of real economy, and they use this money to reinvest. With the inflows of money keep coming, the bubble is growing bigger and bigger, and the market is also getting more and more risky systematically. Moreover, under such market environment, in order to increase earnings, financial institutions tend to invest more on long-term projects. However, the majority of money is deposited for the short term, thus the time span of lending and depositing is not matched, creating an extremely unstable structure. Once there is a sudden increase for market fluidity need, banks would find it difficult to collect enough money back to adjust, facing serious fluidity risk.

Thirdly, fierce competition in the financial industry lowered the standard of risk management. Nowadays, in China, there are around 5000 banking institutions, 3000 rural credit associations, and 1000 rural banks, all of which are competing fiercely to get financial resources. Considering there are little differences between their services, it is unavoidable for them to compete by lowering their prices. In this situation, financial entities find it hard to insist a proper standard of risk management. In order to capture market share, some banks even "co-operate" with their clients to lend in high risk. Some financial institutions provide services in extremely low or even negative margin. From the firm's perspective, although paying the liability is a heavy burden, thanks to the growing economy, their return can still cover the cost of debt as long as they can get stable long-term money support. Meanwhile, these firms can get new loans to pay the old. Both banks and firms prefer more risks, leading to high moral hazard and adverse choice. In the end, the order of credit market is distorted and the system is more fragile.

6.2 Complex Interactive Financial Relation in China's Financial Market

6.2.1 *Financial Reforms Lay the System Foundation for Market Interaction*

China's reform and opening up has reached a deep level and the reform in the financial field is also processing, which is affirmed by the fact that RMB has been admitted in SDR currency blanket. The reform aims to enhance the efficiency of the financial system, optimize resource allocation, and serve the real economy better.

1. Liberalization of interest rate

The price of money is the key factor of enhancing efficiency of the financial system and optimizing resource allocation, providing a sufficient reason to implement reform in the liberalization of interest rate. The reform began in 1996 when banks were allowed to determine the rate of interbank borrowing by themselves. In the past two decades, China has continued this reform according to the need of economy and finance development. Table 6.1 shows the process of this reform. By 2015, the banks were permitted to determine deposit rates on their own, which marks that the reform is almost completed. Rates determined by market help financial institutes to predict dynamically and set the asset price; this is definitely good to the connection of different financial markets.

2. Capital Market Diversification and Opening Up

With the development of market-oriented interest rate, the capital market gradually opens up in an orderly, multi-layered, and diversified manner. In the beginning of 1992, China set up stock exchanges in Shanghai and Shenzhen, respectively, and also established a special regulatory institution, the CSRC. In 1999, the "Securities Law" was enacted to clarify the status of the capital market by law and regulate the issuance and trading of securities.

The first decade of the twenty-first century witnessed deepening of the capital market reform and improvement of the market mechanism. In 2002, the CSRC promulgated "the Administrative Measures for Securities Companies" to impose provisions on the internal control and

Table 6.1 The history of interest rate liberalization (1996–2015)

	Time	*Event*
Rate liberalization in monetary market	June 1996	The PBOC announced that instead of controlling interbank lending rate directly, it manages it indirectly and that commercial banks can determine the lending interest rate. At the same time, the central bank canceled the ceiling control of interbank lending interest rate
	July 2013	The PBOC canceled the restriction of bill discounting. The equation "discount rate = rediscount rate + basis points" doesn't work anymore. The rate is determined by commercial institutes
Rate liberalization in bond market	1996	In security exchange market, the Ministry of Finance began to issue treasury bonds inviting tenders using interest rates or return rates. It was the first-time issue of treasury bonds of CNY195, 200,000,000 in the market way
	1997	In the interbank bond market, treasury bonds, central bank bills, and the policy financial bonds were issued in a market way. Banks could repo or sell bonds freely, and the rate is determined by trade participants
	1998	China Development Bank and Export-Import Bank of China issued their bonds in a market way
	1999	For the first time, the Ministry of Finance issued treasury bonds in interbank market and interest rates was issued by tender

(*continued*)

Table 6.1 (continued)

	Time	*Event*
Rate liberalization for deposit and loan	October 1998	The PBOC carried out market-oriented reform of lending rates for the financial institutions (excluding rural credit cooperatives). The maximum floating range of small business loan rate increased from 10% to 20%, and the maximum floating range of loan interest for the rural credit cooperatives expanded from 40% to 50%
	April 1999	The loan interest rate for financial institutions below the country level could go up to 30%
	October 1999	A Chinese-funded commercial bank legal person could conduct large-scale fixed time deposit with the interest rate determined by both parties on a trial basis for a Chinese-funded insurance company
	September 2000	The foreign currency loan interest rate has been reformed, which completely liberalized foreign currency loan interest rate. Both sides of the supply and demand of funds can determine the foreign currency loan interest rate based on the variation of interest rate, the cost of funds, and risk difference in the international market. The deposit interest rate control for large amount foreign currency has also been released
	July 2003	Commercial banks could independently determine the interest rates on small deposits of some major foreign currencies
	August 2003	The loan interest rates were allowed to go up for the rural credit cooperatives in the pilot areas, but the floating range shall not exceed twice of the benchmark loan interest rate
	November 2003	Commercial banks and rural credit cooperatives could open postal savings agreement deposits
	November 2003	Commercial banks could implement cap management of small deposit interest rate for USD, yen, Hong Kong dollar, and euro, in accordance with the interest rate change of international financial markets
	January 2004	The floating range of the commercial banks and urban credit cooperatives loan rate is expanded to 0.9–1.7 times of the benchmark interest rate. The floating range of loan interest rate of rural credit cooperatives was expanded to 0.9–2 times of the benchmark interest rate
	August 2006	The floating range of commercial individual housing loan interest rate was extended to 0.85 times of the benchmark interest rate
	May 2008	The lower limit of commercial individual housing loan interest rate was extended to 0.7 times of the benchmark interest rate
	June 2012	The lower limit of the loan rate fluctuation range of financial institutions was adjusted to 0.8 times of the benchmark interest rate, and the upper limit of floating range of the deposit interest rate was adjusted to 1.1 times of the benchmark interest rate
	November 2014	The financial institutions' upper limit of the floating range of deposit rates was adjusted to 1.2 times from 1.1 times of the benchmark deposit interest rate. The benchmark interest rates of other loans and deposits were adjusted accordingly, and the grade of the benchmark interest rate term was appropriately simplified
	March 2015	The financial institutions' upper limit of the floating range of deposit interest rate was adjusted to 1.3 times from 1.2 times of the benchmark deposit interest rate
	May 2015	The financial institutions' upper limit of the floating range of deposit interest rate was adjusted to 1.5 times from 1.3 times of the benchmark deposit interest rate
	August 2015	The upper limit of floating rate of one year or longer (excluding one-year term) time deposits was liberalized, while the upper limit of floating rate of current deposit and time deposit below one year was unchanged
	October 2015	The PBOC no longer set the upper limit of deposit floating rate for commercial banks and rural cooperative financial institutions

risk management of securities companies, and allow foreign institutions to set up Sino-foreign joint venture brokers in China. In 2004, implementation of "the Law of the People's Republic of China on Securities Investment Funds" encouraged institutional investors to play important roles in China's capital market, marking a historical stage with laws to be abided by in the fund industry. In 2005, under the guidance of national policy on finance and economic development, China officially launched the split share structure reform where large shareholders transfer part of their shares to exchange for shares of the circulation, which achieves the institutional transition to enable shares of the same class to have the same rights. At the same time, the Shenzhen Stock Exchange established the SME Board and the agency share transfer system to expand the financing functions of the capital market. In 2006, establishment of the China Financial Futures Exchange and the formal implementation of the revised "Company Law" and "Securities Law" together mark legalization of China's capital market and provide basic conditions for CSRC to regulate Chinese capital market with tighter control.

After the global financial crisis, the capital market suffered a heavy blow, and lost more than 60% of the market value. In order to stabilize the market, hedge the risk, and improve the price formation mechanism, China launched its pilot securities margin trading, and had CSI 300 Index listed in China Financial Futures Exchange in 2010. In 2012, in order to lower the listed threshold for high-tech start-ups, Shenzhen Stock Exchange launched out the GEM, pouring fresh blood and vitality into the Chinese capital market.

In 2013, the Third Plenary Session of the 18th Central Committee of the Communist Party of China approved of the "CPC Central Committee's decision on a number of major issues of comprehensively deepening reform", and clearly put forth the goal of "improving the multi-leveled capital market system, promoting stock issuance registration reform, promoting equity financing through various channels, developing and regulating the bond market, and raising the proportion of direct financing". The same year, the National Equities Exchange and Quotations (NEEQ) expanded nationwide with high-tech, high-growth enterprises as the main body; multi-level capital market construction has made substantial progress. In November 2014, in order to promote the capital market opening and expand the scope of the main investors and stocks, Shanghai-Hong Kong Stock Connect was established. In 2015, the 14th session of the 12th NPC Standing Committee examined the revised draft of "Securities Law", and the registration system for stock issuance was just around the corner.

3. Capital account steadily opens up

Against the backdrop of interest rate market-oriented and capital market reform, more space and more opportunities also emerge in China's capital market for future development. Related to this is the issue of capital account liberalization. Figure 6.1 summarizes the basic course of Chinese capital account liberalization. With the development of the capital market, it is inevitable that it put forward higher requirements for the free flow of funds. Risk management and resource optimization require better risk sharing in global markets. The continuous opening of Chinese capital account and the reform of exchange rate formation mechanism have created conditions for further promoting integration of capital market and global capital market and risk sharing, but in the meanwhile, they put forward new problems. In the context of global market integration, cross-border transmission of financial risk makes the risk management, whether macro or micro, become more complex. Improper risk management can

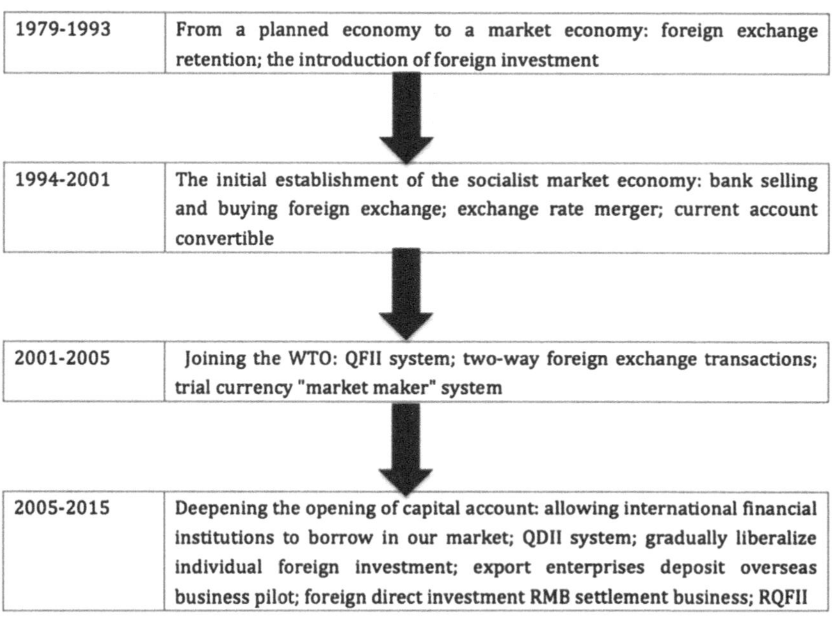

Fig. 6.1 Four stages of Chinese capital account opening (1979–2015)

make the financial system fail to function properly; it will also cause damage to the real economy. In severe cases, it will hinder further advancement of the reform and opening up process. One question that must be answered in the process of capital account liberalization and exchange rate regime reform is how China's financial markets interact with international capital flows and exchange rate volatility, and how risks are transmitted. To ensure that financial reform better promotes the efficiency of the financial system, risk must be well prevented and held under control.

6.2.2 Signs of Market Linkage

Financial market is the carrier of financial assets transaction. We can observe the relationship of intermarket linkage to analyze the correlation between underlying assets' yield and volatility. Chinese financial market mainly includes stock market, foreign exchange market, money market, and derivatives market. Research on its linkage relationship includes both linkage in financial markets and multi-level linkage between financial markets. Just briefly going through the research results of scholars, we would easily find that China has formed a complicated financial market linkage mechanism.

1. Linkage within the money market

The transactions or subjects in China's currency market mainly include interbank lending, repurchasing, commercial paper, bank acceptance notes, large transferable certificates of deposit, and so on. Money market linkage means various transactions or subjects are influenced by the same market benchmark interest rate at the same time. Which interest rate suits the benchmark for the money market? Studies of Fang Xianming and Hua Wen (2009), Jiang Xianling, and others (2012) all have shown that Shibor, to some extent, enjoys its rationality as the benchmark interest rate of the Chinese money market; while Song Fangxiu and Du Ning (2010) believe that the interbank borrowing rates and (seven-day bonds) repurchase rate of the interbank market are representative of the benchmark interest rate of China's money market; Shibor has only a guiding significance for short-term interest rates; Li Hongjin and Xiang Weixing (2010) believe the interest rate of central bank bills is more qualified to be the money market benchmark interest rate.

2. The linkage between capital flow and capital market

Regarding capital flow and financial market linkage relationship, Chen Langnan and Chen Yun (2009) believe major factors influencing short-term international capital flow include the domestic and international rate spreads, the nominal exchange rate of RMB, the expected change rate of RMB exchange rate, stock market investment income, real estate market investment return, and so on. RMB appreciation and the Shanghai Composite Index rise will cause international hot money inflows, but the hot money inflow is not the cause of RMB appreciation and the Shanghai Composite Index rise.

Studies of Wang Guosong and Yang Yang (2006) showed that before the exchange rate system reform in 1994, major factors influencing China's capital flow were RMB exchange rate expectations. However, after 1994, China's current price level and RMB nominal exchange rate have a significant impact on its international capital flows. The RMB exchange rate expectations, the price level, and nominal exchange rate together have become major factors influencing China's capital flow. This means, the actual driver for short-term international capital flows in China's domestic market is their opportunities of arbitrage in stock and real estate and other asset markets, as they wait for RMB appreciation. In terms of internal and external drivers, Liu Lida (2007) argues that Chinese international capital flows are mainly driven by internal factors. The most important external factor, namely, spreads, has little ability to explain capital flows. There is a strong correlation between capital flows and the "GDP difference" (especially the lagged value). Since the reform of the exchange rate regime in 2015, the rise of house prices has led to capital outflow, which has caused de-valuation of the RMB exchange rate and the market depreciation expectation. In the meanwhile, the stock price will fall down, resulting in the "seesaw effect" of stock price and house price.

Currently there are two main conclusions in the academia about the return correlation in international capital market. First, as Eun and Shim (1989) put forward, the US stock market plays a very important role in international stock market information transmission. Second, as Soydemir (2000) proposed, the linkage mechanism for economic entities in capital market and the depth of international trade are positively correlated. In addition to the correlation between the rates of return, liquidity relationship between international markets has also attracted more and more attention from the academic community after the financial crisis in 2008.

Major viewpoints are that the stock market and bond market in the economy tend to be integrated due to non-liquidity problems, and there is a close relationship between market liquidity and the real economy.

3. Linkage between stock price and exchange rate

Linkage between capital market and foreign exchange market is usually reflected by the linkage between stock price and exchange rate. Dornbusch (1980) proposes a flow-oriented view of examining how changes in exchange rate can influence balance of trade and international competitiveness of a country, and then further exploring how they affect performance of listed companies and then get reflected in the capital market. On the contrary, Frankel (1983) suggests a stock-oriented view that on either the micro-economic or macro-economic level, changes in domestic stock prices will affect cross-border capital flows and then cause changes to the exchange rate. After the 1990s, more and more researchers including Ajayi and Mougoue (1996) have discovered foreign exchange market and the stock market influence each other in both short and long term.

Regarding linkage between interest rates and stock prices, many international studies prove that in either developed or developing countries, there is always a significant negative correlation between interest rates and stock prices. Wang Yixuan and Qu Wenzhou (2005) demonstrate through empirical evidence that the linkage between interest rate and stock price in China is very weak. In other words, neither of the two variables changes the other. Jiang Zhensheng and Jin Ge (2001) et al. believe that there is a difference between the transmissions of two markets. The influence from the stock price to interest rate is significant, while the reverse is relatively weak.

4. RMB offshore and onshore market linkage

Onshore market of RMB was formed in 1994 and has been developing with reform of China's foreign exchange system continuously. In 1994, China had its first large-scale exchange rate regime reform, during which China decided to abolish the former practice of foreign exchange retention, turning over, and quota management; impose the foreign exchange settlement system; and establish a unified national interbank foreign exchange market, known as China foreign exchange trading center. That's how the onshore market of RMB was formed. It welcomed a trade-driven soar in trade volume when China joined WTO in 2001. In the 2005 exchange rate reform, it is required that the regime must be a managed floating one based on market supply and demand with reference to the basket of currencies. With this regime, exchange rate fluctuations increase significantly. Then, in the August 11 reform in the same year, further requirements were put forward for improvement of the central parity price quotation mechanism where market makers must refer to the closing exchange rate in the interbank foreign exchange market the day before when they offer a quotation. This is equivalent to set a reference price to the central price and have made clear the sources of quotation for market makers. This reform has tremendously reduced the chance of central bank manipulation of the middle price, thereby leaving the right of price setting to the market. As a result, the onshore exchange rate of RMB has taken an important step toward market-oriented mechanism.

Offshore market of RMB started in 1996, with its origin in the RMB Non-deliverable Forwards (NDF) offered by Singapore, Hong Kong, and other places to Chinese international enterprises. After the expiration, spread is settled in USD to help Chinese internationals fix the exchange rate in advance and to avoid the risk of exchange rate fluctuations. NDF is the most influential offshore RMB trading variety until the early twenty-first century. In 2009, the PBOC announced the "Administrative measures of the RMB settlement for cross-border trade", which has greatly expanded the sources of offshore RMB. In July 2010, the PBOC and the Hong Kong Monetary Authority signed an agreement to enable RMB deposits in Hong Kong to be transferred among banks without the former exchange limit. This move has promoted the offshore RMB settlement and brought China's Hong Kong offshore market of RMB (CNH market) rapid development and created significant substitute for the RMB NDF market. Apart from Hong Kong, Singapore, London, Luxemburg, and other places have also built up their own offshore RMB centers, to jointly help the process of RMB internationalization. In contrast, the onshore RMB market is relatively small and the average daily trade volume is about $60 billion. In the context of RMB internationalization, the offshore market continues to develop and now enjoys an average daily trade volume of more than $200 billion.

Many scholars home and abroad have launched an in-depth study of the relationship between offshore and onshore RMB exchange rate. For instance, Wu Ge and Pei Cheng (2012) have applied the quantitative analyses of the AR-GARCH model to discover the guiding role onshore exchange rate has upon the offshore exchange rate, which means the onshore market is more active in the setting of the RMB exchange rate. Cheung and Rime (2014) have made use of order flow to study the interaction between onshore and offshore exchange rate and discovered that offshore exchange rate had greater impacts upon the onshore one and had significant forecast role on RMB central parity price. Despite all the different ways of research and conclusions, almost all the scholars agree that overseas elements have started to affect the spot RMB market in a more influential way. The transmission mechanism that information of RMB NDF market passes to the domestic spot market makes the RMB NDF exchange rate play the role of price discovery. Domestic financial market and overseas financial market are linked more closely to each other and realization of an independent economic policy system becomes more difficult a challenge. Under the macro-background of a more open domestic financial market, markets are linked more closely to each other and risk also gets transmitted more rapidly. Therefore, compared with capital control, risk management through exchange rate policy adjustment becomes a more feasible choice in the future. Appropriate relaxation of the floating range of RMB exchange rate can increase the cost and risk of hot money flow. It can enhance the independence of China's monetary policy and create conditions for gradual liberation of capital account. The central bank's adjustment of the offshore and onshore RMB market price spread can promote better role of market regulation and prevent financial imbalances and financial risks.

The aforementioned studies have not given full consideration to the non-linear variation of the offshore-onshore exchange rate linkage. To overcome this limitation, Wang Fang (2016) et al. have used a threshold error correction model to discover that when the difference between offshore and onshore exchange rates is small, the onshore exchange rate has a stronger lead to exchange rates of two markets. Self-adjustment of the offshore exchange rate can restore the equilibrium relationship between onshore and offshore exchange rates. The onshore market exchange rate is randomly floating, while the offshore market exchange rate is mainly affected by the onshore market exchange rate, offshore market liquidity, and investors' judgment of the global capital market risk. When the difference between offshore and onshore exchange rate is large, onshore exchange rate loses its guiding effect. The offshore market shows a mean regression characteristic, while the onshore exchange rate chases the winner and cuts the loser. The RMB exchange rates of two markets diverge in terms of their trends. It becomes more difficult and more time-consuming to rebuild the long-term equilibrium relationship through market adjustment. With a huge spread in between, pressure on capital flow increases and the effect of policy factors on the exchange rate strengthens. If the central bank can make good use of the linkage, it will yield twice the result with only half the efforts in intervening the foreign exchange market.

6.3 Cross-Border Capital Flow Drives Up Linkage and Volatility of Markets

To comprehensively analyze relationship between capital flow and the overall financial market, we use a more comprehensive and empirical model based on economic theory (see Appendix 4 for reference) to investigate interaction among short-term capital flow, RMB offshore and onshore spread, capital market yield, excess return with uncovered interest arbitrage in foreign exchange market, and leveraged investment in capital market. Theoretically, changes in the RMB offshore and onshore exchange rate spread, capital market yield, and excess return in foreign exchange market can not only drive short-term cross-border capital flow, but also get affected by short-term capital flow. It cannot be ignored that the leveraged investment in capital market is somewhat an accelerator in this process. Nevertheless, it is difficult to make accurate judgments of the actual situations without reliable empirical study. Previous researches care more about linkage of yields than market volatility and risk, while those two factors are essential to macro-prudential regulation against the backdrop of RMB internationalization, therefore, we take both yield and volatility into consideration for cross-market linkage.

According to the research objectives, we collect and sort out five groups of representative data: short-term cross-border net capital inflow, offshore and onshore RMB exchange rate margin, Shanghai-Shenzhen 300 index yield rate, uncovered interest arbitrage excess return, and security margin balance in capital open market, all on a daily basis. Additionally, the data are divided into two groups by the turning point of exchange rate regime reform on August 11, 2015. On such basis, we examined interactions between these five groups of data and discovered new changes after the reform.

(1) **Influence between market yield and short-term capital flow changes from being one-way to two-way, and short-term cross-border capital has a larger impact upon China's economy with more in-depth influence on the capital market price and leverage.**

Before the August 11th reform, an increase (or decrease) in the Shanghai-Shenzhen 300 index yield can propel a rise (or a drop) of security margin balance in the capital open market, and promote short-term cross-border capital inflow (or outflow). However, this effect cannot have a reverse impact on A-share price or security margin balance by cross-border capital flow, which indicates that before the reform, cross-border capital cannot significantly affect China's capital market or the leverage ratio, but it can be influenced by a rise in share price or leverage ratio and get returns out of it. It is also a prominent characteristic of international hot money.

However, after the August 11th reform, there are some marked changes in the linkage among those five groups of variables. The relationship among Chinese capital market price, leverage ratio, and cross-border net capital inflow has changed from being one-way-driven to being mutually influential in a circular way. Besides, impact upon any of the three variables will cause a reverse strengthening of the trend. This reflects a stronger impact of cross-border capital flow on China's economy, which can cause in-depth influence on the price and leverage level in the capital market.

(2) **Influence of offshore** and **onshore RMB exchange rate margin and uncovered interest arbitrage return in foreign exchange market on capital market yield, leverage ratio, and capital flow declines.**

Before the August 11th reform, an increase (or decrease) in offshore and onshore RMB exchange rate margin will lead to a fall (or rise) in USD, which further causes offshore RMB interest rate margin as well as the leverage ratio to drop (or rise) rapidly and volume cross-border capital flow to decrease (or increase). Yet, after the reform, spread between offshore RMB and USD can no longer cause significant impacts anymore.

(3) **Both relevance of financial market risk and the volatility of the relevance has been strengthened.**

In our empirical model, the volatility of variables represents the uncertainty faced by the market entity, which may bring about economic and financial risks. Before the August 11th reform, three variable pairs are proved to have significantly relevant volatility: offshore-onshore exchange rate margin and uncovered interest arbitrage excess return, share market return and change of security margin balance, and offshore-onshore exchange rate margin and capital flow. Except for these three pairs, other variables' correlations are not significant. Before the August 11th reform, there is no significant correlation between the volatility of capital flow and A-share market index yield.

Nevertheless, after the reform, linkage among variables' volatility increases significantly (refer to Appendix 1 for detailed information), especially among the short-term cross-border capital flow, Chinese capital market yield, and growth rate of margin trading. According to Fig. 6.2, correlation between cross-border capital flow and capital market volatility is almost 0 before the reform, while Fig. 6.3 shows a significant increase of the correlation afterward. For most of the time, volatility of capital flow is positively correlated with uncertainty of capital market, and the correlation itself fluctuates in a big way. It indicates that greater elasticity of RMB exchange rate enhances the correlation between short-term capital flow and the risk of capital market, which needs more macro-prudential regulation.

Under the background of deepening reform, it is particularly necessary to study how capital flow and financial market correlate with each other. Previous researches often examine situations with high inflation and deterioration of fiscal deficit, which have never happened in China. So it is

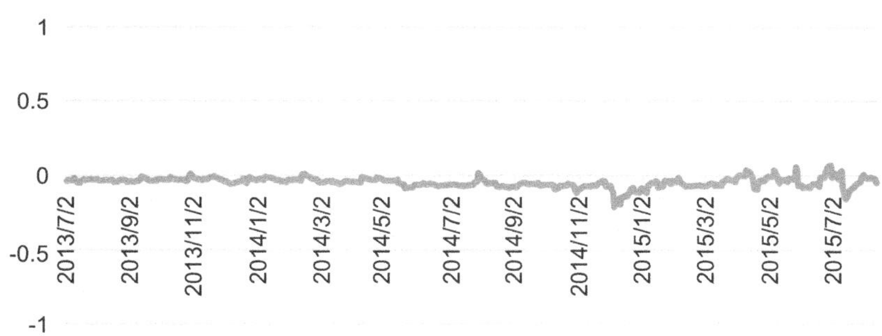

Fig. 6.2 Dynamic correlation coefficients between capital flow and capital market yield volatility. (Before the August 11th reform)

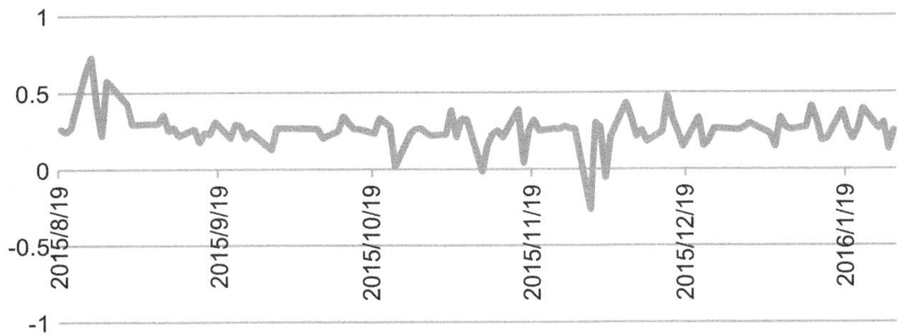

Fig. 6.3 Dynamic correlation coefficients between capital flow and capital market yield volatility. (After the August 11th reform)

difficult to apply previous research results to the study the fragility of China's current financial system. China's financial system is established gradually on the basis of commercial banks as the main body, with barely any channels for private investment. People's savings usually exist in the form of deposits, and the commercial banks do not have enough awareness to fend off liquidity risks. However, over the recent years, with national commercial banks stripping off their bad assets and securitizing credit assets, along with looser regulation on bank entry, rapid progress of interest rate liberalization, and prosperity of Internet finance and shadow banking, ecosystem of the financial system has taken seismic changes and the liquidity risk of commercial banks sharply increased. Generally speaking, financial institutions' risks all focused on the following three aspects. First, increasing investment channels have driven up the cost of liquidity. Second, an increasing capital cost has brought up the market risk appetite. Third, fierce peer competition has reduced the risk control standards of financial institutions. Therefore, in order to accurately evaluate impacts of capital on financial market and understand their correlation, it is necessary to consider business changes in financial institutions and liquidity volatility at the same time, and carry out comprehensive analyses of risk in the market and in financial institutions to find an effective path for macro-prudential management.

CHAPTER 7

Bank Internationalization and Risk Prevention

International Monetary Institute

With the growing of RMB internationalization and opening-up of China's economy, China's banking industry is undergoing significant changes in its external operating environment: it will meet a huge opportunity for international expansion that will further promote its two dimensions: customers and products. The overseas business scale and income sources will be consequently increased. With the rising proportion of overseas operations, assets, and income, banks will face a more complex market environment and regulations. Risk exposure, in both quantity and structure, will be greatly adjusted; banks will be required to strengthen the risk management to prevent impacts inflicted by various risks.

International Monetary Institute (✉)
Renmin University of China, Beijing, China
e-mail: imi@ruc.edu.cn

International Monetary Institute (ed.), *Currency Internationalization and Macro Financial Risk Control*,
https://doi.org/10.1007/978-981-13-0698-3_7

7.1 The Current Situation and Development Opportunities

7.1.1 International Operation Has Become a Trend

Banks in China have long been the major driving force of allocating financial resources and providing financial services. Whether it is the result of marketization after China's opening up or the need of bank transformation, banks are actively pursuing internationalization strategy, and regard internationalization as one of the main indicators to measure their comprehensive competitiveness. Chinese banks highlight international financing, customer searching, business expanding, resource allocation optimizing, and portfolio risk reducing. To that end, banks will start from two dimensions: the financial product diversification and customer base internationalization to enhance the internationalization of balance sheets and overall returns. At present, most commercial and policy banks in China are in the early stage of internationalization. The Bank of China, as the largest state-owned commercial bank with the highest degree of internationalization, its overseas assets in 2015 and overseas profits accounted for 27.01% and 23.64%, respectively, can be hardly considered high compared to other global systemically important banks. In order to echo the internationalization of enterprises and the Belt and Road initiative, policy banks are also going global. By the end of 2014, the international business of National Development Bank stretched to 115 countries and regions around the world, with an international business loans of $319.8 billion; The Export-Import Bank of China granted 921 billion yuan of loans in 2014, and by the end of 2015, more than 520 billion yuan to countries alongside the Belt and Road. However, from perspectives of assets and profits, Chinese banks lagged far behind compared with western mainstream international banks in terms of overseas assets and profits of large commercial banks (see Figs. 7.1 and 7.2).

According to the objective law of the transnational operation, banks mainly choose to follow the cross-border operation of domestic enterprises at the initial stage and provide financial services for multinational enterprises. It was not until 2003 that Chinese enterprises began to go global on a large scale. They lacked long-term transnational operation experience and unevenly operated in different regions. These resulted in their slow international expansion and their over-prudence in M&A. Due

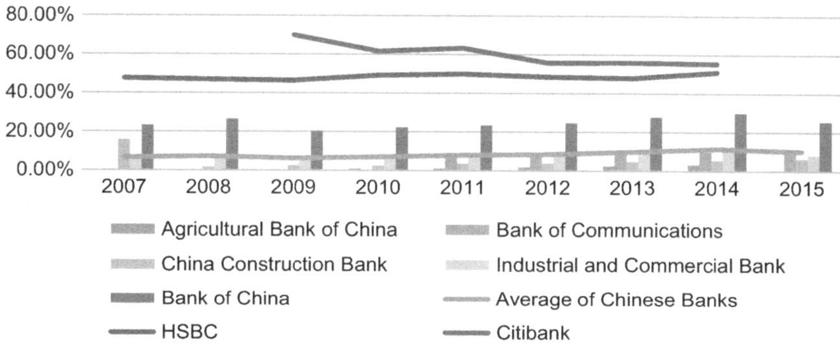

Fig. 7.1 Proportion of overseas assets of commercial banks

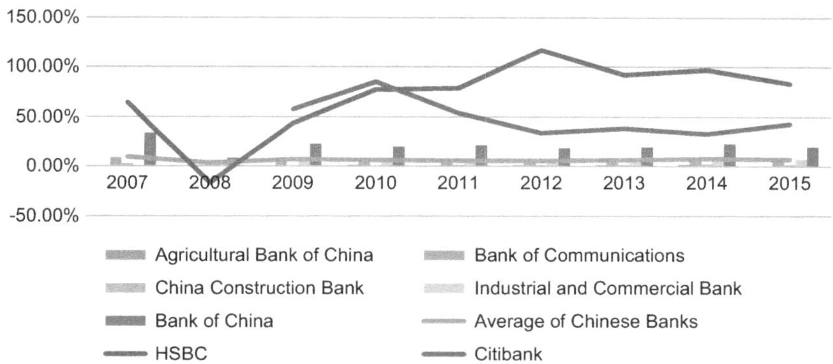

Fig. 7.2 Proportion of overseas profits of commercial banks. (Data Source: Annual Reports of Banks)

to the limited number and level of overseas institutions, Chinese banks suffer from a low level of internationalization, narrow customer source, and small product range. Compared with other mature international leading banks, they have a lower degree of integrated operation and a higher loan business to total asset ratio and interest income to total income ratio. Overseas Chinese banks mainly follow the same business model as their parent banks in domestic market: based on the traditional corporate banking services, traditional loans, syndicated loans, trade financing, international clearing, and settlement as their core business. As the scale still serves as an important indicator in *internal performance appraisal*, the expansion of overseas business of Chinese banks has been mostly reflected in the credit assets with successive years of rapid growth.

7.1.2 Diversification of Financial Products and Financial Services

The rapid internationalization of the RMB has created a favorable condition for Chinese banks to accelerate business innovation and transformation, contributing to increasingly diversified financial products and services. In particular, based on the traditional cross-border services of international clearing and settlement, foreign exchange trading, international credit, and debt issuance, Chinese banks can timely design and provide diversified RMB products according to different market demand.

1. Demand increases significantly in RMB investment and financing products.

With the acceleration in its internationalization, RMB has gradually become an internationally accepted medium of valuation and settlement. Therefore, the demand of RMB investment and financing in both domestic and offshore markets has been stimulated. In 2015, direct investment settled with RMB reached 2.32 trillion yuan, up by 1.21 times than 1.05 trillion yuan in 2014, nearly three times more than that of 2013. FDI from financial institutions reached 1111.631 billion yuan, an increase of 35% over 2014 and of 53% over 2013. In November 2014, the PBOC issued *Notice on Cross-Border Securities Investment by RMB Qualified Domestic Institutional Investors* (RQDII), indicating the official opening of RQDII business to further support innovation of overseas RMB product and development of offshore RMB business.

With the rapid growth of cross-border use of RMB, deposit has expanded year by year in offshore markets including Hong Kong, Taipei, Singapore, London, and Luxembourg, securing funding for offshore RMB investment and financing market. These offshore markets introduced all kinds of products dominated in RMB, which mainly include offshore RMB deposit certificates and bonds, increased from 41.5 billion yuan in 2010 to 564 billion yuan in 2014 in total.

In order to meet the new changes in market demand, Chinese banks have carried out lots of innovation to promote the integration between onshore and offshore market. They have bettered the docking of RMB outflow mechanism and inflow arrangement, forming the interaction and circulation of products and cash flow. In 2014 Chinese banks issued a total 309.4 billion yuan in offshore RMB financing, which is 4.89 times that of 2011, with an average growth rate of 171%. The shareholding commercial banks issued 8.2 billion yuan, accounting for 2% of the overall size.

With the increase in the international recognition of RMB, the demand for investment-related financial transaction products has risen rapidly. The RMB internationalization, formerly driven by trade, will gradually be driven by the development of investment pricing and financial products, which will prompt Chinese banks to speed up developing RMB investment and financing products. Based on the characteristics of the current international financial market, it can be expected that the RMB bond transactions under the capital account will increase substantially. They mainly include:

(1) Fixed-Income Products. Regarding the different opening degree within the onshore market and the classification of offshore RMB products, fixed-income products (e.g., RMB bonds) will gradually become the primary investment targets for foreign institutions to configure yuan assets. Chinese banks have become the main trading institutions of the offshore market and can also enter the onshore bank bond market with a certain investment quota. Institutions can give full play to their advantages in the offshore and onshore trading, and develop more products to meet different investment demand.

(2) RMB Monetary Fund Products. With high flexibility, ideal product yield, and comparatively lower risks, RMB monetary fund products have been popular in quite a period of time. With advantages in products, Chinese banks developed a certain amount of RMB monetary fund products, broadened trading channels for investment products, and intriguing a large amount of non-bank institutional and individual investors.

(3) Derivatives denominated by RMB. Chinese banks, with experience on investment products denominated by dollar and euro,

have begun to explore the possibility of converting dollar and other non-RMB investment products into RMB-denominated ones, thus diversifying products options. At present, some exchanges have launched RMB-denominated derivatives: exchanges in Hong Kong and London offer RMB futures contract products; the CME of the United States, Singapore Exchange, and Brazil Futures Exchange have launched RMB against USD and local currency futures products.

2. RMB foreign exchange trading products increase rapidly.

As the RMB internationalization continues, more international institutions have participated in RMB foreign exchange market and RMB demand in foreign exchange market has increased. Before the full opening up of capital account, the offshore market still plays an important role in obtaining RMB. It is expected that foreign institutions will exchange currencies and allocate assets through CNH markets to manage their exchange and interest rate risk. Additionally, to meet the need of the real economy, they use a variety of offshore RMB derivatives to bring more money into the offshore market. RMB's foreign exchange transactions, exchange transactions, and lending transactions will become increasingly active, with spot and forward RMB exchange volume growing rapidly. It is estimated that offshore foreign exchanges reached approximately $230 billion per day and roughly accounted for about 2.3% of total sum of exchange, ranking fifth globally, well below 42% of the USD and 13.4% of the euro. Increasing demand for RMB financing products will directly stimulate total volume of RMB exchanges. Future foreign exchange will play an increasingly important role in both offshore and onshore RMB market and the trading volume will grow significantly.

3. Establishment of regional RMB settlement platform.

According to the Society for Worldwide Interbank Financial Telecommunications (SWIFT), in December 2015, RMB had a share of 2.31% in the global pay market, an increase of 0.03% from the previous month. And it maintains the world's fifth largest payment currency and the second largest trade financing currency. RMB is increasingly used as international valuation, settlement, and financing currency. In order to meet the demand for RMB international clearing, through designated clearing banks, overseas branches of major Chinese commercial banks serve as the clearing platform to connect foreign financial institutions, creating global RMB clearing networks to provide efficient and convenient financial services. With the diversification of RMB products and expansion of the business, Chinese banks will enrich their RMB clearing business as part of their overseas strategies and enhance ties with foreign counterparts to complement one another. Additionally, expansion and extension in clearing channels and accounts chains enable Chinese commercial banks to accumulate offshore bank accounts and non-resident accounts, which, in turn, will generate more overseas channels and attract a large number of international customers and create further convenience for the internationalization of commercial banks in China (see Table 7.1).

Table 7.1 The distribution areas of yuan clearing banks

Area	*Position*
Asia	Hong Kong, China
	Macao, China
	Taipei, China
	Vientiane, Lao
	Singapore
	Phnom Penh, Cambodia
	Seoul, South Korea
	Doha, Qatar
	Kuala Lumpur, Malaysia
	Bangkok, Thailand
Oceania	Sydney, Australia
Europe	London, England
	Frankfurt, Germany
	Paris, France
	Luxembourg
	Hungary
	Zurich, Swiss
North America	Toronto, Canada
South America	Santiago, Chile
	Argentina
Africa	Johannesburg, South Africa
	Zambia

Source: *2015 Annual Report on the Internationalization of Renminbi*, People's Bank of China

7.1.3 Overseas Expansion and Institutional Layout

Despite successful layout in Asia, America, Europe, Africa, and other regions, international layout of Chinese banks are still imbalanced. Hong Kong and other close areas still remain the primary choice for the bank's international strategy. With its close economic relationship with mainland China, unique historical and cultural factors, and geographical location advantage as the global financial and RMB clearing center, Hong Kong plays a major role in Chinese banks' overseas business. Therefore, realizing diversified profit channels and promoting the internationalization are important for Chinese banks to participate in the international competition with better competitiveness.

The Belt and Road initiative has oriented a new direction for China's international economic cooperation and helps improve the reasonable layout of overseas Chinese bank institutions. On March 28, 2015, with the State Council authorization, the NDRC, the Ministry of Foreign Affairs, and the Ministry of Commerce jointly issued the Vision and Actions on Jointly Building Silk Road Economic Belt and 21st-Century Maritime Silk Road. By supporting countries alongside the belt in infrastructural construction and cooperation, creating regional community of shared interests and destiny, and connecting Asia Pacific and European economic circles, the initiative aims to realize the interoperability of the world. The initiative will stimulate long-term investment and financing in countries alongside the Road, promote convenience for cross-border trading, and enhance capital flows brought by economic interconnection, thus creating a more open cross-border payment and settlement market and providing opportunities for the development of Chinese banks. Chinese banks can select syndicated loans to finance long-term infrastructural construction and large-scale equipment exports based on their strength and layout overseas. They can also provide export buyers' credit, sellers' credit, letters of credit, and other financing products and international settlement service to meet the actual cross-border financing needs.

The implementation of Belt and Road initiative has promoted economy and trading of countries alongside and has created favorable conditions for Chinese banks to further expand and improve their international layout, to better the clearing system, to strengthen cooperation between clearing platforms for foreign exchange funds, and to help construct the international clearing network for domestic and foreign currency. By the end of 2015, among the five major state-owned banks of China, Bank of China had owned 644 overseas institutions; Industrial and Commercial Bank of China (ICBC),

404; Bank of Communications, 15; Agricultural Bank of China, 17; and China Construction Bank, 27. In total, more than 1000 overseas institutions cover more than 50 countries worldwide, most of them being developed countries and regions. Among policy banks, China Development Bank currently has one overseas branch, five international representative offices, and over 50 overseas working groups; The Export-Import Bank of China, by the end of 2015, had set up one overseas branch and two representative offices, and established agency relationship with 1355 domestic and foreign banks and their branches, covering more than 160 countries and regions.

Compared to global banks, Chinese banks are less competitive in the cross-time zone quoting and trading service. In terms of operating time, Chinese banks are yet to provide 24/7 trading service compared with major international banks. Therefore, the market competitiveness should be improved.

7.1.4 RMB Internationalization Brings New Opportunities

During the process of "Going out",[1] Chinese banks are restrained by their weak customer base and the lack of development momentum. Internationalization of the RMB will help improve the customer service of Chinese banks, therefore providing potential for long-term development through accelerating the construction of customer base in terms of organization of internationalized enterprises.

1. Enhancing Chinese banks' ability to provide services for enterprises that go global.

With further internationalization of the RMB, financing cost of Chinese enterprises overseas will be reduced. This is conducive to developing overseas business, accelerating the "going out" process, and creating opportunities for customer base expansion.

Further deepening of China's opening up encourages more and more enterprises to go out, carrying out overseas market expansion and strategic layout. Along with the enterprises' going out, commercial banks in China can proactively enhance their level of internationalization. Based on their advantages in product category and service experi-

[1] Term for reform and opening up launched in 1978, in which Deng Xiaoping urged for internationalization of business sections.

ence, they can complement with development- and policy-oriented finance to diversify innovative financial products and improve their service level. They can form a product house integrated with export credit, project financing, resource and loan swaps, merger financing, syndicated loans, financial leasing, overseas loan under domestic guarantee, and cross-border guarantee.

As Chinese banks have a huge domestic customer base, they are efficient in providing international acquisition, financing, settlement, and other professional financial services for domestic enterprises. Therefore, they will help them take the initiative in regional development by expanding trade and investment, creating opportunity for international business and new resources acquisition. Chinese banks can also provide enterprises with innovative services including various exchange rate derivatives, financial advice, risk management, and investment banking to avert risks and to help enterprises stand on the international stage.

2. Central banks, sovereign funds, super-sovereign institutions, and exchanges will become new strategic clients of Chinese banks.

The RMB, as a new SDR currency, shares the same role of a reserve currency as the USD, euro, and other international currencies. To certain extent, this clears the technical barrier and legal obstacles for central banks to hold RMB on a large scale, enabling them to hold and allocate RMB assets with proper risk management. RMB's joining the SDR will therefore encourage central banks and sovereign wealth funds to proactively absorb RMB assets and promote the allocation of RMB assets in private financial institutions, creating potential customer base of Chinese banks.

Central banks, sovereign funds, super-sovereign institutions, exchanges, and other institutional clients have long set a high threshold for cooperating banks. Consequently, most Chinese banks have been rejected and unable to establish business ties with them. Fortunately, with the strengthening of investment and reserve currency function of the RMB, Chinese banks are gradually accepted due to their experience in RMB product design and relevant business as well as the good understanding of domestic policy and market. Despite the lack of experience, they may well become the bridge through which international clients invest in domestic and overseas RMB products. RMB's joining SDR enables Chinese banks to continuously optimize their business model, enrich their services, and establish stable business ties with central banks, sovereign funds, super- sovereign institutions, and exchanges as well as cultivate new customer base.

Column 7.1 Opportunities and Challenges After RMB's Joining SDR
Lian Ping

Chief economist in Communications Bank of China

RMB's joining SDR will create a rare opportunity for commercial banks, especially large ones, to become more international, integrated and to implement new wealth management strategy. Meanwhile, however, banks will also face challenges in product innovation and risk identification and management. Generally speaking, opportunities will outweigh challenges.

I. **Business opportunities in four major domains favor the development of commercial banks.**

From the micro-business level, commercial banks involved in cross-border-, cross-currency-related business will usher in new development opportunities.

1. **Increasing demand in global asset allocation will promote the development of personal consumption, personal banks, wealth and assets management, RQFII and QDII2 hosting, trust, and other business.**

On the one hand, with the increasing degree of RMB internationalization and openness in domestic and foreign financial markets, personal investment will cover a much broader range of overseas financial products including stocks, securities, funds, insurance, foreign exchange, and other derivatives. Overseas industrial investments in green fields, M&A, and joint investments, together with foreign real estate investment, will create business opportunities for personal financial sector and private banking sector. On the other hand, investment demand of foreign investors for various assets in China will also increase and push the overseas business of commercial banks. Additionally, commercial banks can conduct direct RMB overseas investment through trust subsidiaries. There will be more bank-related trust companies serving as important platforms for international expansion of commercial banks.

2. **Increasing global trading of RMB will promote the development of financial market business, precious metals, and foreign exchange.**

State-owned large commercial banks can play the role as major counterparties and market makers in global RMB trading and become vital price makers in global RMB market. They can develop RMB-related interest swaps, foreign exchange swaps, options, and other derivatives. They can also provide exchange rate and commodity hedging services for domestic enterprises or small- and medium-sized institutions. Research on various RMB or RMB asset–related indexes will not only provide price inferences for market entities, but also to some extent enables banks to have price guidance rights in RMB-related areas. RMB Internationalization Index, jointly issued by Communication Bank of China and Renmin University of China since 2012, has become the representative indicator of RMB's internationalization.

3. **Increasing demand for RMB-denominated international loans will promote the development of financing for trading, international settlement, and securitization of credit assets.**

Cross-border RMB loan business should be flexibly adjusted according to the offshore-onshore RMB interest rate spread. In the first half of 2015, the cost of offshore RMB financing was significantly lower than onshore: cross-border RMB loan business in Shanghai Free Trade Zone, Shenzhen, Qingdao, Quanzhou, Kunshan, and other places gathered a strong momentum, but in the second half, due to the slashing of the interest rate and the heating expectation on the Fed's raising interest rates, offshore-onshore RMB spread inverted occasionally. As the inversion will happen more frequently in the future, adjustments should be made in a timely manner. At the same time, corresponding adjustments should be made in overseas loans under domestic guarantee and vice versa. When cross-border loans reach a certain amount, cross-border RMB loan securitization or credit transfer business can be developed accordingly.

4. **The uprising of international RMB-denominated bonds will accelerate the development of issuance, underwriting, and investment business of investment banks, financial market, and asset management institutions.**

First of all, the offshore RMB bond underwriting business will see many hotspot markets. After a series of mechanisms and strategies including China-UK Economic and Financial Dialogue, China and South Korea Free Trade Agreement, and the Belt and Road initiative, except for Hong Kong SAR, Taiwan, Singapore, Seoul, London, and even Doha and Dubai in the Middle East are expected to become important hubs for offshore RMB deposit and trade, making the distribution of future offshore RMB bond market more balanced. Hong Kong dim sum bonds will continue to lead the market. Besides, renminbi Formosa bonds, Lion City bonds, Emirates bonds, and Sukuk bonds will also see their rapid development. Large commercial banks have accumulated enough experience in issuing dim sum bonds and offshore RMB bonds in Hong Kong market. On the other hand, they have numerous domestic and overseas branches, among which some are regional important RMB clearing centers. So they are more likely to lead the related business. In terms of bond types, in addition to the general enterprise credit bonds, finance bonds, sovereign bonds, and local government bonds (such as municipal bonds) will be more diversified. Second, domestic panda bond market will continue to grow rapidly. In June 2015, the central bank of China clearly suggested "further openness to encourage overseas institutions to issue RMB bonds in China", implying a greater opportunity for panda bonds. Institutions predicted that, after RMB's joining the SDR, the scale of panda bond market may exceed 300 billion yuan by 2020. Third, business consulting, bridge loans, and investment banking business related to these two types of bond will benefit.

II. Challenges in two aspects

On the one hand, more complex and turbulent exchange and interest rate environment requires innovative product designs and operating modes. After the RMB's joining the SDR, there will be more frequent interactions between the domestic and international financial markets. A new environment means that commercial banks can no longer sustain most of their previous products and business models. At the same time, further openness of China's financial and capital account also requires commercial banks to innovate more RMB-related products and services to meet the increasingly diversified needs of customers. If they cannot make timely adjustments, they may face a decline in the customer loyalty.

On the other hand, there will be more requirements on comprehensive risk management for cross-border, cross-shore, and cross-currency business: (1) the default risk: since customers are coming from worldwide including transnational companies and network platform without clear nationality, insufficient information about their credit standing will bring potential risks for domestic banks; (2) local or short-term liquidity risks due to unreasonable setting of the overseas branches or fund procurement; (3) operational risks due to imperfect trading discipline and procedure; (4) risks of interest and exchange rate markets; (5) cross-border legal compliance risks: full awareness of legal risks and market practice in related financial markets is needed when participating in the global commodity and financial derivatives trading; (6) policy risks due to political and economic turmoil, geopolitical conflicts, and differences in regulation. Therefore, commercial banks should take the default risk as the central topic of risk management and implement a comprehensive risk management concerning credit, liquidity, market, operation, policies, laws, and regulations, as well as policies.

7.2 Challenges in the Course of Internationalization

Due to the rising proportion of overseas business assets and revenues, Chinese banks will face a more complicated market environment and regulatory requirements. They will face huge challenges of risk exposure in terms of quantity and structure, which requires them to strengthen risk control mechanism and guard against all kinds of risks.

First, the internationalization of Chinese banks will face information asymmetry: target market differs from domestic market in trading mechanism, regulatory requirements, and compliance control. All these require more time and energy to gradually develop their professional ability and technique to participate in overseas investment, virtually increasing the cost.

Second, Chinese banks will theoretically face market risk, operational risk, political risk, and legal risk during the course of internationalization. In practice, these four risks appear in different forms and need proper identification and management.

Political risk and legal risk are highly destructive, and they may lead to irreparable damage once triggered. Therefore, investors are required to do systematic researches on and be familiar with the laws, regulations, and foreign economic and financial policies of the target country. Investors should timely notice the relevant changes in legal provisions and policies to avoid economic losses due to legal disputes in the process of internationalization.

The operational risk throughout the process of internationalization during the capital inflow and outflow needs special attention due to its various kinds and complex structure. Developed countries are strict on anti–money laundering and compliance regulation. It cannot be ignored that the large number of regulators and regulations in foreign countries could increase the possibility of violating rules in overseas business.

Market risk, including the risks closely related to exchange rate, interest rates, and financial market volatility, is essential to realizing the dynamic balance of the profits and risks in the process of internationalization.

7.2.1 Credit Risks in the Speed-Up Global Asset Allocation

Credit services go along with "going-out" Chinese enterprises. RMB loans have taken shape in the offshore market. RMB loans in total Hong Kong bank loans reached 115.6 billion yuan (2013), 188 billion yuan (2014), and 297.6 billion yuan (2015). RMB discount and loan balance in Taiwan offshore market reached 92.055 billion yuan (2013), 196.297 billion yuan (2014), and 251.95 billion yuan (2015). RMB loans in Singapore exceeded 300 billion yuan in 2013. The British import-export financing in RMB reached 33.9 billion yuan (2012), 38.57 billion yuan (2013), and 33.4 billion yuan (2014). RMB loans in Luxembourg were 235 billion yuan (2013) and 145.8 billion yuan (2014).

Compared with domestic investment, overseas investment of Chinese enterprises increases the political risk, legal conflict, and exchange rate risk, thus bringing a higher default risk and credit risk to Chinese banks. In the Belt and Road initiative, for example, participation in the infrastructure construction projects in countries alongside the belt often requires Chinese banks to provide corresponding financing services and investments. However, Chinese banks may face generally a low yield, long payback period, and possible structural excess risk in investment layout. These imposed stresses on the capability and the comprehensive risk management of commercial banks, making them reconsider whether they can support projects with a long payback period. Since most project target countries are developing countries or emerging markets, they are geopolitically complex and have greater uncertainties in social security, legal environment, and economic development, which may result in delayed completion, suspension of project, excess of budget, and decline in loan quality causing great losses to enterprises and banks.

Since the global financial crisis, the international financial regulatory standards have become increasingly strict. Foreign regulators' adoption of tougher capital and liquidity management requirements imposed stress on international institutions of Chinese commercial banks and restricted the expansion of business to some extent. At the same time, with the increasing integration of global economy and finance, the internationalization of Chinese enterprises and financial institutions is greatly promoted. Hence Chinese banks will face more competition in cross-border loans. On the one hand, Chinese banks have to cope with pressure from local financial institutions and institutions of the developed countries, especially under the adversity of different policy and law environment, higher loan costs, narrower product range, lower service level, and customers' acceptance. On the other hand, horizontal competition among Chinese banks exists, especially when they have similar ratings and low degree of differentiation in product. These imposed huge challenges on cross-border loan business of Chinese banks.

7.2.2 Liquidity Risks Caused by Frequent Capital Flow

1. Stability of bank deposit is challenged by greater openness of capital account.

Gradually losing capital account control makes cross-border capital flow more frequently and increases the volatility of bank deposit. It is fair to estimate that along with the advancement of the RMB internationalization, settlement currency for foreign trade and investment currency will include yuan, investment and financing in securities market dominated by RMB bonds will constantly emerge, and the scale of currency swaps with other countries will be gradually expanded. These factors will result in cross-border flow of bank funds, shaking the stability of the deposit.

From the perspective of deposit and loan ratio, in 2015 the ratio of commercial banks in China was 67.24%. Sixteen listed commercial banks had the average ratio of 73.48%. The figure indicated serious polarization, with the Bank of Communications being the highest at 82.99%, Bank of Nanjing the lowest at 49.82% (see Fig. 7.3). Due to the low deposit yields, bank deposits have been flowing to other financial investment channels. Once the capital account is freed, loss of deposit will be intensified. Therefore, the deposit and lending ratio is worrying (see Fig. 7.4).

2. New round of "financial disintermediation" produces liquidity shock.

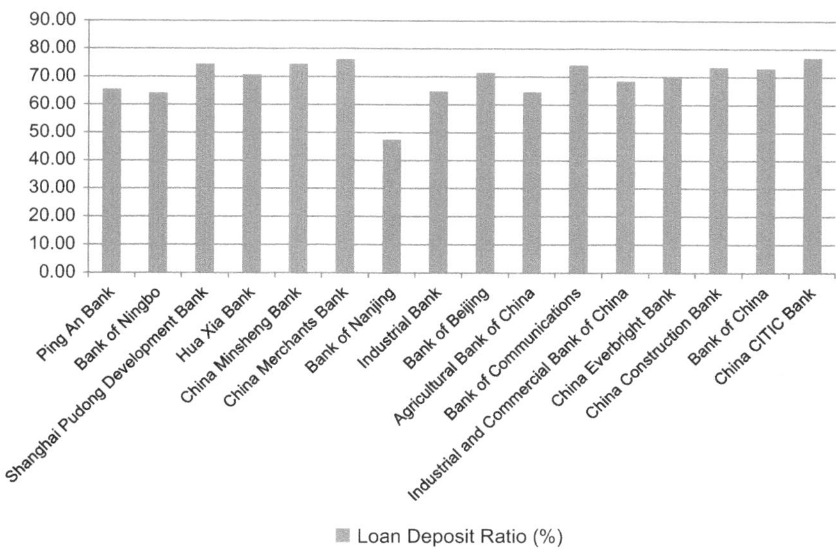

Fig. 7.3 Loan deposit ratio of Chinese-funded listed banks, 2015. (Data Source: Wind Info)

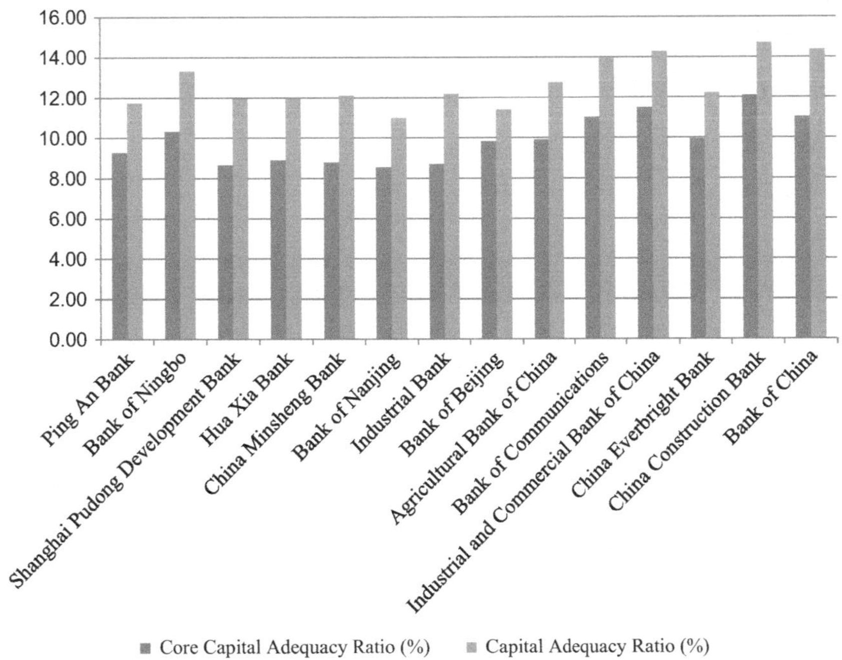

Fig. 7.4 Capital adequacy ratio (CAR) of Chinese-funded commercial banks, 2014. (Data Source: Wind Info)

The internationalization of RMB and the further opening up of capital account will allow enterprises and institutions to finance by issuing offshore RMB bonds. The establishment of a low-cost financing channel could trigger a new round of financial disintermediation and be disadvantageous to banks' assets expansion and profitability. China's economic growth has slowed down since New Normal. To coordinate with the economic transformation and upgrading as well as the supply-side structural reform, since 2015 the PBOC has cut interest rates five times, lowered the deposit reserve ratio four times, resulting in spreads change and exchange rate fluctuations. This increased the net foreign exchange settlement in offshore RMB, tightened the RMB liquidity, and promoted offshore RMB financing at large. A growing number of Chinese banks participated in the offshore financial market, especially the offshore RMB market, to conduct overseas interbank lending. Since more and more market main bodies began to issue RMB debt instruments, coupled with the opening of the SH-HK Stock Connect and the expansion of RQFII, the demand and supply relation has changed within offshore RMB investment and financing market and offshore RMB became less liquid.

Similarly, as the domestic market becomes more open to the outside world, foreign financial institutions will be involved as well. Investment quota of QFIIs increased over the same period by 32.74%, 34.65%, and 21.14% from 2012 to 2015. The number for RQFII was 135.07%, 90.29%, and 48.26% during the same period (see Fig. 7.5 and Table 7.2).

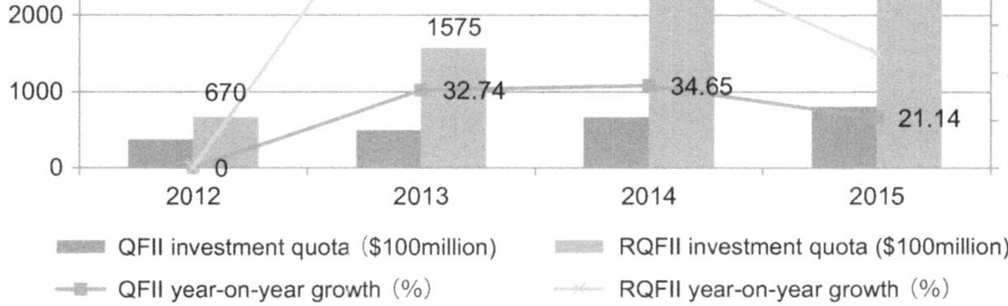

Fig. 7.5 2012–2015 QFII and RQFII. (Source: Wind Info)

Table 7.2 Chinese banks' borrowing and lending from overseas banks and other financial institutions

Year	*2013*				*2014*				*2015*			
Bank	*Index*											
	Borrowing funds		*Lending funds*		*Borrowing funds*		*Lending funds*		*Borrowing funds*		*Lending funds*	
	Amount (100 million)	*Percent*[a]	*Amount (100 million)*	*Percent*	*Amount (100 million)*	*Percent*	*Amount (100 million)*	*Percent*	*Amount (100 million)*	*Percent*	*Amount (100 million)*	*Percent*
Bank of China	2466.61	84.17	770.93	30.34	1121.17	55.61	1003.28	32.35	1121.27	37.02	1032.18	29.38
Industrial and Commercial Bank of China	2708.10	91.67	1023.91	22.02	2613.03	86.82	1329.04	28.42	3065.90	80.45	2282.99	39.21
Agricultural Bank of China	1077.89	73.87	62.40	2.00	1576.12	79.68	201.13	4.85	1642.80	56.57	536.25	10.44
China Construction Bank	1160.81	94.78	1169.60	50.07	1263.63	83.05	1314.83	53.1	2168	71.27	1188.76	35.66
Bank of Communications	878.85	60.71	320.06	15.37	862.86	62.7	279.63	14.71	1031.74	64.47	886.71	22.67

Source: Annual reports of banks

[a]Note: The ratio of overseas interbank borrowing (lending) to overall interbank borrowing (lending)

The entrance of international financial institutions not only intensified competition, but may introduce the external risks into the domestic financial system. Therefore, both Chinese financial institutions' going out to the offshore financial market and the entrance of overseas counterparts to bond market in China could spark the liquidity crisis.

7.2.3 Market Risks Brought by Exchange Rate Fluctuations

Marketization of RMB exchange rate formation mechanism may increase the risk of exchange rate fluctuations and impose challenges to foreign exchange business of commercial banks. On the one hand, foreign exchange investment and trading business of commercial banks will suffer from losses caused by exchange rate fluctuations. On the other hand, foreign exchange wealth management and other foreign exchange derivative business will receive adverse effects. Since the impact of exchange rate fluctuations has been fully analyzed in the previous section, we will not elaborate on it here.

7.2.4 Management Risks Brought by the Expansion of Overseas Institutions

As an inevitable approach to the internationalization of Chinese banks, overseas branches of Chinese banks face the challenge of risk management while creating profit and new business models. The operational risk is especially noteworthy. Due to the differences in laws and regulations in various countries and regions, overseas bank branches need to improve the business system accordingly. Since these branches are just starters of international business such as cross-border RMB settlement, they are unfamiliar with foreign laws and regulations. Their staffs are not adroit in the specific business and the immature service system is likely to cause a loop hole. All these require a better control of operational risk. A typical case is that on February 17, 2016, the Madrid branch of the ICBC was investigated for potential money laundering and tax evasion. Five major persons in charge including the general manager, deputy general manager, and department manager were under custody and the branch was temporarily closed. According to the local law enforcement authority, the investigation aimed to search evidence that "the bank helped a criminal gang transfer 300 million euros from Spain to China." Although till now certain results are yet to be published, it gives warning of risks to overseas Chinese banks in their expansion of business.

In addition to the operational risk, the expansion may cause financial risks, challenging the group management of banks. Overseas branches enable balance sheets to include business in global market and business involving overseas funds enlarges overseas sources in the balance sheet. In the face of the newly developed overseas market, the lack of experience and unfamiliarity with the business model may easily aggravate the maturity pattern of assets and liabilities. Besides, improperly consolidating domestic and foreign statements will trigger financial risks. At the same time, the internationalization of RMB poses challenges on the 24/7 liquidity management since banks will have more foreign customers. Inappropriate use of its own funds, unreasonable allocation of interbank borrowing and lending, and inaccurate capital price valuation will also lead to financial risks.

Lastly, there may be the management risk. Currently Chinese banks are relatively experienced and mature in cross-border RMB business in Hong Kong and the ASEAN countries. With the deepening of the RMB internationalization, the customer base will gradually go international. Transnational trade groups are the most potential new customer base, but they will challenge the market forward-looking and strategic deployment of banks. To perfect global service network and to efficiently screen credit risk of foreign institutions should be given priority in overseas commercial bank branches.

Although Chinese Banks, during the process of internationalization, will encounter many external risks, current risks are mainly from within the country as overseas business and international revenue account for a lower proportion of the entire business. The foreign investment of Bank of China in 2014 accounts for 16.14% of total investment; its total assets in Hong Kong, Macao, and Taiwan account for 16.33% of the total assets of the group, contributing 6.44% of the total profit; its total assets in other countries account for 11.08% of total assets and 6.54% of the total profits. As China's economic growth is in the down side, risks for banks in the future will still be assets and business risks posed by mainland China and regions close to the mainland (Hong Kong, Macao, Taiwan).

7.3 Chinese Banks Still Need to Guard Against Domestic Risks

7.3.1 The Risk of Decreased Asset Quality in Banks

The main business of Chinese banks is credit, and the decline in credit asset quality is the primary risk threatening bank security. Since bank loan is the main financing channel for enterprises, non-performing loans have risen sharply during the process of cutting over-capacity, de-stocking, and de-leveraging as well as shutting down high-polluting and high-energy-consuming enterprises. In the fourth quarter of 2015, total assets of commercial banks grew by 15.6%. The scale of non-performing loans continued to go up while the provisioning level was downing. Commercial banks' caliber provisioning coverage ratio hit 181% and some major state-owned banks nearly reached the minimum line of 150%, imposing larger provisioning pressure in the future. By the end of 2015, the proportion of special-mentioned loan was 3.79%; the overall non-performing loan, 1.67%; and provisioning coverage ratio, 181% (see Figs. 7.6 and 7.7).

From the international experience and the practice of China, institutions can adopt assets securitization and debt-for-equity (commercial banks can convert enterprise's debt to equity under certain standard) to deal with the increasing bad loans. Debt-for-equity provides a new way of handling the bad assets on sheet: it accelerates the clearing of non-performing asset in the short term, alleviates the asset quality of banks, and lowers corporate leverage, thus exerting great influence on banks' risk management. Noteworthy is that the conversion will lead substantially bankrupted enterprises with renewed loans that are not listed into non-performing loans to speed up debt-for-equity restructuring. As a result,

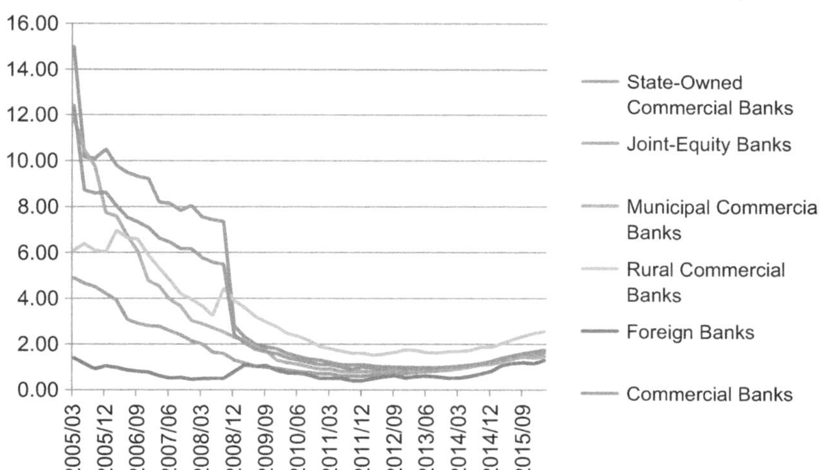

Fig. 7.6 Non-performing loan ratio of commercial banks, 2005–2015. (Data Source: Wind Info)

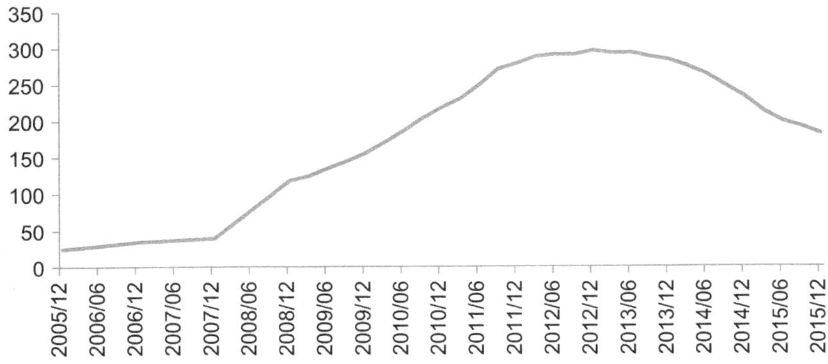

Fig. 7.7 Provision coverage ratio of commercial banks, 2005–2015. (Data Source: Wind Info)

the pressure of asset quality on the bank sheet will rise rather than reduce in the short term. Additionally, the possible moral hazard and the binding interests between banks and enterprises require banks to set up a strict risk isolation mechanism to prevent the tunneling of interests. In the long run, the conversion can help lower the leverage of enterprises and eliminate the zombie companies. However, the shift from creditors to investors forces banks to shoulder the certain cost of de-stocking and cutting over-capacity. Banks must be fully aware of the risks and formulate the corresponding risk control measures.

7.3.2 The Risk of Decreased Profit

The narrowing spreads and decline in asset quality are the two major factors dragging down the growth of bank profit. During the economic structural adjustment of cutting over-capacity, de-stocking, and de-leveraging, the trend will continue for a period of time in the future.

According to figures released by the China Banking Regulatory Commission (CBRC), by the end of the fourth quarter in 2015, commercial banks' net profit in 2015 was 1.59 trillion yuan, increased by 2.43% from the previous year. Their net interest margins (NIM) was 2.54%, up by 1 BP from the third quarter. The revenue-cost ratio was 30.59%, down by 1.03% from the previous year. Commercial banks' non-performing loan ratio was 1.67%, up by 8 BP from the third quarter. Provisioning coverage ratio was 181.18%, down by 9.62% from the third quarter. The loan provisioning rate was 3.03%, basically unchanged from the third quarter (see Table 7.3).

Commercial banks' net profit growth rate was 2.4% in 2015, down by 7.2% compared to the growth rate of 9.6% at the end of 2014. The basically accomplished interest rate marketization, together with the central bank's cutting rates for several times, has negatively affected the NIM. Banking is typically procyclical. The net profit growth has inevitably slowed down due to the macro-economic downturn and deterioration of asset quality. If the asset quality continues to worsen and harm profit, total net profit growth is likely to be forecast close to zero or even negative (see Fig. 7.8).

Table 7.3 2015 major regulatory indicators (corporation)

	1st quarter	*2nd quarter*	*3rd quarter*	*4th quarter*
Liquidity indicator				
Liquidity ratio (%)	47.46	46.18	46.16	48.01
Loan-to-deposit ratio (%)	65.67	65.80	66.39	67.24
RMB excess reserve ratio (%)	2.30	2.91	1.91	2.10
Profit indicator				
Net profit (2015)	4436	8715	12,925	15,926
Asset profit ratio (%)	1.29	1.23	1.20	1.10
Return on capital (%)	17.76	17.26	16.68	14.98
NIM (%)	2.53	2.51	2.53	2.54
Non-interest income to total revenue (%)	24.60	24.61	24.27	23.73
Cost income ratio (%)	26.67	27.21	27.88	30.59
Capital adequacy indicator				
Net core tier 1 capital	95,456	97,062	101,414	106,268
Net tier 1 capital	98,027	99,962	104,463	110,109
Net capital	117,594	119,949	125,073	131,030
Weighted credit risk assets	803,078	833,708	859,033	884,712
Weighted market risk assets	7929	8354	8598	8613
Weighted operational risk assets	68,530	68,672	68,814	77,226
Total weighted risk assets after the application of capital	895,530	926,236	950,921	973,982
Core tier 1 CAR (%)	10.66	10.48	10.66	10.91
Tier 1 CAR (%)	10.95	10.79	10.99	11.31
CAR (%)	13.13	12.95	13.15	13.45

Source: China Banking Regulatory Commission (CBRC)

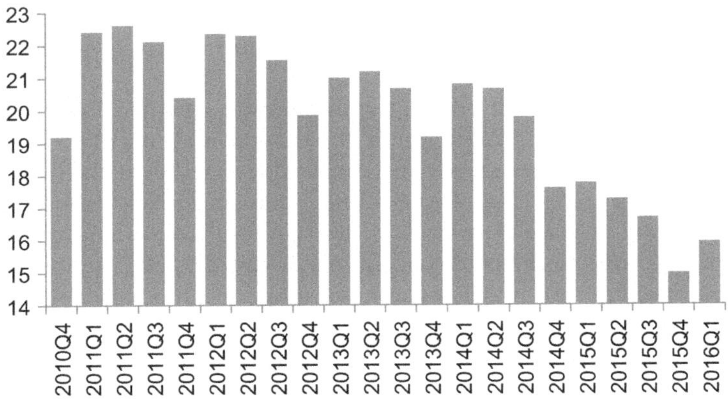

Fig. 7.8 ROE of commercial banks, 2010–2015. (Data source: Wind Info)

With the trend of a slowing profit growth, it is imperative for banks to change the profit pattern. Promoted by the interest rate marketization, off-balance-sheet business has become a key field for the competition among traditional banks. Debts-to-equity, non-performing assets securitization, and the purchase brokerage license to promote integrated management are expected to become the breakthroughs for banks to solve narrowing spreads and the decline in asset quality.

7.3.3 Risks Brought by Interest Rate Marketization

Since the liberalization of controls over the deposit interest rate 20 years ago, Chinese interest rate marketization has been basically accomplished. On the one hand, to meet the needs of macro-economic management, the central bank has repeatedly cut off reserve and interest rates, resulting in a decline in the interest of bank loans; The uprising of Internet finance, on the other hand, joined the competition with higher interest rate and caused a dramatic loss of bank deposits. Banks are facing the pressure from narrowing spreads and the upward deposit-loan ratio. According to CBRC, the deposit-loan ratio of commercial banks was 66.28% in 2015, increased by 1.15% compared to 65.13% in 2014 (see Fig. 7.9). Additionally, asset allocation outside the capital market and Internet financial innovation intrigued much deposit in banks (see Fig. 7.10). Banks will see even more instability in liabilities and liquidity risks.

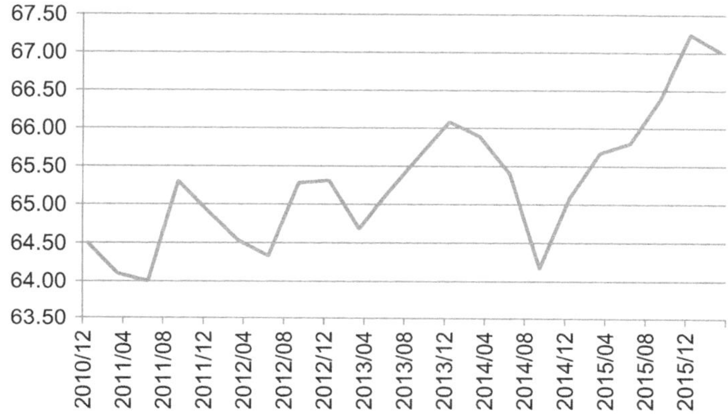

Fig. 7.9 Loan-deposit ratio of commercial banks, 2010–2015. (Data source: Wind Info)

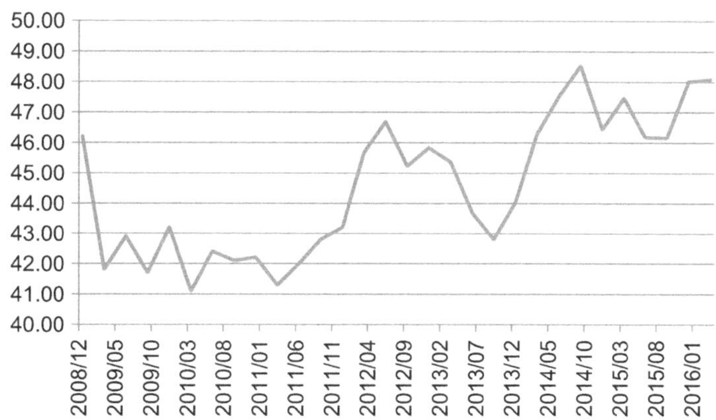

Fig. 7.10 Liquidity scale of commercial banks, 2009–2015. (Data source: Wind Info)

7.3.4 Shadow Banking Risks

In recent years, shadow banks have revealed issues like complexity in transaction and non-standard management while catering to economic and social development. Shadow banks invest their funds to local government financing platforms, real estate, and industries that are highly polluting, energy-consuming and have excessive production capacity. This weakens the effectiveness of the macro-economic adjustment and hinders economic restructuring. The capital source and its use of shadow banks are interconnected with the formal financial system, so poor management will lead the risk to transfer to the formal financial system. In addition, the over-expansion of some shadow banks has obviously caused unreasonable high yields without proper risk warnings, which disrupted the financial order and market environment.

Trust companies are the most important shadow banks in China. They are more sensitive to business cycles and the changes in macro-environment. Against the backdrop of the New Normal in which the economy is in the downturn, with over-capacity seen in many industries including iron and steel, coal, and cement, trust companies ended their rapid growth since 2008 and entered the transition stage. During the early stage of rapid growth, the unreasonably high interest rate and too much focus on businesses such as real estate and infrastructure construction have resulted in severe redemption risk of trust products. As trust companies are faced with the challenge of business accumulation and release, in-depth involvement with trust companies will inevitably bring risks to banks.

Banks should highlight the potential risks in the cooperation with trust companies. First of all, loans initiated by banks and granted by trust companies may have off-balance-sheet risk exposures. Restricted by regulatory requirements and lending targets, banks have the incentive to securitize to remove part of assets from the balance sheet. However, banks will have to bear the losses due to default of trust products. By December 2015, loan trust products accounted for 7.76% of the entire 40,614 trust products with averagely large issuance scale which accounted for 19.52% of overall issuance. Since the current provision rate for off-balance-sheet assets is low, systemic default of trust products will considerably increase banks' non-performing assets. Second, since banks purchase trust products in the form of claiming trust benefit or providing financing channels for other trust business, investment related to these trust products will face losses if default takes place. Third, commission sales of trust products entail potential risks. In the cooperation, banks mainly get commission income from high-net-worth clients: they only need to fulfill the commission agreement and do not participate in product design and fund raising. When default occurs, the bank is not liable for compensation. However, if the bank misleads investors in the sale, it will have to share the responsibility of breaching the contract.

Additionally, the rigid redemption has also developed the risks of shadow banking. Despite that short-term compulsory payment can help promote the business and reassure investors, its long-term effects are: investors will become insensitive to risks; there is an increasing mismatch of risk and return; it will increase the risk of adverse selection; the expected return cannot cover the cost of financing in times of a slowing economy. The rigid redemption is unfavorable to the development of mature financial markets.

In recent years, with the expansion of trust companies' self-operated marketing channels and the increasing competition in asset management industry, trust companies have been less dependent on banks and the proportion of cooperation between trust companies and banks is decreasing gradually. Besides, rules and regulations on real assets transfer, non-standard assets proportion, and methods to count depreciation of assets have been made stricter to put under control the overall risks in the cooperation between trust companies and banks.

It is important to note that the shadow banking businesses that operate credit diversion in the disguise of similar business and entrusted loans are still thriving. By the end of 2014, the size of shadow banks had reached about 46 trillion RMB, among which the overlapping of interbank products and trust products is significant, further enlarging the systemic risk. In this context, on January 16, 2015, the CBRC issued the *Measures for the Administration of Commercial Bank Loans (Draft)*, which specifically stated that entrusted loans cannot be from bank credit funds or issuance of bonds and are not allowed to enter the capital market in any forms. Source, target, and quota are three key elements in the *Measures* to manage the entrusted loans so as to regulate unauthorized leverage lifting and strictly control non-standard credit assets risks. Together with the previously issued *Notice of the CBR C on Relevant Issues concerning Regulating the Investment Operation of Wealth Management Business of Commercial Banks* (2013 NO. 8) and *CBRC Notice on Regulating the Interbank Business of Financial Institution* (2014 NO. 127), regulations upon shadow banking are implemented in both framework and practice.

Promoted by the loosing regulation on local financing platforms and active interbank businesses, the social financing scale expanded to 1.8 trillion RMB by the end of 2015. As is a sign of the recovery in shadow banking, instability and potential risks brought by it are worth attention and vigilance. Additionally, business mode of shadow banking has also gradually entered outside funds allocation in the capital market, Internet financial innovation, and real estate agencies with various and complex forms, further exacerbating the overall risk of the banking industry.

Column 7.2 Compliance Risk Management of Cross-Border RMB Business in Commercial Banks

With the steady progress of RMB internationalization in recent years, cross-border RMB business has been booming. The framework of the international use of the RMB has been completed. Cross-border RMB business in current account has achieved full coverage and great facilitation. A policy barrier for cross-border RMB direct investment no longer exists. And cross-border RMB financing is being orderly released. Commercial banks, practitioners of cross-border RMB business, are actively carrying out cross-border RMB financial services with full implementation of regulatory requirements. They continuously improve the internal management to steadily promote the healthy development of cross-border RMB business.

1. **Full implementation of the "three principles" in operation.**

"The three principles"—namely "to know your customer, to understand the business, and to verify information with due diligence"—are the basic principles of commercial banks in cross-border RMB business. The "three principles" will be implemented throughout each business operation and management of cross-border RMB business with discretion and self-discipline.

Commercial banks will strictly carry out the customer identification ("know your customer"): banks will carefully verify the legitimacy, authenticity, and validity of customers' identity, business conditions, and other documents when establishing business relations with them. Establishing business relationship with foreign residents and overseas financial institutions requires reviews on money laundering, terrorism financing, and other international sanctions. During the business relationship with customers, banks will update customers' information with due diligence in order to ensure the authenticity of identity of customers. Commercial banks should check the contract, background of transaction, product categories, investment target, prices and terms, bills requirement, and other documents while operating the cross-border RMB business ("to understand the business"). Bank should reasonably consider the matching between cross-border financing deadlines and the term of funds turnover. Bank should prevent and control risks through overall understanding of validity of cross-border RMB commodity trade, service exchange, or investment and financing according to the business background and monitoring of cross-border physical distribution, cash flow, and document.

Commercial banks should not only continuously make efforts in verifying the customers' identity and transactions, but also should regularly monitor changes in customers and business indicators. They should review the large, frequent, or abnormal transactions. Once finding suspicious business, banks should timely report to regulators (e.g., the PBOC) and cooperate with the subsequent verification and investigation of the business.

2. **Improving the internal control management system and building a long-term risk management mechanism.**

A sound internal control management system plays an important role in maintaining the healthy development of cross-border RMB business. First, rules and regulations that are within the framework of cross-border RMB regulatory policy and take into account the international practice as well as domestic and foreign laws and regulations are fundamental to internal management. In specific operational instructions, banks should strengthen the prevention and control of major risks, fully implement regulatory requirements such as anti–money laundering and anti-terrorism financing with great prudence. Second, banks should establish institutionalized and feasible risk preview and routine inspection mechanism to identify and avoid high-risk business and the violation of regulations in a timely manner. And they should timely correct the problems found during routine inspections. Third, banks should strengthen the suspicious data analysis and follow-up business management. Banks should build monitoring and reporting system for large and suspicious transactions. Once suspicious transactions are found, banks should timely report to regulators and adjust the customer risk level, access to business, and risk prevention and control strategies to improve the capability of risk control. Fourth, banks should make clear the risk responsibility of personnel at all levels and set up an accountability mechanism. They should strictly implement the accountability mechanism on those who fail to manage and control properly, cross the bottom line, or violate the rules and laws.

CHAPTER 8

Supply-Side Structural Reforms Consolidate the Economic Foundation of RMB's Internationalization

International Monetary Institute

Theoretical research and practices have shown that a strong economic strength is the basis of a country's currency internationalization; the key for the success of RMB internationalization lies in the pivotal international presence of China's economy. However, it is currently faced with arduous structural adjustment tasks and complex international economic environment constraints. New problems and new risks have put continual pressure on sustained economic growth. How can we break the bottleneck of China's economic sustainable development? The supply-side structural reform is the only way. Only by reconstructing the basis of Chinese economy's sustained and efficient development through supply-side reforms will the internationalization of the RMB be able to proceed in a more firmly and longer manner.

International Monetary Institute (✉)
Renmin University of China, Beijing, China
e-mail: imi@ruc.edu.cn

International Monetary Institute (ed.), *Currency Internationalization and Macro Financial Risk Control*,
https://doi.org/10.1007/978-981-13-0698-3_8

8.1 The Real Economy Is the Solid Foundation of the RMB Internationalization

Without a strong real economy, a country's currency cannot be trusted by global currency users for long, and the internationalization of it will become a building on the quicksand, with no solid foundation. From this perspective, so far the RMB internationalization process has been relatively smooth due to the solid foundation of its real economy. In 2015, the RMB joined the SDR basket, which has undoubtedly demonstrated the international community's recognition of China's sustained and rapid economic development over the past 37 years' reform and opening up.

Bergsten (1975) believed that if a country's currency wants to become an international currency, it has to possess a comparative advantage in the international economic system, stable economic strength, and a stable price level. Based on optimum currency areas, Tavlas (1997) considered that the degree of trade integration was the most important factor in the choice of international currencies. Richard Portes and Helene Rey (1998) emphasized that a large-scale and strong economy and intensive foreign trade with a relatively high status are two direct determinants of the international market's recognition of a currency. Bacchetts and Wincoop (2002) found that market share is a decisive factor in choosing the denominated currency. The higher the market share of the exporting country, the more likely it is to price with the currency of the exporting country. On the contrary, enterprises in exporting countries are more likely to be forced to choose a strong foreign competitor's currency for the pricing. Therefore, a strong economic strength and an important position in international trade are necessary prerequisites for the internationalization of a currency.

History has proved that strong economic strength is the driving force and fundamental guarantee for the currency internationalization of a country. Before the pound became an international currency, the United Kingdom had become the factory of the world by virtue of the Industrial Revolution and free trade. The goods produced in the world market, the total economy and its growth were ahead of other industrial countries. The rapid development of the United Kingdom's economic trade had enabled the pound to quickly establish its international currency status. By 1914, 90% of the international trade had been settled in pound, and the United Kingdom's overseas investment had accounted for half of the total investment of western countries. By 1944 when the Bretton Woods system determined the USD as a key international currency, the United

States had established a more modern industrial system with higher economic efficiency by virtue of latecomer advantages, and as early as 1870, its total economic output had been over the United Kingdom's and ranked top in the world. Before euro's official entry, the EU's total economic output had increased from about 6.7 trillion dollars in 1993 to nearly 10 trillion dollars in 2002. Between 1995 and 2000, the economy of the EU countries maintained a steady growth rate of 3%. The EU's overall economic strength had surpassed that of the United States and ranked first in the world. Because of the support from the strong real economy, euro, which formally entered the circulation in 2002, has justifiably become the main international currency after the dollar.

In addition to the economic strength and trade status, currency internationalization also requires the stability of the currency value as the precondition. The essence of currency stability is to maintain a moderate balance between monetary supply and demand, which also means to balance the relationship between the money supply and the growth of the real economy. Before the founding of new China in 1949, the economy of the semi-colonial China had suffered from currency instability and even hyperinflation. After the founding of new China, Chen Yun and other senior leaders in charge of macro-economy took decisive measures based on the needs of the real economy to maintain the balance of supply and demand of daily necessities and important materials through the planned organization of production and smooth logistics, so that RMB currency stability was soon realized. The currency stability had been maintained until China adopted the policy of reform and opening up in 1978. Since then, under the guidance of *Introduction to Comprehensive Balance of Finance and Credit* written by Mr. Huang Da, the former President of Renmin University of China, China's monetary finance is clearly positioned to serve the development of the real economy, with particular emphasis on the balance of monetary supply and demand and the stabilization of RMB purchasing power, preventing financial "off real to virtual" and self-expansion. Moreover, this deep-rooted financial concept affects not only China's domestic inflation management, but also RMB's external pricing, making RMB a currency with smaller exchange rate fluctuation and more stable value in the world since the international financial crisis in 2008. Based on the theories and practices of monetary and financial service in the real economy, RMB has gained the ideological foundation and practical experience of currency stability, and got ready for its internationalization.

The key that a country's currency could play the functions as an international currency lies in the support from powerful national strength, rapid economic growth, and strong export. In international trade and capital flows, the valuation and settlement currency is chosen, to some extent, based on monetary transaction costs, and fundamentally on the trading parties' confidence in the purchasing power of the currency, which mainly derives from the recognition of the issuing country's economic strength and international status. Therefore, since the *RMB Internationalization Report* was released for the first time in 2012, we have always insisted on a basic view that the real economy is a solid basis of RMB's internationalization. Without China's real economy and its indubitable strong strength in the global economy, RMB's internationalization cannot stride forward.

Column 8.1 Indispensable Factors to Cross the Middle-Income Trap

Since the global financial crisis in 2008, there have been unfavorable views in the world about China's development. In the country many Chinese scholars and officials are worried that, due to some institutional and economic deficiencies, China may fall into the middle-income trap despite its rapid development, just like some emerging markets in Latin America, and be trapped in a situation with stagnant economic development, sharp social conflicts, and losing the power for economic growth and its international competitiveness for a long period of time.

Through the history of the world's economic development, it is not difficult to find that there are three groups of developed countries that have successfully overcome the middle-income trap. The first category is traditional old capitalist countries, including the United Kingdom, France, and other old European countries, and the United States. They have fully realized the industrialization with the impetus of the Industrial Revolution, and built a whole set of self-upgrading industrial system in the country and in the regional alliance. In the course of economic development and industrialization, these countries have, through foreign wars and colonization, achieved the plundering of overseas resources and wealth, and thus built a relatively perfect social security system in their own countries, and, to some extent, transferred social contradictions to abroad. The second category is countries like Japan, South Korea, and Singapore.

After the Second World War, they have undertaken technology transfers and large amounts of orders that were made out of international strategic considerations by the countries in the first category, based on which they have established part of self-improving and updated industrial system, and achieved economic growth and consequently successful entry to the rank of developed countries. However, they are not independent in many fields, such as politics, economy, and military affairs. They are taken and won by the countries in the first category in terms of international affairs. The third category is Australia and Canada, countries that have the same type of homology with the first category. They have extremely rich per capita economic resources, and become the essential supply section of resources and intermediate products for the industrialization of the first category, thus entering the group of rich countries. To summarize the experience of these countries that have successfully crossed the middle-income trap, we could find that almost all of them share a common characteristic, which is that they have all completed industrialization, and the strong driving force for sustainable economic development relies on a relatively perfect industrial system with self-upgrading capability.

On the other hand, the countries that fall into the middle-income trap used to reach a high level of per capita income and were very close to the rank of developed countries. Unfortunately, they did not build an innovative and competitive industrial structure or an effective finance-serving-real-economy mechanism, or they lacked the effective management capacity on macro-financial risks after opening the capital account, or they cannot handle the relationship between economic growth and people's livelihood improvement well, all the above had resulted in an over-rapid rise of labor costs, the widening gap between the rich and the poor, the imbalance in the industrial structure, and consequently the loss of economic autonomy and the international competitiveness of goods in the process of economic globalization. Moreover, this even resulted in the handover of their economic artery to foreign capitals, leaving themselves struggling and suffering in the middle-income trap with the constant impacts of the financial crisis.

As the largest developing country, China still has half of its population living in rural areas; although the industrial categories are complete, high-end manufacturing capacity is weak, which means the industrialization is far from being completed. After the great changes in the international economic environment, problems of China's unreasonable economic structures begin to appear; economic growth starts to fall and shift into the new normal. Based on its national conditions, China has drawn up a two-wheel driving strategy of supply-side reform and new-type urbanization, after fully absorbing other countries' experiences and lessons in the process of crossing the middle-income trap. As long as China unswervingly builds an industrialized system with innovation and self-upgrading capacity, and develop a multi-level domestic demand market with strong purchasing power, it will be able to double its national income by 2020 from the level in 2010 and lay a solid economic foundation for successfully crossing the middle-income trap and the internationalization of RMB.

8.2 Major Risks for China's Sustainable Economic Development

Under the previously prevailing traditional economic model, China's economy focused on demand management, and achieved relatively fast development through expanding investment, increasing exports, and stimulating domestic consumption of residents and the government. At present, China's economy is facing formidable challenges simultaneously from the slowdown in economic growth, structural adjustments, and the aftermath of previous stimulus policies. The slowdown of economic growth, the decline of industrial products' prices, the shrinkage of entity companies' profits, the sluggish fiscal revenue growth, and the rising economic risks all these have clearly demonstrated that the previous driving forces of China's rapid economic growth have become ineffective, and it is difficult to sustain the economic model that relied mainly on credit policy for more investments and on favorable policies for more exports. Therefore, it is urgent for China to accelerate the economic transformation and upgrading, and create new economic growth momentum so as to realize the sustainable development of its real economy.

8.2.1 Structural Barriers Brought by Traditional Economic Model

Since the outbreak of the international financial crisis, the world's economy has entered a long period of recession. With relatively high dependence on the international community, China's economy has been severely stricken, and the unreasonable problems of domestic industrial structure have become more prominent. Especially under the anti-crisis economic stimulus plan implemented by the G20 countries, China has experienced extensive economic expansion, which has led to a serious debt management and over-capacity. The economy is heavily burdened, with lots of business closures, decline of investment impetus, and lack of growth momentum. In 2015, China's GDP grew by 6.9% year-on-year, declining for five consecutive years. Industrial value added increased by 5.9%, down by 1% over the previous year; fixed asset investment increased by 10%, 5.7% less than last year's figure. Industrial enterprise profits fell by 2.3% year-on-year; the number of loss-suffering enterprises in November reached 54,459, up by 17.4% year-on-year. Over a long period of time, the important engine of China's economic growth—export—remained sluggish, with its total volume of import and export in 2015 reaching 3.95864 trillion dollars, down by 8.0% year-on-year, imports 1682.07 billion dollars, down by 14.1% year-on-year; and exports 2276.57 billion dollars, down by 2.8% year-on-year. All these have indicated that the unsustainable traditional economic model has caused a structural obstacle for economic growth, which is mainly demonstrated from the following four aspects:

1. Weak innovation ability

Since the reform and opening up, due to the overall backwardness of technology level and the lack of core technologies, most Chinese enterprises can only engage in the "processing and compensation trades (processing with materials or given samples, assembling supplied components)" and low-tech and labor-intensive production, and produce low-value-added products. Moreover, the enterprise's awareness of innovation is weak and the R&D investment is low. In 2000, China's R&D expenditure accounted for only 0.9% of GDP, less than one-third of that in Japan; the contribution of science and technology to GDP growth was less than 20%.

After the outbreak of the international financial crisis, China began to emphasize economic transformation and upgrading, and increased R&D investment, which exceeded that of Germany in 2010, and then become more than Japan's in 2013. In 2015 it reached 1.4 trillion which had made China become a country with the second largest R&D investment, just after the United States. At present, China's R&D expenditure accounted for 2.1% of the GDP, which has exceeded that of the United Kingdom, and reached the Eurozone level. However, it still falls behind compared with the levels in Japan and in the United States (Fig. 8.1). In China, half of the population is rural residents, and the overall education level remains low; the lack of well-qualified talents, especially in the areas of science and technology, is the key reason for the restrictions of China's innovation capacity. According to the World Bank, there were only 547 R&D researchers per one million people in China in 2000, while the figure was 5151 in Japan and 3476 in the United States, which means China's level was only one-tenth and one-sixth of the levels of the latter two countries. Through unremitting efforts, China has made great achievements in the cultivation of scientific and technological personnel and is narrowing the gap with the developed countries rapidly. In 2013, the number of researchers per one million in China doubled to 1089, which was about one-fifth of that in Japan and one-fourth of the United States and one-third of the

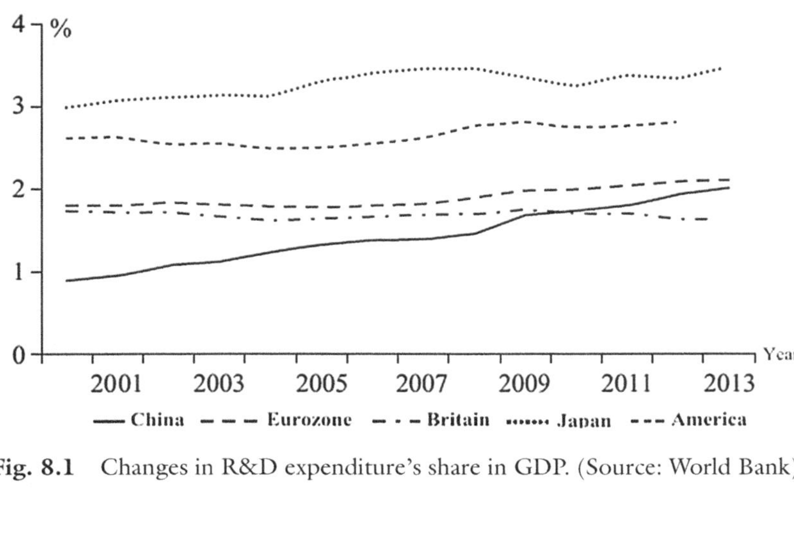

Fig. 8.1 Changes in R&D expenditure's share in GDP. (Source: World Bank)

Eurozone level (Fig. 8.2). China had a large quantity of patent applications in 2014, which was 127,042, and was almost five times more than the 26,560 in 2000, making it the second highest-ranking country in terms of patent applications, right after the United States. Despite this fact (Fig. 8.3), due to the constraints of the mechanisms and institutions, the industrializing of scientific and technological achievements was weak, and many patents remain at the laboratory level, which resulted in a relatively low contribution of science and technology to economic development. The contribution of science and technology to the economic growth in the United States was more than 70%, while in China, this figure was less than 30%. This has become the "Achilles's heel" for China's economic development.

2. Imbalance of economic structure

One of the main manifestations of China's economic structural imbalances is the declining of consumption rate and the rising of saving rate year by year. From 2000 to 2008, because of the increasing pressure from

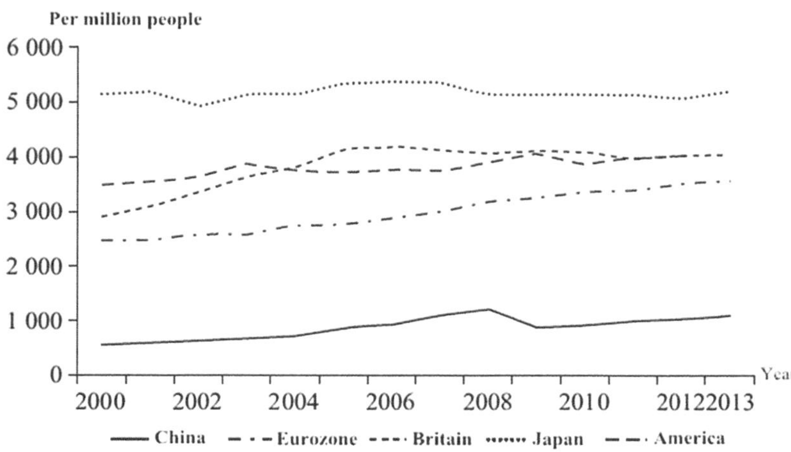

Fig. 8.2 Changes in R&D researchers' quantity. Note: R&D Researchers refer to professionals involved in the concept formation or invention of new knowledge, new products, new processes, new methods or new systems, and related project management, including doctoral candidates involved in R&D practices [ISCED97 Level 6]. (Source: World Bank)

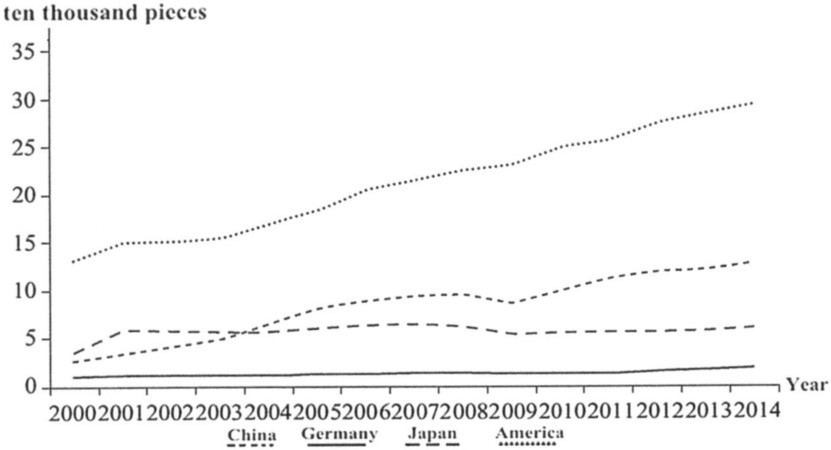

Fig. 8.3 Changes in the quantity of patent application

housing, healthcare, education, and pensions and the unsound social security system, household saving rate will increase sharply, from 36.2% to 51.8%, and the consumption rate declined from 63.1% to 49.7%. The changes in saving and consumption structure caused the shrinkage of China's domestic market and significantly higher dependence on external demand, making China's economic growth to be driven by investment and export. The international financial crisis in 2008 and the follow-up sluggish international market resulted in lower demand in the international market and the fast exposure of problems like structural imbalance of over-supply and over-capacity in part of partial to in some industries. In order to maintain a certain rate of economic growth, the government was forced to adopt a large intensity of expansionary fiscal and monetary policies to increase the proportion of investment-driven economy. As shown in Fig. 8.4, large-scale investment has led to a sharp expansion of production capacity; however, the speed of consumption increase far lagged behind that of capital investment and production capacity, and this worsened the imbalance between insufficient domestic demand and excess production capacity.

Another manifestation of the China's economic structural imbalance is that some industries have serious over-capacity issues, whereas residents' living demands could not be efficiently satisfied. In the process of economic

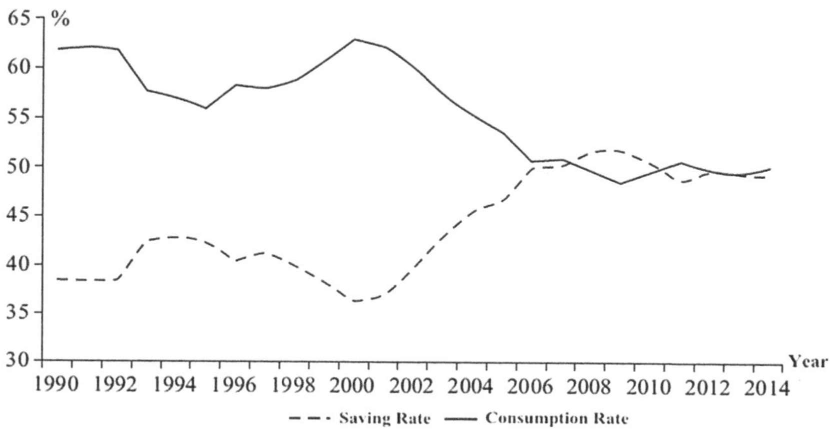

Fig. 8.4 Curves of China's savings and consumption in 1990–2014. (Source: World Bank)

transformation and upgrading, the industries of iron and steel, coal, chemicals, construction materials, and electrolytic aluminum have suffered from serious over-capacities. For example, estimated by the 3.5 billion tons of coal consumption in 2015, China's coal capacity had a surplus of 2.2 billion tons and the rate of capacity utilization was less than 70%. Since 2012, China's crude steel capacity utilization rate has remained under the reasonable level, and this figure in 2015 was less than 67%, which meant significant loss for the steel industry. The member companies of Iron and Steel Industry Association lost 64.5 billion yuan in 2015, reaching a percentage of 50.5% of loss-incurring enterprises. The situation was quite difficult for this business. Nitrogen, chlor-alkali industries suffered from losses as well; industries of inorganic salts, methanol, and tire manufacturing suffered from declining profits consecutively for two or three years. Cement industry profited 33 billion yuan, down by 58% year-on-year, and its production growth turned out negative for the first time in 25 years. Aluminum smelting industry incurred huge losses for many years with a heavy debt burden.

Many coastal enterprises are still engaged in the traditional processing industry. They have adopted inefficient production technologies and methods, resulting in a market space occupied by a large number of cheap and highly eliminable products, and thus bringing about substantially adverse supply. Since the reform and opening up, China has been implementing the development strategy of the "demand guides supply, and supply improves demand" for a long time. In the time with short supply and weak purchasing power, China emphasized too much on meeting the requirement of "quantity", and far from enough on product quality and brands. Once the income level and demand level are elevated, or the number of low-end demand from abroad is decreased, this would result in a strange phenomenon that Chinese people would try to buy high-quality goods like milk powder, toilet lids, and pressure cooker from abroad while many Chinese industries would inevitably undergo over-capacities at home. Whether China would be able to balance the supply side and the demand side, steadily adjust the economic structure, reduce inefficient and low-end supply, and expand effective and high-end supply would be crucial to the future of China's economic development.

3. The decline in private investment

For quite a long time in the past, investment remained the main driving force for China's economic growth. Although the consumption has surpassed investment and exports to become the first driving force of economic growth in recent several years, investment still remains a special engine for China's economy against the background of a negative export growth. Enterprises are the main force of private investment, among which the small enterprises are the most dynamic. As an important component and the basic development power of China's economy, small- and medium-sized enterprises (SMEs) have made important contributions to facilitating market competitions and creating jobs. According to National Bureau of Statistics, SMEs accounted for over 95% of the total enterprises, with the value of their final products and services accounting for more than 50% of the GDP. Due to the problems in ideological concepts and systems, the relationship between the government and the market is unbalanced, and the market is in a secondary position in terms of the allocation of resources. All kinds of constraints and soft conditions have made it impossible for small and medium enterprises to enter high-profit and emerging industries, making them less willing to invest in the process of economic transformation and upgrading. In addition, the bank-led financial system, with "identity discrimination", has contributed little to financially supporting SMEs. Even though SMEs are willing to invest, their capitals are still tight, and it remains difficult for them to finance. Figure 8.5

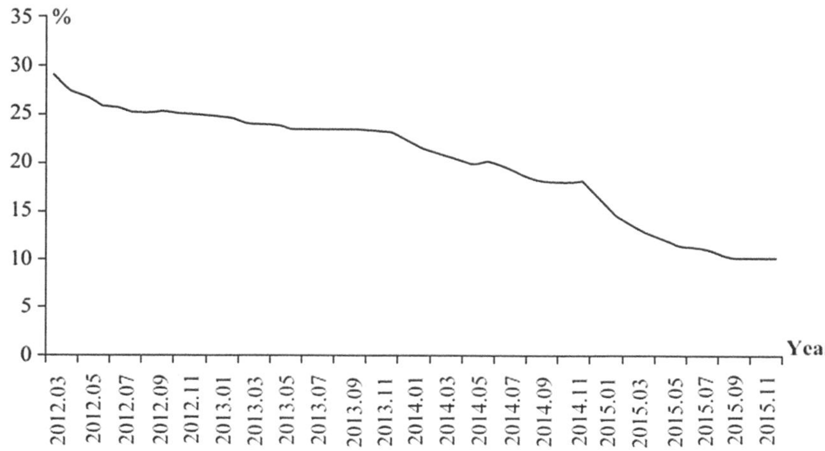

Fig. 8.5 Private investment growth rate curve. (Source: National Bureau of Statistics)

reflects the change in the investment growth of private fixed assets. At the end of 2015, the growth rate was 10.1%, down by 58% from 24.1% in the beginning of 2013. The sharp decline of private investment reflected that the development environment for SMEs became worse, so that the scale expansion, technological research and development, and capital demands cannot be satisfied. SMEs' lack of enough vigor and vitality will bring a great pressure on solving the employment issue and keeping economic flexibility in the process of new urbanization (Fig. 8.6).

4. Large-but-not-strong trade

In 2015, the total value of China's import and export of goods was 24.59 trillion yuan, remaining the top one in the world, and still improving than last year's level. From the perspective of the "quantity", China was the world's largest trading country, and the largest trading partner for more than 100 countries. The volume of its import and export accounted for more than one-eighth of the world's total. In terms of the "quality" of trade, China still has a long way to go before it becomes a trading power given the value-added products of the exported goods, trade competitiveness, and the pricing power. On one hand, China's export products are mostly low value-added and easily replaceable; however, the export volume

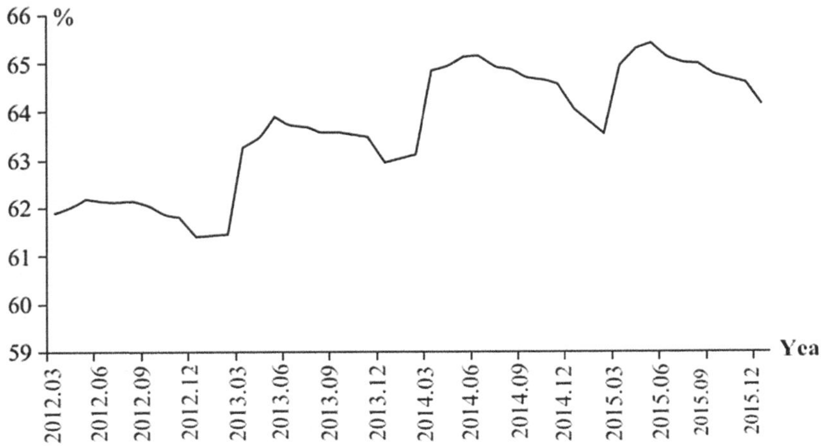

Fig. 8.6 Shares of private investment in fixed assets. Note: Investment ratio of private fixed assets = private investment in fixed assets/national investment in fixed assets (excluding farmers)

could be very sensitive to price changes; traditional cheap-labor-based made-in-China products are losing their glory. In 2015, total export of seven categories of labor-intensive products—namely, textiles, clothing, bags, footwear, toys, furniture and plastic products—reached 2.93 trillion yuan, turning out a rarely seen drop of 1.7% year-on-year. According to the World Bank, while other major countries (regions) were undergoing decline in the export of high-tech products, China has realized a steady rise from 19.0% in 2000 to 25.4% in 2014, which has gradually exceeded the levels of the euro area, Japan, the United Kingdom, and the United States (see Fig. 8.7). Although China's export of high-tech products accounts for a relatively large share of manufacturing products, most of the key technologies and components of these products come from abroad, which means not only that China has to depend on other countries for the production in this area, but also that the margins would be relatively low, and that China will lose its voice in terms of pricing power in trade negotiations. In addition, China doesn't have many famous manufacturing brands, which means this industry would not be very competitive in the international market. On July 22, 2015, the list of world's top 500 enterprises in the *Fortune* was published. A total of 106 Chinese companies were on the list, which was second to the United States, nearly twice as much as Japan. However, these

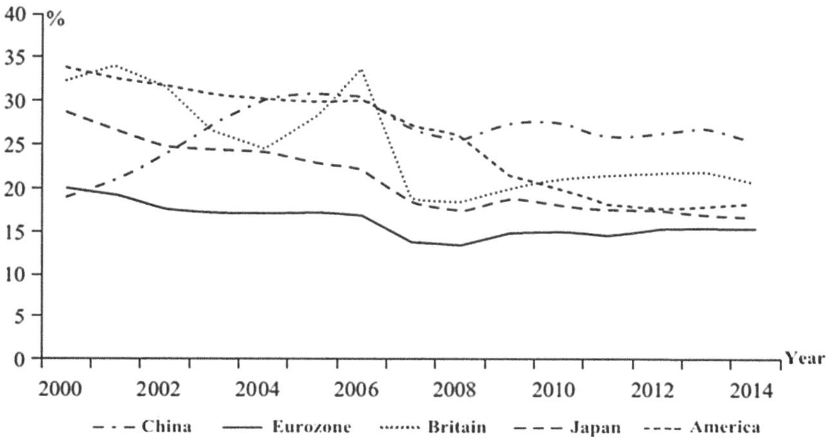

Fig. 8.7 Changes of high-tech exports proportion (of manufactured goods). Note: Exports of high-tech products refer to products with high R&D intensity, such as aerospace, computer, medicine, scientific equipment, and electrical machinery. (Source: World Bank)

companies are mainly concentrated in industries of resources, energy, mining, steel, transportation, telecommunications, and finance, while only two or three of them are manufacturing enterprises (see Table 8.1).

8.2.2 Complex International Environment and External Shocks

1. Outside demand downturn led to export-driven failure

In the United States, the European Union, Japan, and other developed countries or regions; the economy is still in a moderate recovery and the economic growth is weak after the financial crisis stage. The IMF estimated that economic growth in developed economies would be 1.9% in 2015, up by 0.1 percentage point from 2014, but still well below the global average of 3.1%. Developing countries' economic growth rate was 4.0%, down by 0.6 percentage points from 2014 (see Fig. 8.8). World's economic growth rates forecasted by IMF is 3.4% in 2016 and 3.6% in 2017, but still quite slow. Developed countries failed to return to 2007

Table 8.1 Chinese enterprises in global top 500 and their ranking

International ranking	*Company*	*International ranking*	*Company*
2	Sinopec Group	274	Jiangsu Shagang Group Co., Ltd.
4	China National Petroleum Corporation	276	China National Pharmaceutical Group Corporation
7	State Grid Corporation of China	281	China Minsheng Banking Corp., Ltd. (CMBC)
18	Industrial and Commercial Bank of China	282	(Jardine Matheson)
29	China Construction Bank	288	China National Machinery Industry Corporation
31	Hon Hai Precision Industry	296	Shanghai Pudong Development Bank
36	Agriculture Bank of China	304	Bohai Steel Group
37	China State Construction Engineering Corporation	315	Jizhong Energy Group
45	China Bank	316	CPC Corporation, Taiwan
55	China Mobile Communications Corporation	321	China National Aviation Fuel Group
60	SAIC Motor	326	China Metallurgical Group Corporation
71	China Railway Group Limited	328	China Pacific Insurance (Group)
72	China National Offshore Oil Corporation	336	Hutchison Whampoa Limited (HWL)
77	Noble Group	339	Zhejiang Materials Industry Group Corporation (ZJMI)
79	China Railway Construction Corporation	341	Datong Coal Mine Group Co., Ltd.
87	China Railway Construction Corporation	342	China CEFC Energy Company Limited (CEFC)
94	China Life	343	China Guodian Corporation
96	Ping an Insurance (Group) Company of China, Ltd.	344	Xinxing Cathay International Group Co., Ltd.

(*continued*)

Table 8.1 (continued)

International ranking	*Company*	*International ranking*	*Company*
105	Sinochem Group	345	China Huadian Corporation
107	China FAW Group Corporation	354	Jiangxi Copper Corporation
109	Dongfeng Motor Group Co. Ltd.	355	Pegatron
113	China Southern Power Grid Company Limited	358	Lu'an Group
115	China Resources National	362	Guangzhou Automobile Group Co., Ltd.
143	China Post	364	Henan Energy & Chemical Industry Group Co., Ltd.
144	China North Industries Group Corporation	366	China Electronics Corporation
146	Tewoo Group Co. Ltd.	371	China Shipbuilding Industry Corporation
156	Pacific Construction Group	373	Shandong Energy Group Co., Ltd.
159	Aviation Industry Corporation of China	379	Jincheng Anthracite Mining Group
160	China Telecom	380	Shaanxi Yanchang Petroleum (Group) Co., Ltd.
165	China Communications Construction	382	Jinneng Group Co., Ltd.
174	The People Insurance Company Group of China Limited	389	Quanta Computer Incorporated
186	CITIC Group Corporation	390	China Nonferrous Metal Mining (Group) Co., Ltd.
190	Bank of Communications	391	China Energy Engineering Group Co., Ltd.
196	Shenhua Group	392	China Datang Corporation
198	China Minmetals Corporation	393	Formosa Petrochemical Corporation
207	Beijing Automotive Group	400	Kailuan (Group) Co., Ltd.
218	Baosteel Group Corporation	402	Shougang Group

(*continued*)

Table 8.1 (continued)

International ranking	*Company*	*International ranking*	*Company*
224	China Huaneng Group	403	China Power Investment Corporation
227	China United Network Communications Ltd.	409	Yangquan Coal Industry (Group) Co., Ltd.
228	Huawei Investment & Holding	416	Shaanxi Coal & Chemical Industry Group Co., Ltd.
231	Lenovo Group	420	China Everbright Group
234	Shandong Weiqiao Pioneering Group Co. Ltd.	423	Compal Electronics Inc.
235	China Merchants Bank	426	China General Technology (Group)
239	Hebei Iron & Steel Co. Ltd.	432	China Ocean Shipping (Group) Company
240	Aluminum Corporation of China Limited	437	China Aerospace Science and Technology Corporation (CASC)
247	Amer International Group	451	Ansteel Group
253	Power Construction Corporation of China	457	China Poly Group Corporation
258	Greenland Holding Group	464	HNA Group
264	Shanxi Coking Coal Group Co., Ltd.	467	AIA Group
265	China National Chemical Corporation	471	Cathay Life Insurance
270	China National Building Materials Group Corporation	472	Taiwan Semiconductor Manufacturing Company
271	Industrial Bank Co., Ltd.	477	Geely Holding Group
272	COFCO Corporation	500	Wuhan Iron and Steel (Group) Company

levels of growth; developing countries realized only half the rate of growth over the same period. The depressed economic environment in the world means that external demand is difficult to grow. China's exports growth is likely to remain negative, and exports would no longer play a role in driving economic growth.

Among China's major trading partners, the United States has maintained a good momentum of economic recovery; the Eurozone and

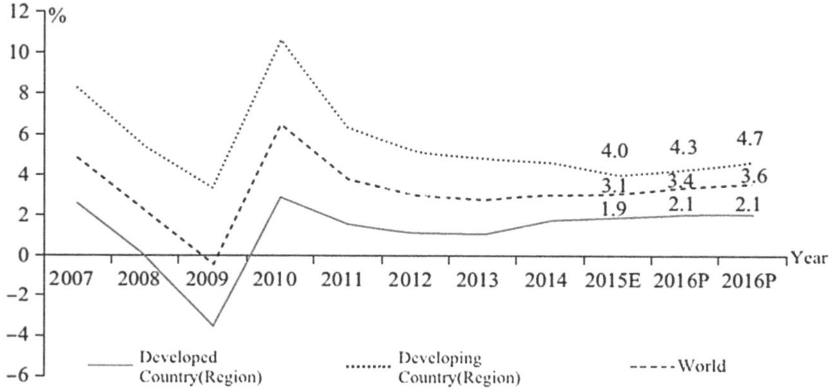

Fig. 8.8 Growth rates and expected GDP of major countries. Note: Figures in 2015 are estimated values; figures in 2016 and 2017 are forecasted values. (Source: IMF, *World Economic Outlook*)

Japan's economies are still weak. According to Gann's ten-year cycle of economy,[1] the US financial crisis had gone through eight years, near to the end of the decline, and it was expected to enter a decade-long rise in 2017. While the 2011 outbreak of the European sovereign debt crisis was only five years ago, considering the plight of the refugee crisis, at least four to five years will be accounted before being completely out of the haze. In 2015, China's total import and export value of goods was 24.59 trillion yuan, down by 7% over 2014. The export was 14.14 trillion yuan, down by 1.8%; the import was 10.45 trillion yuan, down by 13.2%. In fact, since 2010, China's exports growth to major developed countries (regions) had decreased significantly and was very unstable (see Fig. 8.9). For example, its export growth rate to the United States dropped from 28.1% in 2010 to 3.4% in 2015. In the same period, China's export growth rate to Japan fell from 22.7% to −9.1%, and the figure to the euro area was from 33.6%

[1] Ten-year cycle is an important basis for Gann analysis. Gann believes that the ten-year cycle can reproduce the market cycle. A new historical low and a new historical high are a decade away from each other. Any long-term rally or decline cannot last for more than three years, during which there must be three to six months of adjustment. Therefore, the ten-year cycle of the rally process is actually that in the first six years, there would be a top every three years and in the remaining last four years, it occurs the final top would appear (see Baidu Encyclopedia).

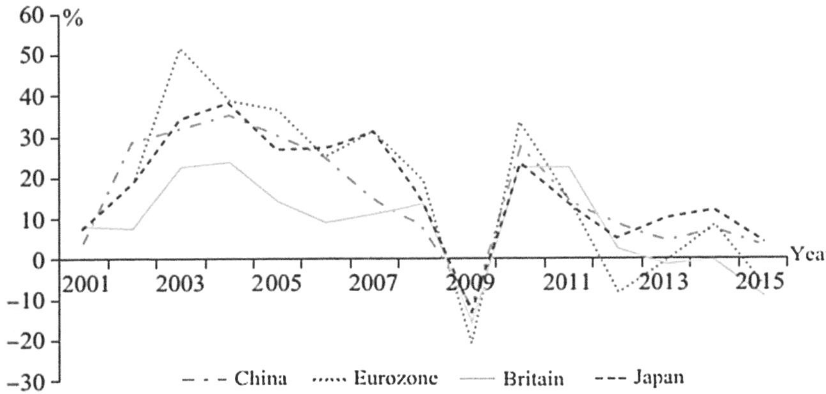

Fig. 8.9 China's export growth rates to major developed countries and regions. (Source: World Bank)

to 6.1%, and 24% to 4.4% to the United Kingdom. As developed countries account for about half of China's foreign trade share, if the economic growth or recovery of developed countries and regions remains sluggish, China's export enterprises will be down to a very difficult situation.

Although the economic growth of emerging markets is faster than that of developed countries, due to their increasing prominent structural contradictions, weak technological innovation capability, higher economic dependence on the external, and weaker risk management capability against external shocks, their economic growth is slowing down against the slow economic recovery, sharp decline of commodity prices, and exacerbated capital outflow in developed countries. At present, emerging markets account for an increasing proportion in China's foreign economy. More than half of its foreign trade is with emerging markets and developing countries. Especially after "Belt and Road" initiative was proposed, China is building closer economic and trade ties with countries along the road, and its investments and trade are also increasingly toward these countries. Due to the close geographical relationship, China's trade with South Korea, India, and ASEAN countries has grown rapidly. Since 2001, the annual growth rates of export to these countries and regions have exceeded 20% (see Fig. 8.10). In 2015, the poor economic performance of the emerging markets led to the decline of their import demands, and thus resulted in a sharp drop in China's exports to these markets. For

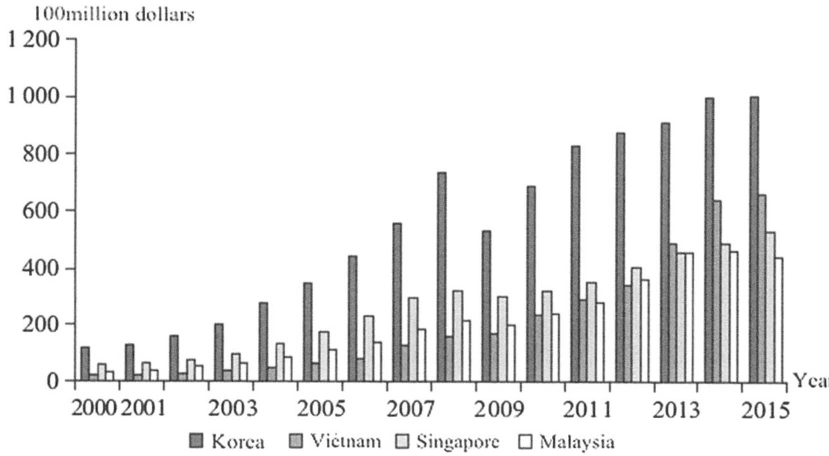

Fig. 8.10 The changes of China's exports to Southeast Asian countries in 2000–2015. (Source: IMF, IFS)

example, export growth rate to South Korea fell from 28.3% in 2010 to 1% in 2015, while that to India fell from 37.7% to 7.4% and from 21.3% to 4.5% to Malaysia over the same period.

Given the current downturn of global economy, and the drop of the external demand of China's major trading partners, if China couldn't take effective measures to enhance its export competitiveness, it will be likely to lose export drivers, which would cause unprecedented pressure on its economic growth and employment.

2. Growing international competition for made-in-China

After the global financial crisis, developed countries started to adjust the industrial structure. They introspected the financial "off-the-real" phenomenon, vigorously strengthened the supervision, and required financial institutions to de-leverage and better serve the real economy. At the same time, in order to maintain their economic and technological leadership, the developed countries have returned to real economy, seeking industrial restructuring, promoting the development of high-end manufacturing, and enhancing the competitiveness of their manufacturing industry in the world. The United States, Japan, Germany, France, and other European countries have developed and promulgated the "Remanufacturing" strategy: the US "Revitalization plan of the manufacturing sector" and "High-end manufacturing plan" focus on developing new energy, new materials, biotechnology, and other emerging industries through innovation; Japan, in addition to maintaining its leading role in terms of machinery and equipment manufacturing, automotive and key parts and components manufacturing, also concentrates on developing robots, new energy vehicles, 3D printing, and IT's role; Germany has launched a high-tech "Industrial 4.0" program to raise the level of smart manufacturing and to build smart factories with adaptability, resource efficiency, and ergonomics; France has proposed a "New Industrial Realization Plan", focusing on seven knowledge-intensive and technology-intensive strategic industries. These practices of these major industrial countries have elevated the threshold for China to enter the high-end manufacturing industry, which may further widen its gap in this area, and brings great challenges to China's development of innovative technology and industrial upgrading. On one hand, due to the rapid increase in labor costs, China's labor-intensive and low-end manufactured goods are losing their edge; on the other hand, developed countries are increasing investment in high-end products, which have created high-technological barriers, making China lose its comparative advantages in the international trade and also lose its income substantially from the international trade. The ratio of trade surplus to GDP had declined from the peak of 10.02% in 2007 to the trough of 1.56% in 2013. In the past two years, import expenditures have declined more than export earnings due to the sharp decline in commodity prices. Despite a negative growth in exports, the trade surplus has widened and the current account balance has increased in proportion to GDP (Fig. 8.11).

3. Greater competition pressure for international capacity cooperation

It is an inevitable choice for the achievement of industrial transformation and upgrading to strengthen the international cooperation of capacity, access to new markets, and prolong the life cycles of some manufacturing industries. Emerging countries are China's main targets of this international capacity. Since the 2008 financial crisis, trade protectionism has become prominent, and the manufacturing industry in emerging economies has borne the brunt. Most trade barriers are created by developing countries. The emerging economies mainly rely on low-cost and low value-added labor-intensive and capital-intensive industries, with

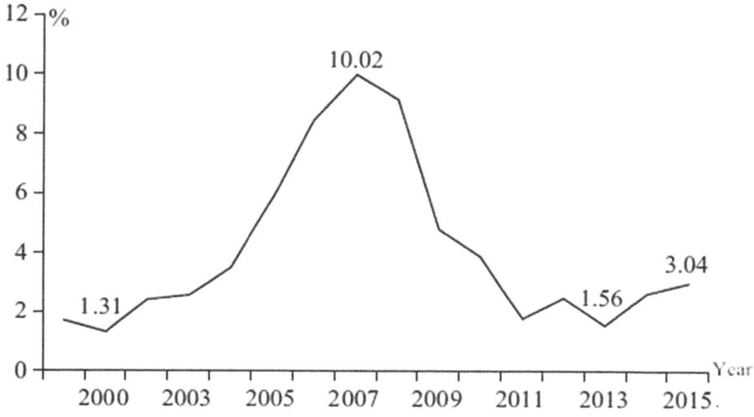

Fig. 8.11 The proportion of China's current account balance to GDP

low-technological barriers, high homogeneity. The competition between them is intensive and the possibility of trade friction is relatively high. Emerging economies are short of the high-tech products of developed countries. Those products are difficult to be substituted, and have little to do with the trade barriers of the emerging economies. At the same time, China's abundant cheap labor does not have obvious advantages in emerging countries. Hence, in order to lead in the emerging markets again, China must improve the technologies of its products. As mentioned above, the major industrial countries have increased R&D investments, and paid more attention to maintaining their manufacturing advantages and international competitiveness. Affected by the US and Japan's return to Asia-Pacific strategy and a new wave of global industry consolidation, developed countries began to gradually transfer their businesses to and increase the investments in Southeast Asia, Africa, and the countries along the "Belt and Road". Compared with China, Europe, the United States, and other developed countries have obvious advantages in technology, which has caused a tremendous impact on China's direct investment and international capacity cooperation in these areas.

8.2.3 Possible Threats of Capital Flows on Economic Stability

RMB's joining the SDR basket has objectively put forward higher requirements for China's financial opening. The PBOC said that China will continue to accelerate financial reform and opening up to the outside world and make positive contributions to promoting global economic growth, maintaining global financial stability, and improving global economic governance. There is no doubt that China's economy will be in a more and more open macro-environment, in which the capital flows, finance, and real economy will have a more complex relationship. The risk that real economy would be affected by the RMB exchange, financial markets, and international capital flows has become greater.

1. Risks of capital flows' effect on the real economy

Capital account has become more open. While acquiring foreign and domestic resources, it is difficult to avoid short-term capital flow arbitrage risk. China's access to the SDR basket means that China provides a reserve asset for the global economy, which will inevitably increase the global asset managers' interest in and demand for RMB. The increase in RMB exchange flexibility will, in return, raise the RMB exchange sensitivity and in short term may lead to more capital flows. From the international experience, the rapid inflow of short-term capital could easily lead to asset bubbles, and will be followed by large-scale rapid outflow of assets, which would result in financial market turmoil and even financial crisis, undermining the real economy, capital chain, and artificial economic fluctuations.

From the perspective of capital inflows' impacts, large-scale capital inflows in the short run may lead to three types of risks: (1) shortage of currency supply in the foreign exchange market, and potential risks of currency appreciation; (2) excess domestic liquidity, low interest rates, and risks of over-heated economy from over-borrowing enterprises. The inflated prices of the bond market, stock market, and real estate market might bring about asset price bubbles; (3) in the background of high exchange rates and low interest rates of domestic currency, domestic enterprises and financial institutions would borrow large amounts of external loans, causing the mismatch risk between currency and its maturity on the balance sheet. These three risks are likely to pave the way for financial crisis. Take South Korea as an example. In order to meet the entrance requirements of the OECD, South Korea carried out free convertibility under current account and capital account in 1993, and opened the capital market and monetary market to foreign investors in 1995. This rapid opening of its financial markets under the circumstances of incomplete domestic financial reform resulted in significant inflows of short-term international capitals. In 1996, South Korea's foreign exchange reserve stood at $33.2 billion, while short-term foreign debt stood at $93 billion. The financial regulatory authorities had underestimated the foreign exchange risks, liquidity risks, derivatives trading risks, and external debt risks from financial opening, which had led to the breakout of Southeast Asian financial crisis from South Korea.

As the flow of short-term capital is highly speculative, once the destination country's economic expectations change, or the expected return on financial market arbitrage declines, or monetary policies change in major currency issuers, or there are any fluctuations in the international community, which will induce a sudden interruption or termination of capital inflows and consequently reverse the flow, causing the large-scale outflow of short-term capitals. Once this occurs, there will be not only large-scale outflow of foreign capitals, but also follow-up outflow of domestic capitals for the sake of seeking profits or mitigating risks. From the perspective of the impacts from the short-term capital outflow, there would be three adverse consequences, including: (1) The domestic interest rate will rise sharply, which will consequently result in the increase of financing costs for physical industries, and breaks of capital chains, and cause bankruptcy consequently, and ultimately deactivation of physical industries; inactivated physical capacities may be then acquired by international capitals at a very low price and become the entity working for foreign companies; (2) Asset prices will drop sharply, breaking the asset bubbles caused by previous capital inflows, and severely damaging the asset sides of the balance sheets of the civil sector, businesses, and government departments that possess domestic assets; (3) The value of domestic currency will be significantly depreciated, which will bring about a rapid increase in exterior liabilities to those domestic financial and physical industries that have borrowed a lot in foreign currencies, and add to their risks of bankruptcy and being merged and acquired by foreign companies.

2. Empirical study about the impact of capital flow on the real economy

Hutchison and Noy (2006) and Joyce and Nabar (2009) found that if "the decline in the net inflow of a country's capital reaches more than 2 standard deviations of its average of capital flow samples within a year" is defined as "the sudden cessation of capital inflow", this kind of sudden cessation will be most dangerous to the real economy. The general currency crisis would lead to a 2–3% decline in output on average in three years, while this "sudden cessation" would cause a 13–15% decline.

In order to quantitatively discuss the impact of capital flows on the real economy, this chapter has chosen G20 countries, which account for 90% of the global economy, as the research objects, and used the panel data model as a tool to do the empirical analysis.

(1) Basic metering model settings:

$$GDP_{it} = \alpha_i + \eta_t + \beta GDP_{it-1} + \sum_{n=0}^{\omega} \gamma_n CAP_{it-n} + \xi_{it.}$$

GDP_{it} is the explanatory variable, which represents the real GDP growth rate of country i in year t;

α_i denotes the fixed effect of country i, and η_t denotes the time effect of year t. Based on test results, the fixed effect model is chosen in this chapter.

$\sum_{n=0}^{\omega} \gamma_n CAP_{it-n}$ represents the sum of the impact from capital flows on the GDP, where CAP_{it-n} represents the capital flow indicator for country i in year t-n. In this study, four indicators are used to model respectively, which are net capital inflow, growth rate of net capital inflow, capital inflow, and growth rate of capital inflow; the values of ω range from 0 to 2 to observe the influences of different lag phases. Therefore, three sub-models can be constructed for each capital flow indicator.

ξ_{it} is the stochastic error term.

(2) Data selection and model grouping

This chapter chooses capital inflow and its growth rate, net capital inflow and its growth rate as the measure index of the impact of capital flows. In order to avoid the influence of the short time series on modeling reliability, this study takes the data from 2002 to 2015, and removes the countries with incomplete data. As the capital inflow characteristics of developed and developing countries are different, China, as a developing country, is possible to have some developed country's characteristics in terms of capital flow with the RMB's internationalization. Furthermore, China is in the transition from relatively strict capital controls to relatively liberal capital management, and it has relatively huge institutional differences compared with other countries, so it is not included in this study. Developed countries and developing countries are grouped for the

Table 8.2 The impact of capital inflow and net capital inflow on economic growth

	Capital inflow		*Net capital inflow*	
	CAPT	*CAPT (−1)*	*CAPN*	*CAPN (−1)*
Developed countries group	0.359**	0.381**	0.138	0.421
	(0.0383)	(0.0443)	(0.5481)	(0.8405)
Developing countries group	0.3068**	0.2387	0.3137**	0.2696*
	(0.0441)	(0.145)	(0.0313)	(0.0882)

Note: CAPT in the table indicates capital inflow, CAPN represents net capital inflow; the figure in the upper part of each cell is a coefficient value; * indicates a significant impact in the level of 10%, ** indicates a significant impact in the level of 5%, and the figures in the bottom are the corresponding P values

modeling. The former group includes Canada, Germany, France, Italy, Japan, South Korea, the United Kingdom and the United States, and the latter includes Argentina, Brazil, Russia, and South Africa.

(3) Empirical results

According to the study, neither the growth rate of capital inflow nor the growth rate of net capital inflow has significant impact on the economic growth of the developed countries group and the developing countries group, so this chapter will not elaborate on this. For developed countries, the changes in net capital inflow do not have significant impact on economic growth, but the amount of capital inflow does on the aggregate output. For developing countries, the modeling results show that both capital inflow and net capital inflow will have prominent impacts on current GDP growth, and at the confidence level of 10%, the impact of the net capital inflow in the previous phase on current GDP growth is also significant (as shown in Table 8.2).

Empirical studies on the past 13 years' data of G20 countries have shown that capital inflows have significant impacts on their economic growth. For each $10 billion increase of capital inflows in developed countries, the GDP growth rate would increase by about 0.36%. Of course, developing countries are mostly countries with net capital inflow; therefore, every additional $1 billion of capital inflows would bring 0.31% increase in the GDP growth rate. On the contrary, if, for some reason, capital outflows occur, every $10 billion outflow in developed countries or developing countries would cause about 0.3% of decrease in their GDP growth rate.

3. Risks of greater economic virtualization

With the progress of information technology and economic globalization, there have been trends of securitization, digitalization, and internationalization in the world's finance since the 1980s. Financial innovations are endless and financial derivatives market is emerging everywhere. Financial transaction has gradually separated itself from the real economy. According to the BIS, the world's stock trade volume accounted for 102.4% of the GDP, while the figure in 1990 was only 32% (see Fig. 8.12). The growth rate of international illiquid debt balances was also much higher than that of the real economy. Before the 2008 financial crisis, the annual gap between the two reached 13%. Since then, the developed countries have worked hard de-leverage, and significantly narrowed the gap (see Fig. 8.13).

Globally, financial activities have been increasingly focusing on product derivatives and transactions over the past 25 years, and paying less attention to credit support for businesses and individuals. In other words, finance is emphasizing more on services for finance rather than for the real economy. Financial industry has separated itself from the real economy to achieve its own prosperity and form a huge virtual economy that is growing rapidly and gathering a huge amount of wealth. With limited

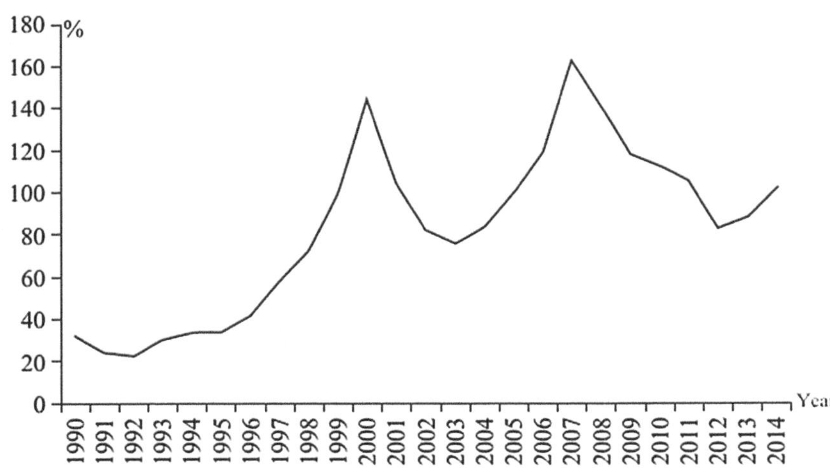

Fig. 8.12 The proportion of world's stock transactions to GDP

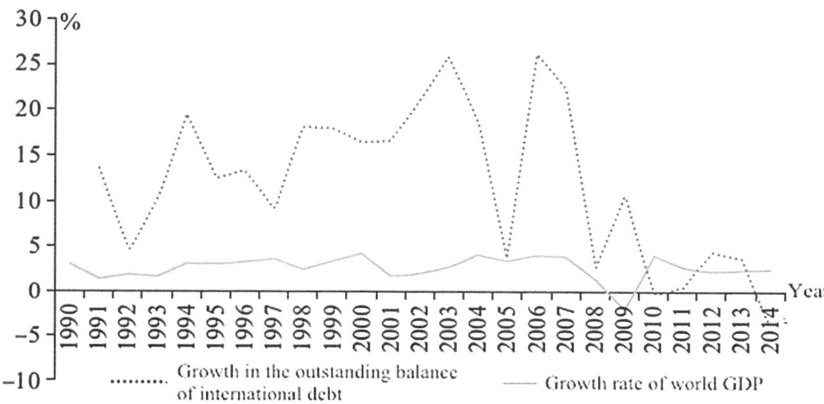

Fig. 8.13 The contrast between the growth rate of world's debt and that of GDP

openness and underdeveloped financial market, China has been less affected by the impact of this economic virtualization. However, with the gradual integration of China's economy and finance into the global economy, especially after the RMB becomes an international currency, the "off real to virtual" issue of finance has become prominent, and the virtual economy has even become popular in certain areas. For example, some local governments are promoting the development of the financial industry in an unrealistic manner and some entrepreneurs prefer to become "rich overnight" through financial management, and financial assets speculation rather than invest in real economy. Affected by the demonstration effect of the virtual economy in Wall Street, finance has become an approach to earn "quick money" through financial products, market innovations, and financial technologies, instead of a tool to serve real economy. This concept has become very popular. Hence, it is not difficult to predict that with more open capital accounts there will be more frequent and greater international capital flows, which will, to some extent, stimulate the expansion of China's virtual economy, and make money that should have been invested in the real economy to be invested in the "quick money" financial products, destroying the development of China's real economy. In addition, because the allocation of resources in the international context is more convenient, money that should have been invested in domestic industries has been invested in foreign industries, leading to the "hollowing of industries" that has once happened in developed countries like Japan and the United States, which would be detrimental to the foundation of RMB internationalization's long-term development.

It is noteworthy that due to the imbalanced development of world's economy and the unsynchronized economic cycles in different countries, the differences in the return on investment (ROI) have always existed. In the past 20 years, the ROIs in emerging countries have been obviously higher than those in developed countries. With a higher level of opening up, overseas investment opportunities for Chinese residents will inevitably increase. Through FDI, external RMB loans, and the issuance of RMB bonds, people will be able to have higher ROI than that of domestic investment. This kind of cross-border investment practices will undoubtedly squeeze domestic funds partially. Experience in developing countries suggests that high-yielding foreign investment, under full market mechanisms, would have a crowding-out effect on domestic investment, or raise domestic investment returns. In current process of industrial restructuring, the average rate of ROI of China's secondary industry is relatively low, which would easily lead the capital to flow to the stock market or financial trading products that have a higher return, resulting in financial asset bubbles and increase the risks of financial system's risks. At the same time, the real economy cannot get the necessary financial support.

In the process of RMB's internationalization, in order to meet the demand of financial institutions with different risk preferences and to build appropriate RMB reflow mechanism, China needs to develop multi-level financial market and diversify the supply of RMB products. These two factors will jointly promote the expansion of China's virtual economy. If we cannot find an appropriate balance between financial development and financial services for the real economy, or effectively control and standardize this financial expansion, it will cause the over-expansion of virtual economy and increase the risks of the industrial investment decline and economic de-industrialization, which would not be conducive to China's economic structural stability and sustainable development.

8.3 The Keys to Supply-Side Structural Reforms

To solve its major economic problems, China must change the concepts of development and economic models. At the Fifth Plenary Session of the 18th CPC Central Committee held in October 2015, five new concepts of development—namely, "innovative, coordinated, green, open and inclusive"—were put forward for the first time, calling for the fundamental role of the market in economic development, and the switch of policy-making focus from the previous demand management to supply-side reform. The essence of the supply-side structural reform is to reduce the inefficient production capacity, revitalize the stock of assets, make up the structural weakness, and improve the total-factor labor productivity through "de-capacity, de-stocking, de-leveraging, cost-reducing, and pitch-up in weak growth areas" from the perspective of production factor supply, so as to develop new impetus to keep the high speed of China's economic development. If China can successfully complete the task of supply-side structural reforms during the 13th Five-Year Plan period and establish a sustainable economic structure that can adapt to the new international and domestic environment, it will consolidate the economic base of RMB's internationalization and avoid the plight of the Japanese yen's internationalization. It will break the currency inertia of the international financial market, and make RMB one of the most important international reserve currencies.

8.3.1 Seizing the Principal Contradiction to Complete De-capacity, De-stocking, and De-leveraging

As mentioned above, over a long period of time, China's economy has been highly dependent on exports and investment. It is featured with the characteristics of extensive economic development. People in some places would pursue economic growth regardless of costs, which has caused great damage to the environment. In order to achieve the goal of economic restructuring and upgrading and to meet the new demands of the people for higher-quality life and a better ecological environment, it is imperative to carry out supply-side structural reforms and realize "subtraction" and "addition". To do "subtraction", that is de-capacity, de-stocking, de-leveraging, and cost reducing. That is, to adjust the industrial structure and to remove the factors violating the economy. Due to a sharp reduction in external demand, some export-oriented enterprises have suffered from over-supply and over-stocking, which has resulted in consecutive losses and hard to survive. The new green economy concept has forced some enterprises with high-pollution, high-energy-consuming and high-resource-consumption to close. Thus, it is essential to lower the burden on enterprise for some unreasonable charges.

From the perspective of demand, there are currently five industries with serious excess capacity: iron and steel, coal, chemicals, building materials, and electrolytic aluminum. Taking the steel industry as an example, according to the National Bureau of Statistics, in 2015 China's crude steel had an output of 804 million tons, down by 2.33%, which was the first negative growth since 1981; steel consumption was 664 million tons, declining for the first time since 1996. Iron and steel production capacity utilization rate is less than 67%, and half of the iron and steel enterprises are at a loss. The industries of coal, chemicals, building materials, and electrolytic aluminum are similar to the steel industry. About 30% of capacity had to be removed in order to achieve balance of supply and demand, and the healthy development of these industries.

Looking into the reasons for the over-capacity of the five industries, it is not difficult to find that they are positively correlated and inherently consistent with the increase of real estate stocks. Since the reform of the housing system in 1998, the enthusiasm of residents for houses have been rising, coupled with 300 million migrant workers into the city, which has brought a huge housing rigid demand. Driven by the strong demand, the average annual growth rate of commercial housing sales during 2001–2007 was close to 30% (see Fig. 8.14). The real estate has quickly become a pillar industry of China's economy, thus driving the rapid growth of the upstream and the downstream 60 industries of steel, building materials,

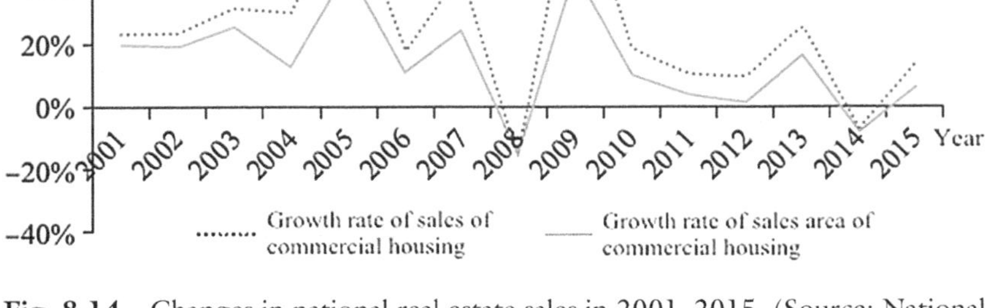

Fig. 8.14 Changes in national real estate sales in 2001–2015. (Source: National Bureau of Statistics)

household appliances, and petrochemical decoration. Since the 2008 international financial crisis, the government has launched 4 trillion economic stimulus plans to further promote real estate sales, which reached its peak in 2009. Since 2010, the government began to control the rapid rise of housing prices to prevent real estate bubbles, thus ending the rapid increase of the real estate industry; investment demand began to decline and the real estate inventory began to increase.

However, after nearly 20 years of rapid growth, real estate supply and demand has become imbalanced. First-tier cities are in short supply with surging housing prices, while in some three-tier and four-tier cities, there have been severe backlogs of commercial housing inventory. According to the National Bureau of Statistics in 2015, the total area of real estate sold reached 1.28 billion square meters, an increase by 6.5% year-on-year. The growth rate of commercial property sales rose by 14.1%. The for-sale area was 718.53 million square meters. In 2011–2015, the average annual growth rate of for-sale areas was up to 22.2% (see Fig. 8.15). Due to the narrow investment channels of residents, commercial housing has gradually deviated from the living function and evolved into a tool for investment. According to China Economic Net, if China's housing area per capita is 30 square meters, currently the "vacant" housing which is uninhabited can supply nearly 240 million people for living. The inventory

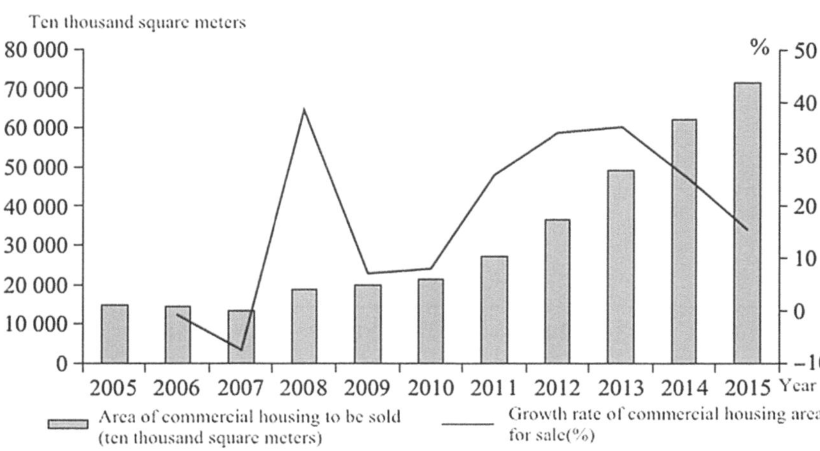

Fig. 8.15 National real estate for-sale areas and growth rates in 2005–2015

increase of commercial housing would directly result in the rises of upstream building materials and steel industry inventories (see Figs. 8.16).

From the micro-cosmic perspective of enterprises, de-capacity means shutdowns or even bankruptcy, and the layoff of workers. The capitals invested could not be recovered, and thus became sunk costs. Many entrepreneurs were not willing to actively take measures to reduce production. From the government's point of view, the five sectors are heavy-capital enterprises, which could make great contributions to local economic growth, taxation, and the settlement of employment, so it is usually difficult for local governments to give up these enterprises. From banks' point of view, these over-capacity enterprises used to be customers that banks have strongly supported and hugely loaned. Hence it is undoubtedly that de-capacity, de-inventory, and de-leveraging mean that banks' non-performing loans are likely to increase substantially. Under the pressure performance appraisal, some banks are hesitant in terms of stopping lending to these enterprises or resolutely calling in the loan (Fig. 8.17).

Faced with this complex situation, we must adhere to the following principles: (1) respect the laws of the market and allow the market to play a decisive role in the allocation of resources. As long as the government does not intervene and leave the problem of over-capacity to be solved by the market, the mechanism of survival of the fittest in the market competitions will force companies to reduce excess capacity, and

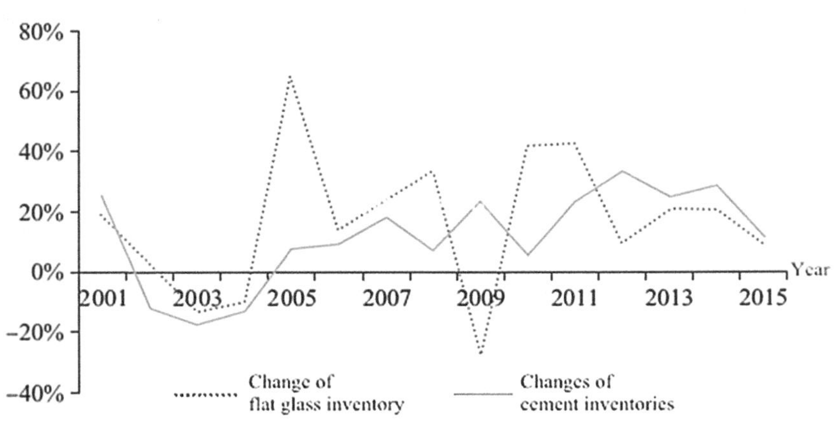

Fig. 8.16 Changes of inventory in building materials industry. (Source: National Bureau of Statistics)

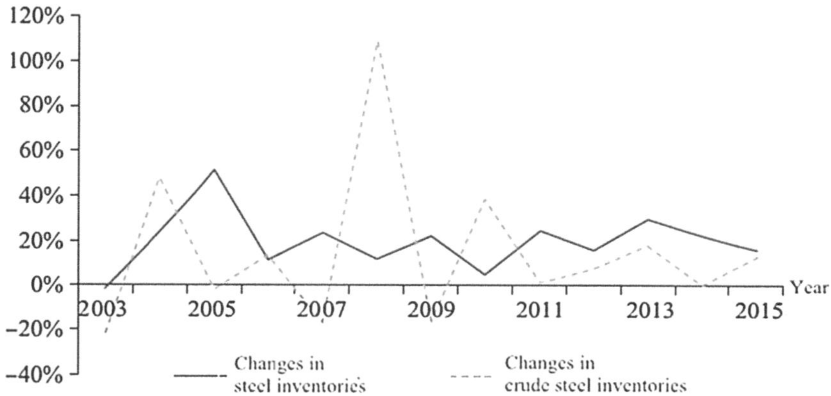

Fig. 8.17 Inventory changes in iron and steel industry in 2003–2015. (Source: National Bureau of Statistics)

bring punishment to the enterprises that do not adapt. (2) Design in an overall manner instead of achieving de-capacity, de-inventory, and de-leverage fragmentarily. De-capacity, de-inventory, and de-leverage is a complex system engineering, involving a number of interrelated industries. Rather than take straight measures, we need to take advantage of a linked effect to make real estate the core of de-stocking. Only by seizing the major contradiction can we achieve good results. Otherwise, carrying out de-capacity separately is easy to result in mutual obstruction and inefficiency. (3) For state-owned enterprises (SOEs), the competent departments should make scientific judgments, follow the market situation, resolutely give up saving the zombie enterprises, strive to merge and reorganize, and, at the same time, solve the laid-off employees' employment and maintain social stability.

8.3.2 Acting Both Inside and Outside to Make Up for the Weakness of Technologies and Brands

To implement supply-side structural reforms, while doing a good job of "subtraction", we must also make great efforts to do the "addition". In addition to raising investments to infrastructure, pension, medical, education, environmental protection, and cultural and sports facilities we need to provide effective supply in response to the people's growing material and cultural needs. We believe that the key to weakness is technological progress. It is essential to implement preferential policies, increase investment in research, focus on short-board technologies, and enhance the contribution rate of science and technology to economic growth from the perspective of improving productivity and labor productivity.

1. Encouraging scientific and technological innovation to enhance industries' core competitiveness

Looking at the major industrial countries, the contribution rates of science and technology in their national economic growth are more than 50% and in the United States the rate is more than 70%. Although China has increased investment in scientific research in the 12th "Five-Year Plan" period and encouraged mass innovation, and has been in sync with or even got ahead of the world's advanced level in the fields of space technologies, 4G mobile communication, high-speed rail, and nuclear power, its overall technological level is still lagging behind compared with advanced developed countries. In China's economic growth, the contribution rate of science and technology is less than 50%. At present, in the nine high-tech fields, China can compete only in the trade of computer and communications technology and biotechnology, while the trade competitiveness of the other seven areas remains poor. In order to obtain high competitiveness in the international industrial chain in the coming decade, China needs to adopt comprehensive measures in terms of fiscal measures, finance, income, and intellectual property rights; encourage the transformation of innovations and scientific and technological achievements into productive forces; continuously improve the industry's technological content and labor productivity; and promote trade and industrial upgrading. The government should encourage investment in high-tech industries, implement a financial accounting system that stimulates investments into R&D, and enhance the tax preferences for high-tech absorption and patent transformation. China needs to enhance enterprises' intrinsic incentives for technology innovation through complete policy support, making them truly become the main players of technological innovation. Specific measures would include: providing tax incentives for independent innovation industries and economic activities; increasing the deduction for pre-tax income for R&D investment; allowing enterprises to accelerate the depreciation of equipment and instruments used for research and development; reducing or exempting high-tech enterprises' income tax; and encouraging financial institutions like banks, securities, insurance, and funds to strengthen financial support for innovation-oriented enterprises. At the same time, it needs to guide foreign investment into high-tech fields, and restrict investments into low-tech industries. While gradually implementing national treatment for foreign investors, China has to launch appropriate tax incentives and restrictive policies to encourage FDI to invest more in the manufacturing of high-tech general equipment, communications equipment, and other electronic facilities. It needs to increase the technical content of trade-related foreign-directly-invested activities, and promote sustainable, stable, and healthy trade development.

China needs to encourage enterprises to increase R&D investment, and strive to achieve the goal of 60% contribution rate of scientific and technological progress to economic growth by 2020, thus transforming "Made in China" into "Quality in China" and "Intelligence in China". Once such economic "transformation" has been realized, China's economy will have a strong international competitiveness, and it would be easier to elevate from the low end to the high end, and consequently, the foundation of RMB's internationalization would be more solid.

2. Promoting the M&A of the high-end manufacturing industry in developed countries to increase high-tech supply

The manufacturing sector in major industrial countries has a long history. Many of their enterprises have world-renowned brands and core technologies. At present, some Chinese enterprises have a strong economic strength and strong ability to absorb advanced technologies; however, they are hunger for core industries for product upgrading in the fierce international competition. The core technology should mainly be obtained through independent research and development. In the cases, it might also be a shortcut to purchase and absorb advanced technology from developed countries. Especially when the international financial crisis has not yet ended, Europe has been hit by the new refugee crisis, which has worsened the uncertainty of its economic recovery. Due to the difficulty of survival under such a shrunken market, many manufacturers have the willingness and motivation to sell their own brands and technology and even the whole company. Chinese enterprises should seize the opportunity and select the ideal target enterprise through M&A on the basis of the actual needs of industrial transformation and upgrading, so as to enrich their technology, brands, and international marketing network and elevate faster from the low end of the international industrial chain to the high end.

However, even purely market-oriented act of M&A aimed at western companies could be hampered by some European and American countries' political prejudice against China. Therefore, it is necessary to play the role of government guidance and support, to coordinate all forces of politics, diplomacy, and community to help Chinese enterprises to complete the M&A activity in developed countries, enhance the technological level of domestic enterprises, build international marketing brands and network, and improve the supply level of domestic enterprises to the global commodity market.

3. Strengthening the quality and brand-building to complement the short board of effective supply

For middle-income stage, quality and brand has been much emphasised in consumption. No brand means no market and no stance. Therefore, developing a large number of well-known brands is the protection for China's real economy to withstand a variety of adverse impacts. Chinese government should formulate laws and regulations to protect intellectual property rights so as to develop a good environment for brands' development, and to strengthen the positive publicity of domestic products and brands from the perspective of public cultural opinion. In fact, Chinese enterprises' existing technology and management level have been sufficient to produce high-quality products that meet the high-end needs. Hence, the crowded overseas shopping shouldn't have happened. However, domestic enterprises lack the awareness of their own brands and pay more attention to the quality of products serving foreign countries than to those for the domestic, thus undermining the reputation of their own brands. In addition, the stereotype that domestic brands are low in quality and prices has affected the choice of high-end consumers, making them more likely to choose imported products. When Chinese people do not want to buy domestic-brand products at high prices, those brands have to provide cheaper products, which correspondingly have lower quality, and that would further deepen the low-quality and low-cost image of domestic brands, constituting a vicious circle that is hard to break. Therefore, to create world-known brands and to cultivate domestic market, Chinese enterprises have to strictly control the quality of production so as to develop brand reputation with long-term high quality. At the same time, the government should follow relevant laws and regulations to protect domestic brands, severely punish fake and other intellectual property infringement, standardize the market environment, and protect domestic brands.

China's industrial transformation and upgrading cannot be separated from the international market. China needs to make long-term national brand development plan while encouraging enterprises to go out. It should make full use of the consulate and local Chinese organizations, regularly organize various exhibitions that attract Chinese and foreign enterprises, help enterprises understand local environment and culture, and make them understand the local market segmentation so as to target accordingly. Meanwhile, it should help enterprises to establish unimpeded overseas sales channels and promote their corporate brands. A common strategy for Chinese enterprises in the past was to first occupy the domestic market, and then to be an original equipment manufacturer (OEM) for foreign companies. They would use OEM production to form the reputation of quality in the international market, and then take advantage of this reputation to seek agents, and gradually promote their own brands. It has become difficult for this kind of approach to succeed today when the unicorn enterprises with Internet thinking prevail. Hence, they have to learn from Unilever, Procter & Gamble, and other multinational companies' brand management strategy, which is to acquire well-known local brands at an appropriate cost, make full use of "Internet +", and develop innovative brand management to establish smooth sales channels and a reasonable model of brand operation and management.

8.3.3 Strengthening the Economic Function of Financial Services Entities

1. Preventing the mismatch of resources and the risk of economic bubbles

Finance is an efficient means of resource allocation. Developed financial markets and various financial instruments are vital promoters for the development of the real economy. After joining the SDR basket, China's financial market has become more open. The RMB covers both offshore and onshore markets; participant, product innovation and varieties will have a leap-type development. Financial industry itself has a greater possibility of separating from the real economy for self-expansion and self-service. Therefore, it is particularly essential to emphasize China's clear long-term positioning of the financial industry and place the relations between finance and real economy rightly. The concept of finance serving the real economy should never be swerved.

In the allocation of capital elements, China should take the advantages of its social system, and comprehensively use fiscal and taxation policies to balance the excess revenues of domestic financial operation and the average profit of industrial entities. It should inhibit the tendency of financial "off-the-real" self-expansion and self-circulation, and prevent the stock market, the gold market, the real estate market, the foreign exchange market, and some derivatives market from breeding asset bubbles or squeezing the real economy investment, so as to ensure that financial institutions are using funds to serve the real economy.

We should strengthen the guidance of foreign capitals, foster a more convenient and legal operating environment, and encourage foreign investors to invest in the commodity market, services, and other real industries, promoting China's related industries to improve technology and management level.

We should strengthen the integration of production and financial cooperation and speed up international capacity cooperation under controllable risks so as to better achieve industrial transformation and upgrading goals of de-stocking and de-capacity. We should rely on the improvement of domestic scientific and technological level to enhance the technological content of overseas investment, and improve the technological spillover effect of China's FDI, thus maintaining the superiority of China's overseas investment. At the same time, we need to encourage the overseas investments' profits to reflow and be invested into R&D and industrial upgrading, and into the scientific and technological innovation of traditional physical industries, upgrading the domestic industrial level. China should learn from the lessons that Japanese economy had in the process of the Japanese yen's sharp inflation and its internationalization, prevent the industry from over-quick transferring to foreign countries, and avoid the hollowing of industry and the de-industrialization. Otherwise, the economy would be likely to lose growth foundation and development momentum, which would inevitably lead to another "two decades lost".

2. Multiple measures to guarantee financial services for the real economy

We need to accelerate the construction of domestic financial market. It is not only necessary to form a capital market that accords with the scale of China's physical industry, but also essential to develop a financial sector and market that matches economic transformation and upgrading requirements, so that the need of investment and production in various types of enterprises and upgraded consumption demands of individuals can get sufficient financial support, and domestic and foreign capitals would be able to find satisfactory financial products in the domestic financial market. At the same time, we need to attach great significance to the degree of financial virtualization; appropriately constrict the development of financial derivatives operating purely within the financial system and aimed at profiting within the financial system or even avoiding financial regulation; and form a relatively safe capital market reliable for physical industry and international capacity cooperation.

We should open capital accounts and financial markets in a prudent, gradual, and controllable manner; strengthen the application of big data technology; integrate the regulations of banking, securities, and insurance; and strengthen the monitoring of capital flows. In the process of opening capital accounts and financial market, we should design and introduce a variety of capital flow detection and management tools, for example, introducing Tobin tax that helps to curb the flow of short-term capitals, or mitigating the shock from short-term capital flows through increasing costs and constraining flow speed.

We should strengthen the implementation of macro-prudence policies. In the event of abnormal short-term capital flows, we should raise or reduce the capital adequacy ratio and provision requirements through imposing a tax on net foreign currency positions of financial institutions, restrain the mismatch between maturity and currency of financial institutions' balance sheets, and mitigate the impact from short-term capital fluctuations on the financial system. We should learn from the lessons that Japan has provided in this regard. After the yen's appreciation, the Japanese government failed to timely adjust the financial market or actively resolve the shocks and risks of the currency appreciation. On the contrary, an unhealthy domestic financial system enlarged that impact and risks, resulting in huge real estate bubbles and severe hollow of industry, and Japan has paid a great price for it.

3. Increasing financial support for micro-, small- and medium-sized enterprises

Micro-, small-, and medium-sized enterprises (MSMEs) have contributed significantly to promoting market competition, enhancing market vitality, and promoting technological innovation. They have become an important player in national economy and market development. However, MSMEs are small in scale, weak in profitability, imperfect in financial system, insufficient in credit concept, and incomplete or incorrect in financial statement information. These have become certain obstacles for banks to conduct pre-credit investigation of enterprises. Difficulty in getting loans has become a major restriction for SME development.

In order to effectively solve the financing problem for SMEs, in June 2015, the PBOC lowered the deposit reserve ratio. It decided to, from June 16, 2014, cut the reserve requirement ratio of RMB by 0.5 percentage points for the commercial banks that meet prudence business requirements and achieve a certain proportion of loans to rural areas and small- and micro-sized enterprises, and guide the credit resources to support the "agriculture, farmer and rural areas" and small and micro enterprises.

The CBRC needs to guide and supervise small and medium enterprises; comprehensively examine the loans for them from three aspects of growth rate, the number of households, and the success rate of application; and establish the three "no less" regulatory standards. The three "no less" mean that, on the basis of effectively increasing the loan increment, we should make great efforts to achieve a loan growth for small and micro enterprises no less than the average loan growth, the number of households in this regard no less than the number of households over the same period last year, and a success ratio no less than the level of the same period last year.

In addition to expanding the accessibility of loans, the capital market also tries to broaden the channels of direct financing for MSMEs. The CSRC has proposed ten opinions on capital market's support for small- and micro-sized enterprises to enable excellent small- and micro-sized enterprises to enter the capital market for financing as soon as possible through vigorously developing the private placing market and expanding the scope of corporate bonds, constructing and improving China's multi-level capital market. The establishment of National Equities Exchange and

Quotation (NEEQ) provides services for the open stock transfers, financing, and M&A of non-listed joint-stock companies and makes great contributions to the development of SMEs. For the private SMEs, the NEEQ not only provides new financing channels, but also introduces strategic investors. It brings in funds and, meanwhile, introduces standardized corporate governance so as to lay a solid capital and governance foundation for enterprises to become bigger and stronger.

In 2015, the Ministry of Finance, the Inland Revenue Department, and the State Administration of Taxation jointly issued *the Notice on Issues Relating to Preferential Income Tax Policies for Small-Sized and Small Profit Enterprises*. From January 1, 2015, to December 31, 2017, for enterprises with an annual taxable income less than 200,000 yuan (including 200,000 yuan) only 50% of their taxable income would be counted with a tax rate of 20%. The loan contracts signed by financial institutions and micro- and small-sized enterprises are exempted from the stamp duty. In addition, a series of policies and measures have been formulated to provide SMEs favorable conditions in terms of value-added tax and business tax, reduce their tax burden, enhance their profitability, improve their financial situation and credit, and develop their financing capacity.

8.4 RMB's Internationalization Benefits China's Economic Transformation and Upgrading

The supply-side reform and the healthy and sustainable development of China's economy are conducive to consolidate the physical foundation of RMB's internationalization. What cannot be ignored is that RMB's internationalization itself is to construct a more robust international currency order and increase the international liquidity supply, and it also provides a sound environment and driving forces for the transformation and upgrading of China's real economy. In fact, there is a good interactive mechanism between China's economic development and the economic-development-based RMB internationalization, which can provide necessary support to consolidate the domestic industry base, resist the adverse impact from the international community, and assist China's economy in completing the structural adjustment as soon as possible.

8.4.1 RMB Internationalization Can Promote Direct Investment and Industrial Upgrading

Actively using foreign capital and introducing advanced technologies are significant factors for China's manufacturing industry to have great progress and become the world's processing factory

China has 1.4 billion people. Its regional economic development is uneven, and it is in the process of new urbanization. Currently, China can provide a broad market to manufacturing enterprises from low end to high end, from primary industries to tertiary industries, from ordinary consumer goods to luxury ones, from material to spiritual, which is a great attraction for international investors. According to data from the Ministry of Commerce, in China's non-financial sector, 837,000 foreign-invested enterprises had been set up and the actual use of foreign capital had reached USD 1.6423 trillion by the end of December 2015. The internationalization of RMB has accelerated, especially after China joined the SDR basket, and the international community maintains an optimistic outlook about China's economy. The global top 500 multinational companies continue to invest in building new enterprises or make additional investment in China. The industries that they invest in have covered automobiles and components, petrochemicals, energy, infrastructure, biology, pharmacy, communications, finance, software services, and so on. The actual use of foreign capital reached 781.35 billion yuan in that year. The amount of foreign investment utilized by China is still among the top in the world.

The progress of RMB's internationalization has strengthened the confidence of foreign investors in China and facilitated RMB Foreign Direct Investment (RFDI). In particular, the expected appreciation of RMB along with the process of RMB's internationalization also encourages and leads foreign investment to play an active role in China's industrial transformation and upgrading. There are two new features of foreign capital utilization: first, higher proportion of green investment. Comparing with the previous investment in manufacturing and real estate, the proportion of foreign enterprises investing in finance, software, medical services, healthcare, and healthcare facilities has increased significantly; higher proportion of high-tech and high value-added products investment. China has been vigorously popularizing the use of information technology, reducing network costs, advocating using "Internet+" technologies to transform traditional industries, and encouraging mass entrepreneurship and mass innovation. The central and local governments have taken measures to encourage R&D investment, and improve the technical level and technology absorption capacity. These measures have in fact elevated the technological benchmark for foreign capitals to enter the Chinese market, which is conducive to improving the structure of foreign investment and introducing high-tech and capital-intensive enterprises.

Since the reform of the RMB exchange rate formation mechanism in 2005, despite the occasional short-term de-valuation, the RMB has been steadily appreciated. After the market-oriented reform of the RMB exchange rate on August 11, 2015, although there was significant depreciation of RMB's value against the USD, the RMB still maintained a slight appreciation according to the comprehensive calculation of the RMB's weighted average exchange rate against a basket of foreign currency based on the CFETS RMB exchange rate index released by China Foreign Exchange Trade Center. In fact, the RMB appreciation trend along with the process of RMB's internationalization has clearly affected the industrial choice of FDI. Over the past decade, due to the steady appreciation of RMB, the international comparative prices of the domestic raw materials and salaries, which are calculated in RMB, have greatly increased, adversely affecting the resource-consuming multinational companies that rely on China's resources. With the rapid increase of the average wage of China's labor force, the advantages of cheap labor in China are gradually weakening. The competition of low-tech and labor-intensive industries has been intensified and the living space for them has been narrowed, which forces foreign capitals to adjust their investment strategies and shift to higher-tech products and industries. The FDI "industries transfer effect" and "technology spillover effect" of RMB's appreciation are playing a leading role on China's industries and products' upgrading.

8.4.2 RMB Internationalization Can Promote International Production Cooperation

China is a developing country. Its practical technology and management experience have a comparative advantage to many developing countries, and are easier to learn by developing countries and more in line with their real demand compared to those in western developed countries. Therefore, using China's capital will not only help these countries to expand the scale of capital formation, increase their economic growth rates, and improve the employment and people's livelihood, but also help these countries to obtain better demonstration effect and technology spillover effect. The whole technical level and production capacity of China's real economy are also in line with the needs of the majority of developing countries in the world, so China's capital, which is carried by China's real estate production capacity to participate in international cooperation, is an international cause for mutually beneficial cooperation. In fact, China's high-speed rail technology, communications technology, aerospace technology, nuclear energy technology, home appliances technology, and infrastructure technology are in a leading position in the world. Both developed and developing countries can benefit from them. Therefore, since China has loosened the restrictions on enterprises' external investment and encouraged enterprises to go out, China has invested in over 180 countries in the world. In 2014, China's overseas investment exceeded the utilization scale of foreign investment in China for the first time, and it has become a net capital outflow country and ranked one of the most important overseas investment countries all in the world.

That RMB joined SDR consolidates the process of RMB's internationalization, expands the international community' demand for RMB, and makes the RMB-denominated investment more acceptable, which has provided overseas investment convenience and income stability for Chinese enterprises and improved the cross-border investment environment. "Going out" for international production cooperation is bound to be more active. Especially those private enterprises which were, in the past, constrained by foreign exchange and had weak risk management capacity of the exchange rate can benefit and can easily, quickly, and directly use RMB to invest abroad. Neither side has to exchange to a third currency. This would both save the exchange cost and avoid exchange rate risks. They can also utilize offshore RMB market more frequently to solve the financing difficulties encountered in transnational operations. It would greatly enhance their incentives in the cooperation of international production capacity, is conducive to changing the status that China's overseas investments mainly rely on SOEs, and promotes the international cooperation of China's capitals carried by industrial entities in a comprehensively and multi-agent manner.

In 2015, the total volume of China's bilateral trade with "Belt and Road" initiative countries reached $995.5 billion, accounting for 25.1% of the country's total trade volume. China's direct investment in those countries reached $14.82 billion, increasing by 18.2% year-on-year, which was much higher than the level of China with countries in other regions. As we have put forward in *RMB Internationalization Report 2015*, commodity trade, infrastructure financing, industrial park construction, and cross-border e-commerce can be RMB internationalization's breakthroughs in the construction of "Belt and Road" initiative. In terms of China's foreign investment and international production cooperation, economic and trade cooperation zones and industrial parks are playing an important role. So far, China has cooperated with the countries along the initiative to build more than 50 overseas economic and trade cooperation zones, of which Belarus-China Industrial Park, Thailand-China Luoyong Industrial Park, and Indonesia-China Industrial Park have achieved prominent effects and begun to serve as important carriers for promoting China's enterprises to go out as a group and for the cooperation of international capacity and equipment manufacturing. In addition, keys projects like the signing of China-South Korea free trade agreement, the success of the China-ASEAN FTA upgrading negotiation, the initiation of Sino-Thailand high-speed rail project, the progress of Turkish East-to-West high-speed railway, and the Kyaukpyu special economic zone in Myanmar are all conducive to a higher-level international cooperation of China's capital and capacity.

The development of the Eurozone shows that choosing a currency that has close economic and trade relations in the regional economy as the key currency can help maintain long-term stability of supply and demand, avoid exchange rate risks, and accelerate the process of economic integration. Therefore, promoting the internationalization of the RMB in the construction of "Belt and Road" initiative can boost the economic integration of the countries along the way, and also add new impetus for China's industrial transferring and its international cooperation of production capacity cooperation.

8.4.3 RMB's Internationalization Can Stabilize the Supply of Commodity Materials

RMB's internationalization is to play RMB's role as an international currency in trading settlement, financial transactions, and official reserves, of which the RMB-denominated settlement of commodities is a breakthrough in this process. At present, gold and iron ore have already begun to be denominated in RMB in the transaction.

Since the establishment of the Bretton Woods system, the USD has been the currency of the commodity. When the dollar and gold de-coupled with each other, the dollar's liquidity is in the tendency of constant expanding; especially after the "9/11", the United States has been implementing a loose monetary policy, leading to the proliferation of dollars. As a result, the determination of commodity prices has been separated from the actual market supply and demand, and, instead, depended largely on changes in liquidity and speculations. Hardly did the commodity producers or consumers have any say in the pricing. As the largest importer and the largest consumer of a variety of commodities, China is often faced with the dilemma of "once bought, the price goes up; once sold, the price goes down", causing a great threat to the steady development of China's economy, and artificially setting obstacles for Chinese economy to transform "from big to strong". Moreover, the resources-oriented developing countries, restricted by their comprehensive national strength, were not strong enough to confront the developed countries in the commodity market for their own destiny. China is developing into a country with economy mainly driven by consumption, and the demand for some commodities is still rising. For example, China now has become the largest trader and consumer of gold and crude oil, and more than 70% of its commodities are imported from the countries along the Belt and Road initiative. Hence, strengthening the cooperation of commodity production between China and the countries along the way and using RMB for denomination is undoubtedly a win-win strategy.

Whether making RMB as a pricing currency for commodities and whether the price of commodities can be determined by the real needs largely depend on whether the future price fluctuation risks of commodities fluctuations can be controlled through the RMB derivative products. By integrating the demand for commodities of the countries along the way, and combining the single demand of China with the regional demand, China has enhanced the pricing right of "Belt and Road" countries in commodity market and consumption through free trading with the countries along the way, controlling transportation, participating in commodity production, providing financial services, and so on. Taking crude oil as an example, China, the Middle East, Central Asia, Russia, and other countries and regions can cooperate to promote the region's crude oil trade to be priced and settled in RMB and to promote the crude oil future price proposed by Shanghai International Energy Center to be another benchmark price like WTI, Brent, Dubai, and Oman, and thereby enhance the pricing right of crude oil of these countries, including China. In fact, the level of commodity prices is not the core issue. The purpose of making commodities RMB-denominated is to make the prices related to the real demand and affordable, make resources controllable, and able to achieve added value, and fairly and reasonably distribute the value between the exporting country and the consuming countries.

In short, given China's current promotion of scientific and technological progress, the optimizing of the resource allocation, and the improvement of effective supply, steadily boosting the RMB internationalization process will help China optimize the allocation of resources in domestic and international markets, accelerate the pace of international production cooperation, and play a positive role in China's industrial upgrading and transformation and in the supply-side reform. It is noteworthy that the implementation of the supply-side reform and the completion of "de-capacity, de-stocking, de-leveraging, and cost reducing" will inevitably lead to economic growth decline, the increase of bank non-performing ratio and the government deficit, and even greater social instability risks in the short run. If these risks cannot be resolved in time, it is likely to impact the entire financial system, deteriorate the financial environment of the real economy, and bring about systemic financial risks. We need to construct the framework of scientific macro-prudence policies, and launch prior-monitoring and evaluation plans in all channels, all aspects and all kinds of risks during the process of supply-side reform to prevent the systemic risks, all channels and all kinds of risks during the process of supply-side reform, and make prevention plans accordingly to defuse risks. These are essential strategic measures to ensure the success of supply-side reform and consolidate the economic foundation of RMB's internationalization.

CHAPTER 9

The Prevention of Systematic Risks and the Framework for Macro-Prudential Policies

International Monetary Institute

9.1 The Necessity of Constructing a Macro-Prudential Policy Framework

In December 2015, RMB joined the SDR basket. Marking international recognition to a greater extent, this event is a milestone in RMB internationalization. Accelerating the marketization of exchange rates and liberalization of capital accounts, it also forces China's financial system to open up further.

The opening up of the financial system would first cause large-scale capital flow worldwide, shocking China's exchange rates and interest rates. To a certain extent, the inflow of international capital has promoted macro-economic development. However, a massive inflow of short-term capital will raise the ratio of short-term external debt to the total external debt, distorting the price of domestic currency and assets, thus resulting in over-investment and possibly excessive credit. The financial system may

International Monetary Institute (✉)
Renmin University of China, Beijing, China
e-mail: imi@ruc.edu.cn

International Monetary Institute (ed.), *Currency Internationalization and Macro Financial Risk Control*,
https://doi.org/10.1007/978-981-13-0698-3_9

face greater risks. In case of a short-term capital outrush, people would sell their domestic assets, dragging down their prices and causing a financial panic. If the panic spread, greater outflow of capital would ensue. When the capital outflow exceeds the foreign exchange reserves, the central government may declare the de-valuation of currencies against foreign currencies, leading to greater panic. And so a vicious circle is formed. Besides, RMB exchange rates face more risks as the financial system opens up. Through capital flows, investment structure, and other factors, a closer interaction between capital and asset investment will bring about a more complicated mechanism of interest rates and exchange rates, rendering the regulation of both rates more difficult. A typical example is the yen. During the internationalization of the yen, the Japanese government tried to rely on appreciation for better international status. However, without strong support from the real economy, the value function of the yen was gradually lost, while the value fluctuated violently. In addition, although China's overall external debt is currently controllable, external debt repayment is also one of the potential risks after the financial system opens up. After RMB becomes convertible, former control over external debt will no longer be feasible. Once the exchange rates fluctuate substantially, problems may arise in terms of debt solvency. When the foreign debt ratio of a country is too high, the decline in solvency will lead to a fall in credit rating, lowering the country's ability to refinance and further reducing financial confidence, thus creating a vicious circle.

After all, with the opening up of China's financial system, exchange rate risks, external shocks, domestic financial market risks, and real economy risks become more intertwined and contagious, thus increasing systemic risks. Since the second half of last year, the stock market and foreign exchange market have shown great volatility. Although the event did not induce systemic risks, it has increased the probability of the chain impact of systemic risk caused by a single market or local risks.

In recent years, China has continuously strengthened the identification and prevention of systemic risks and actively participated in the reform of global macro-prudential supervision and management. Domestically, China has introduced a series of macro-prudential tools and strengthened their coordination with macro-economic policies, effectively preventing the accumulation of systemic risks. However, a potential danger of systemic risk outbreak still exists, as China lacks a macro-prudential policy framework in line with national conditions, and currently undergoes the "triple transition" and economic downturn. Therefore, it is important to speed up the reform of macro-prudential supervision during the present window period.

In fact, "macro-prudential" is neither a new word nor a new problem. It was first coined by the BIS as early as 1979. Nearly three decades later, macro-prudential supervision, as the "macro-economic regulatory guidance", was rarely mentioned, except when "scattered" in reports of international agencies like the BIS and the IMF. It was not until the 1997 Asian financial crisis that the importance of macro-prudential supervision began to be recognized both theoretically and practically. During the 2008 world financial crisis, "macro-prudential supervision" has been further strengthened.

The main objective of macro-prudential supervision is to curb systemic risks, protect financial stability, and reduce the huge economic cost of financial crises. In the narrow sense, macro-prudential supervision is limited to a systematic combination of prudential regulatory policies, emphasizing on the design of regulatory instruments in both the time dimension (or "vertical" dimension) and the cross-sectoral dimension (or "horizontal" dimension). In the broad sense, macro-prudential supervision includes systemic risk analysis, identification and monitoring, policy tools and implementation of conduction and governance structure and institutional basis, and so on. When combined, all these components of macro-prudential management form what is internationally known as the "macro-prudential policy" (Fig. 9.1).

9.2 Systematic Risk Identification and Assessment

The traditional research on systemic risk defines it as a communication risk. It means that the external shock is not limited to the direct impact on the economy, but spread through the financial system and the real economy, ultimately leading to a crisis and damage to the real economy. This view focuses on preventing the collapse of individual institutions and the exogenous nature of risk, ignoring the financial imbalance in the early stages of accumulation and the role of common risk exposure that financial institutions have in the crisis.

In fact, the entire financial system may become volatile due to both external and internal factors; once the system is subjected to systemic risks, every single financial institution will inevitably be affected. Because of the financial crisis, key factors inducing the crisis are considered to include the common risks exposed in the financial system and financial imbalances

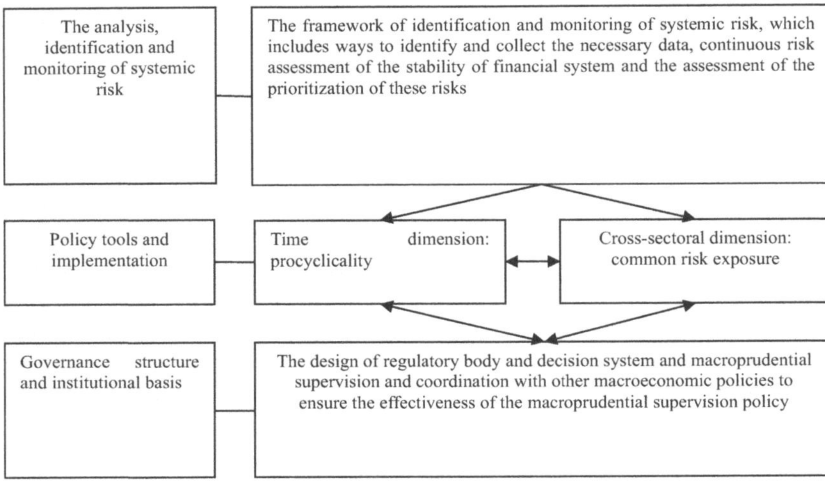

Fig. 9.1 Framework of macro-prudential policy

over time, rather than the spread of risks. Unlike traditional definitions, the definition of systematic risks lays more emphasis on the magnitude of financial imbalances, the procyclicality and relevance of the financial system, the endogeneity of risk, and so on.

According to the IMF, the BIS, and the Financial Stability Board (FSB), systemic risk is lately defined as the discontinuity of financial services (including credit intermediaries, risk management, payment systems, etc.) resulting from the failure of the whole or part of the financial system (possibly imposing serious negative effects on the real economy). However, the definition is not clear about the dependence on time, national environment, the financial system, the effect on the real economy, and the sensitivity of policy intervention. Thus it does not accurately reflect the essence of systemic risks.

In addition, more researches are conducted to describe specific systemic risk from two dimensions, namely, time and space. The cross-sectoral dimension mainly considers the distribution of systemic risks in the financial system at a given point in time, including the common exposure of financial institutions and the contribution of individual or groups of financial institutions to systemic risk. In the modern financial system, financial institutions directly hold the same or similar assets, or indirect exposure to other institutions (e.g., counterparties) and tend to use the same value assessment and risk measurement tools and so on. Thus financial institutions enjoy increasing correlation, homogeneity, and concentration. In this case, risk is more likely to "breed" within the financial system and spread rapidly through a "risk network" woven by the same risk exposure. The time dimension (or "vertical dimension") focuses on how systemic risk changes over time—how systemic risk is constantly amplifying economic cycles through the interrelationship between the financial system and the real economy, leading to financial crises or the "procyclicality" of the financial system. During an economic upswing, financial institutions tend to have more exposures due to the weakening of risk awareness and the reduction of financing constraints, leading to high leverage, excessive market liquidity, and soaring asset prices. Without sufficient buffer, this process will lead to the accumulation of systemic risks and increasing financial imbalances, thus planting the seeds for financial crises. Once the economic trend reverses and the economy turns from upswing to downturn, financial imbalances will lead to large-scale financial turmoil. Consequently, de-leveraging, credit supply, and other financial services shall be substantially reduced, and the turmoil exacerbated. In addition, time and cross-sectoral relationship are not isolated. The common risk exposure of financial institutions has two impacts: first, it strengthens the correlation among financial institutions; second, it enables consistent actions among financial institutions, in which case systemic risks can more easily bring chain reaction to market players, strengthening the periodic fluctuations of economy.

9.2.1 Causes of Interaction Between Financial System and Real Economy

(1) Theoretical explanation of interaction between the financial system and the real economy

In the modern economy, the financial system is an important sector of the national economy. As part of the service sector, finance directly contributes to the real economy output, financing households and businesses and sharing risks. In addition, financial system matters in the rational allocation of scarce resources. It can be said that the establishment of a modern national economic system requires modernization of the financial system.

US economist Merton believes that the primary function of the financial system is to promote the effective allocation of scarce economic elements in an uncertain environment. This mainly involves the rational and efficient use of scarce resources among economic entities, regions, and periods, obtaining greater productivity and return. Relying on this function, companies can gain financing through financial institutions and engage in R&D activities requiring huge capital investment, so as to promote economic development. With promising market prospects, companies can also quickly expand production to achieve rapid growth. The families can better smooth intertemporal consumption through housing loans and other ways to improve welfare. Focusing on the primary function—resource allocation—Merton further summed up the six core functions through which the financial system affects the real economy. First, the financial system provides a payment and settlement system for transactions in goods and services. Upon its birth, the financial system freed people from barter, greatly improving the efficiency of transactions and reducing transaction costs. While the Internet industry has developed in recent years, the network payment, representing new settlement methods, improves in terms of transaction efficiency and transaction security. Second, by pooling small money, the financial system can finance projects that require substantial capital. This feature reflects resource allocation across economic entities, the most typical example of which is the bank's lending process. Without the financial industry, it is hard to imagine how to accomplish many modern big projects and R&D projects requiring huge investments. Third, the financial system can also achieve intertemporal and cross-regional allocation of resources. Certain studies have shown that regional financial strength is positively correlated with FDI and local economic growth. This result shows that the financial system can improve production efficiency and promote economic development through cross-regional resource allocation. Fourth, the financial system provides a platform to manage and control risk. This function mainly involves two aspects: on the one hand, the financial system itself can provide risk hedging tools, such as insurance, futures, and options. On the other hand, the financial system can reduce the risk of the whole economy by optimizing resource allocation for the real economy. Fifth, the financial system provides price signals for the market economy with de-centralized decision-making. Price is the soul of the market economy. Through price signals, a good financial system can accurately and quickly reflect market supply and demand, helping economic entities to make decisions. Sixth, a good financial system can reduce the asymmetric information that hinders smooth transaction.

Lin Yifu grouped the functions of the financial system into three categories: mobilization of funds, allocation of funds, and risk diversification. He pointed out that the most important function is fund allocation. The reason is that efficient allocation of funds increases productivity, encourages savings, and reduces overall economic risk. Therefore, the efficiency of a financial system is mainly concerned with the efficiency of its fund allocation. In theory, to reduce financing costs, a perfect financial system can help by overcoming the moral hazard, adverse selection, and other obstacles to capital flow problems. Thus it is advisable to allocate resources to the most competitive and innovative industries and enterprises, so as to improve the speed and quality of economic development. The most urgent task facing the Chinese economy is the shift from the traditional development mode of high energy consumption and high pollution to the new development mode featuring "Internet +", and "mass entrepreneurship and innovation". To improve the efficiency of capital allocation is an important support for economic restructuring. The importance of an efficient financial system to an innovative and entrepreneurial economy is reflected in two aspects. On the one hand, it can help start-ups to obtain the necessary financing; on the other hand, a good financial system can identify the real prospects for enterprises.

It's not difficult to find out that the financial system and the real economy have mutual influence and a spiral cross-promote relationship. By optimizing the allocation of resources and diversifying risks, the financial system serves the real economy. Furthermore, financial services are part of the real economic output, while the growth of the real economy also increases the demand for financial services and promotes the development of the financial sector. As China transforms from a manufacturing power to an innovation-oriented country, enterprises also need a surge in R&D investments. In general, R&D investments have both high costs and risks. The financial sector can either finance corporate R&D or diversify R&D risks. Therefore, as the real economy grows, its demand for financial services increases, promoting the development of finance. Moreover, as China's economic openness increases, enterprises and investors are more involved in international economic and financial activities, followed by an increase in demand for financial services.

(2) The transmission mechanism of financial risks and real economy fluctuations

1. Financial shock: impact on the real economy and transmission mechanism (taking the sub-prime mortgage crisis as an example)

In terms of several key variables reflecting the overall economy, financial shocks reduce average output, capital, and consumption while increasing the volatility of output, consumption, investment, and labor time. In other words, the financial crisis affected the real economy as well as the first and second moments of the main economic variables, featuring economic recession and increasing uncertainty.

As China's economy has not suffered from the financial crisis, we take the 2007–2009 sub-prime crisis in the United States as an example to examine how the financial shock spread in the real economy. As shown in Fig. 9.2, after the outbreak of the financial crisis, the first affected variables were GDP and private investment. The decline in private investment is

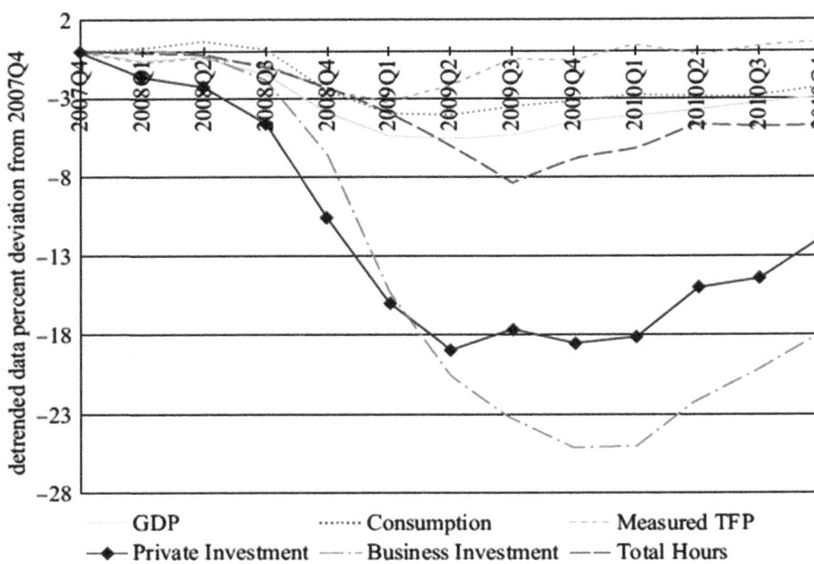

Fig. 9.2 Change of major US economic variables compared with 2007Q4

mainly caused by the decline in real estate investment. Commercial investment, consumption, and total labor time did not begin to plunge until the third quarter of 2008, while private investment had a six-month lag. However, in the second quarter of 2009, or an early stage of the financial crisis, the economic slowdown was not significant. With the bankruptcy of Lehman Brothers in September 2008, GDP, private investment, business investment, labor time, and consumption began to plunge. During the trough, compared to the fourth quarter of 2007, GDP fell by 5.6%, labor input more than 8%, private investment more than 20%, and business investment more than 25%. In contrast to previous economic crises, the major economic variables have not only slowed down but also for a long period of time. Correspondingly, total factor productivity indicators have fallen by more than 3%, but productivity is recovering faster than other major economic variables.

We shall discuss the impact of financial shocks on the real economy from the perspective of two economic micro-entities, namely, household and business. The credit crunch caused by the financial crisis is usually manifested by increasing financing difficulties and cost of carry. In terms of family decision-making, it is through two channels that the credit panic affects household, the most basic entity. First, households with higher debt levels had to cut back on borrowing and lower their debt because of tightening credit constraints, which reduced the demand for credit to some extent. Second, households that are not subject to credit constraints usually take precautionary measures, such as increasing savings to guard against potential financial risks. This will increase the supply of credit. As a result, interest rates will decline, due to the demand for credit, interest rates will decline under balance. Thus when a credit panic occurs, a change in the credit supply–demand relationship will lead to a reduction in the equilibrium interest rate. Studies have found that when an economy suffers from a credit panic, the interest rate slumps before slowly returning to a steady-state level that is lower than before the financial shock. This excessive adjustment of interest rates is made because households with much debt before the onset of the financial shock have to adjust their credit quickly for adapting to new credit constraints. So demands plunge, and lead to a low interest rate. As the distribution of economic agents slowly converges to the new steady level, the pressure on the credit demand gap decreases and the interest rate begins to slowly become steady again. In general, when hit by financial shocks, households with higher debt levels had to cut leverage by reducing consumption and increasing labor supply.

When there is nominal price rigidity, total output is mainly determined by consumer demand. Therefore financial shocks bring about a decline in output. Even worse, the fall in output will be greater when the nominal interest rate is close to zero, or when the central bank cannot further reduce the rate for stabilizing exchange rates and preventing capital outflows in an open economy. Theoretically, when we consider real estate—a consumer durable for investment—the credit panic, on the one hand, forced households with net debt to cut leverage and reduce consumption. On the other hand, preventive measures make other households to increase investment in housing and other durable consumer goods. Therefore, economic theories cannot predict what reactions the real estate investment will raise. However, taking the US financial crisis in 2007 as an example, a large number of empirical studies have shown that the collapse of the real estate market and the credit crisis are closely related, leading to the decline in output, consumption, and employment. At present, although the overall level of debt of China's households is not high, we still have to be vigilant of the rapid expansion of new financial instruments that have not yet been incorporated into the regulatory system, and the resulting rapid increase in household leverage.

Another important micro-entity is the business. Next we will discuss the spread of financial shocks in the real economy from the perspective of manufacturers. In the actual economic operation, manufacturers often cannot invest all willingly in production and research and development activities, but face credit constraints, working capital constraints, and inventory constraints, among others. A well-functioning financial system can help firms to mitigate the negative effects of these constraints so that capital can be well utilized to increase overall economic productivity. Yet developing countries often do not have a sound financial system, leading to more common resource mismatch and lower production efficiency. When an economy suffers a financial shock, it is often followed by the tightening of credit. In turn, the most direct impact is the lack of corporate working capital. Companies have to maintain operations through other measures such as layoff. More seriously, the tightening of credit affects some enterprises that could invest in the best way; now they can only choose sub-optimal investment plans. The choice will result in a decrease in the efficiency of capital allocation and a decline in productivity. For young or entrepreneurial firms, the tightening brings an even bigger impact. Although their productivity is usually high, their lack of capital accumulation often makes them more dependent on external financing.

Conversely, large enterprises, with their own capital adequacy, are not subject to this constraint, even when credit constraints are tightened. They are even able to expand the size of their firms through lower interest rates and relatively safer assets. Studies have shown that the US sub-prime mortgage crisis beginning at the end of 2007 has rendered small enterprises to reduce labor investment by two times that of large enterprises. Because large firms are often less dynamic and less productive than small ones, the mismatch of capital slows the overall productivity of the economy. In an open economy, economies that suffer from financial shocks are less attractive to FDI and less likely to introduce new technologies. In China, we need to pay special attention to the leverage and debt levels of the real estate business. As current capacity, inventory, and leverage fall, we need to prevent the real estate business from using policy loopholes, expanding blindly, and increasing leverage.

Another consequence of the financial shock is that the increase in economic uncertainty, that is, the future returns on investment, becomes more ambiguous and risky. One of the immediate effects of the increase in uncertainty is a decline in the willingness to invest. The reduction of investment willingness is manifested by the decline of investment in the original technology level and by a large decrease in R&D investment. These consequences will cause short-term financial shocks to affect the economy over the medium- to long-term. In an open economy, the increase in uncertainty may also feature an outflow of capital, which may lead to a fall in the exchange rate, causing more capital outflows. Mutual influence and reinforcements may lead a country's economy into recession.

All in all, the financial impact will make enterprises more subject to credit, working capital, inventory, and other constraints, forcing companies to lay off, reduce investment, and reduce R&D and other activities. Under heterogeneity of enterprises, financial shocks have a greater impact on small and entrepreneurial enterprises than on large enterprises, which aggravates the mismatch of capital and reduces the overall productivity.

2. Causes of the previous financial crisis

The famous American economist Alan Blinder (also professor of Princeton University) has summed up seven major factors causing a financial crisis. We will further attribute these factors into five categories, and discuss causes of the Japanese financial crisis.

First, the asset bubble. Asset bubbles can be divided into the real estate bubble and the bond bubble represented by the mortgage-backed securities. According to the Case-Shiller home price index, created by economist Karl Case and Robert Shiller, US real estate prices between 1997 and 2006 increased by 85%, far above the average increase of US home prices recorded. Similarly, the Japanese real estate prices in the late 1980s also experienced great inflation. In the booming real estate market of both countries, due to rising real estate prices, even the mortgage holders with lower repayment ability can easily obtain mortgage refinancing and pay old mortgages with higher interest rates. Therefore, in this period, mortgage default is very rare. The low default rate renders the risk premium of mortgage-backed securities very low. In fact, because of the overall economic prosperity, the risk premium is low, not just for mortgage-backed bonds, but for other bonds as well. Longer market booms and low default rates during the bubble period send a false signal to investors that the default rate of bonds can be maintained at a low level for a long time, thus creating a bond bubble. However, such an ultra-low-risk premium is doomed to be unsustainable, and the bond bubble will eventually burst.

Looking back, we find that the real estate bubble and the bond bubble in the United States and Japan share a common cause—overly loose monetary policy. In response to a small recession in the US economy in 2001, the Fed lowered the federal benchmark rate to 1%. Similarly, the Bank of Japan cut its statutory rate to a record low of 2.5% in 1987, in response to Japan's weak exports following the 1985 Plaza Accord. Ultra-low interest rates drive a large amount of capital into the mortgage securities market (with higher interest rates and lower default rates), and even direct real estate investment. The influx of capital boosted the real estate prices, which gave birth to the real estate bubble and bond bubble.

What comes second is excessive leverage. The fragility of the US financial system before the crisis was mainly reflected in the excessive leverage. The US household leverage increased substantially with the drop in down payment ratio of housing mortgage loans or even the emergence of "zero down payment". In addition, due to the lack of supervision of off-balance-sheet assets of commercial banks, the US banks generally use structured investment instruments for off-balance-sheet assets transactions. These structured instruments often have significant leverage, allowing banks to bypass highly regulated investments in the national financial sector. Moreover, investment banks with higher returns tend to trade at extremely high leverage. For example, five major Wall Street investment banks have an average leverage rate of up to 30:1, or even 40:1. It can be said that before the financial crisis, from the US family and commercial banks to investment banks, all were involved in treacherous investments with high leverage, and a single mistake would result in failure.

Third, the financial system is an irrational incentive mechanism. This mechanism mainly consisted of two parts: the pay system for financial practitioners, and the rating agency incentive system. The pay system is a risk-averse system. Despite great risks, financial transactions, when successful, can reap considerable benefits. For a trader, success brings great rewards, and failure only means loss for investors. Such incentives will inevitably encourage financial practitioners to engage in risky transactions, exposing the entire financial system to greater risks. The gravest problem this mechanism brings in this financial crisis is the relaxation of housing mortgage eligibility, or the emergence of sub-prime loans. The ultimate collapse of financial derivatives based on sub-prime mortgages triggered this financial crisis. On the other hand, because buyers of the rating agencies products are also issuers of evaluation standards, the rating agencies often have some deviations in the evaluation of financial products. Investors cannot make accurate risk judgment because of the excessive reliance on rating agencies due to lack of information. In addition, when assessing the risk of a financial product, rating agencies often focus only on the product itself, while ignoring macro-systemic risks. However, during a systemic risk outbreak, the micro-risk of a single financial product often appears negligible.

Fourth, the highly complex financial derivatives follows, accompanied by the influx of capital and rapid financial innovation. Highly complex financial derivatives make it more difficult for disadvantaged investors to accurately judge investment risk, aggravating the blindness of investment.

Fifth, financial supervision is loose and the shadow banking system wantonly expands. Long before the financial crisis, the US financial regulators are mostly liberalists; more or less, they want to relax financial regulation. A major practice of loosening supervision is excessively relaxing the supervision of sub-prime mortgages, leading to their rapid expansion and setting a time bomb for the US financial system. Looser regulation is also reflected in American International Group's (AIG) case. AIG was the world's largest insurance company, enjoying good credit rating and becoming the most important seller in the market for derivatives, such as credit default swaps. However, back in 2000, the Commercial Futures

Modernization Act explicitly prohibited the regulation of derivative products. Without regulation, the AIG accumulated USD 500 billion of credit risk positions by 2007. Eventually, with the outbreak of the financial crisis, the Fed had to spend tens of billions of dollars on the nationalization of AIG to save it from bankruptcy. In addition, the rapidly growing shadow banking system is beyond regulation and much larger than the traditional banking system. Therefore, a large part of the financial industry is not subject to any regulatory supervision. According to Grammk, in 2005, the shadow banking system held more than 80% of all sub-prime mortgages. Japan's financial system in the late 1980s was not as complex as the US financial system in the early 2000s, but at the time there were also a large number of non-traditional banking institutions. One typical representative is the "housing finance specialized clubs" (also referred to as "Zhu Zhuan"), specialized in providing residential mortgages. Bankruptcy of housing finance specialized clubs in Japan is often considered as the first stage of the Japanese financial crisis. From the experience of the United States and Japan, an important condition for preventing financial risk accumulation and even the financial crisis is setting a regulatory system for the financial sector, especially for the speculative behaviors of shadow banks.

Box 9.1 The Origin and Diffusion of the Financial Crisis: Taking the United States and Japan as Examples

When Lehman Brothers—the fourth largest US investment bank—announced bankruptcy on September 15, 2008, the most serious financial crisis since the Great Depression gradually reached its climax, leading to years of economic recession. The impact of the financial crisis spread quickly to the real economy, and in the first quarter after Lehman Brothers' bankruptcy, the US real GDP declined by 3.7% annually. In the fourth quarter of 2008, the decline widened to an annual average of 8.9%. Then in the first quarter of 2009, the decline in GDP was still 5.3%. This systemic financial risk, caused by the recession in the United States and the world, has a huge and far-reaching impact. In this column, we will review the origins of the 2008 US financial crisis and its spread in the financial system, and then contrast it with the Japanese economic crisis of the 1990s.

Both financial crises originated from the real estate bubble burst. In the United States, real estate prices peaked at the start of 2006, then dropped mildly before plunging in 2007.

With house prices falling, sub-prime mortgage holders cannot pay by refinancing, and therefore can only choose to default. The increase in defaults has created a further pressure to depress real estate prices, so that more home mortgages have to choose default. This in turn leads to falling home prices—an increase in defaults—a further decline in housing prices—more defaults. A vicious cycle finally forms. This cycle not only brought about the burst of the real estate bubble, but also influenced the whole financial system with high leverage through a large number of financial products and derivatives. The first to suffer is a large number of investment banks holding mortgage-backed securities (collateralized debt obligation [CDO]) and Fannie Mae and Freddie Mac, two mortgage giants. In March 2008, Bear Stearns, Wall Street's fifth-largest investment bank, suffered first from a liquidity squeeze due to over-reliance on mortgage-backed securitization and the housing bubble burst. Then, with the loss of market confidence, the problem aggravated into insolvency, leaving the well-known company on the brink of bankruptcy. Eventually, the Fed had to absorb the loss of USD 29 billion, leading to the acquisition of Bear Stearns by JP Morgan Chase Bank. This mitigated the outbreak of systemic financial risks. Fannie Mae, Freddie Mac, and other investment banks on Wall Street suffered greatly, as the collapse of the housing market did not stop. The mortgage-backed securities and their securitization businesses were hit hard. The companies either are been nationalized or acquired by large banks or bankrupted. One of the most famous cases is the bankruptcy of Lehman Brothers in September 2008, which marked a watershed in the crisis and a trigger for the total outbreak of systemic risks. Meanwhile, the major investment banks, Fannie Mae, and Freddie Mac were tortured by the housing mortgage securitization business, and a US international insurance company was not spared too. AIG suffered a severe crisis when the real estate bubble burst as a result of its huge investment in "credit default swaps", a financial derivative that was based on sub-prime mortgages. The crisis eventually died down after the Fed provided 85 billion dollars and took over 79.9% of AIG shares. In addition, Lehman's bankruptcy extended the financial panic to monetary funds because of the close ties between Lehman and money market mutual funds. Then, due to a large number of bad mortgage loans, many commercial banks were also hit. The impact of commercial banks is not limited to bad mortgages or the loss brought about by financial derivatives, but also a loss of public confidence and deposits. Internationally, financial institutions such as the United Kingdom, France, and Germany also suffer great direct losses and indirect losses caused by the financial panic. The hazards of this financial crisis were not confined to the financial system, but spread through the entire real economy. Because of the liquidity drop in the financial market, the real economy was also faced with financing difficulties, causing abnormal operation of the real economy, an increase in unemployment, and negative economic growth.

In Japan, the real estate bubble burst is often attributed to two events: the raising of statutory interest rates by the Bank of Japan in May 1989 and the implementation of real estate financing control by the Japanese Ministry of Finance in March 1990. The fall in real estate and stock prices ensued. Similar to the United States, the decline in real estate prices caused a large number of mortgage defaults. Many housing finance specialized clubs held a large number of bad debts and faced bankruptcy. Failing to clean up these bad debts in time, the Japanese economy entered a 20-year recession.

In the case of the United States and Japan, the laissez-faire of the real estate bubble accumulated great risks for the financial system. The bubble burst impacted first related financial products, then other aspects of the financial system, eventually dealing a huge blow to the real economy. Next, we will analyze the causes of financial crises.

3. The Interaction of Monetary Policies with the Financial Market and Its Impact on the Macro-Economy: A Case Study of the Stock Market

We use the structural vector auto-regression (SVAR) model, which imposes both short-term and long-term constraints, to analyze the concurrency relationship between monetary policies and the financial market (taking the stock market as an example). We examine the interaction of monetary policies with the financial market and its impact upon the macro-economy. Different from the traditional VAR model, in order to incorporate the possible contemporaneous relationship between monetary policy and stock price into the model, we abandon the assumption of traditional SVAR model that the stock price is not affected by the current monetary policy or the monetary policy is not affected by the current stock price. We assume that stock prices and monetary policy mutually influence. In order to make the model identifiable, we also assume that the monetary policy shock has no long-term effect on the stock price. Because in the long run, stock prices are mainly affected by fundamental factors such as the profitability of listed companies, while the neutrality of monetary policy renders it impossible to affect the long-term stock price.

We use the monthly data from 1997 to 2015 as the sample interval to study the impulse responses of major variables such as inflation and GDP to monetary policy shocks and stock price shocks (Figs. 9.3 and 9.4). It can be seen that neither the interest rate shock nor the M2 supply shock has any significant effect on the stock price. To some extent, this shows that the transmission channel between monetary policy and financial market is still blocked, and it is necessary to further promote the reform of monetary policy and financial market. Both monetary policy shocks have significant effects on inflation, but the impact on output is slightly different. M2 supply has a significant positive effect on output after stage 5 of the shock. The impact of interest rates came relatively late, to be shown as a significant negative effect after stage 10. Thus, the two monetary policy instruments are good targets for monetary policy intermediaries. Stock price shocks have a significant effect on both interest rates and M2 supply, but the effect on M2 supply comes later than that on interest rates. This reflects that China's monetary policy takes into account the situation of the stock market. Asset prices contain information on the output of inflation, and monetary authorities should respond to asset price changes. In addition, stock price shocks have a significant impact on inflation and output, and rising stock prices will lead to inflation while stimulating output growth in the short term. This shows that China's stock market has occupied a more important position in the national economy, deserving more attention from policy-makers. This may also be one of the reasons that stock price shocks have a significant impact on monetary policy.

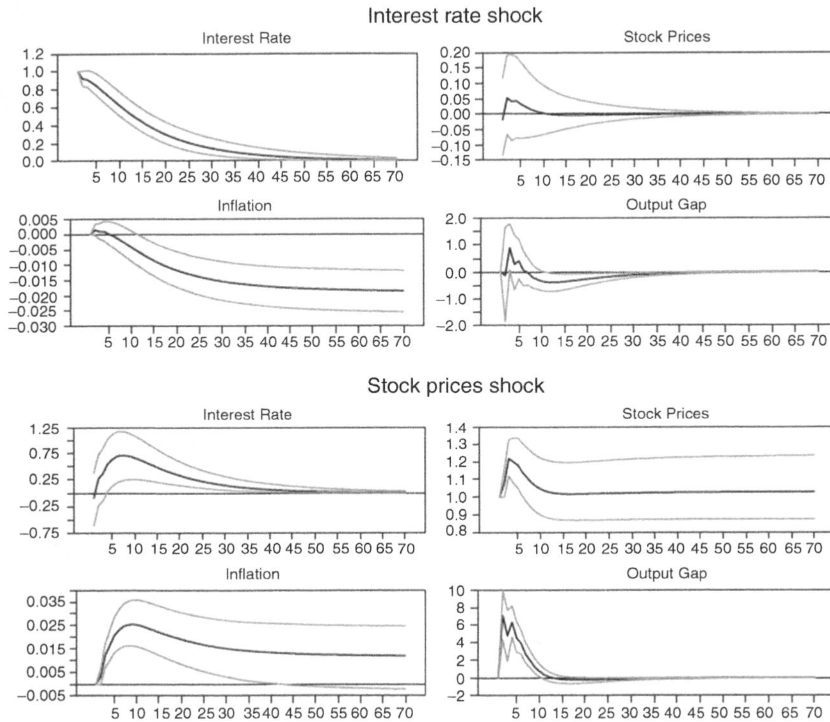

Fig. 9.3 Interest rate shock and stock prices shock

9.2.2 Assessment of Systemic Risk in China

(1) Progress of systemic risk assessment methods

By the end of the twentieth century, international financial institutions and national regulatory authorities began committed to the development of systematic risk assessment methods. The CAEL and CAMEL systems, which measure capital adequacy, capital quality, profitability, and liquidity, were used by national regulatory authorities as early warning tools for individual institutional risk before the 1990s; the IMF and the World Bank started the Financial Sector Assessment Program in 1999. The KLR method, the FR model, and the financial stress index are still used in many

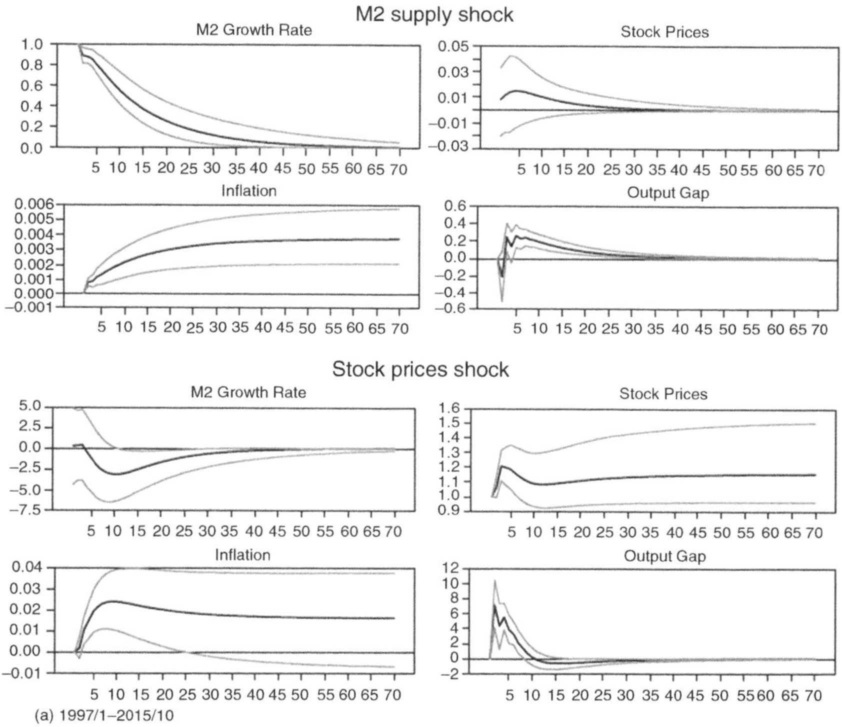

Fig. 9.4 M2 supply shock and stock prices shock

countries. Following the 2008 crisis, the exploration of systematic risk assessment has been strengthened. The IMF, the BIS, and the FSB have summarized the measurement methods into two categories:

1. **Single indicator system or model**

First, the aggregate indicators of economic imbalance. Assessing the accumulation of risks in the financial system or the real economy involves numerous indicators on macro-economic data or balance sheets, such as bank credit, liquidity, and maturity mismatches; exchange rate risks; and external imbalances. For example, the debt-to-GDP ratio, as a core indicator of systemic risks within the banking system, is used as a variable linked to counter-cyclical capital buffering.

Second, the market conditions indicators, such as risk appetite (spreads, risk premiums, etc.) and market liquidity indicators. They focus on recession-causing financial market conditions.

Third, the risk concentration index. These are related to interdepartmental systemic risks, focusing on the transmission and amplification of risk. In addition to measures of size and concentration, they are more concerned with the common exposures and correlations among financial institutions, the public and private sectors, financial market players, and countries. For example, network models are frequently used to measure the association among intermediaries and the potential for contagion. The Basel Committee has developed index-based metrics to identify banks of global importance.

Fourth, the macro stress test. Unlike traditional stress tests, which measure the flexibility of institutions, macro stress testing is used to test the stress of the entire financial system. On the one hand, the method can integrate the extreme scenario (tail risk) of the market and the risk amplification mechanism caused by the network effect into the market dynamic mechanism. On the other hand, it can better assess the relevance of the financial system to the real economy by including multiple rounds of adverse feedback effects.

2. Comprehensive indicator system or model

Compared with a single index, a comprehensive index system or model can more effectively identify and assess systemic risks. The IMF has developed the Global Financial Stability Map, Global Risk Appetite Measures, and the Systemic Risk Dashboard. Other indicators include the Merrill Lynch Global Financial Stability Index, the European Central Bank's Composite Indicator of Systemic Stress, and the Macro Prudential Indicators of Fitch Ratings. The above methods not only consider national conditions, but also include systemic risk indicators like credit and leverage, providing strong support for implementing macro-prudential supervision policies.

The "system risk dashboard" developed by the IMF is able to select a group of indicators according to national conditions in the absence of significant single indicators. The method specifies the possibility and potential impacts of shocks as well as high- and low-frequency monitoring tools, and selects one or two of the most robust and effective analysis tools in early warning practice in each dimension (as shown in Table 9.1). The ECB uses a seven-step approach to assess systemic risk: first, identify

Table 9.1 IMF "system risk dash board" indicators

Aggregate measure	
Low Frequency	*High Frequency*
Crisis risk models	Systemic CCA
Likelihood of shocks	
From asset quality/price deviation	
Low Frequency	*High Frequency*
Credit/GDP deviation	Regime shifts in financial market volatility (e.g., interest rate, currency, and equity markets)
House prices	
From concentrations/connectedness	
Low Frequency	*High Frequency*
Interbank exposures	Distress dependence (JPod, BSI)
Core/non-core liabilities (aggregate)	
Potential impacts	
Through balance sheet exposures	
Low Frequency	*High Frequency*
Leverage measure	EDF measures for main SIFIs
Macro stress tests	
Through interconnectedness	
Low Frequency	*High Frequency*
Network models	CCA-related measures of joint losses
Cross-border exposures of banking systems	

the source of financial vulnerability. Second, set the source as a potential risk scenario. Third, identify the shock events leading to the occurrence of the risk scenario. Fourth, calculate the occurrence probability of the above scenario. Fifth, calculate the estimated loss of the financial system. Sixth, measure the intensity of the impact. And the final step is the risk rating.

On the whole, although a large number of systematic assessment methods have been put into practice, its effectiveness remains to be further investigated. First, quantitative tools alone cannot assess systemic risk and guide macro-prudential regulation that can be effective only when combined with other qualitative tools (e.g., market intelligence and surveillance). Second, the effectiveness of systemic risk assessment relies heavily on the availability and accuracy of data. Currently, the FSB, the IMF, the BIS, and the World Bank are working on data and information availability. Finally, there is no universally applicable assessment method because the assessment of systemic risk is closely related to a country's economic development, financial system structure, monetary policy, exchange rate policy, and economic openness.

(2) China's systematic risk assessment based on the comprehensive index system

After joining the SDR, RMB faced systemic financial risks, including financial policy risk, financial market risk, financial institution risk, and foreign exchange market risk. Therefore, we use the method of Liu Ruixing (2015) to determine the Chinese systemic risk index in terms of financial policy environment, financial market, financial institution, and foreign exchange market. We use the monthly data from July 2005 to December 2015 to measure systemic risks within the sample interval.

1. Financial policy risk. To a certain extent, joining the SDR also encourages the RMB to grow fully convertible. This comprehensive liberalization will not only bring further integration of domestic and international financial markets, but also greater challenges to financial policy-makers and regulators. At the same time, financial development is inevitably affected by macro-monetary and fiscal policies, so we shall measure the financial policy risk first. Specifically, we choose the rate of change of money supply (M2/GDP), the change of real interest rate, and the ratio of fiscal deficit to GDP as measurements of financial policy risks. We shall also use the proportion of

the standard deviation of specific financial risk indicators to determine the weight of the specific index.

2. Financial market risk. After joining the SDR, RMB has brought the domestic financial market with further integration and more in-depth interaction with international capital. On the one hand, this will help the development of China's financial markets, to strengthen the role and influence of the financial system in China. On the other hand, it also means that China's financial system is more vulnerable to fluctuations in international financial markets. Therefore, the financial market risk is also an important source of systemic risk. The index of financial market risk mainly includes the stock price index, the national debt index, and the national real estate climate index. This is because the stock market, the bond market, and the real estate market are main components of the financial market. Internationally and domestically, this will likely lead to financial market bubbles and financial volatility.
3. Risk of financial institutions. Financial institutions are the main body of the financial system, and their operation is also related to the efficiency of the financial system. Because of the great size or involvement with other institutions, some financial institutions can affect the entire financial system through their own security. In addition, after the RMB joined the SDR, China's financial institutions will gradually participate in more international financial activities. Therefore, in the measurement of systemic risks, the risk of micro-financial institutions is essential. At this stage, banks are still the most important financial institutions in China. Therefore, this section uses the ratio of bank loans to GDP, the rate of change of interbank offered rate, and the rate of change of interbank bond trading rate as the main indicators to describe the risks of financial institutions.
4. Foreign exchange market risk. After the RMB joined the SDR, the role of the RMB in world trade and foreign exchange reserves is becoming more and more important, and RMB faces greater risks and challenges. This is because its convertibility symbolizes the interaction between domestic capital and foreign asset investment. In turn, the exchange rate and other mechanisms become more complex and difficult to control. Therefore, the foreign exchange market risk is also included in the measurement of financial systemic risks. The key indicators selected in this section are the rate of change in the USD against the RMB and the rate of change in the foreign exchange reserve.

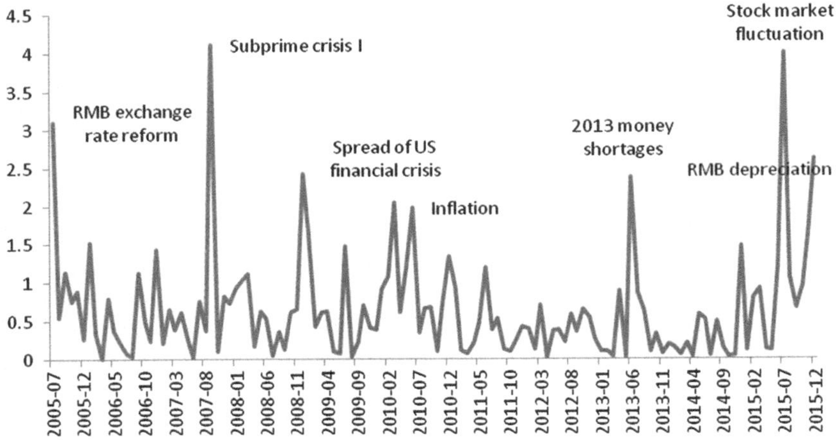

Fig. 9.5 China's systemic risk index

According to China's systemic risk index, during the decade from July 2005 to December 2015, China experienced seven periods of high systemic risks. Specifically, on July 21, 2005, China began to implement the floating RMB exchange rate system based on supply and demand, regulated and managed with reference to a basket of currencies. The yuan is no longer single pegged to the USD. This reform has to a certain extent pushed up the systemic risk of the month. The two systemic risks in October 2007 and December 2008 can be attributed to the emergence and spread of the US sub-prime crisis, while the systemic risk at the beginning of 2010 was due to high inflation. After a stable period from mid-2010 to early 2013, short-term liquidity risks (money shortages) appeared in June 2013 and led to a rise in systemic risks. The last two systemic risks were caused by the volatility in the stock market in mid-2015 and the rapid depreciation of the RMB at the end of the year (Fig. 9.5).

It is not difficult to see that China's systemic risks, despite a number of short-term rises, mainly originate from a single market, without causing an outbreak or a continual rise in risks. It should be noted that in the second half of 2015, China's systemic risk experienced two major increases. This phenomenon is rare in history. Therefore, the relevant departments should strengthen the close monitoring of systemic risk and improve emergency response measures, so that the loss from an outbreak can be controlled within a certain range.

Although systemic risk may come from all aspects of the financial system, we cannot regard any single financial risk as systemic risk. Systematic risk can affect multiple financial sectors at the same time, even the real economy. The basis for risk judgment is whether there are multiple financial sector transactions going on simultaneously. If the impact of a financial sector's risk is limited to the sector itself, however the risk cannot be called systemic risk however large volatility it caused.

Because of the diversity of systemic risk sources and assessment, a holistic grasp is needed. Therefore, the establishment of a unified and comprehensive financial supervision and monitoring system is particularly important. In addition, in modern financial development, due to the existence of high-frequency trading, financial volatility can rapidly become systemic financial risks in a very short period of time. Therefore, we recommend that higher-frequency data, such as weekly data, be used to assess and monitor systemic risk.

9.3 The Main Content of the Macro-Prudential Policy Framework and Operational Mechanism

9.3.1 Choosing the Macro-Prudential Policy Tool: "Time Dimension" and "Cross-Sector Dimension"

The micro-prudential supervision tools aim to protect consumers and investors by internalizing the risks of individual institutions and ignoring their "externalities". However, in a highly correlated financial system, individual institutions are in a tight and complex network system, with very obvious externalities. In this case, it is not possible for an individual institution to "internalize" the cost of pressure generated by other institutions altogether, thus requiring macro-prudential policy instruments to provide additional incentives for financial institutions. Specifically, it is necessary to force individual institutions to "internalize" their "externalities" by enhancing the soundness of the financial system, slowing the procyclicality of the financial system, and suppressing the interrelationship of financial institutions.

Macro-prudential policy instruments are divided into two categories: counter-cyclical policy instruments ("time dimensions") and policy instruments ("cross-sectoral dimensions") that focus on the concentration and relevance of the financial system. The instruments share these features: first, both micro-prudential supervision tools with macro-prudential functions and typical macro-prudential supervision tools must be clearly targeted toward inhibiting systemic risks and protecting financial stability. Second, in order to ensure the effectiveness of the policy, macro-prudential supervision tools should be subject to an institution with macro-prudential regulatory authority, responsibility, and operational independence. At the same time, macro-prudential supervision tools can not only undermine the effectiveness of other policies, but also effectively complement existing policies. Third, the macro-prudential supervision tools are mainly used to prevent financial instability instead of for governance, because the latter belongs to crisis management. Fourth, macro-prudential instruments must be tailored in accordance with institutions' contribution to systemic risks, and any institution of system importance (regardless of their type) should be included in regulation.

From the "time dimension" perspective, the macro-prudential policy tools achieve their policy function mainly through the establishment of sufficient capital buffers during economic prosperity. On the one hand, because the process of capital accumulation is relatively easy and the cost is not high during the economic boom, it can also act as "brakes" to restrain excessive risk-taking by financial market players. On the other hand, during economic recessions, through the accumulated capital buffers can absorb losses and mitigate the endogenous crises that may enlarge the mechanism. At present, the policy tools of "time dimension" mainly include reverse-cycle capital buffer, retained capital buffer, dynamic provisioning system, liquidity requirement, leverage ratio, loan value ratio, and stress testing. From a cross-sectoral perspective, macro-prudential policy instruments use a top-down approach, based on the contribution of individual institutions to systemic risks: first, we measure system-wide tail risk and calculate the impact of a single institution at risk. Policy instruments shall be adjusted accordingly (capital requirements, insurance premiums, etc.). This means that institutions with great impact and contribution need to implement higher regulatory standards. In contrast, micro-prudential regulation is common to all institutions, and is generally achieved in a bottom-up manner. At present, the "cross-sectoral dimension" of the policy tools includes the solution of "too big to fall" and the target policy tools designed based on risk contribution of different institutions.

In fact, the macro-prudential policy tool has long been in existence, but the large-scale application of regulatory practice was applied only after this international financial crisis (see Table 9.1). Recently, the IMF conducted a survey of the use of macro-prudential policy instruments in 119 countries over the period 2000–2013. It was found that the frequency of use in developing countries was higher than that in developed countries, and that the frequency of their use increased with the passage of time. Whether or not the capital account is open or not is not consistent with the frequency of the use of the tools. The frequency of the use of regulatory instruments is not as high as that of the capital account liberalization (Table 9.2).

In recent years, China's regulatory authorities have begun to strengthen macro-prudential supervision and introduce more effective and targeted policy tools (see Table 9.2). Implementation agencies mainly include the PBOC and the CBRC. There are tools to deal with time-dimension and cross-sectoral risks, at both the macro- and micro-levels. These tools work well against systemic risks.

9.3.2 The Coordination Between Prudential Supervision and Macro-Economic Policies

The inclusion of a macro-prudential dimension in the current framework of financial stability means that the current policy framework needs to be completely restructured. It is especially important to clarify the policy boundaries of prudential supervision policy and macro-economic policy, and to ensure the realization of financial stability goal through coordination and cooperation between each other.

In the new framework, various policy instruments have been given new roles to play in financial stability while ensuring that their primary objectives are met (see Fig. 9.6). In the case of monetary policy and micro-prudential supervision, the primary objective of monetary policy is monetary stability, while the primary objective of micro-prudential regulation is to limit the risks of individual financial institutions. In practice, only effective coordination between the two can better serve the financial stability goals. In particular, the central bank cannot take short-term inflation as its sole objective, but should consider the actual situation of credit and asset prices, so as to achieve long-term financial and macro-economic stability

Table 9.2 Frequency of macro-prudential policy instruments

Instrument	*All countries*	*Developed countries*	*Emerging market countries*	*Developing countries*	*Countries with open capital account*	*Countries with non-open capital accounts*
	(1)	*(2)*	*(3)*	*(4)*	*(5)*	*(6)*
Caps on the LTV (%)	21	40	20	6	29	14
Caps on the DTI (%)	15	13	21	0	19	12
Time-varying/dynamic provisioning (%)	9	5	6	19	5	11
Counter-cyclical capital requirement (%)	2	1	3	1	0	3
Leverage (%)	15	13	17	12	28	8
Systemic capital surcharges (%)	1	1	1	1	1	1
Limits on interbank exposures (%)	29	33	32	17	34	26
Concentration limits (%)	75	69	76	77	72	78
Caps on foreign currency lending (%)	14	9	16	13	10	16
Reserve requirements (%)	21	0	24	33	4	32
Caps on local currency lending (%)	12	0	11	26	9	14
Levy/tax on financial institutions (%)	14	14	14	11	17	12

Source: IMF (2015)

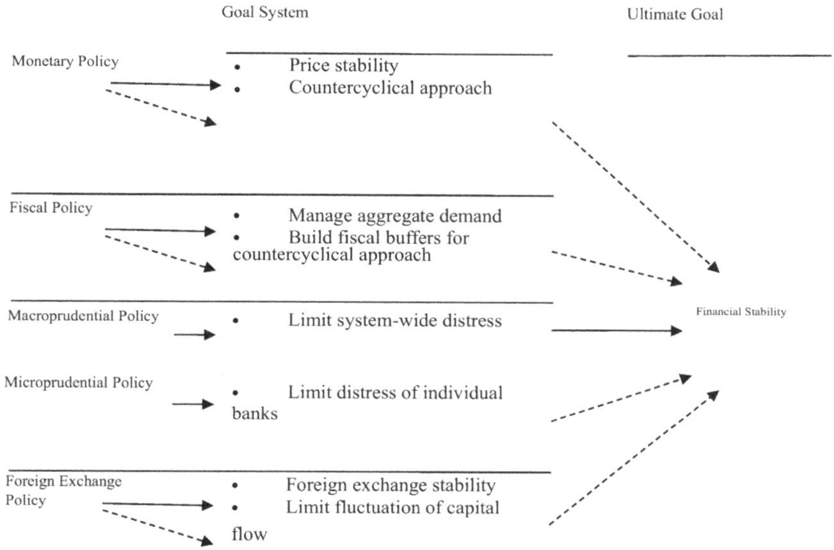

Fig. 9.6 Policy objectives under the new framework of financial stability. Note: The solid line in the figure represents the primary objective of the policy and the dotted line represents the secondary objective of the policy. (Source: Hannoun 2010; Schoenmaker 2010)

through additional policy actions. At the same time, the micro-prudential supervision policy is not limited to individual financial institutions. It will be extended to a macro-prudential perspective. The risk exposure of individual institutions in the whole financial system is taken into account, beneficial for realizing financial stability.

Specifically, we need to redefine the targets for monetary, fiscal, exchange rate, and prudential policies.

(a) **Monetary policy**

When making monetary policies, the central bank must take into account the main and secondary goals, the correct handling of the relationship between the two, and the implementation order. First, monetary policies still use traditional policy tools, the protection of monetary stability as the top priority; Second, through more symmetrical policy operations, including financial stability into secondary goals can help reduce financial imbalances and achieve financial stability. Specifically, to reverse the economic upswing, it is necessary to curb excessive prosperity by raising the statutory interest rate, the reserve requirement ratio, and controlling credit disbursements and liquidity through the issuance of central bank bills and repurchase agreements. In an economic downturn, the economy can be revitalized by a reduction in the statutory interest rate, the deposit reserve ratio, easing credit, and injecting liquidity through open market operations to avoid excessive depression.

In order to ensure financial stability, it is necessary to adopt a more symmetrical approach to monetary policy operations. Be it boom or bust, monetary policy should have a more balanced effect. Of course, this does not mean that monetary policy must include asset prices into policy objectives. In fact, monetary policy can reverse the accumulation of possible systemic risks and financial imbalances by reversing asset prices, rather than directly incorporating this economic indicator into monetary policy objectives.

(b) **Fiscal policy**

As with monetary policy, fiscal policy is often used for counter-cyclical demand management. But in its development and implementation, it is necessary to consider the need to retain or release certain fiscal buffers to deal with the possible expansion or tightening of the financial system. In other words, fiscal policy also needs to achieve its primary functions as tax changer and automatic stabilizer, and implement in a more balanced way to protect financial stability.

In the economic uptrend, the accumulation of fiscal buffers could be achieved by reducing debt and raising the tax rate for the financial sector. This also means that government debt should be kept at a reasonable level so that during periods of economic downturn, the government can use borrowing to smooth the volatility of financial markets. During economic downturns, recession is mitigated by supporting the financial sector through capital injection, deposit and debt guarantees, and crisis relief packages for financial institutions.

(c) **The exchange rate policy**

In most developed countries, especially those adopting inflation targeting, the exchange rate policy is usually linked to monetary policy and more concerned about the impact of exchange rate policy on inflation. However, in some small and emerging market countries, the exchange rate policy is not the same. Mishkin (2008) found that small countries are mostly concerned about the exchange rate and intervened by the foreign exchange market to smooth the fluctuations, which, to some extent, will affect exchange rates. Practice has proved that such an approach works particularly for protecting financial stability and reduces the effect of economic fluctuations. In all previous crises, the volatility of exchange rates caused by that of capital flows or others would seriously jeopardize financial stability and devastate the real economy. In particular, countries with high dependence on trade or more currency mismatches are affected more than others.

(d) **Prudential policy**

The main objective of micro-prudential supervision is to maintain the soundness of individual institutions and correct market failures caused by information asymmetry, limited liability, and other defects like government guarantees. Its role in macro-economics has long been neglected, and financial regulation does not take on the role of macro-economic policy. Since the 2008 crisis, micro-prudential regulation is widely criticized for its lack of supervision on systemic risk, the procyclicality of the financial system, liquidity risk, shadow banks, and so on.

After the crisis, the academia and policy-makers have reached a basic consensus to strengthen macro-prudential supervision. Most countries want to make macro- and micro-prudential supervision policies to ensure financial stability. On the other hand, macro-prudential supervision, as an important means of macro-economic management, is increasingly used together with monetary, fiscal, and other macro-economic policies to jointly maintain financial stability.

9.4 Construct a Macro-Prudential Policy Framework Based on China's Reality

Since the 2008 crisis, China has adopted practical macro-prudential policy tools in line with the global macro-prudential supervision and the trend of financial regulatory reform, which proved effective in preventing and resolving systemic risks. In recent years, important documents of the party and the state have repeatedly proposed to construct a macro-prudential policy framework. However, the current reform initiatives are limited to instrument innovation, without reaching the core of regulatory reform. China hasn't improved the governance structure and basis for macro-prudential policies, and truly ushered a new era of economic and financial development in line with China's macro-prudential policy framework. This has led to volatility in the stock market and the foreign exchange market, among others, and there is a possibility of crisis due to systemic risk. President Xi Jinping stated in the "Instructions on formulating the 13th five-year plan" that "frequent exposure of local risks, especially the recent volatility of the capital market, shows that the existing regulatory framework does not totally support China's financial industry development. We must adhere to market-oriented reform and speed up the establishment of a financial regulatory framework with modern characteristics, coordinated supervision and high efficiency. We shall adhere to the bottom line that systemic risks should be prevented by all means".

Therefore, as RMB joins the SDR and China joins international competition, China should draw upon international experience, clarify the principles of its financial regulatory system reform, and accelerate the construction of a macro-prudential policy framework in line with China's reality.

First, add the term "macro-prudential" to the existing financial regulatory framework and define the departments in charge of macro-prudential policy implementation. Since the 2008 crisis, regulatory reforms have focused on the macro-prudential aspect of the current regulatory framework. Countries have strengthened systemic risk monitoring, assessment, and prevention, and in different ways (e.g., specialized committees or prudential regulators) identified sectors for implementing macro-prudential policies. For example, the Financial Stability Oversight Board, established by the United States under the Dodd-Frank Wall Street Reform and Consumer Protection Act, consists of ten voters and five non-voting members. The voting members include nine members of the Federal Financial Supervisory Authority and an independent member with insurance expertise. The Chairman is the Minister of Finance, accountable to Congress. The Commission is responsible for identifying the institutions, tools, and markets that are important to the system, comprehensively monitoring systemic risks and proposing appropriate response measures. It also coordinates the resolution of disputes in member sectors and facilitates information sharing and regulatory coordination. In accordance with the Pan-European Financial Regulation Reform Act, the European Commission established the European Systemic Risk Committee. The

European Central Bank governor served as chairman of the committee. Members of the committee include central bankers, vice president of the European Central Bank, the European Commission representatives, and managers of EU micro-prudential regulatory bodies. The Committee collects and analyzes data and information; conducts systematic risk monitoring, analysis, and evaluation; and advises Member States on the implementation of macro-prudential policies, while strengthening communication and coordination among member countries. Under the new Financial Services Act, the Bank of England Board of Governors has a Financial Policy Committee, chaired by the governor of the Bank of England. The Committee consists of the Chairman of the Monetary Policy Committee, the Chairman of the Prudential Authority, and the Chairman of the Bureau of Financial Conduct. Its main functions include identification, assessment, and monitoring of systemic risks; protecting financial stability; and conducting macro-prudential supervision. Specifically, the functions include making macro-prudential policy instruments and asking new prudential regulation or the financial supervision authorities to exercise the "power of direction" and the "Power of recommendation". In accordance with the Law on Economic Modernization and the Law on Banking and Financial Supervision, France has established a regulatory framework with the central bank as its core and including the Prudential Regulatory Authority and the Financial Market Supervisory Authority. At the same time, France established the financial supervision and systemic risk committee, responsible for monitoring and identifying systemic financial risks, coordinating domestic and foreign regulatory actions, cooperation, and exchanges.

Second, in addition to maintaining monetary stability, the central bank should be more empowered to maintain financial stability and strengthen financial supervision. Before the crisis, to solve financial and monetary policy conflicts and protect its independence, the central bank is divested of the financial regulatory functions. However, monetary stability did not lead to financial stability, but to frequent financial crises. In the past 30 years, both developed and developing countries have suffered from the financial crisis. After the crisis, all countries set the prevention of systemic risks and financial stability as the core objectives of the regulatory reform, strengthen the functions of central bank in financial stability and financial supervision, and promote the macro-prudential supervision reform and its coordination with macro-economic policies. For example, the Federal Reserve is given regulatory authority over systemically important institutions, financial holding companies, and important financial infrastructures. The Eurozone established a single regulatory mechanism (SSM), giving the ECB financial regulatory authority. Since November 2014, the ECB has had direct control over the systemic importance of member states under the SSM framework. Non-member countries have established credit institutions, financial holding companies, hybrid financial holding companies, and credit institutions. The Bank of England is responsible for prudential regulation of systemically important financial infrastructures as well as micro-prudential supervision. The new "Bank of Korea Act" clearly gives the central bank a role to maintain financial stability and correspondingly more regulatory authority.

Third, it is necessary to clarify the relationship among monetary policy, macro-prudential, micro-prudential, and behavioral supervision. Their coordination and cooperation shall be strengthened.

Since the 2008 crisis, the reform of financial supervision system has mainly focused on how to combine monetary policy, macro-prudential, micro-prudential, and behavioral supervision with rational institutional arrangement. In the present situation, there are several following models: first, the "great central bank's model", in which central bank is responsible for monetary policy, macro-prudential and micro-prudential supervision. For example, according to the "UK's Bank of England Bill: Technical Advisory Draft" released last year, the country's financial regulatory system was upgraded by replacing the Monetary Policy Committee on Monetary Policy, the Financial Policy Committee responsible for macro-prudential policies, and the Prudential Regulatory Commission on Micro-Prudential Regulation under the Bank of England. At the same time, the Prudential Regulatory Authority, formerly a subsidiary of the Bank of England, was fully integrated within the bank, creating a centralized supervisory system dominated by the central bank. Similar is Russia's post-crisis system of supervising banks, securities, insurance, and other non-banking financial institutions by the central bank. The second model is the "Commission + enhanced version of the central bank", in which case the Financial Stability Supervision Committee is established with strengthened financial supervision from the central bank. The model retains the supervision pattern by the Financial Stability and Supervision Committee to assume systemic risk prevention, mitigation, regulatory coordination, and other functions. The Fed is given more regulatory functions. Of course, the reason to adopt this model includes that the United States has the most developed and complex financial system, with long-term implementation of the state-level regulatory system. So the reform of a single regulatory system will face many institutional and legal barriers. In fact, the newly established European Commission on new systemic risk in Europe and the ECB model, given more regulatory functions, have some similarities with the regulatory reform in the United States. The third model is the "prudential supervision + behavior supervision" model. The key feature of the model is a strict distinction between prudential regulation and behavioral regulation, as well as the central role of the central bank in prudential regulation. Australia's regulatory model: the central bank is responsible for macro-prudential policies. The Prudential Regulatory Authority and the Securities and Investments Commission, independent from the central bank, assume the functions of micro-prudential and behavior supervision. In the Netherlands, the central bank is responsible for macro- and micro-prudential supervision, and the FSB is responsible for regulatory oversight.

Fourth, comprehensively improve the availability and accuracy of financial data to provide comprehensive and timely information for systemic risk monitoring, analysis, and evaluation. The outbreak and spread of the international financial crisis is largely because of policy-making departments. Lacking comprehensive financial information, they cannot accurately follow the risk accumulation and evolution before the crisis, missing the opportunity to provide warning signals and policy intervention. The macro-prudential policy implementation department can make more effective judgments and decision-making only by grasping a large amount of economic and financial data in a comprehensive, timely, and accurate manner and by learning the overall operation and development of the financial industry as a whole. At present, the FSB, the IMF, the BIS, the World Bank, and major economies are strengthening data and information availability by improving central bank functions, revising the legal framework, improving statistical systems, and expanding the scope of statistics while promoting financial information sharing and coordination.

Fifth, establish an effective crisis management mechanism and strengthen financial consumer protection. Since the 2008 crisis, in order to prevent the recurrence and spreading of the crisis, countries have strengthened their ability to deal with the crisis. The Federal Reserve and the Bank of England have taken on risk disposal. In the new regulatory system, the Federal Reserve and the Federal Deposit Insurance Corporation are jointly responsible for US systemic risk disposal. In accordance with the EU "Bank Restoration and Disposal Directive", the Bank of England, as the UK financial crisis disposal authority, is responsible for the development of disposal strategies. The new regulatory approach specifies that the Bank of England should provide critical information to the Ministry of Finance when the Bank develops or updates a financial institution's disposal strategy, so that the government can timely assess the risks posed to public funds. Through the construction of the European Banking Federation, the European Union combines the regulatory, disposal, and deposit insurance mechanism of the banking industry. In addition, some countries have set up special institutions to further strengthen the protection of financial consumers. For example, the Federal Reserve has unified the protection of consumer rights through establishing an independent Consumer Finance Protection Bureau.

Appendix 1 Global Macro-Prudential Instruments

Instruments	*Conceptual basis*
Time dimension	
Caps on the LTV	The LTV imposes a down payment constraint on households' capacity to borrow. In theory, the constraint limits the procyclicality of collateralized lending since housing prices and households' capacity to borrow based on the collateralized value of the house interact in a procyclical manner. Set at an appropriate level, the LTV addresses systemic risk whether or not it is frequently adjusted. However, the adjustment of the LTV makes it a more potent counter-cyclical policy instrument
Caps on the DTI	The DTI represents prudential regulation aimed at ensuring banks' asset quality when used alone. When used in conjunction with the LTV, however, the DTI can help dampen the cyclicality of collateralized lending by adding another constraint on households' capacity to borrow. As in the LTV, adjustments in the DTI can be made in a counter-cyclical manner to address the time dimension of systemic risk
Caps on foreign currency lending	Loans in foreign currency expose the unhedged borrower to foreign exchange risks which, in turn, subject the lender to credit risks. The risks can become systemic if the common exposure is large. Caps (or higher risk weights, deposit requirements, etc.) on foreign currency lending may be used to address this foreign-exchange-induced systemic risk

(*continued*)

(continued)

Instruments	*Conceptual basis*
Ceilings on credit or credit growth	A ceiling may be imposed on either total bank lending or credit to a specific sector. The ceiling on aggregate credit or credit growth may be used to dampen the credit/asset price cycle—the time dimension of systemic risk. The ceiling on credit to a specific sector, such as real estates, may be used to contain a specific asset price inflation or limit exposure to a specific risk—the cross-sectional dimension of systemic risk
Limits on net open currency positions/ currency mismatch	Such prudential regulation tools limit banks' common exposure to foreign currency risks. In addition, the limits may be used to address an externality—sharp exchange rate fluctuations caused by a convergence of purchases/sales of foreign exchange by banks. This externality increases the credit risk of unhedged borrowers with heavy foreign currency debt
Limits on maturity mismatch	These prudential regulation tools may be used to address systemic risk since the choice of asset/liability maturity creates an externality—fire sales of assets. In a crisis, the inability of a financial institution to meet its short-term obligations due to maturity mismatches may force it to liquidate assets, thus imposing a fire sale cost on the rest of the financial system. The funding shortages of a few institutions could also result in a systemic liquidity crisis due to the contagion effect
Reserve requirements	This monetary policy tool may be used to address systemic risk in two senses. First, the reserve requirement has a direct impact on credit growth, so it may be used to dampen the credit/asset price cycle—the time dimension of systemic risk; second, the required reserves provide a liquidity cushion that may be used to alleviate a systemic liquidity crunch when the situation warrants
Counter-cyclical capital requirement	The requirement can take the form of a ratio or risk weights raised during an upturn as a restraint on credit expansion and reduced during a downturn to provide a cushion so that banks do not reduce assets to meet the capital requirement. A permanent capital buffer, which is built up during an upturn and deleted during a downturn, serves the same purpose. Both can address the cyclicality in risk weights under Basel II based on procyclical external ratings
Time-varying/dynamic provisioning	Traditional dynamic provisioning is calibrated on historical bank-specific losses, but it can also be used to dampen the cyclicality in the financial system. The provisioning requirement can be raised during an upturn to build a buffer and limit credit expansion and lowered during a downturn to support bank lending. It may be adjusted either according to a fixed formula or at the discretion of the policy-maker to affect banks' lending behavior in a counter-cyclical manner

(*continued*)

(continued)

Instruments	*Conceptual basis*
Restrictions on profit distribution	These prudential regulation requirements are intended to ensure the capital adequacy of banks. Since undistributed profits are added to bank capital, the restrictions tend to have a counter-cyclical effect on bank lending if used in a downturn. The capital conservation buffer of Basel III has a similar role
Cross-sectoral dimension	
Systemic capital surcharges	Basel III stipulates the need for systemically important financial institutions to extract 1–2.5% of additional capital
Levy/tax on financial institutions	Levy on global banks and financial institutions and creating bailout funds are meant to cover salvage costs for future financial institutions such as banks, including financial stability contribution (FSC), financial activities tax (FAT), financial transaction tax (FTT), and so on
Limits on interbank exposures	Restrictions on interbank exposures can reduce the risk of bank-to-bank transmission and address the risk of large-scale outbreaks caused by excessive exposure
Concentration limits	Risk concentration is a risk exposure that may affect the normal operation as a result of an individual risk or risk set that is not fully de-centralized relative to bank capital, total assets, and overall risk level. Concentration limits on the financial institution can reduce the formation probability of the overall risk concentration degree
Higher capital charges for trades not cleared through CCPs	Basel III raised the capital requirement for bilateral OTC exposure and encouraged OTC derivatives to focus on central counterparties to address the systemic risks that may arise from derivatives markets such as banks and other financial institutions

Source: IMF (2011, 2015); sorted by the author

Appendix 2 China's Macro-Prudential Instruments

Instrument	*Institution*	*Policy objective*
Time dimension		
Personal housing loan value ratio requirements	PBOC, CBRC	Real estate prices, real estate–related assets business
Differential reserve dynamic adjustment mechanism	PBOC	Credit growth, asset prices
Dynamic provisioning requirements	CBRC, PBOC, Ministry of Finance	Alleviate procyclical business behavior, improve the absorptive capacity of losses, and credit growth

(*continued*)

(continued)

Instrument	*Institution*	*Policy objective*
Counter-cyclical capital regulation	PBOC, CBRC	Relieve procyclical business behavior; improve the absorptive capacity of losses, credit growth (secondary target)
Leverage rate requirements	CBRC	Relieve procyclical business behavior
Adjustments to specific portfolio capital requirements	CBRC	Fine-tune the growth of a particular portfolio
Cross-cyclical risk-weighted asset measurement	CBRC	Mitigating the procyclicality of capital measurement
Desirable loan management mechanism	PBOC	Regulate the pace and the scale of the total amount of loans over a period of time of banking financial institutions
MPA	PBOC	The upgraded version of the desirable loan management mechanism and differential reserve dynamic adjustment mechanism. Focus on the seven aspects of capital and leverage, assets and liabilities, liquidity, pricing behavior, asset quality, external debt risk, and credit policy implementation, and strengthen counter-cyclical regulation and systemic financial risk prevention through comprehensive evaluation
Cross-sectoral dimension		
Strengthen the supervision of the systematically important financial institutions	PBOC, CBRC	Mitigate the impact of failures by systematically important financial institutions on the financial system
Liquidity risk management	PBOC, CBRC	Macro-level liquidity risk
Limiting interbank transactions	PBOC, CBRC	Reduce the contagious effect between financial institutions
Risk isolation ("Fence Principles")	PBOC, CBRC	Reduce the contagious effect of intermediate business and high-risk business on the traditional business
Early warning system	PBOC, CBRC	

Source: Liao Min (2014), sorted by the author

CHAPTER 10

Conclusions and Proposals

International Monetary Institute

10.1 Major Conclusions

Conclusion 1 Incorporating RMB into the SDR basket represents a milestone in RMB internationalization. Jointly driven by five impetuses, RMB Internationalization Index (RII) jumped to 3.6, an increase of over ten times over five years. At this new stage, China needs to step up macro-financial regulation to avoid the waxing and waning of RMB internationalization.

The year 2015 saw rich fruits for RMB internationalization. Accumulated RMB cross-border settlement reached RMB 7.23 trillion, accounting for 29.36% of China's trade volume and 3.38% of global trade settlement. ODI settled in RMB reached RMB 736.2 billion, a year-on-year growth of 297.53%. Overseas loan balance for domestic financial institutions reached RMB 315.347 billion, a year-on-year increase of 58.49%. The PBOC has signed swap agreements with monetary authorities of 33 countries and regions, with the swap balance being RMB 3.31 trillion. RMB-denominated financial assets are more attractive to foreign investors.

International Monetary Institute (✉)
Renmin University of China, Beijing, China
e-mail: imi@ruc.edu.cn

International Monetary Institute (ed.), *Currency Internationalization and Macro Financial Risk Control*,
https://doi.org/10.1007/978-981-13-0698-3_10

There are 295 QFIIs and 186 RQFIIs, representing rapid expansion of both schemes. Foreign governments started to issue RMB-denominated panda bonds in China and incorporate RMB-denominated assets into their official reserves. As RMB took on more functions of an international currency, on November 30, 2015, the IMF announced the inclusion of RMB in the SDR currency basket. This is a milestone for RMB internationalization. In 2015, the RII (an indicator of RMB international usage) reached 3.6, an increase of over ten times over five years.

Five impetuses drive the rapid rise of RII: first, China's economy has maintained a medium- and high-speed growth of 6.9%, boosting the confidence in RMB of the international society. Second, China has been deepening its financial reform and pushing forward capital account convertibility. In 2015, China liberalized its interest rates. In August, China started the market-oriented reform of the exchange rate formation mechanism. China has relaxed the limits on enterprises to issue bonds overseas and allowed more foreign institutions to participate in China's interbank forex market according to laws and regulations. China's capital market openness has reached 0.6502, an increase of 34% over 2011. Third, China has improved the infrastructure for RMB internationalization and aligned supporting systems with international standards. The Cross-border Interbank Payments System (CIPS) was launched, completing a worldwide RMB settlement network. China adopted the IMF's Special Data Dissemination Standard to enhance standardized and transparent economic/financial statistics. Fourth, China has been pushing forward the Belt and Road initiative and achieved huge success in Sino-European economic and financial cooperation. China has signed cooperation agreements and MOUs with 31 countries and regions. Many major projects have been implemented and the Asian Infrastructure Investment Bank (AIIB) has been put into operation. All these have laid a solid foundation for using RMB along the Belt and Road. The EU has become China's largest trading partner, largest source of technology introduction, and major investment partner. It is worth noting that RMB-denominated ODI and cross-border loans have become a new impetus driving RII up. Fifth, RMB has been more widely used in commodities pricing. Against a strong USD, the Middle Eastern countries have increased their use of RMB. In 2015, the use of RMB has become common: UAE's and Qatar's use of RMB comprised 74% and 60%, respectively, of all payments to Mainland China and Hong Kong. RMB has become the third most popular currency, next only to the USD and euro, in transactions with

Russia. Moscow exchange has launched the ruble-RMB futures. London Metal Exchange has accepted RMB as cash collateral. Shanghai FTZ has launched RMB-denominated spot trading for international commodities transactions.

In 2015, major currencies showed divergent developments. As the Federal Reserve hiked interest rates, the USD greatly went strong, driving the USD Internationalization Index up to 55.82 and recovering the loss since the sub-prime mortgage crisis in 2007. Difficulties in Greece, the refugee crisis, and Brexit have led to a bleak future for the euro and the Euro Internationalization Index dropped to 24.29. Japan has been recovering slowly with substantial growth of business revenue. The Yen Internationalization Index kept at 4.06, showing a consolidated status of the yen. The United Kingdom's economy has been better than expected, with rapid growth of trade and investment. The GBP Internationalization Index was 4.82, showing a slightly enhanced position of the pound.

It should be noted that RMB being included in the SDR basket doesn't mean that RMB has been fully internationalized. The goal of RMB internationalization is to match the status of RMB with that of China's economy and trade. This will take a long time. Although the IMF officially recognized RMB-denominated assets as international reserve assets, the use and holding of RMB in the international financial market still decides whether RMB can become a major international currency. Seen from the development of yen internationalization after being included in the SDR basket, the official recognition as an international currency would not necessarily bring about matching market status. China should draw lessons from the waxing and waning of yen internationalization. China should stick to its policy positions, seize opportunities of the market, prepare to break containment, and strive to stand out in the competition of international currencies. In this way, China can avoid similar setbacks witnessed during yen internationalization.

Conclusion 2 Classic theories and Germany's and Japan's experience show that as RMB becomes increasingly internationalized, the monetary authority will necessarily face severe challenges in macro-financial policy adjustments and related macro-financial risk management. China should establish a macro-prudential policy framework as the institutional foundation and focus on exchange rate management in macro-financial risk management. Managing capital flow should be the starting point for macro-financial risk management. China should also try its best to fend off and prevent systematic financial crises that are extremely damaging. By doing all these China can ensure the ultimate RMB internationalization.

As a currency becomes internationalized, the issuance country will have to choose again among three macro-financial policy goals, namely, capital account convertibility, exchange rate stability, and monetary policy independence. In history, Germany and Japan have chosen different policy pathways, resulting in different and profound implications on the two countries' economy and finance. A gap thus emerged in the currency internationalization of these two countries.

Germany first internationalized mark and then totally liberalized its capital account. In the process, Germany has been incessantly pursuing the stability of exchange rate and monetary policy. Germany has been prudent in gradually opening and adjusting its capital account. This approach has helped Germany win a golden period of improving the core industrial competitiveness; it has also allowed for adequate technical and policy instruments in tackling financial market fluctuations after mark's internationalization. Ultimately, this approach contributed to the solid status of mark and Germany in the international financial market. However, Japan has been radical. Since the 1960s, Japan has made big strides in opening its capital account and has over-valued the real economy's resistance against yen appreciation. Japan has failed to maintain exchange rate stability. Yen's rapid appreciation has led to industrial transfer and the economy has been hollowed out, which severely damaged Japan's real economy. In the 1980s, Japan tried to stimulate the economy through adopting easy monetary policy and opening its financial market. However, the contraction of the real economy was inevitable at that juncture. At last, yen internationalization was only imagination and the Tokyo financial market was also harmed.

When a currency becomes a major international currency, the monetary authority can only adopt the policy combination of "free capital flow + floating exchange rate + independent monetary policy". This also applies to China. However, abruptly liberalizing the capital account and the RMB exchange rate will easily lead to systematic financial crises and severely damage the real economy and the financial sector, which would halt the RMB internationalization. Therefore, policy adjustments should be patient. Exchange rate and capital account can be liberalized only when the economy, financial market, and regulator are fully prepared against international capital.

As a currency becomes internationalized, the first challenge for the issuance country is exchange rate volatility. Excessive volatility will negatively impact the financial market and hamper the stable growth of the real economy. In this regard, China should learn from Germany and prioritize exchange rate stability at the preliminary stage of RMB internationalization.

With the gradual opening up of capital account, China's forex market and capital market will be the main targets for hot money and speculative capital. China should draw lessons from the financial crises of emerging markets caused by international capital flow. China should remain vigilant against international capital flow, especially short-term capital flow. Therefore, managing capital flow should be the starting point of macro-financial risk management. Priority should be given to identifying and monitoring the chain effect in domestic financial market caused by cross-border capital flow. China should step up macro-prudential regulation to avoid systematic financial crises.

Currently, the core task of macro-financial management is to establish a more sophisticated and targeted policy framework of macro-prudential management. China should seek financial stability and thus lay the necessary foundation for RMB internationalization. On the one hand, China should coordinate exchange rate policy with monetary and fiscal policies. In pursuing financial stability, China should bear in mind the stability of price, exchange rate, and macro-economic growth. On the other hand, it should continue to improve micro-prudential regulation and heed the risk control and management of financial institutions. China should better protect the rights of financial consumers. Meanwhile, it should explore policies of macro-prudential regulation and focus on the stable operation of the financial sector. We emphasize the coordinated and harmonious development of both the real economy and the financial sector. We take fending off systematic financial risks as an import support of realizing financial stability.

Conclusion 3 Continuing RMB internationalization will lead to severe financial risks. Medium-, short- and long-term exchange rate determinants become more complicated and exchange rate fluctuation and central bank's exchange rate management become the world's focal point. The linkage of financial asset prices among domestic sub-markets and between domestic and foreign financial markets has been more evident and the contagion of financial risk has been intensified. The financial sector has become more sensitive to cross-border capital flow. Banks, in their internationalized operation, face dual risks of domestic and foreign markets and face more difficulties in balancing market expansion and risk control.

As China continues to improve the mechanism of RMB exchange rate formation and liberalize the capital account, the determinants of RMB exchange rate will change evidently. International experience shows that the fundamentals of the macro-economy can better explain and determine long-term exchange rate but has limited influence on short-term fluctuations. Short-term fluctuations are mainly caused by cross-border capital flow and the spillover effect of the policy of other countries. But market arbitrage can bring the exchange rate back to the long-term equilibrium. Exchange rate volatility has no obvious impact on short-term capital flow but has substantial increased influence on stable economic growth and especially FDI.

As RMB takes on more functions of an international currency, its exchange rate will not only influence domestic economic and financial market but also create substantial spillover effect on currency exchange rates of neighboring countries, regional trade and investment as well as the international financial market. Therefore, it is necessary to step up expectation management of RMB exchange rate. On December 11, 2015, the China Foreign Exchange Trading Centre launched the RMB exchange rate index, or the CFETS index. Previously, the market used to refer to RMB/USD exchange rate but now with this index would mainly refer to the effective exchange rate based on a basket of currencies. This index helps the market in understanding and accepting new formation mechanism of RMB exchange rate.

A more RMB exchange rate system will enhance the correlation between cross-border capital flow and the financial market: prices in forex, money, and capital market and in onshore and offshore financial market will be more closely linked and risks will become more contagious. All these will result in substantial vulnerability of the domestic financial market. Studies show that before the 2015 reform of exchange rate regime, price in China's capital market, leverage ratio, and net cross-border capital inflow were driven single-directionally; since then, these three variables show cyclical interaction and positive correlation where shocks on one variable are reflexive and continuously intensifying. Bi-directional influence exist in market returns and short-term capital flow, which shows that shocks of short-term capital flow can influence the price and leverage level of the capital market. Previously, the price gap between CNH and CNY and returns ratio of uncovered interest arbitrage had a huge influence on the returns and leverage ratio of the capital market and capital flow; now such influence is waning.

The SDR inclusion will boost the willingness of more countries and regions to cooperate with Chinese financial institutions and bring about more space for the internationalized operation of Chinese banks. With more clients and products, these banks can rapidly expand their overseas business and income. In this process, Chinese banks will inevitably face more complex market environment and regulation. As a result, the risk exposure of banks will show new features both quantitatively and structurally. As China's economy is still restructuring to reduce excessive capacity and de-leverage, banks will face both domestic and international risks in their internationalized operation. They may face difficulties including deteriorating asset quality, slowing profit increase, rising liquidity risks, and so on. Banks may be less capable in bearing the risks. If they cannot step up risk control, systematically important banks will lose international competitiveness and miss the opportunity for internalized development. This will also harm the stability of the domestic financial system.

Conclusion 4 China's economy faces difficulties including inappropriate development model; backward innovation capability; large, yet not strong, external trade; and contraction of private investment. China should focus on key contradictions to push forward the supply-side reform and lower the real economy risk. By doing so China can consolidate the physical foundation for RMB internationalization. RMB internationalization and supply-side reform can reinforce each other in terms of direct investment, technological advancement, trade upgrading, and so on; with RMB internationalization and supply-side reform, China seeks opportunities in the face of risks and promotes the restructuring, transforming, and upgrading of its economy.

Sustainable growth of the real economy at a medium- to high-speed is the solid foundation for RMB internationalization. Real economy is the basis for currency internationalization. Preconditions for currency internationalization include strong economy, large international trade, stable currency value, free use of capital, and effective macro policies.

Since the 2008 international financial crisis, international economic context has changed and China's traditional growth model that relied heavily on export and investment faced severe difficulties. Structural barriers exist for the real economy and risk points continue to appear. The difficulties are mainly due to the following reasons: (1) China has weak innovation capability and cannot take up the middle and high ends of the international industrial chain. (2) China faces structural imbalances where the savings rate is excessively high, consumption does not sufficiently drive economic growth, and certain industries suffer excessive capacity. (3) SMEs face difficulties in financing and private investment is contracting. (4) China lacks the organizing and pricing power of international trade, resulting in a large, yet not strong, international trade for the country. Meanwhile, China's main trading partners face sluggish growth and difficult recovery. Export has lost its effectiveness in driving the economy. Developed countries have taken measures to boost their manufacturing economy, to de-leverage, and to turn the focus back on the real economy. All these have brought about fierce competition for China's manufacturing industry.

Meanwhile, studies on the cross-border capital flow among G20 countries show that since the RMB started to internationalize, capital flow volatility has become more complex and frequent, exacerbating real economy volatility. Nowadays, the world economy is highly fictitious. Against this backdrop, China needs to fend off the risk of a more fictitious domestic economy.

Supply-side reform would help tackle the accumulative risks in China's real economy. Innovative industrial system would ensure sustainable growth and the solid foundation for RMB internationalization. The stable progress in RMB internationalization will boost international society's confidence in and demand for China's economy. RMB internationalization will facilitate trade, pricing, settlement, investment, and settlement. This helps expand foreign trade and international cooperation and promote international M&A and technological advancement. With RMB internationalization, a new supply model of commodities can emerge and optimized resource allocation can be achieved in both domestic and foreign markets. Especially, RMB steadily appreciates in its internationalization, forcing China's trade to transform and upgrade and to emerge from the low to the middle and high ends of the industrial chain. Outside pressure will push the transformation of China's growth engines. Therefore, RMB and supply-side reform are mutually reinforcing with mutually supportive institutional arrangements. RMB internationalization itself is an important force in pushing forward the transformation of China's real economy.

Conclusion 5 External shocks like cross-border capital flow become interwoven with the risk of domestic financial market, of financial institutions, and of the real economy; these elements are also mutually contagious. Therefore, the chain effects of shocks in a single market and of local risks are more likely to lead to systematic risks. China's Systematic Risk Index needs to be drafted to better assess and monitor such risk, and a policy framework of macro-prudential regulation that suits China's conditions should be established to fend off and manage systematic risks with institutional arrangements.

Faced with interwoven external shocks and internal risks, the whole financial system may fluctuate or even suffer crisis. With China's financial reform and RMB internationalization, cross-border capital movement leads to substantially increased systematic risks in domestic financial market. Faced with systematic risks, any financial institution will be inevitably implicated. In other words, systematic risks can influence multiple sectors of the financial industry and even the real economy at the same time. The criterion for systematic risk is whether abnormal volatility appears concurrently in multiple sectors of the financial industry.

As multiple factors lead to systematic risk, we need to consider the whole picture when assessing systematic risks. We undertake a comprehensive analysis of weighted average on the policy environment, financial market, financial institutions, and forex risks. In this way, we establish China's Systematic Risk Index, offering a scientific basis in measuring and assessing systematic risks. Research results show that from July 2005 to December 2015, China has experienced high systematic risk for seven times. On July 21, 2005, China started the managed floating exchange rate regime based on market supply and demand and in reference to a basket of currencies. RMB was no longer anchored only to the USD. This reform brought about severe shocks and drove up the systematic risk index for that month. October 2007 and December 2008 saw two exacerbations of systematic risks due to the eruption and expansion of the sub-prime mortgage crisis. The high systematic risk in 2010 was the result of high inflation. After a stable period from mid-2010 to early 2013, June 2013 saw short-term liquidity risk (money crunch) and rising systematic risk. Recently, the stock market crisis in mid-2015 and rapid RMB depreciation in late 2015 led to two periods of rising systematic risk.

Although the index goes up shorted for several times, risks originated from a single market and did not result in concurrent risks in multiple financial sectors or the outburst and continuous exacerbation of systematic risk. But it is worth noting that only in the second half of 2015, twice did the systematic risk index go up substantially. Such frequent volatility is rarely seen and calls for attention.

The international financial crisis fundamentally changed the long-term understanding of financial regulation. Around the globe, people agree that monetary stability does not ensure financial stability and individual prudence does not ensure systematic prudence. The appeal for financial stability leads to profound changes in macro-prudential regulation. China actively participated in this global reform and rolled out multiple policy tools in domestic macro-prudential regulation. This helps to fend off the accumulation of systematic risks. Under new circumstances, China needs to add a "macro-perspective" to the existing micro-prudential regulation and coordinate financial regulation and other macro-economic policies. In this way, China should build a policy framework of macro-prudential regulation suited to its current conditions to fend off the appearance and expansion of systematic risk and ensure financial stability.

10.2 Policy Proposal

Proposal 1 **China should further promote the market-oriented reform of the exchange rate and improve the RMB exchange rate regime. China should step up the management of market expectation. While maintaining long-term stability of RMB exchange rate at an equilibrium level, China should pursue exchange rate goals that are in line with optimized monetary policy goals.**

First, China should improve the formation mechanism of exchange rate and further liberalize RMB exchange rate so that RMB exchange rate becomes more flexible and fluctuates bi-directionally. China should enhance the credibility of CFETS index and encourage enterprises and institutions to use and refer to the index. In this way, it can change the market's previous practice of referring mainly to RMB/USD exchange rate. China should allow exchange rate to flow within a wider range and enhance enterprises' awareness of managing exchange rate risks and increasing the use of RMB in their overseas business. China should help financial institutions innovate in instruments to manage exchange rate risks and RMB asset management around the globe.

Second, the exchange rate regime should gradually transition from a managed floating system to a freely floating system. The implementation of exchange rate goals should change from direct to indirect intervention. Market arbitrage can help exchange rate to return to long-term equilibrium and the central bank should exit from normalized direct intervention. Meanwhile, China should prevent the negative impact on the financial market and real economy due to excessive volatility of exchange rate. To improve China's managed floating exchange rate system and gain time and space for China's real economy transformation and growth, exchange rate management should try to realize three goals: firstly, exchange rate should reflect market supply and demand and should be given full play in adjusting international balance of payments and better allocating domestic and foreign resources; secondly, China should avoid large-scale volatilities of RMB exchange rate to create a favorable environment for a stable financial and economic operation; thirdly, China should stabilize the market expectation of RMB exchange rate and enhance communication with the market to enhance government credibility and policy effectiveness. Against the gradual and orderly liberalization of capital account, China should maintain a stable long-term rate at the equilibrium level through an appropriate combination of monetary, fiscal, and income policies. Meanwhile, in case of speculation and crisis in the forex market, China should keep necessary forex intervention and capital control and enhance the application of technical instruments. It should take decisive and effective measures to secure stable RMB exchange rate. All these are necessary steps to contain financial crises and prevent systemic financial risks.

Third, in implementing exchange rate policies, China should prioritize international policy communication and coordination. It should pay close attention to the spillover effects of US macro-policies and enhance communication with the US government. China should establish a USD-RMB exchange rate coordination mechanism to reduce the negative impact of excessive exchange rate volatilities on the economy and finance of both countries. China should take effective measures to cope with the negative interest rates in the Eurozone and Japan. A coordination mechanism of monetary policies is called for among the issuance countries of SDR basket currencies to avoid currency wars among major countries. By doing so, the "beggar-thy-neighbor" effect can be reduced. At the same time, the spillover effect of China's monetary and exchange rate policies on other emerging markets should also be considered. While prioritizing domestic needs, China should consider the interests of other emerging economies through proper communication and coordination. In this way, China can reduce policy frictions and achieve win-win cooperation.

Proposal 2 **China should not rush to liberalize the capital account. It should heed the effect of cross-border capital flow on the price linkage and risk contagion of the domestic financial market and step up the full-blown monitoring on capital flow. Chinese banks should seize the current opportunity to expand overseas business and improve the comprehensive mechanism of risk management; they should avoid magnifying external risks or breeding systematic risks.**

Capital account liberalization should be in line with the reform of exchange rate regime. China should take a "gradual, controllable and balanced" approach and adapt to the needs of its financial and economic development and the situations of the world economy. With unsophisticated domestic financial market and regulation system and limited and less effective means to tackle cross-border capital flow, China cannot suddenly liberalize its capital account. China should have a clear understanding of the net capital outflow over the short term and the influence of bi-directional cross-border capital flow on its economy. It should continue the prudential regulation on capital account and contain the risk of capital flow to a tolerable extent.

Currently, the linkage between forex and capital market and between onshore and offshore market has been further enhanced and the risk contagion among markets has been exacerbated. China should pay close attention to the possible systematic risk due to large-scale, short-term capital flow. It should understand and utilize the linkage between capital market returns and exchange rate. It should step up the coordination between monetary and exchange rate policies and enhance the government's capability in managing short-term capital flow. In addition to controlling speculative capital flow, China should also increase the cost of such activities. It should closely monitor capital inflow and all possible channels so that it can take effective measures upon capital outflow. As QFII capital is the pilot indicator for other funds, China should use big data technology and better collect and analyze high-frequency data. In this way, China can enhance the monitoring and guidance concerning QFII.

The SDR inclusion creates better conditions for the enterprises' overseas investments. Chinese banks should seize the opportunity to become internationalized and offer all-round financial services to Chinese enterprises with overseas business. Chinese banks should help these enterprises to take hold and build their own brands in the international market. Chinese banks should, based on their own characteristics and external environment, draft and adjust the direction and strategy for operation; they should offer more diversified products and services and achieve a diversified income structure; the banks should improve their core competitiveness in the international market and increase the international influence of China's financial institutions. As they face more complex operation environment and larger risks overseas, Chinese banks need to nurture the awareness of risks and the proper understanding of performance. These banks should establish a comprehensive information system of risk management covering domestic and international business. The banks should standardize their overseas business to avoid operational risks. Political and compliance risks are outstanding in the banks' overseas operation. China should draft at the earliest juncture law and regulations concerning the cross-border operation of financial institutions and establish an insurance mechanism for overseas investments. Regulatory authorities should raise the standards on banks' capital adequacy ratio and liquidity and step up cross-border cooperation. In this way, regulatory authorities help Chinese banks to avoid the magnifying effect of external risks and losses. Such risks and losses will further hamper banks' prudent operation, undermine the safe operation of the domestic financial market, and even lead to systematic financial crises in the domestic market.

Proposal 3 **Currently, multiple regulatory authorities lead to problems like scattered policies, overlapping functions, opaque responsibilities, and compromised standards. China should draw upon international practices and identify the principle for the current reform of its financial regulation. China should establish a policy framework of macro-prudential regulation that is suited to its conditions. By doing so, it can offer institutional guarantee to better manage systematic risks.**

China should add a "macro-prudential" perspective to the current framework of financial regulation and identify competent authorities for macro-prudential policies. Since the 2008 financial crisis, multiple countries' reforms have been focusing on adding a macro-prudential aspect to the existing regulatory framework to step up the monitoring, assessment, and prevention of systematic risks. And special committees, prudential regulatory authorities, and similar organs have been designated as the competent departments of macro-prudential policies.

Apart from securing exchange rate stability, central banks should be given more responsibility to safeguard financial stability and enhance financial regulation. After the crisis in the year 2008, major economies have taken steps to prevent systematic risks and safeguard financial stability as the core task of the regulation system reform. Economies have been enhancing the central banks' function of safeguarding financial stability and undertaking financial regulation; economies have been further pushing forward the reform of macro-prudential regulation and its coordination with macro-economic policies.

We should identify the relationship between monetary policy and macro-prudential, micro-prudential, and behavioral regulation according to their different functions and institutional arrangements; we emphasize the coordination between these four aspects. This has become the major task for the reform of financial regulation system in various countries. There are different models of "super central bank" where the central bank is responsible for monetary, macro-prudential, and micro-prudential policies; of "a committee + enhanced central bank" where a financial stability supervisory committee is established and the central bank takes up more responsibility in financial regulation; and of "prudential + behavioral regulation" where emphasis is laid on both sides.

We should improve the availability and accuracy of financial statistics to offer full- and in-time information for the monitoring, analysis, and assessment of systematic risks. The FSB, IMF, BIS, World Bank, and major economies—through enhancing central banks, amending laws, improving statistical arrangements, and expanding statistical coverage—are enhancing the availability of data and information and the sharing and coordination of financial information.

China should also establish an effective mechanism of crisis management and step up the protection for financial consumers. It may refer to the regulation reform in major economies: The Federal Reserve and the Federal Deposit Insurance Corporation jointly manage the systematic risks of the United States; the Bank of England takes care of the financial crises in the United Kingdom and is responsible for setting up procedures and strategies to resolve financial institutions; the EU wants to establish its banking union to combine the mechanisms of banking regulation, resolution, and deposit insurance. In addition, some countries have established specific organs to enhance the protection for financial consumers. For instance, the independent Consumer Financial Protection Bureau, funded by the Federal Reserve, is responsible for consumer protection in the financial sector.

Proposal 4 **China should step up RMB offshore markets to build the channels for the international circulation and use of RMB. It should boost RMB's role in multilateral financial institutions and expand RMB transactions. China should thus establish RMB's network effect in the international financial market.**

China should grasp the opportunities provided by the rapid RMB internationalization to develop RMB offshore markets. It should provide more investment instruments and channels to satisfy the increasing demand for trade and investment. It should establish a self-sustained circulation mechanism for RMB funds to offer enough liquidity for offshore markets. Through specific policy arrangements, China should promote the coordination between onshore and offshore markets and establish the mechanism where onshore prices offer guidance for offshore prices.

Mechanisms of RMB backflow provide new historic chances for Hong Kong and Shanghai. The two financial centers can, focusing on RMB back flow and their respective advantages and needs, undertake deeper cooperation and offer mutual support. The virtuous RMB circulation will boost the RMB internationalization. In establishing the mechanism of RMB international circulation, China should now focus on Hong Kong. It should nurture RMB international capital market through the Shanghai Hong Kong stock connect to establish overseas circulation mechanism of RMB under capital account. From a broader perspective, China should work to establish a Greater China currency area that includes the Mainland, Taiwan, Hong Kong, and Macau, taking regionalization as the strategic focus at the current stage.

China should enhance RMB offshore markets in major international financial centers in Europe. It should promote the cooperation between domestic exchanges of securities and commodities with the exchanges in Frankfurt, Luxembourg, and London. The priority should be launching RMB-denominated financial products including international bonds, stocks, funds, and structured securities and RMB-denominated futures for commodities including gold and oil. China should give full play to local marketing channels to expand the transaction of RMB products. China should accelerate the RMB network effect and help RMB offshore markets to gain width and depth.

After the SDR inclusion, the international society has higher expectations for China to play its role as a major country. The demand for RMB to take more of the functions of an international currency will also increase. Through the effective operation of the AIIB, Silk Road Fund, and CIPS, China is guiding international capital to support major projects under the Belt and Road initiative and increasing the international use of RMB. Upon RMB inclusion, China should be more active in international financial governance and play a larger role in the policy-making and negotiation of international financial institutions like the IMF, World Bank, and BIS. Therefore, China should try to increase its voice in the reform of the international financial system.

Proposal 5 **China should identify key areas of supply-side structural reform and push forward technological advancement at home and abroad. The financial sector should continue to serve the real economy and China should prevent economic bubbles and the over-reliance on the financial sector. All these will add to the mutually reinforcing interaction between RMB internationalization and supply-side reform.**

Supply-side reform is the necessary choice to nurture new drivers for China's economy and restructure toward sustainable development. China should make breakthroughs in three key areas of supply-side reform: first, increasing R&D investment and overseas M&A to promote technology advancement. One core task for supply-side reform is making up for short links in the economy and this should be undertaken at home and abroad. Domestically, with increased R&D investment and institutional reform, China should encourage enterprises to build up their technology and innovation capability and increase total factor productivity. In this way, it can enhance the core competitiveness of its manufacturing industry. Internationally, it should encourage its enterprises to go global. China should increase the M&A of high-end manufacturing businesses in developed countries to introduce high technology from abroad. Secondly, it should push forward financial restructuring and broaden financing channels. China could thus lower the cost of funds and make the financial sector better serve the real economy. It should avoid the excessive reliance on the financial sector and especially potential bubbles. It should develop factor markets and use interest rates as a leverage to adjust the supply and demand of funds. Resource allocation can thus become more efficient. China should promote financial openness and liberalization. As long as it can control the risk, it should encourage its enterprises to raise funds overseas and make use of the low interest rates in overseas markets. In this way, China can help enterprises with high debt/asset ratio to deleverage. It can also reduce substantially the cost of funds and help its enterprises become more dynamic and competitive. China should accelerate the internationalized operation of its financial institutions to offer comprehensive financial services to its MNCs and enterprises overseas. It should help these enterprises explore overseas markets and enhance their status and influence in the international division of labor. These enterprises can thus have more initiative and voice in their international trade. Third, China should coordinate financial and fiscal measures and encourage the ODI of private enterprises and utilize domestic and foreign markets in optimizing the allocation of production factors. On the one hand, China's enterprises should build their brands and enhance their management to satisfy the domestic demand for high-quality daily commodities and luxury goods. It could thus realize import substitution. On the other hand, it should design appropriate models for offering foreign assistance. With effective public–private partnership, China should explore overseas markets and help domestic enterprises participate in international capacity cooperation. In this way, it can extend the life cycle of products with traditional advantages and increase the total factor economic efficiency.

China should insist on the guiding principle that both the financial sector and RMB internationalization should serve the real economy. The progress in RMB internationalization will boost the international community's confidence and investment in China. Meanwhile, Chinese enterprises can use RMB more easily and acquire more stable returns in their overseas investments. Especially RMB internationalization will help change the practice that commodities are priced in USD terms, offering a more stable model of resource supply for China's economy. As the Belt and Road countries are more willing to use RMB, China can cooperate with Middle Eastern and Central Asian countries as well as Russia to push forward RMB invoicing and settlement in the bilateral trade of crude oil. China should help the crude oil futures price of Shanghai International Energy exchange to become another benchmark price for crude oil in addition to WTI and Brent. As a result, China can increase the pricing power of crude oil for itself as well as the above-mentioned countries.

Appendix 1: Experience on the Yen's Internationalization After Joining in the SDR Basket

After the collapse of the Bretton Woods system and the forming of the floating exchange rate regime, the international monetary system gradually evolved from a single polar system to a multi-polar system. In the following years, the internationalization of Japanese yen was about to begin. In 1981, yen joined the SDR basket which marked the internationalization of yen officially started.

The internationalization of yen followed the rise of Japanese economy (Graph A.1). In the 1970s, Japan surpassed Germany to become the world's second largest economy. In the 1980s, Japan achieved a more rapid economic growth. During this period, Japan's economy maintained a high growth rate with relatively reasonable inflation and stable customer price compared with other countries that issued the international currency. Along with the sharp appreciation of yen due to the Plaza Accord, economic bubbles were accumulated rapidly. The property bubbles further dragged the economy down to recession since the middle of the 1990s, indicating the failure of yen's internationalization.

The following three parts show the history of the Japanese yen's participation in global asset allocation after joining the SDR basket. They are the cross-border trade settlement in the commodity market, the capital allocation in the financial market and the capital market, and the allocation of reserve assets.

International Monetary Institute (ed.), *Currency Internationalization and Macro Financial Risk Control*,
https://doi.org/10.1007/978-981-13-0698-3

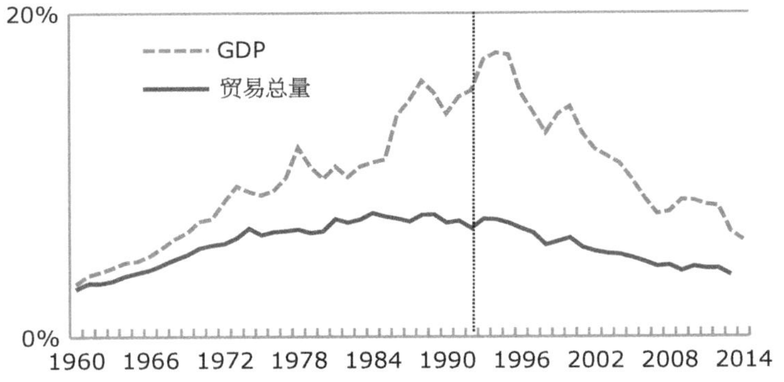

Graph A.1 Proportion of Japan's economy to the global GDP. (Source: World Bank)

Joining the SDR Basket Did Not Obviously Promote the Development of Yen in the Cross-Border Trade Settlement in the Commodity Market

Linda S. Goldberg and Cédric Tille (2005) theoretically and empirically showed the interaction between industry features and invoice currency selection. They concluded that producers in industries with high-demand

Table A.1 Major international currencies' share in the trade settlement of certain countries in 1995 (%)

Country	*USD*	*JPY*	*DEM*	*F*	*GBP*	*ITL*	*NLG*	*Others*
Export								
United States	92.0	2.4	0.9	0.6	0.9	0.3	0.6	2.3
Japan	52.2	36.0	2.4	0.7	1.4	0.3	0.9	5.8
Germany	9.5	0.9	74.7	3.2	2.6	2.2	1.3	5.6
France	18.6	1.0	10.5	51.7	4.2	3.1	1.5	9.4
United Kingdom	23.1	1.1	4.0	3.1	61.6	1.6	2.3	3.0
Italy	21.0	0.6	18.0	8.0	3.5	40.0	1.5	7.4
Netherlands	20.6	0.6	18.5	4.5	4.1	1.5	43.8	6.4
Import								
United States	80.7	2.8	3.8	0.9	1.7	0.8	0.3	9.0
Japan	70.2	22.7	2.7	1.0	1.3	0.8	0.3	1.0
Germany	19.5	1.4	51.5	2.5	1.7	1.0	0.9	21.5
France	23.1	1.0	10.1	48.5	2.9	3.7	1.4	9.3
United Kingdom	24.6	2.0	11.1	4.6	43.0	1.8	2.5	10.7
Italy	29.0	1.0	14.0	7.0	3.8	37.0	2.4	5.8
Netherlands	25.4	1.3	17.5	2.8	3.4	1.0	42.8	5.8

Source: Bekx, P., The Implications of the Introduction of the Euro for Non-EU countries [R]. Euro Papers No. 26, European Commission, 1998 elasticities are more likely to display herding in a single currency as their choice of the invoice currency. They are more likely to choose the same currency as their competitors to reduce risks as much as possible. Both the primary commodity and financial product are highly homogeneous with high-demand elasticities and are traded in a highly competitive international environment. Inevitably, such features will lead to the settlement in a single currency since businesses in all countries choose the most widely used invoice currency with the minimum transaction cost. Gradually, the settlement in a single currency takes shape; the USD that dominates the primary market presents a case. Compared with other international currencies, the yen's development as a medium in the international trade clearly lagged behind.

The graph below shows the use of yen in the domestic trade settlement was much less than that of the USD, English pound, and Deutsche mark. In Japan's export, 52.2% of trade was settled in the USD, the largest proportion except that in the United States. This number reached even 70.2% in terms of the import (Table A.1 and Graph A.2).

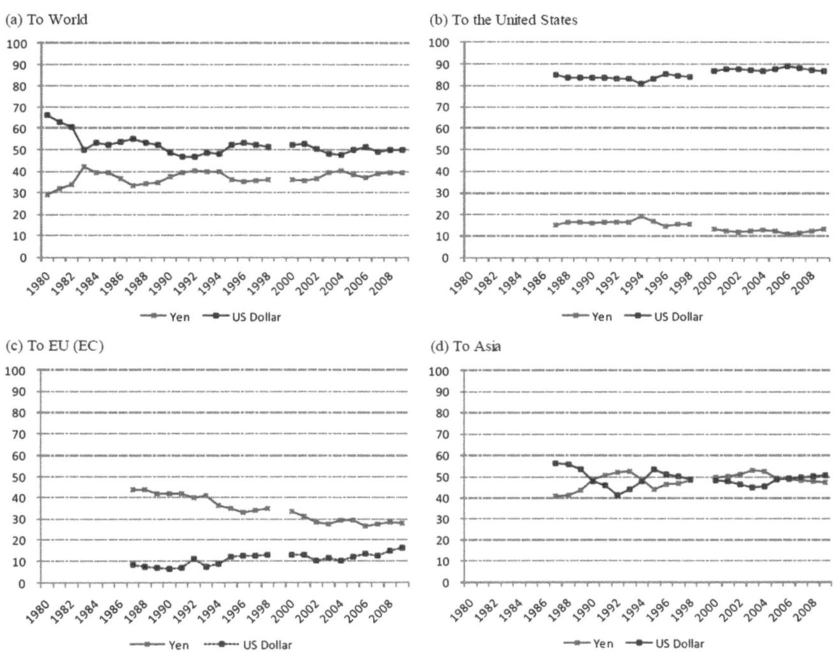

Graph A.2 Japan's export settled in yen and the USD. (Source: Takatoshi, I., Kiyotaka, S. and Junko, S., Determinants of Currency Invoicing in Japanese Exports: A Firm-Level Analysis [R]. RIETI Discussion Paper, 10-E-034, June, 2010)

Joining the SDR Basket Promotes the Yen's Development in the International Financial Market and Capital Market

In the 1970s, a large amount of money trading and trading on financial products gradually disconnected from the production and circulation of the physical products. The subject of the global capital activities also started to change, and the global capital entered a new era of "the fictitious capital". Financial expansion has been the main feature of the global economy since the 1970s. With the development of economic globalization, the fictitious economy has expanded in scale and gradually separated from the real economy. The most important feature of the fictitious economy is the market value of the financial instruments separates from the financial instruments' own value. Trade of the financial instruments has created a system relatively independent to the real economy, in which currency plays an important role. Foreign exchange transactions and the capital market have also gradually disconnected from the real economy and increasingly expanded, exerting larger influences on global economy than that of the real economy.

It is in such context that yen entered the multi-international-currency system, after the collapse of the Bretton Woods system, and became one of the second-echelon currencies that is only second to the USD, just like the Deutsche mark, the French franc, and the English pound. Before

Table A.2 Currency trading's composition in major Forex (%)

	New York				*London*		*Tokyo*	
	1980	*1983*	*1986*	*1989*	*1986*	*1989*	*1986*	*1989*
	March	*April*	*March*	*April*	*March*	*April*	*March*	*April*
Against the USD								
DM	31.8	32.5	34.2	32.9	28.0	22.0	10.4	9.7
JPY	**10.2**	**22.0**	**23.0**	**25.2**	**14.0**	**15.0**	**77.0**	**72.1**
GBP	22.7	16.6	18.6	14.6	30.0	27.0	3.0	4.3
CHF	10.1	12.2	9.7	11.8	9.0	10.0	5.6	4.4
FRF	6.9	4.4	3.6	3.2	4.0	4.0	0.3	0.2
Others	18.3	12.1	10.9	12.3	12.0	13.0	3.7	3.2
Crosses	–	0.2	–	–	3.0	9.0	–	6.1

Source: BIS, *Triennial Central Bank Survey of foreign exchange and OTC derivatives markets*, 1990–2005; Tavlas and Ozeki (1992)

joining the SDR basket in 1981, the internationalization of yen was only about to begin. The use of yen in the foreign exchange market and the capital market was limited. However, since 1981, trading in yen in the financial market increased largely. Statistics (Table A.2), in a review report jointly issued by the Federal Reserve, the Bank of England, and the Bank of Japan in September 1989, showed that after yen joined the SDR basket, the yen's involvement in transactions of the foreign exchange market in New York increased by 111.57% after two years, and the number rose to 147.1% eight years later. Compared with the yen, the involvement of the German mark in the foreign exchange transactions was stable after it joined the SDR basket, failing to exert a significant spur. The statistics of trading in yen in the Tokyo foreign exchange market showed that trading in yen has been weak since the late 1980s: from 1986 to 1989, trading in yen decreased from 38.5% to 36%, a drop of 6.4%; since the 1990s, the number dropped from 15.5% in 1989 to 6.9% in 1998. Trading in yen also shrank gradually in the global foreign exchange market since the 1990s (Table A.3).

Table A.4 shows that after entering the SDR basket, yen-denominated assets had a new round of fast development in the international bond market. In 1975, yen-denominated assets accounted for only 0.4% of the international bond market. However, in 1981, the number reached 6.6% (Table A.3). The reason for such achievement lay in a fast growth of the Japanese economy and the development of yen's internationalization. It was also because lots of Japanese enterprises went abroad to find financing as the downturns of the Japan's stock market made it difficult for the Japanese enterprises to get financing, thus many

Table A.3 Shares of yen trade and Forex trading of Tokyo in the global Forex trading (%)

	1970	*1975*	*1989*	*1992*	*1995*	*1998*	*2001*	*2004*
JPY trade	0.0	0.5	13.5	11.7	12.1	10.1	11.4	10.1
Forex trading of Tokyo Forex trading	–	–	15.5	11.2	10.2	6.9	9.1	8.2

Source: BIS, *Triennial Central Bank Survey of foreign exchange and OTC derivatives markets*, 1990–2005; Takagi, S., Internationalising the Yen, 1984–2003: Unfinished Agenda or Mission Impossible? prepared for BIS/BoK seminar on Currency Internationalization: Lessons from the Global Financial Crisis and Prospects for the Future in Asia and the Pacific, Seoul, 19–20 March 2009

Table A.4 Currency composition of the international bond market (%)

	1975	*1980*	*1985*	*1986*	*1987*	*1988*	*1989*	*1990*	*1991*
USD	50.6	42.7	54.0	53.9	38.8	41.2	52.0	37.9	28.5
JPY	**0.4**	**4.8**	**9.1**	**10.4**	**13.7**	**8.4**	**8.3**	**13.3**	**12.6**
GBP	0.2	3.0	4.0	4.6	7.8	9.4	7.1	8.6	9.1
CHF	17.1	19.5	11.3	10.7	12.9	11.1	7.5	9.4	7.3
DM	16.4	21.9	8.5	8.0	8.0	10.1	6.3	7.4	7.1
ECU	–	–	5.2	3.4	4.0	4.9	4.9	8.1	11.1
Others	15.3	8.1	7.9	9.0	14.8	14.9	13.9	15.3	24.3

Source: BIS, *Triennial Central Bank Survey of foreign exchange and OTC derivatives markets*, 1990–2005; OECD, Financial Market Trends, Various Issues, 1981–1998

Table A.5 Issues of euro-yen bonds and Samurai bonds (in billion yen)

Issuer	*1980*	*1984*	*1985*	*1986*	*1987*	*1988*	*1989*
The Euro-yen bond							
Non-residence	55	227	1446	2551	2994	2213	3558
	–	–	140	442	555	127	–
The Samurai bond							
Public sector	261	915	1115	590	420	635	926
Private sector	–	199	157	195	78	162	74

Source: Nomura Research Institute, Ministry of Finance, Japan; BIS, *Triennial Central Bank Survey of foreign exchange and OTC derivatives markets*, 1990–2005; OECD, Financial Market Trends, Various Issues, 1981–1998

investors of yen-denominated bond were overseas branches of the Japanese enterprises. Besides, Table A.5 shows that although yen's joining of the SDR basket largely promoted the development of yen-denominated bond, the issue of euro-yen bond was relatively faster. From 1980 to 1984, non-resident euro-yen bond increased three times. However, in the middle and late 1990s, the development of yen-denominated bond slowed down quickly. In 1997, yen-denominated bond accounted for less than 5% of the international bond market (Graph A.3).

In the 1970s, almost all the international loans took the form of the USD, with few yen-denominated loans. Since the 1980s, the yen-denominated loan increased rapidly, especially in East Asian countries. Yen-denominated loan's share in external loans of South Korea, Thailand, Malaysia, Indonesia, and the Philippines increased from

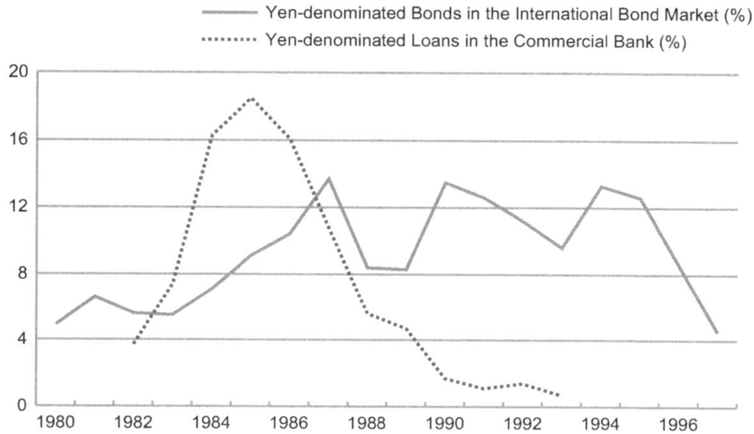

Graph A.3 Yen's role in the global assets allocation. (Source: OECD, Financial Market Trends, Various Issues, 1981–1998)

Table A.6 Shares of dollar-denominated loan and yen-denominated loan in external loans of the East Asian countries (%)

	1980	*1981*	*1982*	*1983*	*1984*	*1985*	*1986*	*1987*	*1988*	*1989*	*1990*
Indonesia											
JPY	**20.0**	**19.3**	**21.0**	**23.3**	**25.0**	**31.7**	**33.9**	**39.4**	**39.3**	**35.2**	**39.3**
USD	43.5	44.4	43.1	42.3	41.4	30.7	26.0	19.2	18.5	19.5	18.5
South Korea											
JPY	**16.6**	**14.1**	**12.3**	**12.5**	**12.8**	**16.7**	**22.0**	**27.2**	**29.5**	**26.6**	**29.5**
USD	53.5	60.2	63.7	64.4	66.0	60.3	49.4	33.8	32.4	35.1	32.4
Malaysia											
JPY	**19.0**	**16.9**	**13.3**	**14.2**	**21.2**	**26.4**	**30.4**	**35.7**	**37.1**	**36.6**	**37.1**
USD	38.0	51.5	62.3	65.8	61.5	50.6	45.0	36.3	35.6	34.2	35.6
The Philippines											
JPY	**22.0**	**20.6**	**19.2**	**20.0**	**20.0**	**24.9**	**25.5**	**35.2**	**40.5**	**32.6**	**40.5**
USD	51.6	51.1	53.9	51.2	52.7	47.8	48.1	42.4	34.7	36.9	34.7
Thailand											
JPY	**25.5**	**23.2**	**24.0**	**27.3**	**29.2**	**36.1**	**39.9**	**43.1**	**43.5**	**40.9**	**43.5**
USD	39.7	40.5	38.0	32.5	29.9	25.5	20.6	17.8	20.8	23.6	20.8
Average											
JPY	**19.5**	**17.8**	**17.2**	**18.5**	**20.3**	**25.8**	**29.3**	**36.0**	**37.9**	**35.7**	**37.9**
USD	47.3	51.3	53.4	53.2	52.9	44.7	38.5	29.0	27.0	28.1	27.0

Source: World Bank; Tavlas and Ozeki (1992)

19.5% in 1980 to 37.9% in the end of 1990 (Table A.6). During this period, although the Japanese commercial banks were in expansion overseas and the Plaza Accord in 1985 made the yen appreciate against the USD and the scale of yen-denominated assets expand, the positive effects of joining the SDR cannot be neglected. The rising demand of yen increasingly lifted the yen's role in the global asset allocation. But such trend did not last for a long time as in the late 1980s, the yen-denominated loans decreased quickly. In 1997, the share of the yen-denominated loans in the external loans of the global commercial banks decreased to 0.2%.

Joining the SDR Basket Increases the Share of the Yen in the International Reserves

Compared with the functions of a medium of exchange and a unit of account in the financial market, yen's function as a store of value became more obvious after it joined the SDR basket. Table A.7 shows that before 1980 the share of yen in global foreign reserves was near zero; from 1980 to 1991, yen's share in the international reserve increased quickly; in 1991, the share of yen in the international reserve reached 8.5%. The share of yen in the foreign exchange reserve of other Asian countries also increased rapidly; especially, after the Plaza Accord the number reached 30%. It was because the export of other Asian countries excessively depended on the Japanese market; it was also because after the Plaza Accord, a fast yen rise increased the burden of the yen loans on some Asian countries, and in order to avoid the foreign exchange risks, some countries had to increase the share of yen in their foreign exchange reserve. In the 1990s, as Japan entered the "Lost Decade", the positive effects of joining the SDR basket gradually disappeared. Yen's role in the international foreign exchange reserve gradually declined. At present, the share of yen in the global foreign exchange reserve has decreased to less than 4%, less than that of the English pound (Graph A.4).

Table A.7 Currency composition of the international foreign exchange (%)

	1970	*1975*	*1980*	*1981*	*1982*	*1983*	*1984*	*1985*	*1986*	*1987*	*1988*	*1989*	*1990*
The world													
USD	77.2	79.5	68.6	71.5	70.5	71.4	70.1	64.9	67.1	67.2	64.9	60.3	56.4
JPY	**0.0**	**0.5**	**4.4**	**4.2**	**4.7**	**5.0**	**5.8**	**8.0**	**7.9**	7.0	**7.1**	**7.3**	**8.0**
DM	1.9	6.3	14.9	12.3	12.4	11.8	12.7	15.2	14.6	14.4	15.7	19.1	19.7
GBP	10.4	3.9	2.9	2.1	2.3	2.5	2.9	3.0	2.6	2.4	2.8	2.7	3.2
FF	1.1	1.2	1.7	1.3	1.0	0.8	0.8	0.9	0.8	0.8	1.0	1.4	2.1
CHF	0.7	1.6	3.2	2.7	2.7	2.4	2.0	2.3	2.0	2.0	1.9	1.5	1.5
Other	8.7	7.0	4.3	5.9	6.4	6.1	5.7	5.7	5.0	6.2	6.6	7.7	9.1
Asia													
USD	–	–	48.6	54.4	53.2	55.7	58.2	44.8	48.4	41.2	46.7	56.4	62.7
JPY	–	–	**13.9**	**15.5**	**17.6**	**15.5**	**16.3**	**26.9**	**22.8**	**30.0**	**26.7**	**17.5**	**17.1**
DM	–	–	20.6	18.9	17.6	16.7	14.6	16.4	16.7	16.7	17.4	15.2	14.2
GBP	–	–	3.0	2.5	2.7	2.9	3.5	4.1	3.6	3.9	4.2	6.4	4.9
FF	–	–	0.6	0.6	0.7	0.8	0.6	0.9	1.1	1.0	0.5	0.5	0.2
CHF	–	–	10.6	5.1	5.6	6.6	4.9	4.9	5.1	5.7	3.4	3.0	0.5
Other	–	–	2.7	3.0	2.6	1.8	1.9	2.0	2.3	1.5	1.1	1.0	0.4

Source: IMF, Annual Report, 1990

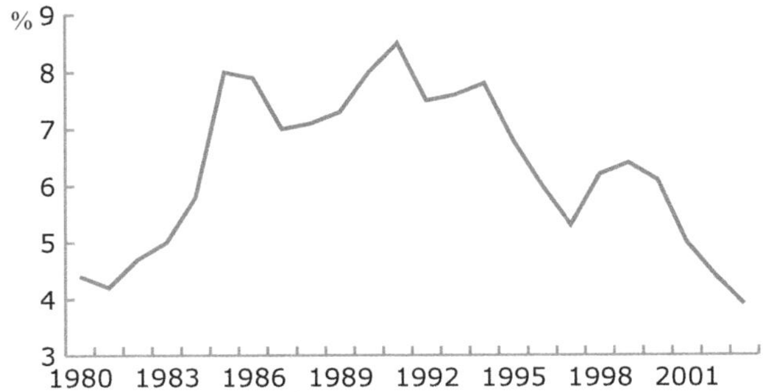

Graph A.4 The share of yen in the international foreign exchange. (Source: IMF Annual Report)

Appendix 2: Foreign Exchange Risk Management in Bank of Communications

Diversified Demands for Foreign Exchange Management Under New Situations

On August 11, 2015, People's Bank of China (PBOC) announced to further improve the quotation mechanism of RMB central parity against the USD toward a market-oriented direction and benchmark status. As of opening quotation that day, the RMB/USD central parity depreciated sharply by 1136 base points compared to the previous trading day, registering a daily decrease of almost 2%, and subsequently both RMB spot exchange rates and offshore RMB exchange rates declined. On September 1, the PBOC issued the *Notice on Enhancing the Macro-Prudential Management of Currency Forward Contracts* ([2015] No. 273), which requires that financial institutions handling foreign currency forward contracts should provide relevant risk reserves. The RMB exchange rate showed even larger fluctuations since the start of 2016—the RMB/USD central parity dropped to a five-year low of 6.5646 on January 7.

Due to the above-mentioned changes in market and policy, clients have shown divergent expectations on RMB exchange rates, and diversified demands for foreign exchange management. Some clients without awareness of hedging begin to realize that risks and opportunities go hand in hand in the area of exchange rates; some clients with strong awareness of hedging and established institutions have effectively locked in risks, and

International Monetary Institute (ed.), *Currency Internationalization and Macro Financial Risk Control*,
https://doi.org/10.1007/978-981-13-0698-3

continue hedging against risks more firmly than ever before; and other customers, due to their loss incurred by the trend reversal, increasingly demand for the study on the future trends as well as innovative products for new situations.

Bank of Communications' Foreign Exchange Risk Management Services for Clients

Bank of Communications (BoCOM) has always been committed to providing comprehensive wealth management and risk management solutions for its clients. To meet the diversified demands for foreign exchange risk management, Bank of Communications provides innovative, tailored financial services for different groups of clients.

1. For customers without awareness of hedging, BoCOM focuses on building the risk consciousness by imparting the idea of fiscal neutrality; that is, both forward exchange sales and settlement aim at locking in risks. BoCOM introduces to its clients a comprehensive package of hedging tools including spot and forward contracts, swaps, options, and combined options, and helps them manage the foreign exchange risks easily with those basic instruments.
2. For clients with some knowledge about hedging against risks, BoCOM develops, a combination set of services of FOREX purchases and sales, FOREX transactions, and financing and wealth management that are tailored to the specific management of clients under new situations. By taking advantage of favorable policies including the expansion of Shanghai Free-Trade Zone (FTZ), the Belt and Road initiative, financial support for domestic enterprises to "go global", combined with BoCOM's advantage of "business networks all over the world" and featured FTZ products such as "comprehensive banking consortium", "offshore M&A loan", "cross-border financing", and "lease receivables factoring", BoCOM designs a comprehensive service programs focusing on cross-border finance and foreign exchange risks for clients with authentic trading background.
3. Innovation in procedures and channels. In recent years, BoCOM adheres to its service philosophy of "One BoCOM, One Client". BoCOM has improved its customer experience through system development, innovative channels as well as optimized processes, and has built its overall strength by integrating products, talents, price-making, brand, and other elements. Guided by the principle of

"serving the real economy and facilitating cross-border transactions", BoCOM persists in innovating in procedures, channels, and services to provide enterprises with FOREX risk management products, such as FOREX settlement via corporate e-banking, a product that helps corporates purchase foreign exchanges conveniently in this rapidly changing market. That's how expertise creates value.

Foreign Exchange Risk Management for Bank of Communications

While providing FOREX risk management products and programs for customers, BoCOM, as a sound operating joint-stock commercial bank, continues to pay attention to risk management and compliance operations.

1. BoCOM implements the regulation intentions correctly. Currently, China's economy is slowing down but still keeps a sound and steady momentum. Despite the pressure on capital outflows for some time, the overall economic performance is under control. The national prudent macro-economic management will help bring about correct market expectations and regulate market behavior. In this regard, BoCOM will continue to improve price transmission and lead the customers on the right track of following the regulatory policy intentions.
2. BoCOM increases the awareness of the overall situation, carries out authenticity checks, and meets regulatory requirements under new situations. The Bank facilitates the FOREX settlement and sale for corporates, and at the same time strictly takes up its duty of regulation subrogation, so as to balance business development and risk control.
3. BoCOM strengthens its internal control system and policy training, and improves its capacity to guarantee the internal management. Besides, the Bank reinforces the mechanisms of accountability, assessment, and monitoring, so as to increase the consciousness and initiative of complying with foreign exchange policies. BoCOM requires that all branches strengthen their business risk management, and reasonably quote their customers by factoring in the price fluctuation incurred by volatile markets. Furthermore, the Bank strictly collects deposits of forwards, swaps, options, and improves the business prevention and control of mark to the market; closely monitor market trends and unusual activity in large positions; and increase authenticity and compliance checks in foreign exchange business.

Appendix 3: Empirical Analysis of Capital Flow's Impact on China's Financial Market Co-movement

Definition of Variables

This part mainly analyzes the dynamic relation between net equity inflows, CNYCNH FX difference, China equity returns, the interest difference of USDCNH, and equity market's margin balance. We will define the variables first and introduce the impulse response function as well as the VAR-MGARCH-DCC Model for further analysis.

We define the United States as the home country and investors holding USD as home investors as we are analyzing the short-term cross-border flow and equity market of China. If a home equity investor holding dollars invests on stock markets in China at time t, sell it at time $t + 1$, the excess return R_t will be calculated as: $R_t = \ln \dfrac{\frac{P_{t+1}}{e_{CNY,t+1}}}{\frac{P_t}{e_{CNY,t}}} - r_{USD,t}$

P_t stands for China's equity portfolio price at time t; $e_{CNY,t}$ stands for CNY FX rate (all exchange rates are in direct quotations); $r_{USD,t}$ stands for the risk-free rate of dollar. Therefore, it is easy to understand the above equation: the stock indexes denominated in USD at time t is $\dfrac{P_t}{e_{CNY,t}}$ and at

International Monetary Institute (ed.), *Currency Internationalization and Macro Financial Risk Control*,
https://doi.org/10.1007/978-981-13-0698-3

time t + 1 is $\frac{P_{t+1}}{e_{CNY,t+1}}$, the return of a stock investor is $r_{USD,\,t}$ and we will get the logarithm of excess return. To identify the risk factors of equity investing, the excess return can be reconstructed as:

$$R_t = \ln P_{t+1} - \ln P_t - r_{CNY,t} - \ln e_{CNY,t+1} + \ln e_{CNY,t} + \ln e_{CNH,t+1}$$
$$- \ln e_{CNH,t}, - r_{CNH,t} + r_{CNY,t} - \ln e_{CNH,t+1} + \ln e_{CNH,t} + r_{CNH,t} - r_{USD,t}$$

$r_{CNY,\,t}$ indicates the onshore CNY interest rate; $r_{CNH,\,t}$ indicates the offshore CNH interest rate; $e_{CHN,\,t}$ indicates the USDCNH exchange rate at time *t*.

Then we denote China's equity return in CNY, CNY/CNH spread and *USD/CNH* UIP as follows:

$$Equity_t = \ln P_{t+1} - \ln P_t - r_{CNY,t}$$
$$Spread_t = - \ln e_{CNY,t+1} + \ln e_{CNY,t} + \ln e_{CNH,t+1} - \ln e_{CNH,t}, - r_{CNH,t} + r_{CNY,t}$$
$$UIP_t = - \ln e_{CNH,t+1} + \ln e_{CNH,t} + r_{CNH,t} - r_{USD,t}$$

Excess return can be rewritten as:

$$R_t = Spread_t + Equity_t + UIP_t$$

To be more specific, $E_{quity}\ y_t$ stands for China equity's excess return in CNY; $\ln P_{t+1}$—$\ln P_t$ stands for its log return while $r_{CYN,\,t}$ is CNY's risk-free rate.

Spread *t* stands for CNH/CNY holding spread. The spread is made of two components: the exchange rate change and the original interest rate difference denote USDCNY and USDCNH respectively. Thus, the exchange rate change part can be calculated as and the interest rate difference part as, which add up together to, denoting the return of a CNH holder if he chooses to take CNY.

UI P_t standing for *USD/CNH* uncovered interest rate parity, in which $\ln e_{CNH,\,t+1} - \ln e_{CNH,\,t}$ is the log exchange rate change of *USD/CNH*, $r_{USD,\,t} - r_{CNH,\,t}$ stands for their interest rate difference, and the two add up together to the carry trade earning of *USD/CNH*, which is often called UIP, that is, uncovered interest rate premium. UIP is an important part of the return of exchange rate unhedged portfolios, and it has undertaken default risk of different countries, and so on.

As for China, some scholars consider equity finance balance (EFB) as a significant influencing factor in the equity market, because liquidity to a large extent dominates the short-term price trend. Therefore, we define the growth of EFB as:

$$EFB_t = \ln Margin_{t+1} - \ln Margin_t$$

$M\arg in_t$ stands for the equity finance balance at time t, $M\arg in_t + 1$ stands for the net grow rate of EFB from time t to $t + 1$. EFB would go up when EFB_t is positive, meaning that more money was invested into the equity market, and vice versa.

In conclusion, we choose 5 variables, namely, *Flow, Spread, Equity, UIP,* and *EFB*, which respectively represent the short-term cross-border capital flow of China, *USD/CNY* spread, equity market's excess return of China, uncovered interest rate parity of*USD/CNH*, and equity finance balance growth respectively. We believe these five variables could effectively measure the co-movement of China's equity flow and market. Considering that economic theory cannot give solid proof to the variables' co-movement and endogenous variables can appear at either sides of the equation, we will use the modified VAR model to analyze the variables afterwards.

Data Description

Data of short-term international net equity inflows originates from the EPFR data, from which we find the Equity Country Flow to China of the non-China residential funds. EPFR gets the daily net change of each fund and gets the net flow to certain countries according to a set proportion. Here we get the flow of non-China equity funds to China, which can be viewed as the net capital change of China's equity market from funds abroad.

EFB data is from Wind and USD Libor, CNY Shibor, CNH Hibor, USD/CNY, USD/CNH, and CSI300 data from Bloomberg. Samples are recorded daily from June 25, 2013, to January 28, 2016, excluding unmatched data, in a total of 612 observations.

In terms of units, the flow is in billion dollars while others are all in %.

Data Analysis

Table A.8 describes the mean, standard deviation, min, median, and max of the sample data. As mentioned before, flow represents short-term cross-border capital flow of China, spread is CNHCNY spread, equity is equity market's excess return of China, UIP is uncovered interest rate parity of USDCNH, and EFB is equity finance balance growth.

Table A.9 describes the Augmented Dickey-Fuller (ADF) test results, and *** stands for a 1% significance level. According to Table A.9, the variables all denied the original assumption under 0.01 significance level without unit root. Therefore, the variables can be viewed as stationary variables in the sample time window.

In order to study the interaction of the variables above, this part constructs the model based on the statistic property of the data and takes all endogenous variables as a function of their hysteresis value in the system. Thus, the single-variable VAR model is extended to a VAR model composed of multiple time series variables. VAR model is one of the easiest models to deal with the analysis and prediction of many related economic indicators. Here we further use the VAR-MGARCH-DCC extension of the VAR model in order to use the more realistic GARCH method to get

Table A.8 Descriptive statistics

Variable	*Mean*	*Std Error*	*Min*	*Median*	*Max*
Flow	−0.0489	0.2186	−1.2597	−0.0312	0.8193
Spread	0.00002	0.0016	−0.0122	0.0001	0.0091
Equity	0.0003	0.0197	−0.0918	0.0005	0.0667
UIP	0.000003	0.0022	−0.0274	0.0001	0.1524
EFB	0.0023	0.0128	−0.1104	0.0032	0.0438

Table A.9 ADF test results

	No trend	*With trend*
Flow	−5.4646***	−5.8266***
Spread	−13.8068***	−13.9169***
Equity	−10.3272***	−10.3620***
UIP	−13.2254***	−13.2737***
EFB	−6.2183***	−6.4308***

its volatility at a higher accuracy rate. In the specific data analysis, we choose the lagging order as 4 by the optimization test, and analyze the relationship between the variables before and after the point of the exchange rate reform of the PBOC as the cut-off point on August 11, 2015.

Figures A.1 and A.2 describe the relationship between the five variables before and after the "8.11 Reform", which indicates the impact of a unit exogenous shock after Cholesky decomposition and degree of freedom adjustment on each variable, and record the current influence instead of the cumulative impact amount.

Except for the fact that we can see autocorrelations between the above variables and their past values, it can be seen from Fig. A.1 that the increase (or decrease) in the price index of China's capital market can significantly influence the EFB growth rate before the "8.11 Reform", and therefore impact the short-term cross-border flow, but this effect cannot go backward from the cross-border capital flows to A-share prices or financing balance. This suggests that before the "8.11 Reform" cross-border capital flow did not have a significant impact on China's capital market and its

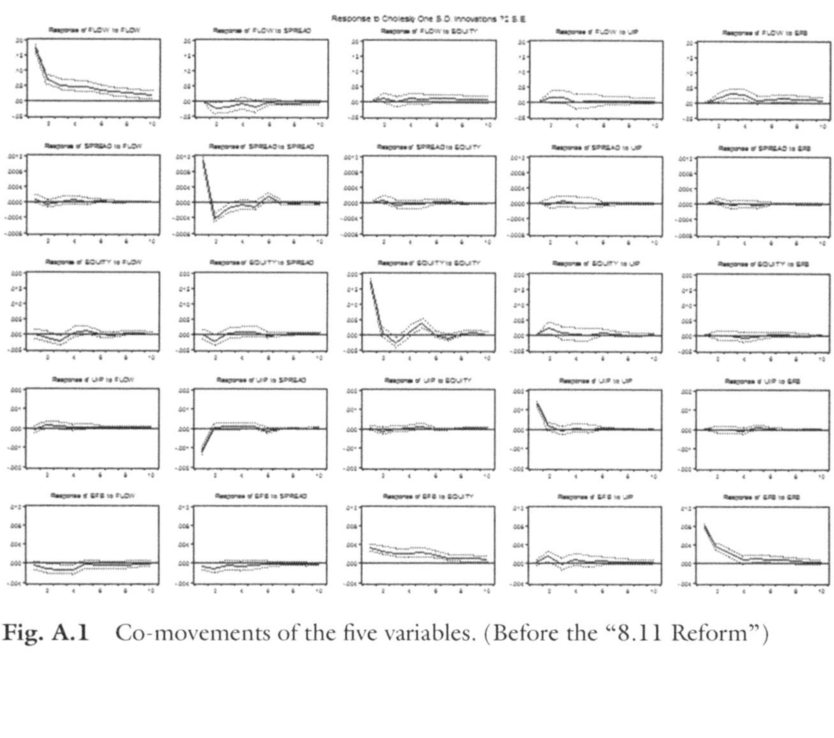

Fig. A.1 Co-movements of the five variables. (Before the "8.11 Reform")

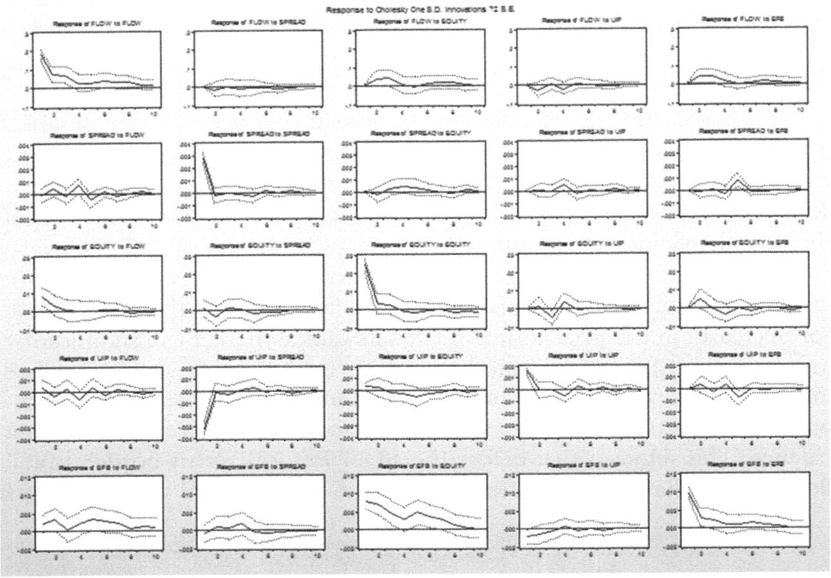

Fig. A.2 Co-movements of the five variables. (After the "8.11 Reform")

leverage growth; rather, it was affected itself by the rising stock price before driving the leverage ratio up. In this case, it also shows the significant characteristics for hot money to make the profit.

In addition, we can see from Fig. A.1 that the CNHCNY spread increase (or decrease) will significantly lower (or raise) the USD and offshore RMB spreads, leading to the decrease (or increase) of the Chinese capital market prices, leverage growth, and cross-border net capital inflows, which may be related to the widely expected convergence of the RMB exchange rate onshore and offshore.

It can be seen from Fig. A.2 that after the "8.11 exchange rate reform", the linkage between the five variables significantly changed. First of all, China's capital market price, leverage ratio, and cross-border net capital inflow's interaction has changed from the previous one-way relationship into a circular positive interactive relationship, and the impact of a variable would be strengthened by itself. This reflects the deeper impact of cross-border capital flows on China's economic growth after the "8.11 Reform", including the capital market prices and leverage levels.

Meanwhile, the USD and offshore RMB spread are still significantly and reversely driven by the exchange rate differentials of CNHCNY spread, but the USD and offshore RMB spread no longer have a significant impact on the other three factors after the reform.

Figures A.3 and A.4 depict the dynamic conditional correlation coefficients for the five-variable simulation under the VAR-MGARCH-DCC model. Comparing the two graphs, we can find two straightforward points: first, the coefficient of the five variables before the exchange rate reform was relatively stable, and after the reform all the ten coefficients started to show different degrees of volatility enhancement; Secondly, after the "8.11 exchange rate reform", the uncertainty between the variables showed a significant increase in the proportion of significant correlation. Before the reform there were only three correlation coefficients out of ten which are significantly not zero, and after the reform the number jumps to five. What's more, the correlation coefficients of two groups showed an increase in the absolute value after the reform. We believe that the above changes can reflect that after the "8.11 Reform", the five groups of variables' correlation increased, and so did the degree of uncertainty for their correlation.

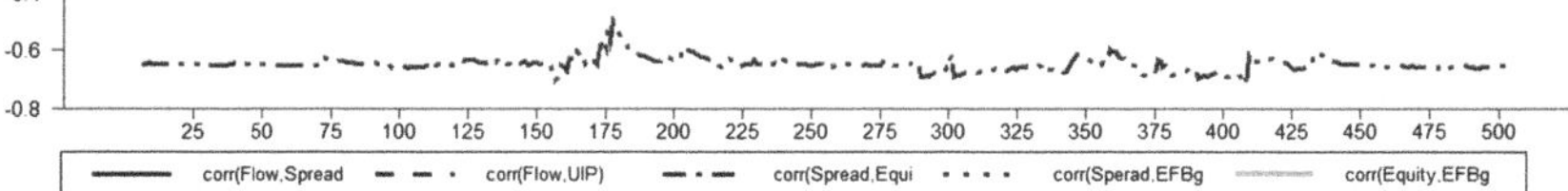

Fig. A.3 Co-movements of the five variables' volatility. (Before the "8.11 Reform")

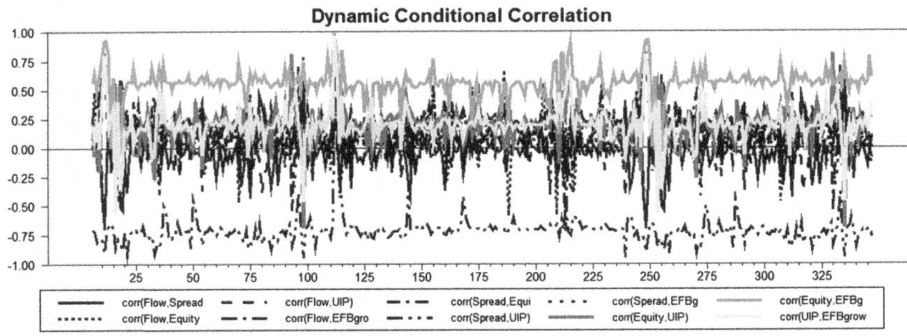

Fig. A.4 Co-movements of the five variables' volatility. (After the "8.11 Reform")

Appendix 4: Businesses Internationalization of the Chinese-Funded Banks

A Summary of Chinese Banks' Overseas M&A

Against the backdrop of rapid economic growth and increasingly fierce international competition, financial institutions in the banking sector in China have been improving their level of internationalization to address challenges and to achieve leapfrog development. In recent years, they have accomplished lots of achievements in terms of the international financial business varieties, the depth and breadth of international layout, and comprehensive cross-border services.

After China's entry into the World Trade Organization in 2001, Chinese banks have gradually started overseas expansion with the listing of major state-owned banks in 2005 through share reforms. According to the "Annual Social Responsibility of Banking in China 2014" of the China Banking Association, by the end of September 2015, Chinese-funded financial institutions opened more than 1200 overseas branches, covering 55 major countries and regions worldwide with a total asset of over \$1.5 trillion. Overseas branches of the five major state-owned banks account for more than 90% of the total. Bank of China has branches in 41 countries and regions, the Industrial and Commercial Bank of China 41, China Construction Bank 15, Agricultural Bank of China 11, and Bank of Communications 11. According to the data issued by the CBRC, by the end of June 2015, a total of 11 Chinese banks set up 55 primary branches

International Monetary Institute (ed.), *Currency Internationalization and Macro Financial Risk Control*,
https://doi.org/10.1007/978-981-13-0698-3

(31 subsidiaries, 15 branches, 8 representative office, and 1 joint-equity bank) in 23 regions and countries along the Belt and Road.

M&A have such advantages as avoiding the host country's regulatory restrictions, easy access to the local market, and complementing transnational cooperation. M&A have become a common choice for many Chinese banks to expand international businesses. After China implemented the reform and opening up policy, the earliest M&A could be dated back to 1984 when Bank of China purchased 50% equity of Banco Tai Fund. M&A thereafter can be roughly divided into four stages: the first stage (1994–2000) began as state-owned specialized banks transformed to state-owned commercial banks, marked by the establishment of policy banks, namely, National Development Bank, Agriculture Development Bank of China, and the Export-Import Bank of China; the second stage (2001–2004) began after China become a member of the World Trade Organization, which brought several challenges and competitions from international financial institutions; the third stage (2005–2008) was the listing of major state-owned commercial banks by share reforms, and the rapid development in joint-equity commercial banks; the fourth stage (from 2009 till now) was triggered by the subprime mortgage crisis which caused profound changes in global economy.

Additionally, according to statistics of 38 M&A by major overseas financial institutions (excluding outperformance after the merger) by Chinese banks from 1984 to 2015, M&A have been increasing rapidly in recent years in number, regional and target diversity, and centralization.

From the perspective of time series, there were only six cases of overseas M&A from 1984 to 2000, with an annual average of 0.375 cases; from 2001 to 2007, due to joining the WTO and the listing of state-owned commercial banks through equity reforms, the number of M&A reached 19, with an annual average of 2.71 (five in 2001 and seven in 2007); in 2008 the outbreak of the global financial crisis led to the decrease in the number of overseas M&A; however, the situation has stabilized since 2010 with an average of 1.6 annually.

From the perspective of regional distribution, the Asian region, including Hong Kong, Macao, and southeast Asia, has been a conventionally most-preferred market for M&A carried out by Chinese banks, accounting for more than 63% of the total; since 2007, however, Chinese banks have begun to involve in the developed regions such as Europe and America and emerging markets; especially since 2010, seven out of the ten cases of M&A cases took place in Western Europe and America, and one case in Taiwan.

Diversification of targets and entities is also noticeable. Although foreign commercial banks are the major targets of M&A for Chinese banks, gigantic banks like the Industrial and Commercial Bank of China and Bank of China have begun to focus on high-quality overseas financial institutions with non-bank business charters of securities, insurance, and financial derivatives trading and leasing so as to further enhance the ability of multinational integrated service management. Additionally, part of listed joint-equity banks with enormous assets also came to prominence in the overseas M&A (see Figs. A.5, A.6, A.7, and Table A.10).

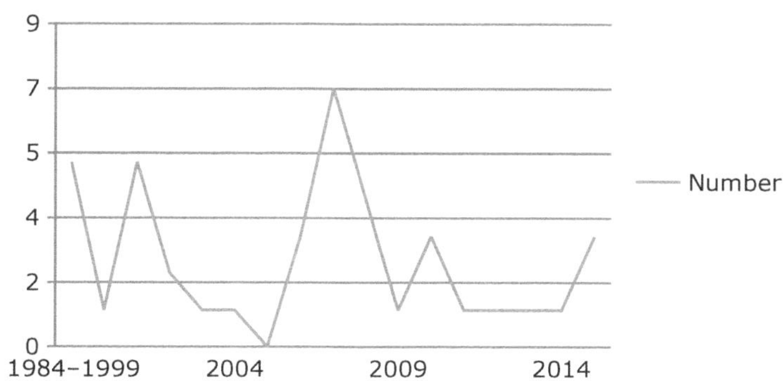

Fig. A.5 Major overseas M&A cases of Chinese-funded banks by number 1984–2015. (Resource: Public information)

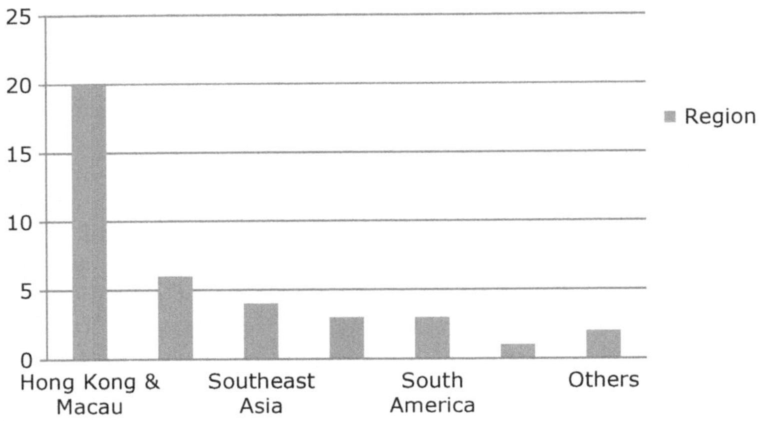

Fig. A.6 Major overseas M&A cases of Chinese-funded banks by region 1994–2015. (Resource: Public information)

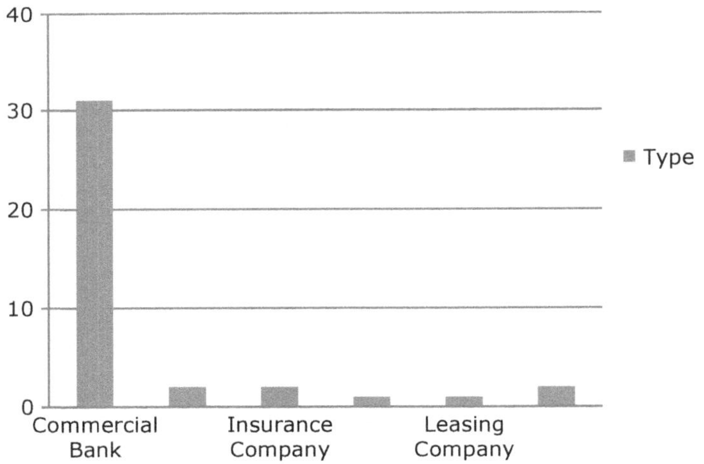

Fig. A.7 Major overseas M&A cases of Chinese-funded banks by type 1994–2015. (Resource: Public information)

Table A.10 Four stages of overseas M&A

Stages	*M&A time*	*Acquirer party*	*Acquired party*
Early stage of reform and opening up	1984.09	Bank of China	Banco tai fund
Transformation of specialized banks	1994.04	China Construction Bank	Natwest Securities Asia Ltd.
	1998.02	Industrial and Commercial Bank of China (ICBC)	Hong Kong Industrial and Commercial Bank
	1998.01	China Construction Bank	Jian Sing Bank
	1998.11	China CITIC Bank	Ka Wah Bank
	2000.04	Industrial and Commercial Bank of China (ICBC)	Union Bank of Hong Kong Ltd.
	2001.08	Bank of China	Central Indonesia Asia bank
	2001.09	Bank of China (Hong Kong) Limited	Nanyang Commercial Bank
	2001.01	Bank of China	Bao Shen Bank
After joining the WTO	2001.11	Bank of China (Hong Kong) Limited	Chiyu Banking Corporation Limited
	2001.11	CITIC Ka Wah Bank	Hongkong Chinese Bank
	2002.02	China Construction Bank	Jian Sing Bank
	2002.02	Industrial and Commercial Bank of China (ICBC)	China Pacific Insurance (Group) Co., Ltd.
	2003.12	ICBC (Asia)	Belgian Bank
	2004.12	ICBC (Asia)	China Merchant Bank (HK)
Listing of major commercial banks	2006.08	China Construction Bank	Bank of America (Asia)
	2006.12	Bank of China	BOC Aviation
	2006.12	Industrial and Commercial Bank of China (ICBC)	Indonesia Halim Bank
	2007.08	Industrial and Commercial Bank of China (ICBC)	Banco de Seng Heng
	2007.09	ICBC (Asia)	JEC Investment company
	2007.01	China Development Bank	Barclays
	2007.01	China Minsheng Bank	United Commercial Bank (Failed)
	2007.01	Industrial and Commercial Bank of China (ICBC)	South Africa Standard Bank Group
	2007.11	Bank of China (Hong Kong) Limited	Bank of East Asia

(*continued*)

Table A.10 (continued)

Stages	*M&A time*	*Acquirer party*	*Acquired party*
	2007.11	Ping An Bank	Fortis Group (Failed)
	2008.06	China Merchants Bank	Wing Lung Bank
	2008.08	Bank of China	HFM
	2008.09	Bank of China	LCF Rothschild Group
	2008.09	China CITIC Bank	CITIC International Financial Holdings Limited
	2009.05	China Construction Bank (Asia)	International Credit (Hong Kong)
	2010.01	Industrial and Commercial Bank of China (ICBC)	Bank of East Asia (Canada)
	2010.04	Industrial and Commercial Bank of China (ICBC)	ALC Bank of Thailand
	2010.01	Industrial and Commercial Bank of China (ICBC)	AXA-Minmetals Assurance Co., Ltd.
	2011.01	Industrial and Commercial Bank of China (ICBC)	Bank of East Asia (America)
	2012.11	Industrial and Commercial Bank of China (ICBC)	Standard Bank Group (Argentina)
	2013.04	Industrial and Commercial Bank of China (ICBC)	Bank SinoPac
	2014.08	Industrial and Commercial Bank of China (ICBC)	ICBC Brazil
	2015.02	Industrial and Commercial Bank of China (ICBC)	Standard Bank Group
	2015.07	Bank of Communications	Banco BBM
	2015.08	Industrial and Commercial Bank of China (ICBC)	Tekstil bank

From the perspective of the concentration of overseas M&A, according to data from 1994 to 2015, the Industrial and Commercial Bank of China has played a dominant role among the five major state-owned commercial banks, followed by the Bank of China and China Construction Bank. Bank of Communications accelerated its pace of internationalization in 2015, and launched its first overseas M&A of Banco BBM in May. Agricultural Bank of China still has not yet initiated its own overseas M&A project. Among joint-equity banks, China CITIC Bank took the leading role, China Merchants Bank made several attempts, and the M&A attempt made by China Minsheng Bank to United Commercial Bank and PingAn Bank to Fortis Group failed (see Fig. A.8).

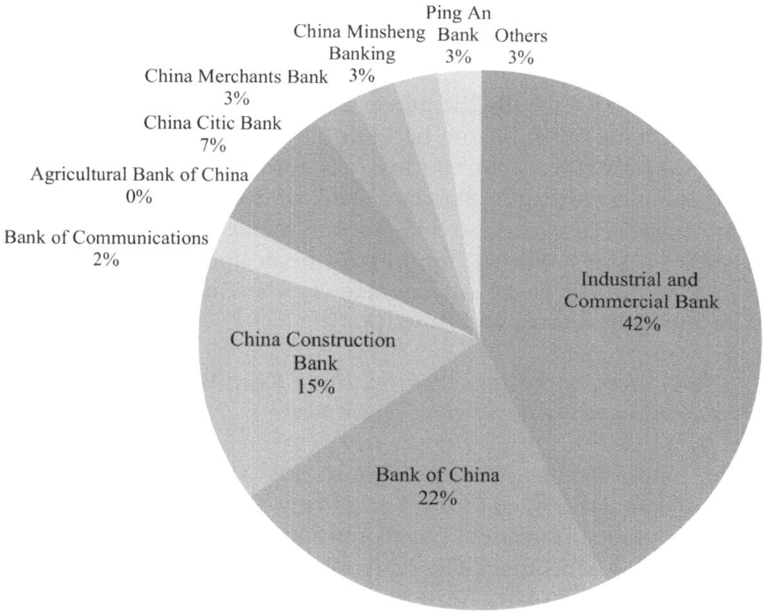

Fig. A.8 Major overseas M&A cases of Chinese-funded banks by bank 1994–2015

Cases of Overseas M&A Made by the Chinese Banks

1. *M&A of Bank of America (Asia) by China Construction Bank—attempt based on Hong Kong Business*

In August of 2006, China Construction Bank launched an overall acquisition of Bank of America (Asia) Co., Ltd. with 9.71 billion HK dollars. Business scale of Construction Bank in Hong Kong doubled, and customer loans rose to the ninth in Hong Kong. Bank of America (Asia), with its Hong Kong banking charter, is a medium-sized retail bank for individual customers and SMEs. It has rich experience in management, excellent financial statement, and strong profitability. Acquisition by Construction Bank was primarily for integrating its HK retail business, learning from advanced management experience, and seeking further international opportunities based in Hong Kong.

2. *Industrial and Commercial Bank of China shareholding of Standard Bank of South Africa—China to Africa*

In October 2007, ICBC acquired 20% equity of Standard Bank of South Africa with $5.46 billion, becoming the biggest shareholder of the bank, and making the case by far the largest transnational M&A project of Chinese commercial banks. Standard Bank of South Africa is the largest bank in Africa and is experienced in precious metals and mineral resources investment in Africa. This acquisition can be deemed as ice-breaking for China's access to the South African market, where is dominant by developed countries in Europe and America.

3. *China Merchants Bank Acquired Hong Kong Wing Lung Bank—the internationalization of joint-equity banks*

From June 2008 to January 2009, China Merchants Bank accomplished total acquisition of Hong Kong Wing Lung Bank, and the latter became one of its subsidiaries. The acquisition was arduous due to the exit and return of Merchants Bank in bidding and the competition from ICBC. Wing Lung Bank is one of the oldest Chinese-funded family banks in Hong Kong, the acquisition of which helped China Merchants Bank rapidly increase its influence in Hong Kong and create the operating synergies. It laid a good foundation for the follow-up internationalization strategy.

4. *Failed acquisition of United bank by Minsheng Bank—reflecting the risk of overseas M&A.*

United Commercial Bank mainly provides financial services for Chinese community and is one of the three major Chinese banks in the United States. Inspired by China Merchants Bank's acquisition of Wing Lung Bank, Minsheng Bank hoped to be the pioneer acquirer among Chinese banks to enter the US market. In September 2007, Minsheng decided to launch a step-by-step acquisition of United Commercial Bank, and raise its stake to 20% through subsequent capital injection. However, in September 2009, executives of United Commercial Bank were suspected of intentional concealment of financial situation, and were accused of fraud. In November, the bank declared bankruptcy. The application of rescue capital injection from Minsheng Bank after the scandal was rejected for political reasons. Minsheng Bank announced later the failure in acquisition and confirmed the investment and impairment losses amounted to 824 million RMB. The failure revealed the information asymmetry, strategic immaturity, and unfamiliarity with local legal regulatory environment in overseas bank M&A.

5. *The Industrial and Commercial Bank of China's acquisition of Standard Bank of Argentina—entering Latin American and emerging market countries*

In November 2012, ICBC's acquisition of 80% equity of Standard Bank of Argentina with no more than $650 million in cash was approved by Argentina's central bank, making the Standard Bank of Argentina a subsidiary of ICBC thereafter. This is the first shareholding acquisition of a Latin American financial institution and a globally mainstream commercial bank by a Chinese bank. The subsidiary has become the largest Chinese-funded bank in Latin America, and the acquisition has made ICBC more competitive.

6. *The Industrial and Commercial Bank of China took a stack in Taiwan Sinopac Bank—the cross-strait financial cooperation broke the ice*

In April 2013, ICBC signed the contract to acquire 20% of equity of Taiwan Sinopacco, Ltd., which broke the ice of cross-strait financial cooperation, and made ICBC the first mainland bank to invest in Taiwan's financial industry by shareholding. The acquisition played a positive role in investment in Taiwan's financial circle and in promoting the internationalization of RMB.

Appendix 5: International Experience on Financial Regulation Reforms in the Post-Crisis Era

The United States

In July 2010, the United States enacted the Dodd-Frank Wall Street Reform and Consumer Protections Act to promote all-round financial regulatory reforms.

First, the Financial Stability Oversight Council (FSOC) was established to identify and prevent systemic risks. The Council provides comprehensive monitoring of systemic risks; identifies and regulates systemically important institutions, instruments, and markets; and also facilitates dispute settlement among the member agencies, information sharing as well as regulatory coordination.

Second, the Federal Reserve is designated as the regulator of systemically important financial institutions.

The scope of regulation and supervision is expanded. The Fed is responsible for supervising banking agencies with assets over $50 billion, all non-bank financial institutions (see Appendix 7) that are important to the financial system such as securities and insurance companies, and systemically important payments, clearing, and settlement activities as well as market infrastructures; meanwhile, the Fed retains the authority to regulate small banks. The Fed also has the backup examination authority for those non-bank financial institutions to determine whether they are threatening financial stability, and whether they need to be regulated.

International Monetary Institute (ed.), *Currency Internationalization and Macro Financial Risk Control*,
https://doi.org/10.1007/978-981-13-0698-3

Stricter standards of prudential regulation are set. Targeting at systemically important institutions, the Fed leads the formulation of stricter regulatory standards of capital, leverage ratio, liquidity, risk management, and so on.

High-risk banking business operations are strictly controlled. Banks are constrained from doing high-risk proprietary trading of securities, derivatives, and commodity futures, and a commercial bank's investment in hedge funds and private equity funds is restricted to 3% of its primary capital.

Supervision on financial holding companies is strengthened. The Fed has the authority to directly examine a financial holding company and any of its subsidiaries (including non-depository subsidiaries), thereby having direct access to detailed information about this company and its counterparts.

Third, putting in place a universal risk disposal and clearing settlement mechanism, and securing the orderly exit of unhealthy institutions. It makes clear that the Federal Reserve and the Federal Deposit Insurance Corporation are jointly responsible for treating systemic risks in the United States.

Fourth, regulation and supervision are extended, and loopholes are filled. Investments advisors of hedge funds and private equity funds are required to register with the Securities and Exchange Commission (SEC), and to provide information about transactions and portfolios of the funds. Companies with over $150 million in assets must be supervised and examined regularly by the SEC. If hedge funds and private equity funds are considered too large or too risky, they will be regulated by the Fed.

The SEC retains its authority to supervise credit rating companies, and conflicts of interest between credit rating companies and issuers as well as underwriters are reduced. The issuers that have been poorly rated for a long time may be de-listed. Investors are allowed to charge credit rating companies with misconduct.

Established under the US Department of the Treasury, the Federal Insurance Office is vested with the duty to submit the list of systemically important insurance companies to the FSOC. Besides, the Office of the Thrift Supervision ceased to exist, and most of its functions have been merged into the Office of the Comptroller of Currency.

Fifth, consumer financial protection agencies are established to reinforce financial shelter for consumers. As a relatively independent bureau in the Federal Reserve System, the Consumer Financial Protection Bureau assumes responsibilities and authorities that previously spread out among seven other federal financial regulators to protect consumers' rights and interests.

EU

In 2010, EU passed the Pan-European Financial Regulatory Reform Bill, a comprehensive reform of the regulatory system. First, the Bill proposed to establish the European Systemic Risk Board (ESRB) to strengthen macro-prudential management. The Board had several responsibilities: to carry out macro-prudential management, data collection and analysis; to identify and assess systemic risks; to provide warnings and recommendations to the European Banking Authority, the European Securities and Market Authority, European Insurance Occupational Pensions Authority and regulatory authorities of member states; and to set up a special inspection team to track and assess their adoption of recommendations. The Board required member states to determine by law the institutions accountable for macro-prudential management. It also required the central bank to play a leading role in macro-prudential policies. In addition, the Board offered member states guidance and suggestions on macro-prudential management, and released each member state's experience in order to promote policy communication and coordination. Second, the Bill extended the ECB's responsibility from maintaining currency stability to financial stability. The international financial crisis and the European debt crisis caused difficulties in interbank financing, strained market liquidity, and a sharp rise in bond yields in certain countries. In order to alleviate the impact of the crisis and safeguard financial stability, the ECB began to implement a series of unconventional relief measures in addition to conventional monetary policies such as reducing the benchmark interest rate. The ECB played an irreplaceable role in fully leveraging the functions of lender of last resort, injecting liquidity into the financial market, improving the financing conditions and liquidity situation in the Eurozone, restoring market confidence, and ensuring the financial infrastructure, such as the payment and clearing system, was fully functional. Third, the Bill proposed to establish a Single Supervisory Mechanism (SSM) and endow the ECB with financial regulatory functions. Therefore, the ECB could directly supervise credit institutions, branches of financial holding companies, and mixed financial holding companies of systematic importance in SSM member states, as well as branches of credit institutions set in non-SSM member states. Meanwhile, regulatory authorities in member states, under the guidance of the ECB, supervised small and medium banks of no systemic importance, and continued to play the role in consumer protection, anti-money laundering, and payment services. The ECB, when necessary, could take over any bank and implement early intervention. All banks in the Eurozone were covered by the single regulatory mechanism, and regulatory authorities of EU member states in the non-Eurozone could also voluntarily choose to join the mechanism. Fourth, the Bill proposed to build the European Banking Union, and to unify the banking supervision, deposit insurance, and disposal mechanisms. The Union consists of three regulatory pillars: a Single Regulatory Mechanism, a Single Resolution Mechanism, and a Unified Deposit Insurance Mechanism. Fifth, the Bill proposed to strengthen coordination and cooperation between EU regulators. Three micro-prudential regulatory institutions—namely, the European Systemic Risk Board and Banking Authority, the Securities and Market Authority, and Insurance and Occupational Pensions Authority—established a mechanism for exchanging and sharing information. Through the Joint Committee, the three institutions strengthened interindustrial and interdepartmental coordination and cooperation. In 2008, regulatory authorities, the central banks, and Ministry of Finance of each EU member state jointly signed a memorandum of crisis management. The memorandum emphasized the cooperation in financial regulation among all the member states, and set up the Cross-Border Stability Group and a cross-border cooperation mechanism. It also emphasized that public allocation of resources should be based on the principle of equality and balance, and that the quota for public resource expenditures should be determined by the impact of the crisis on national economies and the distribution of regulatory powers between home and host countries.

The United Kingdom

Since the crisis, the United Kingdom has adjusted the framework of financial regulation twice. On April 1, 2013, the new *Financial Service Law* took effect, new financial management system began to officially operate, and the Bank of England became the core member responsible for the currency policy, prudent macro-regulation, and prudent micro-regulation. Internally, Financial Policy Committee (FPC) was established to be responsible for prudent macro-regulation; and under FPC,

Prudent Regulation Administration (PRA) was established to replace the original Financial Service Authority (FSA) and be responsible for prudent micro-regulation with Financial Conduct Authority (FCA). In July, 2015, the United Kingdom published *The Proposal of the Bank of England: Technical Consultation Draft* (abbreviated as "Proposal"), planning to further the financial supervision reform and adjust the financial supervision architecture.

First, establishing Prudent Regulation Committee (PRC) to strengthen the prudent regulating function of the Central Bank. The Proposal intends to fully integrate the PRA, a former affiliated organization of the Bank of England, into the internal structure of the Bank, and meanwhile set up the new PRC. The name, legal objective, and way of regulation of PRA remain unchanged, and the Bank of England continues to use the regulation charge of the PRA as its source of fund in order to perform its prudent regulating function while PRC is responsible for establishing the charging standards. Besides, the Proposal proposes to upgrade the FPC from a branch committee under the Board of Directors to a committee directly under the Bank of England, parallel to the Currency Policy Committee and PRC. Therefore, a framework of Policy Currency Committee directly subordinate to the Bank of England, PRC, and FPC is formed, with three branches respectively responsible for the currency policy, prudent macro-regulation, and prudent micro-regulation.

Second, improving the regulation structure and efficiency by streamlining the Board of the Bank of England. The Proposal suggests bringing down the number of non-executive directors from nine to seven, and correspondingly, changing the number of the Board members to 12; abolishing the Legal Supervision Committee, a subordinate Committee of the Board of Directors under the Bank of England, and including it in the Board of Directors, which directly regulates the operation of the Bank of England. The Proposal will also reform the current system of Vice President appointing and removing, and adjust the position of the Vice President through secondary-level legislation, so the Bank of England will be able to resize the scale and constitution of its senior executives in light of requirements.

Third, strengthening information sharing and perfecting the financial crisis disposal. The Proposal intends to further improve the crisis management and disposal mechanism in the perspective of strategies, policies, and crash projects.

Fourth, increasing the transparency and clarifying responsibilities and obligations. The meeting minutes and inflation reports will be decided and discussed through publicizing the currency policies and decisions of the Bank of England, and the confidential duration of the decision-making meeting records will be extended to eight years. The Proposal intends to include the Bank of England in the review range of the National Audit Office for the first time, but policy-making function of the Bank will be excluded from review, so as to ensure the independence of its decision-making.

Germany

After the financial crisis, Germany has reformed its financial regulatory system based on its own financial development and other countries' experience. First, the country has strengthened Bundesbank's financial regulatory rights, especially its part in stabilizing the finance. Bundesbank continues to play a significant role in financial regulation. It takes advantages of its numerous branches to regularly supervise financial institutions, monitor and evaluate their risks, and do auditing. Representatives are dispatched to the management commission of BaFin to supervise its management, decide its budget, and offer suggestions for special regulatory missions. Bundesbank cooperates with BaFin to carry out stress testing, on-site examination, and other major regulations. It establishes a forum on financial market regulation and sets up mechanisms for high-level officials to consult regularly, discuss on relevant policies, and formulate measures. Meanwhile, BaFin will consult with Bundesbank before issuing regulatory laws and regulations and must be consistent with it in fields closely related to monetary policies. In addition, the German Banking Act stipulates that Bundesbank has an exclusive access to financial statistics and information. BaFin alone is not entitled to access statistics of any forms from financial institutions.

Second, macro-prudential management has been enhanced. In 2013, Germany adopted Financial Stability Act and charged FSC with the responsibility of macro-prudential management. FSC members come from the Ministry of Finance, Bundesbank, BaFin, and FMSA and its working mechanism is similar to that of the ESRB. Bundesbank is critical in the macro-prudential management and in defining financial stability risks, evaluating performance of macro prudential policies, and submitting discussion reports and initial policy suggestions to the FSC meetings. It also possesses the power to veto FSC's issuance of warnings and decisions. Third, a more efficient financial institution disposal mechanism has been established. FMSA is set up to manage stabilization fund, provide liquidity for markets, and supervise new non-performing assets of management companies. It is planned to be upgraded to a regulatory institution, responsible for reorganizing financial institutions. The 500 billion euro bailout plan and SoFFin will assist institutions which have suffered from the financial crisis. Two asset management companies, FMS-WM and EAA, are set up to strip bad assets off, relieve the pressure on balance sheet from banks, and ensure that banks continue to offer credit for the real economy.

France

After the financial crisis, France adopted the Economic Modernization Act and Banking and Financial Regulatory Act, respectively, in 2008 and 2010. The country again reformed its financial regulatory system, where the Central Bank is at the core and ACP and AMF go hand in hand. First, the Central Bank is critical in financial regulation. Despite assigning a deputy governor to assume the presidency of ACP, the Central Bank offers other supports concerning resources, staffs, information, financial, and economic analysis. It is also responsible for signing legal documents on behalf of ACP. In addition, it takes advantages of its numerous branches to help ACP and AMF supervise their efforts in consumer protections. Second, financial supervision and systematic risk commission is established to supervise and identify systematic risks and predict their development trends. It also coordinates the country's regulatory actions in Europe and the world, so as to promote cooperation and information exchanges among different domestic departments.

Third, the country merges the regulatory institutions of the banking industry and the insurance industry. It sets up ACP to supervise the two industries, to stabilize the financial market, and to safeguard consumers' rights and interests. ACP can make on-site and off-site inspections of supervised institutions and punish illegal ones through a sanctions committee. Fourth, AMF better assumes its responsibilities to protect investors' interests and ensure financial product safety. It supervises financial markets in terms of safe operations, information issuance, fair transactions, and positive competition. Despite these regulations on security markets, AMF also supervises credit rating agencies, and cooperates and exchanges information with regulators in other member states in EU.

Russia

In July 2013, Russia adopted the Revised Russian Federation Act on Shifting the Right of Supervising and Managing Financial Markets to CBR (251-FZ). The multi-pronged financial regulation system has also been reformed. First, financial regulatory rights are all transferred to CBR. FFMS has been withdrawn (FSIS was merged into FFMS in 2011) and its rights of supervising capital markets and insurance industry have been shifted to CBR. CBR supervises banks and non-bank financial institutions, including securities companies, insurance companies, small financial organizations, exchanges, and pension funds as a whole. It has to submit reports on the stability and developments of financial markets' key areas to Duma. As CBR possesses more power, the previous "Banking Regulatory Commission" is renamed "National Financial Commission". CBR's governor assumes its presidency and its members are selected from officials of CBR's other departments. They evaluate systematic risks, supervise financial affairs of systemically important financial infrastructures and major non-financial institutions, and consider financial stability reports. Meanwhile, the tenure of CBR's governor and director is extended from four to five years and the number of its board of directors is expanded from 13 to 15. In addition, to better supervise all kinds of non-bank financial institutions, the country establishes relevant self-regulatory organizations and unifies the standards on risk management, company governance, internal control, and protection of financial consumers' interests.

Second, the country unifies the planning of financial policies and the supervision over its enforcement. CBR takes over some rights to formulate supervisory standards for financial markets from government departments including the Ministry of Finance, and participates in drafting relevant laws and regulations. It is also responsible for approving accounting standards for credit institutions and non-credit institutions, managing securities issuance and registration, supervising enforcement of securities laws and regulations, and combating insider trading, market manipulation, and money laundering. Non-credit financial institutions include professional securities players like brokers and underwriters (banks can also carry out securities business), investment funds management companies, mutual funds, private pension funds and related depository agents, insurance and actuarial agencies, micro-credit companies, credit consumer cooperatives, housing and savings cooperatives, agricultural credit consumer cooperatives, and credit rating agencies. CBR will also supervise joint stock companies and regulate their affiliated business operations.

South Korea

In 2009, South Korea resumed the revision of the Bank of Korea Act to strengthen the power of Central Bank. The new version of the Bank of Korea Act was officially issued in September 2011, which further strengthens its power to stabilize the finance through the increased supervision rights and macro-prudential tools. First, the Act gives Bank of Korea the power to stabilize the finance. Despite "stabilizing the commodity prices", Bank of Korea has the power to "stabilize the finance". Second, the Act enlarges Bank of Korea's supervisory power. Bank of Korea can get information from not only national commercial banks, but all other financial institutions included in the Act of Financial Industry Structural Optimization. It also improves the efficiency of its joint inspection with Financial Supervisory Service through setting time limits, and strengthens the on-site inspection right. Third, the Act improves emergent liquidity support tools and broadens the access to support. For financial institutions which face tight liquidity due to imbalanced financing and capital usage, Bank of Korea will offer them emergent liquidity support whether they possess eligible collateral or not. Securities lending is included in open-market operations to provide short-term financing for Bank of Korea settlement system when it faces shortage of settlement fund. Fourth, the Act enlarges Monetary Policy Committee's discretion over legal reserves. The Committee has the power to decide the forms of legal reserves; required reserve ratio is now decided by both the liability type and scale rather than liability type alone (Resource: Yongxiang, Bu, 2016.)

Appendix 6: International Practices on Financial Transaction Taxes

Introduction

Tax is a source of government revenue, as well as an important means to of achieving financial stability and restraining investment behavior. It is one of the most important tools in macro-prudential policy. Taxes on financial transactions are usually imposed on the sale of securities, which means that buyers, sellers, or both parties need to pay normally ad valorem tax, that is, a certain percentage of the market value of the securities traded. There are many types of financial transaction taxes (FTTs): securities transaction taxes (STTs), which apply to the issuance and/or trading of financial securities and possibly stocks, bonds, and related derivatives; currency transaction tax, also known as the Tobin tax, imposed on transactions involving foreign exchange and its associated derivatives; bank transaction tax or bank debit tax, commonly seen in Latin America and Asia, which apply to deposits and withdrawals from bank accounts as well as check accounts normally. In addition, some countries tax on insurance, real estate transactions, or increased operating capital.

Taxes on financial transactions have a long history. The British stamp duty was enacted in 1694 and remains in effect today. The United States imposed a non-trivial stock transactions tax from 1914 to 1965, as did New York State from 1905 to 1981. An extremely small securities transfer tax currently funds the Securities and Exchange Commission (SEC). FTTs

International Monetary Institute (ed.), *Currency Internationalization and Macro Financial Risk Control*,
https://doi.org/10.1007/978-981-13-0698-3

have long been popular in less developed countries as a way to raise significant revenue from a small number of relatively sophisticated financial entities.

The FTT is experiencing a resurgence in the developed world. Eleven members in European Union have agreed to enact a coordinated FTT, which is scheduled to go into effect in January 2016. France adopted an FTT in 2012 that will be integrated with the EU tax if and when it takes effect. In the United States, several recent congressional proposals for FTTs have been introduced by Representatives and Senators, including Democratic presidential primary candidate Bernie Sanders.

Proponents advocate the FTT on several grounds. The tax could raise substantial revenue at low rates because the base—the value of financial transactions—is enormous. An FTT would curb speculative short-term and high-frequency trading, which in turn would reduce the diversion of valuable human capital into pure rent-seeking activities of little or no social value. They argue that an FTT would reduce asset price volatility and bubbles, which hurt the economy by creating unnecessary risk and distorting investment decisions. It would encourage patient capital and longer-term investment. The tax could help recoup the costs of the financial sector bailout as well as the costs the financial crisis imposed on the rest of the country. The FTT—called the "Robin Hood Tax" by some advocates—would primarily fall on the rich, and the revenues could be used to benefit the poor, finance future financial bailouts, cut other taxes, or reduce public debt.

Practices in Several Countries

At present, there are two main views on the feasibility of fully implementing FTT: one is from the firm proponents such as Germany, France, and other countries who believe that FTT has such advantages as suppressing short-term speculation by increasing speculative cost, and reducing moral hazard; that is, the profits of the financial sector and remuneration of managers have increased tremendously, but when crisis happens, taxpayers shoulder the relief costs. These countries also believe that the international community should be aware of the urgency of stabilizing the financial markets and thus strengthening cooperation. Taxes on financial transactions will increase the effectiveness of financial regulation so that countries can avoid investing heavily in economic activities. The other is from the opponents such as the United States and Canada, who believe that the introduction of FTT is not a realistic choice and will inhibit the development of financial markets. In addition, its tax system is complex and difficult to define, which could cause tax evasion while increasing the burden of retail investors.

1. **Brazil: Financial Transaction Tax**

Brazil announced the introduction of FTT in 2009, the first among the BRICS countries. The Brazilian government implemented the Tobin tax twice in the 1990s and this century to regulate cross-border capital flows, thus reducing domestic inflation. The practice of FTTs in Brazil can be divided into two stages: the first stage is from 1993 to 1999. In the early 1990s, inflation continued to rise in Brazil; meanwhile, differentiated interest rates implemented to meet the Brazilian government's financing demand continued to attract foreign capital into Brazil, largely fueling the inflation. In December 1993, Brazil began to impose FTT and adjusted the tax rate over time according to the flow of international capital. In addition, other measures were used to control capital inflow, such as capital inflow tax. The Brazilian government began to gradually cut the FTT rate since the 1998 Asian financial crisis when it experienced a large number of capital outflow. At the end, Brazilian government had to cancel the tax. The second stage is from 2009 till now. Due to the international financial crisis in 2008 and the subsequent quantitative easing policy of the United States, the Brazilian financial market once again was confronted with the impact of capital inflows. In 2009, the government announced another introduction of FTT, expanded the taxation scope, and adjusted the tax rates in the following three years. Overall, Brazil's FTTs have played a positive role as they have increased the costs of speculative capital, effectively maintained the stability of the financial markets, and mitigated the impact of capital flows.

2. **Sweden: Financial Transaction Tax**

Sweden introduced securities transaction tax to its financial market in the 1980s and 1990s. Beginning in early 1984, Sweden levied a tax of 1% on financial transactions. Two years later, it was raised to 2%. Although the FTT has brought tax revenue for Sweden, tax avoidance became more serious due to severe tax burdens. At the same time, as long as the transaction parties do not use the brokers registered in Sweden, they do not need to pay taxes. This design flaw enables a large number of traders to avoid tax. From 1984 to 1991, Sweden's domestic securities trading volume declined continuously as a large number of transactions were moved to the London market. In addition, the narrow tax base led to the emergence of many derivatives in order to avoid tax, and this was ultimately reflected in the reduction of tax revenue. Since then, Sweden has tried to halve the tax rate on financial transactions, but the effect was still unsatisfactory. Under heavy pressure the Swedish government had to cancel the FTT. The problems arising in the process of collecting FTT in Sweden reveal that the system design of FTT plays a crucial role in the effectiveness of this tax policy.

A good system design should be able to maintain market liquidity while inhibiting excessive speculation. FTT burden in Sweden was so heavy that it led to increased transaction costs and reduced market liquidity, which did harm to the development of its financial industry. Some experts and scholars who oppose the introduction of FTT often cited the failure of the Sweden as an example of its risks.

3. **Chile: Interest-Free Deposit Reserve in the Quasi-Tobin Tax Nature**

Since the 1970s, Chile has attempted to carry out economic liberalization, for which the authorities have taken a series of measures to maintain a competitive exchange rate on real term. For instance, in 1984, Chile adopted "crawling pegged exchange rates" to keep domestic interest rates higher than the international market, thus gradually reducing inflation. The results were significant in the early 1980s, but when Chile gradually entered the international market, a large number of international capital flowed into the Chilean market; coupled with the poor regulatory capacity of the government, the overheated investment and surging consumption caused inflation and brought great pressure on the domestic interest rates and exchange rates. In order to alleviate the economic and financial strains, curb speculative financial transactions, and optimize the investment structure, the Chilean government adopted a series of policy initiatives in 1991 to prevent capital inflows. One of the most important measures was the interest-free reserve system, requiring that foreign investors pay the Chilean Central Bank local or foreign currency deposits at a certain proportion of the investment amount, and the deposits are interest-free. This is an indirect taxation of capital flows due to which costs of capital inflow were increased. Chile initially demanded a 20% interest-free reserve for short-term foreign borrowings, and later adjusted the deposit ratio along with the exchange rate changes. In 1998, due to the Asian financial crisis, Chile gradually reduced the proportion of deposit reserve until it was canceled. In addition to non-interest reserves, the Chilean government has also implemented measures such as gradually relaxing foreign exchange controls, harmonizing foreign exchange markets, implementing a single exchange rate system, and allowing capital outflows. Chile's domestic situation indicates that the interest-free reserve system has a positive effect in curbing capital inflows and stabilizing the domestic financial markets, but in the long run, the actual effects of this policy need to be reconsidered. For example, the impact on short-term capital inflow was significant, but the total amount of capital inflows has not changed much because of this system. In addition, the influence on long-term real exchange rate and real interest rate of the deposit reserve system is also limited.

4. **Malaysia: Capital Outflow Tax**

The Malaysian government abandoned control of capital inflows in the early 1990s, which was intended to promote economic growth. The financial crisis in Asia that occurred in 1998 greatly impacted Malaysia's financial market and exchange rate market, followed by the currency devaluation and a large amount of capital outflow. Since then, the Malaysian government has imposed strict foreign exchange controls and implemented Tobin tax in 1999 in order to encourage normal investment and long-term investment and to curb short-term speculative investment. Due to the Tobin tax, the exchange rates were 10% higher than previous level, consumption started to rise, and soon the Malaysian exchange rate market and financial market returned to stability. It can be said that the Malaysian government implemented the Tobin tax very timely, thus not only buying more time for government policy adjustments, but also enhancing the confidence of the market and the investors. After the Asian financial crisis, the recovery of the Malaysian economy was significantly better than that in Thailand and Indonesia, which were also hit by the crisis.

5. **EU: Financial Transaction Tax**

After the financial crisis in 2008, some EU member states such as Germany and France and other countries have repeatedly proposed to establish within the EU a unified FTT. After the financial crisis, FTT, especially STT, has caught global attention. France, Germany, and other countries in G20 actively supported the practice of FTT; the European Parliament requires the European Commission to develop an FTT collection plan; a large number of NGOs also actively advocated for a comprehensive collection of FTTs on securities trading and foreign exchange trading. In September 2011, the EU formally released an FTT proposal and suggested it be implemented since January 2014. The proposal includes a uniform minimum tax rate of 0.1% for transaction of all types of financial products (0.01% for financial derivatives trading). The purpose of the proposal was to ensure the financial sector makes more equitable contribution to tax revenues while curbing those financial transactions that are not conducive to the efficiency of financial markets. The European Commission said that the FTTs may bring €57 billion in revenue, part of which would be used to increase the EU budget. Whether the introduction of the FTTs would help ease the current debt crisis and mitigate the impact of the financial crisis on the global economic growth, there were lots of skepticism. France and Germany are strongly supportive of this, but some EU member states are still opposed to it. There is still a lot of uncertainty whether the FTTs can be uniformly implemented in the EU.

In 2012, France introduced a 0.20% tax on stock purchases of French publicly traded companies with a market value over €1 billion, a tax of 0.01% on high-frequency trading, and a tax of 0.01% of the nominal value on some sovereign credit default swaps. The equity transfer tax was seen as a way to raise revenue, and the high-frequency trading and credit default swap taxes were seen as ways to reduce rent seeking and speculation. The French government was sensitive to the possibility of transaction flight to other EU states. As a result, the French FTT exempts market makers and excludes corporate bonds, sovereign bonds, and derivatives. Despite these efforts, evidence suggests that the FTT reduced trading volume significantly, as discussed below.

On October 23, 2012, the European Commission officially expressed support for ten euro countries including France, Germany, Austria, Belgium, and others in collecting FTT through the "enhanced cooperation" mechanism. European Commission data show that if the FTT is levied within the EU in 2014, the revenue will increase by €57 billion annually.

On January 22, 2013, the EU Finance Ministers authorized 11 EU member states to prepare collecting FTT by "strengthening cooperation" in Belgium, Germany, Estonia, Greece, Spain, France, Italy, Austria, Portugal, Slovenia, and Slovakia. On February 14, 2013, the European

Commission formally introduced the FTT, which means that the sales of all financial instruments in the 11 countries are taxed. It is projected to increase € 30 billion to 35 billion in revenue each year. This is a major milestone in the FTT reform since the recent financial crisis.

In May 2014, several EU countries led by France and Germany pledged to start taxing transactions of stocks and some derivatives by 2016. But there are other countries that strongly oppose this practice, expressing concerns about the economic impact and legal foundation of the FTT. A number of supporting countries have submitted their latest political agreements to the EU Finance Ministers Meeting, in which they argued that the FTTs should be implemented in a step-by-step manner. The agreement said that stocks and some derivatives would begin to be taxed before January 2016, but the types of derivatives involved are not yet identified. It also said the parties would agree on a final proposal for the FTT by the end of the year. In addition, countries such as Italy that already have FTTs may continue the practice.

6. The United Kingdom: Financial Transaction Tax

The UK has a long history with FTTs that is mostly positive. The British stamp tax, first enacted in 1694, is one of the earliest instances of financial transaction taxation. The tax is paid on stock transfers, which are made legally enforceable only with an official stamp. The tax is currently 0.50% and applies to securities issued by UK companies, regardless of whether the parties to the transaction reside in the UK. Original issuance is exempt, as are intermediaries such as "market makers". In addition, the UK does not attempt to tax derivatives, which provides incentives for derivatives trading to replace other securities transactions.

As a result, derivatives trading in the United Kingdom has seen a huge rise, which in recent years accounted for about 40% of the trading of UK securities. The tax raises a modest amount of revenue: about £3 billion per year, or 0.6% of total revenues. Administrative costs are very low—less than 0.05% of revenue—according to the UK Revenue Service.

7. The United States: Financial Transaction Tax

From 1914 to 1966, a federal FTT was levied on sales and transfers of stock. The rate was originally 0.02% of the stock's par value (the value stated in the charter, which is usually lower than current market value). In 1932, the tax rose to between 0.04% and 0.06% depending on the type of transaction. In 1959, after firms had become practiced at manipulating par value to avoid tax, the base was changed to market value, and the rate was cut to 0.04%. From 1960 to 1966, stocks were taxed at the rate of 0.10% at issuance and 0.04% on transfer.

Three historical points about the American FTT are worth noting. First, this tax was in place during the 1920s; whatever its effects, it did not reduce speculation sufficiently to avert the stock market crash in 1929. The tax, however, was only 0.02% at that time, which might not have been large enough to deter speculation. Second, it was in place at 0.04–0.06% when Keynes called for a more substantial FTT in the 1930s. Third, US Treasury economist Carl Shoup studied the tax and, in a 1934 report, found it did not raise much revenue and "except as a check on speculative activity, the tax probably has little to justify it".

In 1934, the Securities Exchange Act granted the SEC the authority to fund its oversight operations with fees on self-regulatory bodies such as the New York Stock Exchange. At present, a 0.00184% fee is levied on sales of securities, and a $0.0042 fee per transaction is levied on futures transactions. Debt instruments are exempt from the tax.

The State of New York imposed a stock transfer tax from 1905 to 1981. The tax is still levied, but since 1981 it has been refunded upon request. The tax is $0.0125 per share for stocks with prices under $5, rising in steps to $0.05 per share for stocks with prices of $20 or more.

8. **FTTs in other countries**

Many G20 countries tax some financial transactions. The most common form is a tax on secondary market equity sales at a rate of 0.10–0.50%. Such taxes were imposed in China, India, Indonesia, Italy, South Africa, South Korea, and the United Kingdom. Russia and Turkey imposed taxes and/or capital levies on debt financing, typically on issuance rather than on secondary markets. But many developed nations have repealed FTTs in recent decades, presumably because of competitive pressures stemming from globalization and technological changes that have made remote trading less costly. Germany, Italy, Japan, the Netherlands, Portugal, and Sweden have repealed STTs in the last 25 years.

Conclusion

With the development of global financial integration, the accumulated financial risks have made it necessary to take appropriate measures to curb speculation and maintain the stable and healthy development of financial markets. Practices of other countries and China's national realities suggest that as long as the system design is done properly, the FTT can play a due role in China. The Fifth Plenary Session of the Eighteenth Central Committee of the CPC proposed to realize the modernization of the system and capacity of financial governance, including building a financial regulatory framework to meet the development of modern financial markets, improving a set of regulatory rules in line with national standards, and establishing a national financial security mechanism to prevent systemic financial risks. Therefore, China should start collecting the FTTs as soon as possible and establishing a complete FTT system that can be incorporated into China's financial macro-prudential supervision toolkits, so that it can fully contribute to risk prevention and control, and ensure the sound development of China's financial system and the financial markets (Tables A.11 and A.12).

Table A.11 Status of financial transactions taxes in G-20 and major economies worldwide

Country	*FTT type*
Argentina	0.60% on stocks, corporate, and government bonds, and futures
Australia	N/A at a federal level; states may levy transaction taxes
Brazil	0.38% on foreign exchange trading; 6% on short-term foreign loans and bonds (less than 180 days)
Canada	N/A
China	1% on stocks
European Union	0.1% on stocks and bonds assessed on buyer and seller (total 0.2%), 0.01% on derivatives (forthcoming)
France	0.2% on stocks; 0.2% on OTC trading and stock derivatives; 0.02% on the revised amount of stock statement of big traders
Germany	N/A
Japan	N/A
Mexico	N/A
India	0.1% on stocks assessed on buyer and seller (total 0.2%), 0.017–0.025% on sale of options, 0.01% on sale of futures
Indonesia	0.1% on stocks
Russia	0.2% on value of new share and bond issues
Saudi Arabia	N/A
South Africa	0.25% on stocks
South Korea	0.3% on stocks and corporate bonds
Turkey	0.2% on stocks, 0.6–0.75% bond reissuance fee
United Kingdom	0.5% on stocks
United States	0.00184% on stocks

Source: Leonard E. Burman, et al. Financial Transaction Taxes in Theory and Practice

Table A.12 Major features of selected FTTs and proposals

	United Kingdom (current)	*France (current)*	*Sweden (repealed)*	*European Union proposal*	*Harkin-DeFazio proposal*	*Baker proposal*
Tax based on:						
Issuer	Yes	Yes	No	Yes	Yes	Yes
Buyer/seller	No	Yes	No	Yes	Yes	Yes
Location of transaction	No	Yes	Yes (brokerage)	Yes	Yes	Yes
Tax rate:						
Equities	0.5%	0.2%	1.0%	0.2%	0.03%	0.5%
Debt	N/A	N/A	0.002–0.03%	0.1%	0.03%	0.01%
Currency	N/A	N/A	N/A	N/A	N/A	N/A
Derivatives	0.5%	0.01%	2.0%	0.01%	0.03%	0.02, 0.5%
Value	Premium price	Notional value	Premium price	Notional value	Actual value	Varies
Tax on original issuance?	No	No	No	No	No	No
Tax on secondary markets?	Yes	Yes	Yes	Yes	Yes	Yes
Market makers included?	No	No		Yes	Yes	Yes
Government debt included?	Yes	Yes	Yes	Yes	Yes	Yes
International coordination?	No	No	No	Yes	No	No

Source: Leonard E. Burman, et al. Financial Transaction Taxes in Theory and Practice

Appendix 7: Timeline of RMB Internationalization 2015

Time	*Event*	*Details*	*Significance*
January 5, 2015	The PBOC designated Bank of China (BOC) as the RMB business clearing bank in Kuala Lumpur	According to the memorandum of understanding (MOU) between the central banks of China and Malaysia, PBOC designated BOC (Malaysia) as the RMB business clearing bank in Kuala Lumpur	This will encourage the cross-border use of RMB and help promote liberalization and facilitation of trade and investment
January 6, 2015	PBOC designated Industrial and Commercial Bank of China (ICBC) as the RMB business clearing bank in Bangkok	According to the MOU between the central banks of China and Thailand, PBOC designated ICBC (Thailand) as the RMB business clearing bank in Bangkok	This will promote the cross-border use of RMB in Thailand and ASEAN
January 12, 2015	Serbia began to use RMB in international settlement	Serbia began to use RMB in international settlement	This will promote cooperation in trade and economy between China and Serbia. RMB will play an increasingly important role in the economic relation and cash flow

International Monetary Institute (ed.), *Currency Internationalization and Macro Financial Risk Control*,
https://doi.org/10.1007/978-981-13-0698-3

Time	*Event*	*Details*	*Significance*
January 21, 2015	HSBC launched free trade account service	HSBC (China) announced that its free trade account and business procedure had been approved and that it will begin to serve the Shanghai FTZ clients. HSBC hereby becomes one of the first foreign banks that provide this innovative account service	The account system opens up a passage between the FTZ and offshore market, helps enterprises to set foot in overseas market, and facilitates trade settlement and transfer in cross-border investment and financing. It also helps to prevent risks for the FTZ in exploring more financial innovation
January 21, 2015	PBOC signed an MOU with the Swiss National Bank. Switzerland was granted 50 billion yuan RQFII quota	PBOC and Swiss National Bank signed an MOU on RMB clearing arrangement in Switzerland. Switzerland was granted 50 billion yuan RQFII quota	This signals a new step in financial cooperation between the two countries. It will promote the use of RMB in cross-border transactions for the enterprises and financial institutions, and facilitate the bilateral trade and investment
January 28, 2015	The qualified domestic investment enterprise (QDIE) project was implemented	China Credit Equity Investment Fund Management Co., Ltd., a subsidiary of China Credit Trust Co., Ltd, was qualified as QDIE and became the first qualified trust company	The broad investment scope of QDIE will meet the demand of overseas acquisition and purchase. It will promote the opening up of capital account to create higher foreign exchange demand and help the RMB exchange rate to be more balanced and market-oriented
February 9, 2015	The RMB clearing bank in Sydney opened	BOC held the opening up ceremony of RMB business clearing bank in Sydney. It signifies RMB internationalization has made a substantial progress in South Pacific region	This will promote the bilateral trade and optimize the cooperation structure

Time	*Event*	*Details*	*Significance*
February 13, 2015	Trust company was approved to provide RMB international investment loan service for the first time	A wholly owned subsidiary of CITIC Trust was approved to provide RMB FDI and overseas loan service. CITIC Trust became the first trust company in China to conduct RMB international investment loan business	Along with RMB internationalization and the policy easing for RMB overseas business, the foreign market demand of Chinese institutions and individual investors will expand. Trust companies will accelerate to go global and their overseas business expansion will welcome a "golden era"
February 16, 2015	China Foreign Exchange Trade System (CFETS) provided standardized RMB exchange swap in the interbank foreign exchange market	CFETS provided standardized RMB exchange swap in the interbank foreign exchange market. Standardized RMB exchange swap was realized through C-Swap in foreign exchange trading system	This is an initial result for the CFETS to implement the principle of using various techniques and trading methods to meet various market demand
February 19, 2015	Hungarian National Bank launched RMB projects	Hungarian National Bank launched RMB projects to promote financial infrastructure construction and expand investment scope and financing channel	This will strengthen financial cooperation, promote trade and investment, and maintain regional financial stability
March 4, 2015	China Construction Bank (CCB) became the first Chinese institution to acquire an RQFII license in Europe	CCB (London) was qualified RQFII by CSRC. CCB became the first Chinese institution to acquire an RQFII license in Europe	This will facilitate CCB to promote more RQFII-related products, strengthen the leading position in London market, and bring overseas RMB business to new fields, which is significant for RMB internationalization in Europe

Time	*Event*	*Details*	*Significance*
March 6, 2015	The first non-financial institution issued RMB bonds in Korea	HNA Group Global and CCB Seoul branch issued RMB bonds in Korea. This is the first time for a Chinese non-financial enterprise to issue RMB-denominated bonds in Korean financial market, and the first non-financial institution in the world to issue RMB bonds in Korea	This signifies that South Korea has made important progress in establishing offshore RMB center, and will accelerate the process of putting in place a diversified offshore RMB bond market in South Korea
March 16, 2015	Samsung participated in the direct RMB/won transactions	Samsung began to settle direct transactions between headquarter and Chinese subsidiaries through buying and selling RMB/won in the Seoul market	This will promote the development of RMB-won direct transaction market
March 17, 2015	Moscow Exchange launched RMB/rubble futures transactions	The financial derivatives market of Moscow Exchange launched RMB/rubble futures transactions	This is an important step in developing RMB hedging instruments and will expand trade between China and Russia
March 18, 2015	PBOC signed a bilateral currency swap agreement with the Central Bank of Suriname	PBOC and the Central Bank of Suriname signed a bilateral currency swap agreement worth 1 billion yuan/520 million Surinamese dollars	This will strengthen financial cooperation, facilitate trade and investment, and maintain regional financial stability
March 19, 2015	BOC took the lead to release the Credits Investing & Financing Environment Difference Index (CIFED)	BOC took the lead to release the CIFED. CIFED is the first price index BOC released to the market, following CRI and ORI which reflect the level of RMB internationalization	The release of CIFED is an important step for BOC in researching and developing financial market index and improves the RMB internationalization–related index system of BOC
March 24, 2015	The China–Myanmar currency exchange center was established in Ruili, Yunnan	The China–Myanmar currency exchange center was established in Ruili, Yunnan. The center engages in RMB/kyat exchange under current account and RMB/other currencies exchange under individual account	The center established an effective platform to promote the standardization and legalization of China–Myanmar currency exchange business

Time	*Event*	*Details*	*Significance*
March 25, 2015	PBOC signed a bilateral currency swap agreement with the Central Bank of Armenia	PBOC and the Central Bank of Armenia signed a bilateral currency swap agreement worth 1 billion RMB/77 billion Armenia yuan	This will facilitate trade and investment and promote RMB internationalization
March 25, 2015	ICBC signed an MOU with Toronto Stock Exchange	ICBC signed an MOU with Toronto Stock Exchange. According to the MOU, Toronto Stock Exchange and ICBC Canadian branch will cooperate in financial product development and clearing and settlement and risk management, and establish the RMB financial service system based on the clearing network to promote offshore RMB investment and financing products, RMB derivatives trade, RMB bonds issuance, RMB index, and bulk commodity	The MOU is an important breakthrough of RMB internationalization in Canada. The joint hands of ICBC and Toronto Stock Exchange will deepen and broaden the RMB offshore market in Canada and America
March 25, 2015	The first RMB RQFII exchange-traded fund (ETF) in Europe was listed	The first European RMB RQFII ETF was listed in London Exchange	This will improve the usage and recognition of RMB in European market, and therefore will build a complete and sustainable RMB business environment
March 28, 2015	The One Belt and One Road roadmap was officially disclosed	The One Belt and One Road roadmap was disclosed by National Development and Reform Commission, the Ministry of Foreign Affairs, and the Ministry of Commerce	The disclosure of the roadmap will promote understanding and identification of countries involved in the meaning, goal, and task of One Belt and One Road, and therefore helps implement the strategy

Time	*Event*	*Details*	*Significance*
March 30, 2015	PBOC and the Reserve Bank of Australia renewed the currency swap agreement	PBOC and the Reserve Bank of Australia renewed the currency swap agreement worth 200 billion yuan/40 billion Australian dollars	The agreement aims to support trade and investment especially that denominated in local currency, strengthen financial cooperation, and increase the opportunity for RMB settlement and denomination
April 7, 2015	China launched the China–Ukraine currency swap agreement to aid Ukraine out of economic predicament	China launched the China–Ukraine currency swap agreement signed in June 2012 to aid Ukraine out of economic predicament. The agreement is worth 15 billion yuan/19 billion hryvnia	This will promote RMB to become the reserve currency and hedge currency
April 10, 2015	PBOC and South African Reserve Bank signed the currency swap agreement	PBOC and South African Reserve Bank signed the currency swap agreement worth 30 billion yuan/54 billion rand	This will facilitate trade and investment and maintain regional financial stability
April 14, 2015	The first RMB clearing bank in the Middle East was launched	Qatar Central Bank and ICBC launched the RMB clearing service in Doha. ICBC Doha branch became the first RMB clearing bank in the Middle East	This signifies the strengthening of China–Qatar cooperation in trade and finance, and will stimulate RMB investment in the Middle East
April 14, 2015	The RMB clearing bank in Kuala Lumpur was launched	BOC launched the RMB clearing business in Kuala Lumpur	This will help to deepen bilateral economic and trade cooperation, reflect the vision of the two government leaders; accelerate the process of internationalization of RMB; help Malaysia to better play to its advantages and potential, and enhance its status as a financial center in the ASEAN; and improve BOC's global network of renminbi clearing and settlement, thus providing better financial services for clients

Time	*Event*	*Details*	*Significance*
April 17, 2015	The PBOC and Bank Negara Malaysia renewed the currency swap agreement	The PBOC and Bank Negara Malaysia renewed the currency swap agreement worth 180 billion yuan/90 billion ringgit	This will facilitate trade and investment and maintain regional financial stability
April 21, 2015	Guangdong Free Trade Zone opened	Nansha Free Trade Zone, the largest area in the Guangdong Free Trade Zone, will face the world, especially developed countries in Europe and America. In the areas of shipping and logistics, international trade, and high-end manufacturing and other fields, Nansha will launch a number of key projects and introduce a series of innovative measures	This will deepen and broaden the use of RMB in trade and investment
April 22, 2015	The RMB clearing bank in Bangkok was launched	ICBC (Thailand) launched the RMB clearing service in Bangkok. Commercial banks in Thailand and related countries will be able to handle RMB business through their accounts in ICBC (Thailand)	This will improve the RMB remittance efficiency and convenience, and effectively broaden the channels for using RMB funds
April 29, 2015	Luxembourg was granted 50 billion yuan RQFII quota	Luxembourg was granted 50 billion yuan RQFII quota	It marks a new step in the financial cooperation between the two countries, which is conducive to the use of the RMB cross-border transactions for enterprises and financial institutions and facilitate bilateral trade and investment

Time	*Event*	*Details*	*Significance*
May 1, 2015	The *Deposit Insurance Regulations* was implemented	The *Deposit Insurance Regulations* was implemented. Deposit insurance shall be limited to a maximum of 500,000 yuan	The introduction of deposit insurance system will further enhance the stability of the financial system, promote the reform of the banking industry, improve the level of development and competitiveness of banking industry, and enhance the level of service of the real economy
May 10, 2015	PBOC and the National Bank of Belarus renewed the currency swap agreement	PBOC and the National Bank of Belarus renewed the currency swap agreement worth 7 billion yuan/16 trillion Belarus rubles	This will strengthen financial cooperation, facilitate trade and investment, and maintain regional financial stability
May 15, 2015	PBOC and the National Bank of Ukraine renewed the currency swap agreement	PBOC and the National Bank of Ukraine renewed the currency swap agreement worth 15 billion yuan/54 billion hryvnia	This will strengthen financial cooperation, facilitate trade and investment, and maintain regional financial stability
May 20, 2015	The Ministry of Finance issued RMB national debt in Hong Kong	The Ministry of Finance issued RMB national debt of 14 billion yuan to institutional investors in Hong Kong	This is expected to warm up the dim sum bond market
May 22, 2015	The *AIIB Constitution* was released	The 57 intentional founding members of AIIB announced in Singapore that they had reached an agreement on the *AIIB Constitution* and will hold the signing ceremony in Beijing at the end of June	The constitution directly determines the future work efficiency of AIIB. The most important part is the decision-making system of AIIB, the establishment of the equity allocation and loan system. These three aspects directly affect the members' voice and decision-making power, and provide institutional guarantee for the operation and implementation

Time	*Event*	*Details*	*Significance*
May 25, 2015	The yield curve of the RMB Formosa Bonds was disclosed	The yield curve of the RMB Formosa Bonds was disclosed. The yield curve is based on nine major quotations. It provides a pricing milestone for RMB bond products in primary market, and index for trading evaluation and risk management, and also an important foundation for the development of Formosa bond index and commodity index	This will help establish mid- to long-term interest index in Taiwan offshore market and is one of the major financial infrastructures in Taiwan for developing into an offshore RMB center
May 25, 2015	PBOC and the Central Bank of Chile signed the currency swap agreement. Chile was granted 50 billion yuan RQFII quota	PBOC and the Central Bank of Chile signed the currency swap agreement worth 22 billion yuan/2.2 trillion Chilean pesos. On the same day, the two sides signed an MOU on the RMB clearing arrangement in Chile. Chile was granted 50 billion yuan RQFII quota	This marks a new step in the two countries' financial cooperation, and will promote the use of RMB in cross-border trade and investment
May 25, 2015	PBOC designated CCB as the first RMB business clearing bank in South America	PBOC designated CCB as the first RMB business clearing bank in South America	This will promote the efficient use of RMB in Latin America, enhance economic cooperation, and push forward the building of Chile offshore RMB market
June 3, 2015	PBOC released the *Notice on the Participation of Overseas RMB Business Settlement Banks and Overseas Participating Banks in the Bond Repurchase Transactions in the Interbank Foreign Exchange Market*	PBOC approved the overseas RMB business clearing banks and overseas participating banks to participate in the bond repurchase transactions in the interbank foreign exchange market. The financing balance of the repurchase is no more than 100% of the balance of the bond value. Repurchase fund can be used outside of China	This measure connects RMB onshore and offshore markets and expands the demand for bond investment and liquidity management and thus accelerating RMB internationalization

Time	*Event*	*Details*	*Significance*
June 24, 2015	Japan issued the first RMB bonds "Fujiyama Bonds"	Japan issued the first RMB bonds "Fujiyama Bonds". The bonds, with a two-year maturity and annual interest rate of 3.64%, target Japan's institutional investors. It is expected to finance 350 million yuan (7 billion yen) to help Japanese enterprises in China to raise RMB	Japanese institutions will raise RMB funds at a lower cost to conduct business in China. The Japanese domestic insurance companies and local banks will find an investment channel for the RMB on-hand
June 24, 2015	Mongolia first issued RMB bonds	Mongolia first issued RMB bonds worth 1 billion yuan, with a three-year maturity on par value and the yield of 7.5%	This reflects the higher recognition of RMB in the international market. The closer cross-border cooperation and enhanced capability will increase liquidity and reduce financial risk. As an increasing number of governments and official institutions are using renminbi and pursuing macro-economic and macro-prudential reforms, a solid foundation is built for the sound functioning of the renminbi financial system
June 27, 2015	PBOC and the Central Bank of Hungary signed an MOU on RMB clearing arrangement in Hungary. Hungary was granted 50 billion yuan RQFII quota	PBOC and the Central Bank of Hungary signed an MOU on RMB clearing arrangement in Hungary. Hungary was granted 50 billion yuan RQFII quota	This marks a new step in the two countries' financial cooperation, and will promote the use of RMB in cross-border trade and investment, thus facilitating bilateral trade and investment

Time	*Event*	*Details*	*Significance*
June 30, 2015	CCB launched the first RMB-denominated RQFII currency market exchange fund in Euronext in France	CCB launched the first RMB-denominated RQFII currency market exchange fund in Euronext in France. The fund is invested through RQFII in fixed-income securities in Chinese domestic market. It meets the demand of European investors for relatively stable income and also provides liquidity	This will promote the sustainable use of RMB in European market and increase the recognition of RMB
June 30, 2015	ICBC and Euronext signed a strategic cooperation agreement	ICBC and Euronext signed a strategic cooperation agreement worth 3 billion euros. According to the agreement, ICBC and Euronext will cooperate in European capital market, especially foreign RMB bonds, IPO, GDR, QFII and RQFII, and so on	This will enrich offshore RMB investment products and promote the cross-border use of the RMB and the opening up of Chinese capital market
July 3, 2015	A bank in Switzerland announced, for the first time, to provide RMB account service	Bank of Geneva became the first bank in Switzerland to open up RMB saving account. The account has no lower limit, with 2% annual interest rate and an upper limit of OTC extraction amount of 50,000 Swiss franc (330,000 yuan)	This gives investors and depositors more options under the negative interest rate environment and fluctuations of euro
July 7, 2015	PBOC signed the MOU on RMB clearing arrangements with South African Reserve Bank	PBOC and South Africa Reserve Bank signed the MOU on RMB clearing arrangements	This will promote the use of RMB in cross-border trade and facilitate trade and investment

Time	*Event*	*Details*	*Significance*
July 8, 2015	PBOC designated BOC as the RMB business clearing bank in South Africa	PBOC designated BOC Johannesburg branch as the RMB business clearing bank. This is the first clearing bank PBOC designated in Africa, which will strongly support RMB internationalization in Africa	The establishment of RMB clearing system will promote the use of RMB in settlement and financial transactions
July 9, 2015	Korea launched the real-time RMB bond clearing system	The real-time RMB bond clearing system developed by Bank of Communications and Korea Securities Depository was officially launched	This is significant to push forward the Korean RMB offshore bond market and marks the diversified development of the market
July 10, 2015	The central banks of BRICS signed the *Contingency Reserves Arrangement*	The central banks of BRICS signed the *Contingency Reserves Arrangement*, which provides technical details on the operation of the contingency reserves arrangement	The arrangement provides multilateral financial support to the BRICS countries and makes great contribution to global financial security network
July 13, 2015	The cross-border RMB loan policy of Nansha Hengqin Free Trade Zone was implemented	PBOC implemented the cross-border RMB loan policy of Nansha Hengqin Free Trade Zone	This will help Chinese enterprises to explore cross-border financing channel, facilitate cross-border investment and financing between mainland and Hong Kong and Macaw, and promote RMB internationalization and capital account convertibility
July 14, 2015	Quanzhou Financial Reform Pilot Zone was authorized to carry out the cross-border RMB loan pilot project	Quanzhou Financial Reform Pilot Zone was authorized to carry out the cross-border RMB loan pilot project	This will accelerate economic transformation and development and benefit RMB fund cross-border cash flow and therefore push forward the development of RMB offshore center in Taiwan

Time	*Event*	*Details*	*Significance*
July 14, 2015	PBOC printed and issued the *Notice on Issues Concerning the RMB Investment in the Interbank Foreign Exchange Market of Overseas Central Banks, International Financial Institutions and Sovereign Wealth Funds*	The notice simplifies entry procedure for overseas central banks, cancels the limit and allows them to choose PBOC or interbank market settlement agency to settle transactions, and broadens the variety of investment products	This will raise the efficiency of overseas central banks, international financial organizations, and sovereign wealth funds to invest in interbank market
July 20, 2015	The Singapore branch of ICBC finished the first RMB bond repurchase	The Singapore branch of ICBC finished the first RMB bond repurchase worth 200 million yuan. This is first bond repurchase in domestic interbank bond market by a foreign banking institution	This facilitates investment and financing in RMB for local banks and enriches RMB products in Singapore and increases liquidity of RMB market
July 20, 2015	BOC Hong Kong prolonged the clearing service period for RMB Real Time Gross Settlement System (RMBRTGS)	BOC Hong Kong prolonged the clearing service period for RMBRTGS	This will help improve liquidity management for the participating banks and push forward RMB business in global offshore markets
July 22, 2015	Xiamen launched the pilot of cross-border RMB loan services for Taiwan	Xiamen launched the pilot of cross-border RMB loan services for Taiwan. Companies and projects registered in Xiamen can borrow RMB from financial institutions in Taiwan and deal with fund settlement through banks in Xiamen	This will open up a new channel for RMB assets, expand RMB investment and backflow channel, enrich RMB products in Taiwan, and support Taiwan RMB offshore market
July 23, 2015	ICBC launched an RMB clearing mechanism in Pakistan	ICBC launched an RMB clearing mechanism in Pakistan	This will facilitate transfer and use of RMB

Time	*Event*	*Details*	*Significance*
July 24, 2015	Crude oil futures trade was denominated and settled by RMB inside China	PBOC announced crude oil futures trade inside China will be denominated and settled by RMB	This will accelerate the process of building a direct pricing mechanism of RMB and crude oil, enhance Chinese power in crude oil market, and support the role of RMB as an international reserve
July 28, 2015	London Metal Exchange accepted RMB as a pledge currency	London Metal Exchange accepted RMB as a pledge currency	This will promote the pricing role of RMB in the area of bulk commodity, which is an important step in RMB internationalization
July 31, 2015	Shanghai Free Trade Zone cross-border RMB commodity spot transactions were launched	Shanghai Free Trade Zone cross-border RMB commodity spot transactions were launched	This will benefit the normalization of factor market in the FTZ, absorb investment institutions inside and outside China, and enhance Shanghai as the pricing center for the transactions of bulk commodity factors
August 4, 2015	ICBC Singapore branch launched a 24-hour RMB clearing service	ICBC Singapore branch launched a 24-hour RMB clearing service which covers the time zone of Asia, Europe, and America	This is an important measure for Singapore to consolidate the position of RMB offshore center
August 9, 2015	The Suifenhe ruble cash use pilot project was launched	The Suifenhe ruble cash use pilot project was launched	This will promote the standardization of the use of ruble, enhance frontier trade and tourism development, and push forward the use of RMB cash in the frontier area

Time	*Event*	*Details*	*Significance*
August 11, 2015	PBOC improved the quotation of RMB/USD mid-rate	PBOC made an announcement to improve the quotation of RMB/USD mid-rate. The opening quotations in the interbank exchange market that market makers make to the China Foreign Exchange Trading Center must refer to the closing rate in the prior day and adjust to the main currencies' exchange rate and supply-demand status	This will benefit RMB internationalization. The reform of the mechanism for setting the RMB exchange rate will be more market-oriented; supply-demand relations will play a more important role in the mechanism. This will also enhance the flexibility of the two-way floating RMB exchange rate and maintain relative stability of the rate on a reasonable equilibrium level
August 13, 2015	The Mongolian tugrik cash exchange service was officially launched in China	The Mongolian tugrik cash exchange service was officially launched in China	This will stimulate the exchange rate formation mechanism of the two currencies and therefore set a foundation for the circulation and use of RMB in Mongolia
September 3, 2015	PBOC and the Central Bank of Tajikistan signed the currency swap agreement	PBOC and the Central Bank of Tajikistan signed the currency swap agreement worth 3 billion yuan/3 billion somoni	This will promote cross-border trade and investment in RMB for companies and financial institutions of the two countries
September 7, 2015	PBOC adjusted the cross-border two-way RMB capital pool business policies	PBOC adjusted the cross-border two-way RMB capital pool business policies. In principle, multinational companies can establish only one cross-border two-way RMB capital pool inside China; PBOC will implement upper-limit management on this business	This will stimulate more RMB demand and expand the range and scale of RMB use

Time	*Event*	*Details*	*Significance*
September 14, 2015	The filing system of foreign bonds issued by corporations was introduced	The quota approval in foreign bond issuance was substituted by registration and filing system.	This is an important step in the opening up of capital account and a great support for OBOR strategy and for Chinese companies to go global. This will enrich RMB investment instruments in offshore market
September 17, 2015	The new currency basket of the ECB granted RMB a bigger weight	The new currency basket of the ECB granted RMB a bigger weight from 14.8% to 17.7%	This marks the further development of RMB internationalization
September 17, 2015	PBOC signed an MOU on RMB clearing arrangements with the Central Bank of Argentina	PBOC and the Central Bank of Argentina signed an MOU on RMB clearing arrangements	This will promote cross-border transactions in RMB and facilitate trade and investment
September 18, 2015	ICBC launched the RMB clearing business in Argentina	ICBC launched the RMB clearing business in Argentina	This will deepen financial cooperation between the two countries, raise settlement efficiency, reduce trade cost, and prevent financial risk
September 19, 2015	The establishment of the RMB International Investment Loan Fund made new progress in Guangxi	*The Cooperation Framework of RMB International Investment Loan Fund in Beibuwan in Guanxi* was signed which marks a new progress in the establishment of the fund	The assignment of the framework set a foundation for the establishment of the fund
September 22, 2015	International commercial banks are authorized to issue RMB bonds in the interbank foreign exchange market	HSBC and BOC (Hong Kong) were authorized to issue RMB bonds in the interbank foreign exchange market with the value of 1 billion yuan and 10 billion yuan respectively	This expands the range of the issuer in interbank bond market, broadens the RMB financing channel for the international commercial banks, and will promote the opening up of the bond market and the cross-border use of RMB

Time	*Event*	*Details*	*Significance*
September 23, 2015	BOC Xinjiang branch started the list transactions on RMB against Pakistan rupee cash exchange rate	BOC Xinjiang branch started the list transactions on RMB against Pakistan rupee cash exchange rate	This is an important step in promoting the local currency settlement in the bilateral trade, and will raise trade efficiency, save the cost, prevent risks, and increase income
September 29, 2015	HSBC and BOC (Hong Kong) issued "panda bonds"	HSBC and BOC (Hong Kong) issued "panda bonds" valued 1 billion yuan respectively with a three-year maturity and 3.5% interest rate	This is a milestone in RMB internationalization and the opening up of China's capital market
September 29, 2015	PBOC and the Central Bank of Zambia signed an MOU on RMB clearing arrangements	PBOC and the Central Bank of Zambia signed an MOU on RMB clearing arrangements	This will promote cross-border transactions in RMB and facilitate trade and investment
September 30, 2015	PBOC allowed overseas central bank institutions to enter interbank foreign exchange market	According to a notice of PBOC, China will allow overseas central banks and monetary authorities, international financial organizations, and sovereign wealth funds to enter interbank foreign exchange market to conduct foreign exchange transactions including spot, forward, swap, and options	This is an important step in the convertibility of RMB capital account and RMB internationalization. It will stimulate foreign central banks to hold RMB as reserves. It will also increase the RMB trading volume in onshore market which makes RMB exchange rate more representative in interbank market and therefore win the RMB international pricing power
October 6, 2015	RMB surpassed Japanese yen to become the fourth largest payment currency	According to a report by SWIFT, RMB surpassed Japanese yen to become the fourth largest payment currency	The raise of RMB payment position is a milestone for RMB internationalization

Time	*Event*	*Details*	*Significance*
October 6, 2015	China will begin to release data according to the Special Data Dissemination Standards (SDDS)	China completed the adoption procedure of SDDS and first released some statistics data according to the standard	The adoption of SDDS is an important step to improve statistical system and transparency, reliability, and international comparability. It will be beneficial for the international public to understand Chinese economy in depth and enhance China's participation in global economic cooperation
October 8, 2015	The RMB Cross-border Interbank Payment System (CIPS) was officially launched	The RMB Cross-border Interbank Payment System (CIPS) was officially launched. The first direct participating institutions include 19 Chinese and foreign banks within China; indirect participating institutions include 38 domestic banks and 138 foreign banks in Asia, Europe, Oceania, and Africa	This is a milestone in RMB internationalization. CIPS will become a green channel for global RMB payment and support RMB clearing transactions
October 20, 2015	BOC disclosed the RMB bond trading index	BOC disclosed the RMB bond trading index in Beijing, London, and Singapore	The index will guide global institutional investors to invest in China's interbank bond market as an important reference for global central banks and regulators to understand China's financial market and therefore make new contribution to financial market and RMB internationalization

Time	*Event*	*Details*	*Significance*
October 20, 2015	PBOC and the Bank of England renewed the currency swap agreement	PBOC and the Bank of England renewed the currency swap agreement. The swap scale expanded from 200 billion yuan/20 billion pound to 350 billion yuan/35 billion pound	The renewal of the agreement provides liquidity support for London RMB market. It will promote local RMB asset transaction and management and facilitate trade and investment
October 20, 2015	PBOC issued RMB-denominated central bank bills overseas for the first time	PBOC issued RMB-denominated central bank bills of 5 billion yuan overseas for the first time	The issuance enriches investment variety in RMB offshore market and therefore pushes forward RMB internationalization
October 22, 2015	The executive meeting of the State Council decided to launch the overseas QDII2 pilot program	The executive meeting of the State Council decided to launch the overseas QDII2 pilot program	This will speed up RMB internationalization and broaden wealth appreciation channel for investors
October 23, 2015	Cross-border transportation channels of RMB cash to Russia were established	China transported 5 million yuan in cash to Russia by air which signifies the establishment of cross-border transportation channels	This is an important step in RMB regionalization and internationalization. The channel will deepen economic and financial cooperation with countries along the Silk Road
October 23, 2015	The first non-financial corporation offshore RMB bond of mainland China was issued in Singapore	The first non-financial corporation offshore RMB bond of mainland China was issued in Singapore	This will push forward the construction of RMB offshore market and establish a new channel to finance for domestic infrastructure corporations
October 24, 2015	The deposit interest rate cap was liberalized	The deposit interest rate cap was liberalized	The liberalization of the deposit interest rate cap marks the elimination of the control of interest rate and is a substantial development in interest rate marketization. This is a milestone in the history of financial reform

Time	*Event*	*Details*	*Significance*
October 29, 2015	Shanghai Stock Exchange, Deutsche Börse, and CFFEX jointly signed the agreement in Beijing on establishing the CEINEX	Shanghai Stock Exchange, Deutsche Börse, and CFFEX jointly signed the agreement in Beijing on establishing the CEINEX	CEINEX will provide more convenient financial services for Chinese and European companies, meet the demand of foreign investors to RMB security products, and play an important role in the opening up of China's capital market and RMB internationalization
October 30, 2015	Shanghai Free Trade Zone released 40 regulations on the new financial reform	According to the regulations, the FTZ can conduct pilot program on RMB capital account convertibility	This will promote the convertibility of RMB capital account, expand the overseas use range of RMB, and promote RMB internationalization
November 2, 2015	Korea's RQFII quota was increased to 120 billion yuan	Korea's RQFII quota was increased to 120 billion yuan	This will enhance the development of Chinese and Korean financial market and expand the use of local currencies
November 2, 2015	Taiwan relaxed the regulation on close position for RMB participating banks and clearing banks	Taiwan relaxed the regulation on close position for RMB participating banks and clearing banks, and expended the trading types to spot, forward, and swap	This will increase the opportunity to provide more RMB service to local residents, raise RMB trading volume, and therefore promote the construction of RMB offshore market in Taiwan
November 9, 2015	The interbank foreign exchange market carried out RMB and Swiss franc direct transactions	The interbank foreign exchange market carried out RMB and Swiss franc direct transactions	This will form direct exchange rate of RMB against Swiss franc, reduce exchange cost, promote the use of RMB and Swiss franc in trade and investment, and support economic and financial relations between China and Switzerland
November 16, 2015	PBOC and the Central Bank of Turkey renewed the currency swap agreement	PBOC and the Central Bank of Turkey renewed the currency swap agreement. The swap scale expanded from 10 billion yuan/3 billion Turkish liras to 12 billion yuan/5 billion Turkish liras	This will facilitate trade and investment and enhance financial cooperation

Time	*Event*	*Details*	*Significance*
November 17, 2015	Singapore's RQFII quota was increased to 100 billion yuan	Singapore's RQFII quota was increased to 100 billion yuan	This will meet the asset allocation requirements of Singapore investors, promote the opening up of domestic capital market, and facilitate trade and investment
November 18, 2015	CEINEX opened for business in Frankfurt	CEINEX opened for business in Frankfurt. The first products included ETF and RMB bonds	This marks the official initiation of the operation of European offshore RMB security market. This is an important part in RMB internationalization
November 23, 2015	Malaysia was granted 50 billion yuan RQFII quota	Malaysia was granted 50 billion yuan RQFII quota	This will broaden RMB asset allocation channel for foreign investors, promote the opening up of China's capital market, and facilitate trade and investment
November 25, 2015	The first batch of overseas central bank institutions entered China's interbank foreign exchange market	The first batch of overseas central bank institutions entered China's interbank foreign exchange market. The institutions include overseas central banks (monetary authorities), reserve management institutions, international financial organizations, and sovereign wealth fund	This will facilitate currency exchange, accelerate China's foreign exchange market to integrate into the global market, and promote the use of RMB as reserve and settlement currency
November 26, 2015	PBOC and the ECB finished the bilateral currency swap test	PBOC and ECB carried out the bilateral currency swap test in April and November 2015. The two sides will launch the swap service under necessity	The swap arrangement will provide liquidity support to the currency markets and facilitate trade and investment. It marks a new progress in financial cooperation between the two central banks
November 27, 2015	British Columbia of Canada registered in China's interbank foreign exchange market and issued RMB bonds worth 6 billion yuan	British Columbia of Canada registered in China's interbank foreign exchange market and issued RMB bonds worth 6 billion yuan	This will further expand the range of bond issuers, promote the opening up of bond market, and push forward RMB cross-border use

Time	*Event*	*Details*	*Significance*
November 27, 2015	The Ministry of Finance disclosed the three- and six-month treasury yields	The Ministry of Finance disclosed the three- and six-month treasury yields, which completed the short-term treasury yield curve	This removed a technical obstacle for RMB to join the SDR basket, and is an important step to strengthen domestic financial market. It will better coordinate the fiscal policy and monetary policy, enrich the money market instruments, and benefit the monetary policy transmission
November 30	The IMF Executive Board decided to incorporate RMB into the SDR basket	Effective from October 1, 2016, the RMB will be included in the SDR basket as a fifth currency, along with the USD, the euro, the Japanese yen, and the British pound. The RMB will have a weighting of 10.92% in the new SDR basket, while respective weightings of other currencies in the basket are 41.73% for the USD, 30.93% for the euro, 8.33% for the Japanese yen, and 8.09% for the British pound	This marks a milestone in the RMB global march and a vote of confidence in China's ongoing financial reforms. The joining of RMB in the SDR basket means the international community has greater expectations on China to play an active role in the world economic and financial arena
November 30, 2015	The Working Group on US RMB Trading and Clearing was established	The Working Group on US RMB Trading and Clearing was established	The establishment of the working group will advance a mechanism to trade the Chinese currency in the United States and improve the competitiveness of US companies, while furthering America's financial sector and economy. It will push forward the development of RMB internationalization in the United States

Time	*Event*	*Details*	*Significance*
December 3, 2015	BOC released the first One Belt One Road exchange rate index	BOC released the first One Belt One Road exchange rate index which reflects the fluctuation trend of RMB against currencies of the OBOR countries	This will promote the settlement and transactions between RMB and currencies of the OBOR countries, facilitate trade and investment, and enhance the recognition and use of RMB in the OBOR countries
December 13, 2015	The cross-border currency settlement between China and Tajikistan was launched	The cross-border currency settlement between China and Tajikistan was launched. Companies, individuals, and banks can make financial transactions using the two currencies	This will enhance trade between Xinjiang and Tajikistan, and promote the exploration of advantageous resources and energy strategic cooperation
December 14, 2015	PBOC and the Central Bank of UAE signed the currency swap agreement. The UAE was granted 50 billion yuan RQFII quota	PBOC and the Central Bank of UAE signed the currency swap agreement worth 35 billion yuan/20 billion UAE dirham. The two countries signed an MOU on establishing RMB clearing arrangement in the UAE. The UAE was granted 50 billion yuan RQFII quota	This will promote the use of RMB in cross-border transactions and facilitate trade and investment
December 15, 2015	Korea issued the first "panda bonds" in China	Korea issued RMB bonds of 3 billion yuan in China's interbank bond market, with a three-year maturity and 3% interest rate	This will enrich the types of products in interbank bond market, promote the opening up of the bond market, and enhance economic and financial cooperation between China and Korea
December 17, 2015	Thailand was granted 50 billion yuan RQFII quota	Thailand was granted 50 billion yuan RQFII quota	This will broaden RMB asset allocation channel for foreign investors, promote the opening up of China's capital market, and facilitate trade and investment

Time	*Event*	*Details*	*Significance*
December 18, 2015	The US Congress approved the IMF's 2010 Quota and Governance Reform	The US Congress approved the IMF's 2010 Quota and Governance Reform, indicating that the 2010 reforms, after protracted delay, are expected to take effect soon. The 2010 reforms will double the IMF's quota resources from SDR 238.5 billion (about USD 329.83 billion) to SDR 477 billion about (USD 659.67 billion), while shifting 6% of quota shares to dynamic Emerging Market of Developing Country (EMDCs). China's quota will increase from 3.996% to 6.394%, making the country the third largest shareholder in the IMF from the previous sixth	The 2010 reforms will increase the representation and voice of EMDCs in the IMF, thus helping maintain the IMF's credibility, legitimacy, and effectiveness. Going forward, China will work closely with other member countries to support the IMF in continuously improving the quota and governance structure and ensuring its status as a quota-based and adequately resourced institution
December 21, 2015	China exempted Zimbabwe from debts worth 260 million yuan	China exempted Zimbabwe from debts worth 40 million USD/260 million yuan. RMB will circulate like USD in Zimbabwe from 2016	This will promote the circulation of RMB in Zimbabwe as a payment method
December 25, 2015	The AIIB was officially established	AIIB, prepared by 57 countries, was officially established. This is the first multilateral financial institution proposed by China	This is a milestone in international economic governance reform and will drive up RMB capital flow in Asia and expand the international use

The manufacturer's authorised representative in the EU is Springer Nature Customer Service Centre GmbH, Europaplatz 3, 69115 Heidelberg, Germany. If you have any concerns regarding our products, please contact ProductSafety@springernature.com

Printed and bound by CPI Group (UK) Ltd, Croydon, CR0 4YY
25/09/2026
02222881-0007